ADULT SOCIAL CARE
LAW AND POLICY

Law, Society, Policy

Series Editor: **Rosie Harding**,
University of Birmingham

Law, Society, Policy offers an outlet for high quality,
socio-legal research monographs and edited collections
with the potential for policy impact.

Also available in the series:

- *Mental Capacity Law, Sexual Relationships, and Intimacy*, edited by Beverley Clough and Laura Pritchard-Jones
- *Children's Voices, Family Disputes and Child-Inclusive Mediation*, by Anne Barlow and Jan Ewing
- *Observing Justice*, by Judith Townend and Lucy Welsh
- *Egalitarian Digital Privacy*, by Tsachi Keren-Paz
- *Fragile Rights*, by Anne Revillard
- *Polygamy, Policy and Postcolonialism in English Marriage Law*, by Zainab Naqvi
- *Intersex Embodiment*, by Fae Garland and Mitchell Travis
- *Unsettling Apologies*, edited by Melanie Judge and Dee Smythe
- *Death, Family and the Law*, by Edward Kirton-Darling
- *Deprivation of Liberty in the Shadows of the Institution*, by Lucy Series
- *Women, Precarious Work and Care*, by Emily Grabham
- *Pandemic Legalities*, edited by Dave Cowan and Ann Mumford

International Advisory Board:

Dr Lynette Chua, National University of Singapore, Singapore
Professor Margaret Davies, Flinders University, Australia
Professor Martha Fineman, Emory University, US
Professor Marc Hertogh, University of Groningen, The Netherlands
Professor Fiona Kelly, La Trobe University, Melbourne, Australia
Professor Fiona de Londras, University of Birmingham, UK
Dr Anna Mäki-Petäjä-Leinonen, University of Eastern Finland, Finland
Professor Ambreena Manji, Cardiff University, UK
Professor Linda Mulcahy, University of Oxford, UK
Professor Vanessa Munro, University of Warwick, UK
Professor Debra Parkes, University of British Columbia, Canada
Dr Antu Sorainen, University of Helsinki, Finland
Professor Dee Smythe, University of Cape Town, South Africa
Professor Michael Thomson, 'University of Leeds, UK and University of Technology Sydney, Australia
Dr Bridgette Toy-Cronin, University of Otago, New Zealand
Dr Lisa Vanhala, University College London, UK

Find out more at:
bristoluniversitypress.co.uk/law-society-policy

ADULT SOCIAL CARE LAW AND POLICY

Lessons from the Pandemic

Jean V. McHale and Laura Noszlopy

First published in Great Britain in 2025 by

Bristol University Press
University of Bristol
1–9 Old Park Hill
Bristol
BS2 8BB
UK
t: +44 (0)117 374 6645
e: bup-info@bristol.ac.uk

Details of international sales and distribution partners are available at bristoluniversitypress.co.uk

© Jean V. McHale and Laura Noszlopy 2025

The digital PDF and ePub versions of this title are available open access and distributed under the terms of the Creative Commons Attribution-NonCommercial-NoDerivatives 4.0 International licence (https://creativecommons.org/licenses/by-nc-nd/4.0/) which permits reproduction and distribution for non-commercial use without further permission provided the original work is attributed.

British Library Cataloguing in Publication Data
A catalogue record for this book is available from the British Library

ISBN 978-1-5292-2986-8 paperback
ISBN 978-1-5292-2987-5 ePub
ISBN 978-1-5292-2988-2 OA Pdf

The right of Jean V. McHale and Laura Noszlopy to be identified as authors of this work has been asserted by them in accordance with the Copyright, Designs and Patents Act 1988.

All rights reserved: no part of this publication may be reproduced, stored in a retrieval system, or transmitted in any form or by any means, electronic, mechanical, photocopying, recording, or otherwise without the prior permission of Bristol University Press.

Every reasonable effort has been made to obtain permission to reproduce copyrighted material. If, however, anyone knows of an oversight, please contact the publisher.

The statements and opinions contained within this publication are solely those of the authors and not of the University of Bristol or Bristol University Press. The University of Bristol and Bristol University Press disclaim responsibility for any injury to persons or property resulting from any material published in this publication.

Bristol University Press works to counter discrimination on grounds of gender, race, disability, age and sexuality.

Cover design: Andrew Corbett
Front cover image: Shutterstock/ARMMY PICCA

Contents

Series Editor's Preface		vi
Table of Cases		vii
Table of UK Statutes, Statutory Instruments, and Related Legislation		ix
Acknowledgements		xi
Preface		xiii
1	Adult Social Care in England in a Time of Turbulence	1
2	Foundational Paradigms in Adult Social Care Law and Policy	26
3	Legal Regulation of Adult Social Care Provision in England	62
4	Pandemic Preparedness Planning and the Development of Emergency Legislation	116
5	'Easing' the Care Act: Responding to COVID-19 in the West Midlands	173
6	Pandemic Legacies: 'Living with COVID-19' in Adult Social Care	231
7	Adult Social Care Law and Policy: Learning Lessons from the Pandemic	280
Bibliography		304
Index		342

Series Editor's Preface

The Law, Society, Policy series publishes high-quality, socio-legal research monographs and edited collections with the potential for policy impact. Cutting across the traditional divides of legal scholarship, Law, Society, Policy offers an interdisciplinary, policy-engaged approach to socio-legal research which explores law in its social and political contexts with a particular focus on the place of law in everyday life. The series seeks to take an explicitly society-first view of socio-legal studies, with a focus on the ways that law shapes social life, and the constitutive nature of law and society. International in scope, engaging with domestic, international and global legal and regulatory frameworks, texts in the Law, Society, Policy series engage with the full range of socio-legal topics and themes.

Table of Cases

Barnett Primary Care Trust v X [2006] EWHC 787 QB
BP v Surrey CC [2020] EWCOP
Callin, Heather and Ward v Leonard Cheshire [2002] EWCA Civ 366
Davey v Oxfordshire [2017] EWCA Civ 1308; [2017] EWHC 354 (Admin)
HL, R (on the application of) v Secretary of State for Health and Social Care [2023] EWHC 866 (Admin)
Kings College Hospital NHS Foundation Trust v C [2016] COPLR 50
Louisa Watts v UK [2010] ECHR 793
McDonald v United Kingdom (2015) 60 E.H.R.R. 1
P, R (on the application of) v London Borough of Croydon [2022] EWHC 2886 (Admin)
R (on the application of) Antoniak v Westminster City Council [2019] EWHC 3465 (Admin)
R (Bernard) v Enfield LBC [2002] EWHC (Admin)
R (on the application of Care England) v Essex CC [2017] EWHC 3035 (Admin)
R (BG) v Suffolk County Council [2022] EWCA Civ 1047
R (GS) v LB Camden [2016] EWHC 1762
R v Commissioner for Local Administration ex parte Eastleigh BC [1988] 3 WLR 113 CA
R v Gloucestershire CC ex parte Barry [1997] 2 WLR 459
R v Manchester City Council ex parte Stennett; R v Redcar and Cleveland Borough Council ex parte Armstrong; R v Harrow London Borough Council ex parte Cobham [2002] UKHL 34
R (McDonald) v Kensington and Chelsea RLBC [2011] UKSC 33
R v North West Lancashire Health Authority ex parte A D and G [2000] 1 WLR 97
R (on the application of Alexander Thomas Condliff) v North Staffordshire PCT [2011] EWCA Civ 910
R (SG) v Haringey Council [2015] EWHC 2579 (Admin)
R (Patrick) v Newham LBC (2008) CCLR 48
R (Peters and Findlay) v Secretary of State for Health and Social Care [2021] EWHC 3182 (Admin)
R (X) v Tower Hamlets LBC [2013] EWHC 482 (Admin)

R (Peters and Findlay) v Secretary of State for Health and Social Care [2021] EWHC 3182 (Admin)
R (Peters and Findlay) v Secretary of State for Health and Social Care [2021] EWHC 3182 (Admin)
Re Ellenborough Park [1955] EWCA Civ 4
Sussex Community NHS Foundation Trust v Price [2016] EWHC 3167

Table of UK Statutes, Statutory Instruments, and Related Legislation

1531 Poor Law of Henry VIII
Autism Act 2009
Care Act 2014
Chronically Sick and Disabled Persons Act 1970
Civil Contingencies Act 2004
Coronavirus Act 2020
Disability Discrimination Act 1995
Down Syndrome Act 2022
Equality Act 2010
Health and Care Act 2022
Health and Social Care Act 2008
Health and Social Care Act 2012
Human Rights Act 1998
Localism Act 2011
Local Government Act 1974
Local Authority Social Services Act 1970
Local Government and Public Involvement in Health Act 2007
Mental Capacity Act 2005
Mental Health Act 1983
National Assistance Act 1948
National Health Service Act 1946
National Health Service Act 2006
National Health Service and Community Care Act 1990
Poor Law Amendment Act 1834
Public Health Act 1984
Regulation and Inspection of Social Care (Wales) Act 2016

Statutory instruments

Care and Support (Assessment) Regulations 2014 (SI 2014/2827)
Care and Support and After-care (Choice of Accommodation) Regulations 2014 (SI 2014/2670)
Care and Support (Eligibility) Regulations 2015 (SI 2015/313)
Down Syndrome Act 2022 Commencement Regulations 2024 (SI 2024/373)
Health Protection (Coronavirus) Regulations 2020 No 129
Health Protection (Coronavirus, Local COVID-19 Alert Level) (Very High) (England) Regulations 2020 (2020 SI No 1105)
Health Protection (Coronavirus, Local COVID-19 Alert Level) (High) (England) Regulations 2020 (2020 SI 1104)
Health Protection (Coronavirus, Local COVID-19 Alert Level) (Medium) (England) Regulations 2020 (2020 SI No 1103)
Local Authority Social Services and National Health Service Complaints (England) Regulations 2009 309
National Health Service Commissioning Board and Clinical Commissioning Groups (Responsibilities and Standing Rules) Regulations 2012 (SI 2012/2996)
Social Workers Regulations 2018 (SI 2019/893)

International legal instruments

European Convention on Human Rights 1950/53
UN Convention on the Rights of Persons with Disabilities 2006
Universal Declaration of Human Rights 1948
International Health Regulations 2005, World Health Organisation

Acknowledgements

This book draws upon our research project 'Removing rights from the vulnerable? The impact of COVID-19 social care "easements"', funded by an Economic and Social Research Council COVID-19 Rapid Response Grant (No. ES/V015486/1). We gratefully acknowledge the funding support of the ESRC for this work, which took place between November 2020 and July 2022, while the world was still deep in the throes of the pandemic and its immediate aftermath.

We would also like to thank our project partner Central England Law Centre for their support, and we are particularly grateful to Sue Bent, Emma Austin, and Amie MacDonald. It was the encouragement of Sue and Emma that led to this project being initially developed in the early summer of 2020 in response to unfolding events. Sincere thanks also go to our expert Advisory Board members: Emma Austin, Steve Broach, Kellie Jones, Elssa Keegan, Naomi Madden, and Alex Rook for their wise counsel. Many thanks are also extended to Birmingham Law School graduates Eleanor Ford, Anant Rangan, and Elin Short, who provided excellent research assistance in collecting and collating data from council databases at the start of our ESRC project. Special thanks also go to Richard Young for his, as ever, insightful comments on our original ESRC grant application which led ultimately to the development of this monograph. We would also like to thank our professional services colleagues at Birmingham Law School and in the College of Arts and Law at the University of Birmingham for their support in both pre- and post-award stages. Particular thanks go to Tania Cleaves, Richard Hughes, Sheena Robertson, and Ann Evans. We would also like to thank Grace Carroll and Helen Davies at Bristol University Press for their constant help and support in enabling this book to be written. Our thanks also go to Lee-Ann Ashcroft and the team at New Gen for their great help in making the production process so smooth.

We are immeasurably grateful to our interviewees and workshop participants, who very kindly gave us their time and shared their experiences of what was an exceptionally challenging period for all, both personally and professionally. Their insights greatly enriched our understanding of how the emergency legislation and statutory guidance was received and interpreted on the ground throughout the first 18 months of the pandemic, and their accounts of implementing or responding to these directives and of navigating other operational changes under extreme pressure form the core of this book.

We also benefitted greatly from the input of the anonymous reviewer of this volume, and from the generosity of Alan Greene, Rosie Harding, Catherine Needham, and Laura Pritchard-Jones, who provided very helpful comments on draft chapters. Any errors and omissions are of course the sole responsibility of the authors.

Finally, we would like to thank our respective friends and families for their kindness and patience throughout the long research and writing process. Laura thanks Mella Sirah Noszlopy, and Jean's thanks go to James Sullivan-McHale.

Preface

The aim of this book is to critically explore the impacts of the COVID-19 Pandemic on the delivery of adult social care law and policy in England. Drawing upon original empirical research undertaken in the West Midlands in England it examines the changing landscape of adult social care in England, with a particular focus on the impact of emergency legislation invoked in March 2020.

We began the original ESRC project upon which this book is based in late 2020 while people in England, as in many parts of the world, were experiencing very high rates of COVID-19 infection and mortality, with consequent lockdowns and other restrictions on activity and liberty. It was a time when new vocabulary and behaviours, born of emergency public health protocols, seemed to have been almost normalized at an incongruous pace. As we finish writing it, the UK COVID-19 Inquiry is ongoing and new evidence is still emerging about the nature and extent of pandemic planning, along with further evidence of profound suffering and loss. These accounts serve as sharp reminders of how this health crisis affected all aspects of life, and of the importance of up-to-date, evidence-based contingency planning and the maintenance of robust and responsive systems that can help protect us from the impacts of the next pandemic.

At its core, this book is about human vulnerabilities, fundamental rights, and accountability. Drawing from the experiences of those involved in adult social care during COVID-19 — whether people who receive care and support services, or carers, care providers, or policy makers — we hope this book will offer some useful analysis and lessons for those with responsibility for building a sustainable system of adult social care and for mitigating future crises.

The law is as stated on 30 April 2024.

1

Adult Social Care in England in a Time of Turbulence

I. Introduction: The pandemic and its impacts on adult social care in England

Adult social care in England has been under sustained pressure for decades, with heavy consequences for people who draw on care and support services, for carers, and for the workforce alike. Arguably it has long functioned in crisis mode but since early 2020 the sector has experienced a period of almost unprecedented turbulence. People who draw on care and support services – including many older people, people living with disabilities, or with mental or physical illness, and also carers – were disproportionately impacted by the COVID-19 pandemic. Many of these people were subject to an increased risk of infection. They were further impacted through the social isolation and deprivations associated with mitigations such as lockdowns and shielding, as well as changes in the provision and availability of services.

The Coronavirus Act was passed in March 2020 in response to the global public health emergency. Included in section 15 and schedule 12 of the Act were provisions which enabled local authorities in England to depart from the operation of aspects of their statutory powers and duties under the Care Act 2014.[1] The associated Guidance documents described these as 'Care Act easements'. In relation to the duties placed on local authorities to provide support, the extent to which they could be 'relaxed' or limited was subject to a floor below which failure to provide support would constitute a breach of human rights under the European Convention on Human Rights (ECHR).[2] In making reference to these provisions during the second reading in the

---

[1] See further Chapter 2 of this book for a detailed discussion of the Care Act 2014, and Chapter 4 on the background to the Coronavirus Act 2020 and its implementation.

[2] Department of Health and Social Care (2020) *Care Act Easements: Supporting Guidance*, updated 29 June 2021; withdrawn 22 July 2021, s 4.

House of Commons of the 2020 Act the then Secretary of State for Health and Social Care, Matt Hancock, stated that:

> The purpose of these measures is to make sure that when there is a shortage of social workers, those who need social care to live their everyday life get it and can be prioritised ahead of those who have a current legal right to social care under the Care Act 2014 but for whom it is not a matter of life and death.[3]

These so-called 'Care Act easements', which legally enabled such utilitarian rationing decisions, were extremely controversial from the outset.[4] They were only formally operated for a short period of time by a limited number of local authorities nationally. Yet, as we shall see in later chapters of this book, the delivery of social care services was changed across many local authorities, and not solely in those which formally activated these 'easements'.

This book contributes to socio-legal literature in this area by providing an in-depth analysis of the development of pandemic planning with specific reference to adult social care, and how adult social care law, policy, and service delivery in England developed and adapted in response to the COVID-19 pandemic from 2020 onwards. The analysis is contextualized within an exploration of the theoretical paradigms and principles which inform our understanding of adult social care provision, the existing legal regulation of adult social care in England at the onset of the pandemic and the legislative changes made in 2020. The book draws upon our empirical case study of local authorities in the West Midlands, the region in England which saw the largest number of local authorities formally operating Care Act easements, before considering what can be learnt from the experiences at national level. The book critically interrogates the legacy of the pandemic for adult social care and seeks to identify lessons for future pandemic planning concerning adult social care and for adult social care law and policy more broadly. We are very conscious of the fact that while this book was being written, the UK COVID-19 Inquiry began its work. The Inquiry was established under the Inquiries Act 2004 and is chaired by the Right Honourable Baroness Heather Hallett DBE, a former Lady Justice of the Court of Appeal who was appointed as chair in December 2021.[5] At a very late stage in the production of this book, we were able to include some reflections on relevant findings

---

[3] M. Hancock (2020) HC Coronavirus Bill Debate, Hansard Volume 674, Column 59, March 2020.
[4] See for a more extensive discussion of this issue Chapters 4, 5, and 6 of this book.
[5] See https://covid19.public-inquiry.uk/about/, accessed 25 July 2024.

of the first Report from that Inquiry into Module 1 of its work on the 'Resilience and Preparedness of the United Kingdom', which was published on 18 July 2024.[6] The Inquiry remains ongoing with, as of summer 2024, hearings scheduled into spring 2025. Module 6 of the Inquiry will consider the care sector but the Inquiry hearings for that Module have not as yet been scheduled.

The pandemic changed life for everyone and proved deadly for far too many. As the then Prime Minister Boris Johnson declared on 23 March 2020 that we needed to stay at home 'to protect our NHS and save lives',[7] local council buildings up and down the UK were closed to the public and to the majority of staff. While some face-to-face social care adult services remained in place, these were strictly restricted on public health grounds and, as with many other areas of work, social work teams pivoted to operating primarily online.[8] It was not yet fully understood how the virus was transmitted and personal protective equipment (PPE) was in short supply. Agency care workers maintained a level of domiciliary care services, but these were also restricted in forms of contact and in any case many people declined to have care workers enter their homes. Residential care homes remained open for residents with some care home staff remaining on site to care for residents.[9] In that first COVID year, the whole health and social care sector, those who relied on it for support, and their families and social networks experienced a profound shock.

The impacts of NHS decisions relating to adult social care in the early stages of the pandemic were rapidly felt. Having recognized that hospitals would quickly be overwhelmed by COVID-positive patients, one tactic to 'protect our NHS' was to initiate more rapid discharge of patients. Sending patients into care homes in the early, pre-mass testing, days of the pandemic

---

[6] UK COVID-19 Inquiry (2024) *Module 1: The resilience and preparedness of the United Kingdom: A Report by the Rt Hon Baroness Hallett, DBE Chair of the UK COVID-19 Inquiry*, 18 July 2024, HC 18.

[7] Prime Minister's Office 10 Downing Street (2020) 'Prime Minister's Statement on Coronavirus (COVID-19)', 23 March.

[8] See, for example, K.M. Pascoe (2022) 'Remote service delivery during the COVID-19 pandemic: questioning the impact of technology on relationship-based social work practice', *British Journal of Social Work*, 52(6): 3268–87. See also T. Kingstone (2022) 'Exploring the impact of the first wave of COVID-19 on social work practice: a qualitative study in England, UK', *British Journal of Social Work*, 52(4): 2043–62.

[9] See further A. Comas-Herrera (2020) 'The COVID-19 long-term care situation in England', International Long-Term Care Policy Network, CPEC-LSE, 19 November, at pages 16 and 31; and also C.Ó. Néill (2022) '"This is no country for old (wo)men?" An examination of the approach taken to care home residents during the COVID-19 pandemic', *Medical Law Review*, 31(1): 25.

was viewed as necessary to free up NHS beds.[10] The 'NHS test and trace' system was not launched until the end of May.[11] The consequences of these factors in combination were devastating.[12] The decisions made under this rapid discharge policy in the early months of 2020 ensured that the virus was seeded in care homes, whose residents were precisely those deemed most clinically vulnerable to COVID-19. During the first wave of the pandemic there were some 26,035 excess deaths in care homes.[13] The situation was compounded by the lack of available PPE, with devastating shortages across health and social care sectors and for the wider public.[14]

Heavy reliance on agency and bank staff amid a workforce crisis resulted in a higher level of transmission due to movement across multiple care homes and in domiciliary care.[15] Hudson comments that 'the reliance on zero-hours contracts in the home care sector heightened the risk that those workers who were sick with the virus would feel unable to afford to stay at home and isolate'.[16]

Care home managers also had to deal with rapidly changing and poorly communicated guidance and regulations around infection control and social distancing, while many of the usual sources of external support for staff and residents were effectively cut off.[17] At the same time, it has been suggested that some care home managers were willing to respond positively to the rapid transfer of patients and accept them into their care homes as providers were concerned to sustain income levels in a very fragile care home market.[18] Such

---

[10] There is an interesting parallel with 1939, when the decision to provide additional hospital bed capacity led to 140,000 people being discharged from hospital following the declaration of the Second World War; see G. Dalley (2022) *Caring in Crisis: The Search for Reasons and Post-Pandemic Remedies*, Cham: Palgrave Macmillan, p 69.

[11] Launched on 28 May 2020; see further UK Health Security Agency (2020) *Research and analysis NHS Test and Trace statistics (England): methodology* (updated 18 May 2022).

[12] See, for example, discussion in G. Dalley (2022), ch 7.

[13] Office of National Statistics (2020) *Deaths involving COVID-19 in the care sector, England, and Wales: deaths registered between week ending 20 March 2020 and week ending 21 January 2022*.

[14] See, for example, M. Nayashanu, F. Pfende and H. Ekpenyung (2020) 'Exploring the challenges faced by frontline workers in health and social care amid the COVID-19 pandemic: experiences of frontline workers in the English Midlands region, UK', *Journal of Interprofessional Care*, 34(5): 655.

[15] See University of Strathclyde (2022) 'Care homes reliant on agency staff more than twice as likely to spread COVID-19, study confirms', Web news, 25 January.

[16] B. Hudson (2021) *Clients, Consumers or Citizens: The Privatisation of Adult Social Care in England*, Bristol: Policy Press, p 120.

[17] F. Marshall, A. Gordon, J. Gladman and S. Bishop (2021) 'Care homes, their communities, and resilience in the face of the COVID-19 pandemic: interim findings from a qualitative study', *BMC Geriatrics*, 21(102).

[18] G. Dalley (2022), p 220.

excess deaths were however not the sole preserve of residential adult social care. A further 2,726 excess deaths were recorded among those receiving domiciliary care services during the same period, a 96 per cent increase over the years 2017–19.[19] Locked down and isolated, the quality of life for those who were not struck down by the virus was also severely affected.[20]

The consequences of some of the measures taken at that time had disproportionately damaging impacts on older people, those with disabilities, and those in residential care, and they have come under fierce criticism.[21] It was found that there was unjustified application by some NHS healthcare professionals in the early months of the pandemic of do not attempt cardio-pulmonary resuscitation orders (DNACPR) to people with disabilities or of advanced years.[22] It was also claimed that restrictions on family members being able to visit people in care settings were disproportionate and that these could be seen as a violation of the individual's rights to home and family life.[23] Similarly, Amnesty International reported that the Westminster Government's decision to halt inspections of care homes undertaken by the Care Quality Commission in the early months of the pandemic, and family visits for far longer, had 'increased the risk that care home residents would be exposed to abuses that would not be identified, reported and investigated'.[24]

---

[19] See further P. Dunn et al (2021) *Adult social care and COVID-19 after the first wave*, Health Foundation Briefing, May, p 25.

[20] House of Commons and House of Lords (2022) Joint Committee on Human Rights Protecting Human Rights in Care Settings Fourth Report of Session 2022–23, HC 216, HL Paper 51, 22 July, p 25.

[21] See, for example, C.Ó. Néill (2022): 25.

[22] H. Bows and J. Herring (2022) 'DNACPR decisions during COVID-19: an empirical and analytical study', *Medical Law Review*, 30(1): 60–80. See also Learning Disability England (2020) 'Do not resuscitate notices and people with learning disabilities. January–April 2020 in COVID-19: Findings from our survey', May; and the discussion in Learning Disability England (2020) 'Disabled peoples' rights, DNR, and COVID-19'.

[23] The House of Commons and House of Lords Select Joint Select Committee on Human Rights also indicated that they 'did not believe that there are sufficient measures to ensure adequate respect for the right to private and family life (Article 8 ECHR) in relation to care users and visiting arrangements in care settings', House of Commons House of Lords Joint Committee on Human Rights (2020) *The Government's response to COVID-19: human rights implications*, Seventh Report of Session 2019–20, HC 265; HL Paper 125, 21 September, paras 74–81; Care Quality Commission (2021) *Protect, respect, connect – decisions about living and dying well during COVID-19*, April.

[24] Amnesty International (2020) *As if expendable: The UK Government's failure to protect older people in care homes during the COVID-19 pandemic*, October, pp 24–7. See also contemporary media reports, such as BBC News (2020) 'Coronavirus: Care workers "shocked" by virus treatment guidance', 3 April.

Local authorities, which have care and support duties in relation to adult social care under the Care Act 2014, had to adapt to new working practices and methods of service delivery in rapidly changing circumstances.[25] COVID-19-related staff illness, and absences where workers needed to shield themselves or vulnerable family members, or where they took leave to care for sick relatives or self-isolated after testing positive, had a major impact on workforce capacity just as need grew sharply. Private care providers, whether local authority funded or self-funded – including domiciliary care and support agencies, residential care homes, nursing homes, and some day centres and other non-residential opportunities – were also hit by increased and changing demands and reduced workforce capacity.[26] This, as Hudson notes, intensified the 'fragility in the care market'.[27] As we will see in the next section of this chapter these cumulative effects added further pressure to what was arguably already a 'crisis' situation for this chronically overstretched and under-resourced sector.

II. Contextualising adult social care: definitions and delivery

This section of the chapter places adult social care in England in context. First, we explore definitional issues regarding adult social care in England today. Second, we examine the different forms of delivery of adult social care placing this in its broader historical and regulatory context.[28] We then consider the extent to which adult social care can be claimed to be 'in crisis'.

As Humphries comments of adult social care, 'it is hard to pin down a clear definition of what the term actually means'.[29] A very useful working definition, however, was provided by the Law Commission in its review of the legal regulation of social care published in 2011, which stated that:

> Adult social care means the care and support provided by local social services authorities pursuant to their responsibilities towards adults who need extra support. This includes older people, people with learning disabilities, physically disabled people, people with mental health problems, drug and alcohol misusers and carers. Adult social

---

[25] See discussion in Chapters 5 and 6.
[26] See further Migration Advisory Committee (2022) *Adult Social Care and Immigration: A Report from the Migration Advisory Committee*, April, CP665.
[27] B. Hudson (2021), p 120.
[28] We explore the nature of 'care' as a theoretical paradigm later in this volume in Chapter 2.
[29] R. Humphries (2022) *Ending the Social Care Crisis: A New Road to Reform*, Bristol: Policy Press, p 53.

care services include the provision by local authorities and others of *traditional services* such as care homes, day centres, equipment and adaptations, meals, and home care. It can also extend to a range of so-called *non-traditional services* – such as gym membership, art therapy, life coaching, personal assistants, emotional support, and classes or courses. Adult social care also includes services that are provided to carers – such as help with travel expenses, respite care, and career advice. Finally, adult social care also includes the mechanisms for delivering services, such as assessment, personal budgets and direct payments.[30]

This is the description on which the analysis in this book is predicated. While the domain of adult social care is very broad and not easily amenable to statutory definition, social workers are in contrast a defined legal category. Social workers are required to be regulated by the Health and Care Professions Council by Social Work England[31] and a social worker for the purposes of the statutory instruments is one which is regulated under the Register.[32] The role of Director of Adult Social Services is also recognized by statute as a role which designated local authorities must establish, although this is not subject to separate professional regulation.[33] Those employed as 'care workers' in the social care sector in England are also not subject to professional regulation.[34] One further definitional question here is the use of the term 'personal assistants', which in this context is used to describe a person employed directly by another person for the purpose of providing care and support, often funded by a personal care budget.[35] The words used to describe those who draw upon care and support services are also contested. People are core to all these roles and relationships, and there has been a conversation and debate about the appropriate way in which to speak of people who draw on care and support services, given that this is only one aspect of their self. This conversation is underpinned by

---

[30] Law Commission (2011) *Adult Social Care Law*, Law Com No 326, HC 941, 10 May.
[31] See further the discussion in A. Bramner (2020) *Social Work Law*, London: Pearson, ch 1.
[32] Social Workers Regulations 2018 (SI 2019/893), para 2(5) and see also para 2(6).
[33] Local Authority Social Services Act 1970, s 6.
[34] Regulation does exist in Scotland and Wales. See further Part 3 of the Regulation and Inspection of Social Care (Wales) Act 2016. The issue as to whether such regulation can be seen as a positive remains subject to debate. See further discussion in N. Hemmings, C. Oung and L. Schlepper (2022) *New horizons: What can England learn from the professionalisation of care workers in other countries?*, Research report, Nuffield Trust.
[35] For a discussion of the role of personal assistants, see J.G. Woolham et al (2019) *Roles, responsibilities, and relationships: hearing the voices of Personal Assistants and Directly Employed Care Workers*, NIHR Policy Research Unit in Health and Social Care Workforce, The Policy Institute, King's College London, p 5.

concerns around how the state determines that this grouping of individuals should be characterized.³⁶ Terms such as 'service user', 'client', and even 'customer' are still routinely used, although such terminology is increasingly considered to be outmoded and damaging;³⁷ the nuance of this debate however, goes beyond the scope of the present volume. Here we are taking the approach that we will refer to those persons who are attempting to use or who are using statutory services as people seeking to use or drawing upon such services.

Secondly, we provide context for the later analysis of adult social care in the context of the pandemic by examining the nature of the delivery of adult social care in England over time. The provision of social care to adults is multi-faceted in nature. In considering some of the typologies in which care has been conceptualized, Razavi in a classic analysis suggested that the delivery of care, 'the architecture through which care is provided', can usefully be viewed in terms of a 'care diamond'.³⁸ At one point of the diamond is the family/household, at another point are the markets, the third point of the diamond is not-for-profit organizations, and the final point of the diamond is that of the state – whether 'federal or local'. The actual delivery of care provision can involve aspects of some, or all, of these aspects of the diamond. They are not, however, static; they may be, and frequently are, multi-layered and changeable systems.

The 'family carers' aspect of Razavi's 'care diamond', as we shall see in this book, plays a critically important part in the provision of adult social care in England.³⁹ But what actually is a 'family'?⁴⁰ Herring comments that 'the notion of a family is notoriously difficult to define'.⁴¹ Societal conceptions of what constitutes 'a family' in England have evolved over time reflecting changing approaches to the nature of personal relationships and

---

[36] This also needs to be seen in the context of the historical trends in evolution of adult social care policy and notably the movement from the 1970s onwards – generally the discussion in in B. Hudson (2021), chs 1 and 2.

[37] B. Shannon (2019) 'Words that make me go hmmm: Service user', Rewriting Social Care Blog, 30 November.

[38] S. Razavi (2007) *The Political and Social Economy of Care in a Development Context Conceptual Issues, Research Questions and Policy Options*, United Nations Research Institute for Social Development, Gender and Development Programme Paper, Number 3, p 21.

[39] Carers UK (2024) *Unpaid Carers in Employment: Occupation and Industry*, Research report, April. Those carers who spend at least 35 hours each week caring for someone with an illness or disability, and who earn below a certain threshold, may be eligible to claim Carer's Allowance.

[40] L. Murray and M. Barnes (2010) 'Have families been rethought? Ethic of care, family and "whole family" approaches', *Social Policy & Society*, 9(4): 533–44.

[41] J. Herring (2019) *Family Law* (9th edn), London: Pearson, pp 2–5.

the consequent alteration of the formal legal status of some relationships, such as through civil partnership and same-sex marriage. Furthermore, an individual's own definition of their own family may well differ from that of another.

A further aspect of the provision of care, as noted by Humphries and others, is that the majority of care within families is provided by women – as indeed it is among those working in the professional care sector.[42] As we shall see in subsequent chapters, the role of family and unpaid carers became even more widespread and invaluable during the pandemic. Some care and support is also provided via voluntary sector organizations – another point of the diamond that shone during the pandemic. However, the majority of adult social care provision today is undertaken through the private sector care market.[43] This market is often interconnected with the state, through a local authority commissioning or purchasing services, or alternatively services may be purchased by self-funding individuals.[44]

In England, the state's involvement in adult social care is a complex picture, with a long history. The roots of adult social care in England can be traced from the provision of welfare in medieval Christian Europe with 'welfare houses' and hospitals when the obligation to care for those in need started to separate from monasteries and churches,[45] and there has long been a complicated relationship between the state and provision for 'the poor' or those who are unable to support themselves.[46] The backdrop to the developments from the second half of the twentieth century in relation

---

[42] R. Humphries (2022) *Ending the Social Care Crisis: A New Road to Reform*, Bristol: Policy Press, p 53. See also Chapter 2 (this volume) on feminist approaches to the ethic of care.

[43] See further discussion in B. Hudson (2021).

[44] Sometimes there are also partial funding arrangements. See M. Henwood (et al) (2022) 'Self-funders: still by-standers in the English social care market?', *Social Policy and Society*, 21(2): 227–41.

[45] The historical antecedents of today's debates concerning social care provision do, however, date back much further. See for example discussion in: S. Watson (2020) *On Hospitals: Welfare, Law, and Christianity in Western Europe, 400–1320*, Oxford: Oxford University Press; P. Slack (1995) *The English Poor Law, 1531–1782* (2nd edn), Cambridge: Cambridge University Press; W.P. Quigley (1996) 'Five hundred years of the English Poor Law 1349–1834', *Akron Law Review*, 73; P. Thane (2000) *Old Age in English History: Past Experiences, Present Issues*, Oxford: Oxford University Press; K. Woodruff (1977) 'The Royal Commission on the Poor Law and the unemployed (1905–09)', *International Review of Social History*, 22(2): 137–64; M. Ward (2011) *Beatrice Webb and Her Quest for a Fairer Society: A Hundred Years of the Minority Report*, Oxford: The Smith Institute; Sir William Beveridge (1942) *Social Insurance and Allied Services*, Cmnd 6404.

[46] See further: P. Slack (1995); W.P. Quigley (1996).

to adult social care is formed by the various pieces of Poor Law legislation and the evolution of the Workhouse.[47]

Since 1945 there have been five major pieces of legislation which set the trajectory of and formulated the operational structures for the delivery of care and support for adult social care in England. These are the National Assistance Act 1948, the Local Authority Social Services Act 1970, the Chronically Sick and Disabled Persons Act 1970, the National Health Service and Community Care Act 1990, and the Care Act 2014. While the reforms of the post-war Labour government provided an extensive legal and policy framework for health and social care in the late 1940s, these formed two specific streams whose distinctions remain largely in place today. The NHS was established to provide health care that was free at the point of use,[48] but that approach was not adopted in the National Assistance Act of 1948, which included provisions concerning adult social care and recognized that individuals who had the financial means would need to contribute to their own care.[49] The assessment of needs and related duties and powers concerning the provision of various services that were to be undertaken by local authorities were included in the Local Authority Social Services Act 1970, some of whose provisions, such as those requiring the establishment of a Director of Adult Social Services, are still in force today.[50] This was also accompanied by the passage of the Chronically Sick and Disabled Persons Act 1970 which placed obligations on local authorities to provide services for persons who had disabilities in their area.

While delivery structures have always been complex, the 1980s and 1990s saw critical changes in the formula of adult social care delivery. There was a movement, favoured by the Conservative Thatcher Government, towards community care, or 'care in the community'.[51] However, Dalley comments:

---

[47] See further, for example: L. Clements (et al) (2019) *Community Care and the Law* (7th edn), London: Legal Action Group, para i.4; S. Ottaway (2013) 'The Elderly in the Eighteenth-Century Workhouse', in J. Reinarz and L. Schwarz (eds) *Medicine and the Workhouse*, Rochester, NY: University of Rochester Press; P. Thane (1983) 'The history of provision for the elderly to 1929', in D. Jerrome (ed) *Ageing in Modern Society: Contemporary Approaches*, London: Croom Helm/St Martin's Press.

[48] There are some exceptions to this in that, for example, charges are made for such things as NHS prescriptions, subject to means testing.

[49] See also the discussion in G. Dalley (2022), p 72.

[50] See further Chapter 3 and for background to this Act see F. Seebohm (1968) *Report of the committee on local authority and allied personal social services*, Cmnd 3703.

[51] There was an examination of the role of the social worker and the need for a community-based approach in P. Barclay (1978) *Social Workers: Their Role and Tasks*, London: National Institute for Social Work; and see further C. Hallett (1983) 'Social workers: the role and tasks 1982', *British Journal of Social Work*, 13(4): 395–404.

Since 1980 Conservative Governments of the time had actively encouraged the development of privately owned care homes despite their official policy favouring community care. Their growth had been facilitated by the ability of potential residents to claim the cost of fees from the social security system, as already noted, thus by-passing the involvement of local councils.[52]

Sir Roy Griffiths,[53] in his influential report on community care for the Thatcher Government, saw merit in a multiplicity of provision with a 'mixed economy' of care and stated that 'social services authorities should see themselves as the arrangers and purchasers of care services – not as monopolistic providers'.[54]

Partnership at local level between the NHS and social care was viewed as possible, albeit with distinct but complementary roles for district health authorities, social services departments, and family practitioner committees. The need for partnership between, and indeed the integration of, health and social care has been a running theme revisited during restructuring over the decades, leading to the development of today's Integrated Care Boards, which we consider in Chapter 3. Yet these remain problematic, not least due to the fundamentally different approaches taken to health and social care funding. Another formative feature of the Griffiths report was the stress placed upon what was seen as the need for an acknowledgement of financial realities and the need for appropriately managed funding.[55] This theme also echoes down the years. Griffiths famously referred to community care as being 'a poor relation; everybody's distant relative but nobody's baby'.[56] This characterization remains pertinent today.

The National Health Service and Community Care Act 1990 (the legislation which followed the Griffiths Report) provided that local authorities would be required to produce community care plans in consultation with

---

[52] Dalley (2022) *Caring in Crisis*, p 107.
[53] R. Griffiths (1983) *NHS Management Inquiry*, London: Department of Health and Social Security; see further discussion in M. Gorsky (2013) ' "Searching for the people in charge": appraising the 1983 Griffiths NHS Management Inquiry', *Medical History*, 57(1): 87 and F. Macfarlane, M. Exworthy and M. Willmott (2011) 'The 1983 Griffiths Inquiry', in M. Exworthy et al (eds) Shaping Health Policy: Case Study Methods and Analysis, Bristol: Policy Press, pp 135–50; and R. Griffiths (1988) *Community Care: Agenda for Action. A report to the Secretary of State for Social Services*, London: HMSO; and see discussion in D.J. Hunter and K. Judge (1988) *Griffiths and Community Care: Meeting the Challenge*, London: Kings Fund Institute.
[54] Griffiths (1988), para 3.4.
[55] Griffiths (1988), para 38.
[56] Griffiths (1988), para 38.

local populations. The local authorities would be required to undertake assessments of care needs for local residents. Such assessments should, where appropriate, involve the NHS and housing authorities. Those living in care homes were no longer able to claim fees through the social security system; rather, grant funding was paid directly from central budgets to local authorities. As a result, before being admitted to care homes, people would be subject to both needs assessments and means testing[57] to ascertain how their fees would be paid. Alongside this shift, local authority care homes were steadily transferred into the private sector throughout the 1980s and 1990s. As Needham and Glasby note: 'social workers became "care managers", assessing people's needs and securing a subsequent "care package" from a mixed economy of private, voluntary and public services'.[58]

There were a number of other attempts to restructure the form of care delivery and funding in England over the decades that followed, although proposals for and legislation in relation to free personal care and a national care service were never taken forward.[59] Legislation was introduced to enable direct payments to those using care services in the Community Care (Direct Payments) Act 1996, and this approach continues today.[60] The use of direct payments further characterizes those making use of care and support services as 'customers'.[61] It was not, however, until 2014 that the next radical restructuring was introduced in the form of the Care Act 2014, a far-reaching piece of legislation which underpins the operation of adult social care provision in England and remains in force today.[62]

The Care Act 2014 followed the Law Commission's review of adult social care legislation.[63] It replaced the previous provisions of the National

---

[57] See Dalley (2022), p 107.
[58] C. Needham and J. Glasby (2023) 'Forgotten, neglected and a poor relation? Reflecting on the 75th anniversary of adult social care', in M. Exworthy, R. Mannion and M. Powell (eds) *The NHS at 75,* Bristol: Bristol University Press, p 199.
[59] See further Royal Commission on Long Term Care *(1999) With Respect to Old Age: Long-Term Care: Rights and Responsibilities,* CM 4192, London: HMSO; and H.M. Government (2008) *Shaping the Future of Care Together,* Cm 7673, London: HMSO Royal Commission on Long Term Care; The Personal Care at Home Act 2010; see further B. Cooper and A. Harrop (2023) *Support Guaranteed: The Roadmap to a National Care Service,* London: Fabian Society.
[60] See further Chapter 3.
[61] See C. Needham (2007) *Reform of Public Services Under New Labour: Narratives of Consumerism,* Basingstoke: Palgrave Macmillan. As Needham and Glasby comment, their use is controversial with tensions between those who see this in terms of civil rights as exercising autonomous choice and those who see this as 'privatisation by the back door'. See further Needham and Glasby (2023), p 202.
[62] We examine the Care Act 2014 in detail in Chapter 3.
[63] See further Law Commission (2008) *Adult Social Care Scoping Review;* Law Commission (2010) *Adult Social Care Consultation Paper* No 192; Law Commission (2011) *Adult Social*

Assistance Act of 1948 and aimed to clarify and streamline the plethora of complex, disparate provisions which applied to social care. It roots the provision of adult social care and support in a core 'well-being principle' and sets out a series of duties and powers incumbent upon local authorities in relation to the provision of services to meet the needs of both adults who draw on care and support and of their carers.[64]

One aspect of the Care Act 2014 which has still not yet been brought into force is that which relates to a cap on the lifetime care costs which could be borne by an individual. Instead, contributions remain subject to means testing.[65] Funding remains a source of huge controversy, with debates ranging from the extent to which public funding of care provision is sustainable, how such funds should be generated and allocated, to concerns around the division between those who can and cannot afford to self-fund. The details of the reform of care funding go beyond the specific focus of this book.[66] Nonetheless, as we shall see later, the rising costs of care can be seen as part of the broader 'crisis' in adult social care.

The language of 'the state' can at times obscure the roles of people who are employed in this process. Social workers remain critically important actors in the delivery of care and support,[67] as are their Directors of Adult Social Services (DASSs) who manage their departments at strategic level. All these roles demand a high level of professional discretion and responsibility. As we shall see in subsequent chapters, DASSs, along with principal social workers (PSWs), had a crucial role in re-setting local policy and operational decisions during the pandemic including the operation of Care Act easements.

The adult social care delivery model is very complex. An individual person's care may not fall within a single point of Razavi's 'care diamond',

---

Care Law No 326. See for an evaluation of the operation of the Act J. Tew et al (2019) *Implementing the Care Act 2014: Building Social Resources to Prevent, Reduce or Delay Needs for Care and Support in Adult Social Care in England. Final Report for the Department of Health and Social Care*, University of Birmingham Department of Social Work and Social Care.

[64] See further discussion in Chapter 3.
[65] See discussion in Chapter 3.
[66] This remains an ongoing issue in England. See further Cabinet Office HMG (2021) *Build Back Better. Our Plan for Health and Social Care.* CP 506, 7 September 2021; and Department of Health and Social Care (2021) *People at the Heart of Care. Adult Social Care Reform White Paper.* CP 560, 1 December; updated 18 March 2022.
[67] See further in relation to the evolution and development of the role of the social workers, the Barclay Report in 1982 – P. Barclay (1981) *Social Workers Their Role and Tasks*, London: National Institute for Social Workers, and see further C. Hallett (1983) 'Social workers: the role and tasks 1982', *British Journal of Social Work*, 13(4): 395–404; and D. Tanner, P. Beedell, P. Willis, G. Nosowska, L. Noszlopy, J. Powell, M. Ubhi and M. Wakeham (2024) *Social Work with Older People: SWOP Project Final Report*, University of Birmingham, University of Bristol, Effective Practice.

but rather is likely to involve multi-faceted care provision – with some care being provided through the private sector funded at local authority level, and some provided by family members, who may in turn make use of services and support provided via the voluntary/charitable sector.

While much of the media focus during the early years of the pandemic concerning adult social care in 2020 and 2021 was on the acutely distressing events which took place in care homes involving spread of the virus, loss of life, and individuals being unable to see loved ones due to visiting restrictions, what happened outside in the broader community was far less visible.[68] As noted previously, only one portion of social care provision is delivered in the residential care sector. Beyond this, local authority and private providers work to support people in their own homes living independently or with family. In such situations, support may be provided through the employment of personal assistants[69] or by visiting carers employed via domiciliary care agencies. At the start of the pandemic some families decided to cancel their existing care provision. Amid rising infection rates and as many people were furloughed from their jobs, some took on the role of caring for their relatives.[70] This decision was often driven by concerns about the risks of contact and contagion, and to avoid having social care workers in their homes. Of course, many others were already functioning as unpaid, informal carers to spouses, relatives, or friends, and the pandemic isolated them even further. While these 'unpaid carers' are formally acknowledged as an essential and integral part of the UK's adult social care system, they are not always well supported and, during the pandemic, they were 'neglected' and 'felt abandoned as services closed'.[71] As the House of Lords Adult Social Care Committee commented in its 2022 report:

> The term 'unpaid carers' is a barely adequate description of the many millions of women and men who provide care and support to disabled adults for a lifetime, or who become carers for older people who, sometimes suddenly through stroke, dementia or many other causes, become reliant on care and support. Their voices are hardly heard and

---

[68] House of Lords Adult Social Care Committee (2022) *A 'Gloriously Ordinary Life': Spotlight on Adult Social Care*, Adult Social Care Committee Report of Session 2022–23, HL Paper 99, at para 48.

[69] See further C. Needham and J. Glasby (2024) *Debates in Personalisation*, Bristol: Policy Press.

[70] See Carers UK (2020) *Carers Week 2020 Research Report. The Rise in the Number of Unpaid Carers during the Coronavirus (COVID-19) Outbreak*, and further discussion of this in relation to our West Midlands case study in Chapter 5.

[71] J. Onwumere, C. Creswell, J. Livingston et al (2021) 'COVID-19 and UK family carers: policy implications', *The Lancet Psychiatry*, 8(10): 929–36. See also S. Razavi (2007), n 33, p 6.

they are, for the most part, invisible to those of us who are not in the same situation.[72]

This multi-faceted complexity in the scope and delivery of social care creates notable challenges for law and policy. These challenges can be amplified when some or all points of the 'care diamond' come under pressure. In 2020, the pressures grew intense and multitudinous, but they were pressing upon a state of 'crisis' already manifest. Needham and Hall identify how the strain on social care has developed over two decades, moving from a state of 'slow collapse' into what is claimed to be 'urgent crisis'.[73] They pinpoint five 'crisis claims' which have been made in relation to adult social care.[74] First, Needham and Hall identify a 'crisis of demand' in the context of an ageing population. One of the great success stories of modern medical science is that we have been, for the most part, living longer, but at the same time we cannot assume that all this increased life span will be enjoyed in good health.[75] In fact, life expectancy in the UK has recently fallen, having slowed since 2011 following decades of steady increase, then declining sharply since the pandemic.[76] While 'healthy ageing' is obviously viewed as a positive, in reality an older population is likely to have increasing co-morbidities – as seen, for example, in the changing needs of people in residential care who may require more healthcare support, and the likelihood of such care needs being considered as 'critical' or 'substantial'.[77] This in turn raises questions around who will deliver that care to an ageing population.[78] Humphries has commented that the number of people over 65 who are in receipt of publicly funded social care has fallen in recent years, while there has been a rise in working-age adults receiving support, due to the rising number of working-age people with disabilities or long-term health conditions.[79]

---

[72] House of Lords Adult Social Care Committee (2022) *A 'gloriously ordinary life': spotlight on adult social care*, Report of Session 2022–23, HL Paper 99, para 11; and Chapter 7 on the need for support and recognition of unpaid carers.

[73] C. Needham and P. Hall (2024) *Social Care in the UK's Four Nation*, p 89.

[74] See Needham and Hall (2024) *Social Care in the UK's Four Nations*, chapter 3.

[75] See World Health Organization (2022) 'Ageing and Health', factsheet, 1 October.

[76] This downward trend should be viewed against a backdrop of austerity and growing health inequalities; see V. Raleigh (2022) *What Is Happening to Life Expectancy in England?*, King's Fund Long Read, 9 August and Warren, S. (2022) 'Austerity 2.0: why it's critical for our health that the government learns the lessons of Austerity 1.0', *King's Fund blog*, 1 November.

[77] See Needham and Hall (2024) *Social Care in the UK's Four Nations*, pp 90–6; and also the discussion in University of Birmingham Policy Commission (2014) *Healthy Ageing in the C21st the best is still to come*, Birmingham.

[78] See, for example, the discussion in M.D. Fine (2007) *A Caring Society? Care and the Dilemmas of Human Service in the 21st Century*, Basingstoke: Palgrave Macmillan, ch 5.

[79] See further Humphries (2022), pp 1–2.

Overall, it is clear that the need for a sustainable approach to funding and providing care and support for all cohorts has rarely been more pressing.

Second, Needham and Hall identify a 'crisis of family',[80] which is usually construed in one of two ways:

> Discussion of the crisis of family tends to focus on one of the following; first, family changes that have eroded traditional patterns of informal care provision, raising concerns for some that families are doing too *little*; and second, the continued and unsustainable pressures on unpaid (usually family) carers, generating concerns that families are doing *too much*.[81]

Dalley argues that the Care Act 2014 and the related Guidance assumes that 'family "care and support" is the norm of most caring – with the implication that formal, mostly residential, care is the last option to be chosen'.[82] Arguably, some strengths-based approaches reinforce this view.[83] This is not a model that neatly serves a population which by and large has to work to survive, as juggling work with caring responsibilities can be extremely stressful and difficult to balance.

The third crisis identified by Needham and Hall is the 'crisis of the state'.[84] The framing of the nature of this crisis depends on how one views the role of the state, and whether it is regarded as 'doing too much or spending too little'.[85] In the decade leading up to 2020, there is ample evidence that austerity policies impacted on adult social care provision. Ferguson and Lavelette highlight how by 2012, after the cuts in government funding to welfare spending, and local authority spending some 33 of the most well-known British charities such as the British Red Cross, Mencap, and the Royal National Institute for the Blind had written to *The Observer* stating that the system was in crisis and that '[e]very day, people tell us they are being let down by the care system – unable to access services, finding their care reduced and relying on family and friends to provide support'.[86]

The House of Commons Select Committees for Health and Social Care and Levelling Up Housing and Communities in their 2018 report on the

---

[80] See Needham and Hall (2024) *Social Care in the UK's Four Nations*, pp 96–104.
[81] See Needham and Hall (2024), p 96.
[82] Dalley (2022), p 136.
[83] See Chapter 3.
[84] See Needham and Hall (2024), pp 104–10.
[85] See Needham and Hall (2024), p 112.
[86] I. Ferguson and M. Lavalette (2013) 'The crisis in adult social care', in I. Ferguson and M. Lavalette with responses from B. Jordan, M. Lymbery, D. Whitfield, I. Hood, B. Smith, and C. Cairns, *Adult Social Care,* Bristol: Policy Press at p 5.

funding of adult social care noted that overall 'real terms' adult social care expenditure fell from £15.8 billion to some £14.9 billion in the periods 2010–11 and 2016–17.[87] In evidence for the Select Committee's subsequent 2022 report on Adult Social Care Funding, Charles Tallack, assistant director of the REAL Centre at The Health Foundation, commented that:

> Since 2010, the amount of funding for social care has increased by almost exactly 0% in real terms. That is despite demand pressures. There is an ageing population, a growing population. That means that per person, adjusting for age, funding is about 12% less than it would be had we met the demographic pressures.[88]

In subsequent chapters, we shall see further the impacts of austerity in relation to the West Midlands' local authorities in our case study, most notably in Birmingham since 2010.[89]

The next crisis which Needham and Hall identify is the crisis of 'the market', which in this context they define as being 'the provision of care by non-state providers' stemming from the National Health Service and Community Care Act 1990. They agree with the characterization of the 'trifurcated market' identified by Gingrich as providing a 'reasonable summary of patterns of delivery'.[90] Gingrich summarizes the trifurcated market as being one in which:

> Wealthy users could buy high-quality care at high prices from exclusive private providers, low-income users received public funding for low-quality care, while middle-income users were stuck paying high fees while receiving the same low-quality care as the publicly funded users.[91]

The very existence of this trifurcated market should be viewed in relation to a consequent further crisis in the 'quality' of adult social

---

[87] House of Commons Health and Social Care and Housing and Communities and Local Government, First Joint Report of the Health and Social Care and Housing, Communities and Local Government Committees of Session 2017–19.

[88] House of Commons Levelling Up, Housing and Communities Committee and Health and Social Care Select Committee (2022) *Long-term funding of adult social care*, Second Report of Session 2022–23, HC 19, para 23.

[89] See J. Harris (2024) 'Birmingham's cuts reveal the ugly truth about Britain in 2024: the state is abandoning its people', *The Guardian*, 17 March; and further Chapter 5.

[90] Needham and Hall (2024) *Social Care in the UK's Four Nations*, p 116.

[91] J.R. Gingrich (2011) Making Markets in the Welfare State: The Politics of Varying Market Reforms, Cambridge: Cambridge University Press, pp 183–4.

care provision, as identified by, for example, Ferguson and Lavalette and Harding.[92] There have been major scandals regarding care provision, such as that of Winterbourne View, a private hospital for adults with learning disabilities on the outskirts of Bristol, with abuse revealed due to a BBC *Panorama* programme investigation which resulted in six staff being given prison sentences in relation to the physical and psychological abuse of residents.[93] Sadly, this is far from an isolated example as the subsequent events at Whorlton Hall, a private institution in County Durham, where abuses by care workers of residents with learning disabilities and autism were again uncovered due to a BBC *Panorama* investigation in 2019.[94] This subsequently led to successful criminal prosecutions against the care workers concerned.[95]

The fifth crisis is characterized as the 'crisis of community', a broad sweep which belies the multi-faceted, interconnected nature of the sector:

> Community means many different things. It can be a companion with family care, as part of the informal provision of support for people. It can also be a term for the formal services provided through the not-for-profit sector which includes charities and social enterprises which are also part of the market of providers.[96]

Needham and Hall comment that 'community' can be still seen as an important aspect of care; they also suggest that co-production has become an important means through which community can be developed.[97] Community can also be seen to have been fostered through the increase in volunteering for those with care needs during the pandemic. In the early early months of the pandemic many people came forward to undertake volunteering in their local area and this provided some support to neighbours with day-to-day tasks

---

[92] See I. Ferguson and M. Lavalette (2013), pp 1–3; R. Harding (2021) 'COVID-19 in adult social care: futures, funding and fairness', in D. Cowan and A. Mumford (eds) *Pandemic Legalities: Legal Responses to COVID-19 Justice and Social Responsibility*, Bristol: Bristol University Press, pp 123–4.

[93] See further NHS South West of England (2012) *Report of the NHS Review of the commissioning of care and treatment at Winterbourne View*; A. Hill (2012) 'Winterbourne View care home staff jailed for abusing residents', *The Guardian*, 26 October.

[94] J. Plomin (2019) 'Whorlton Hall hospital abuse and how it was uncovered', *BBC News*, 22 May.

[95] S. Jagger and P. Harris (2024) 'Whorlton Hall: four carers sentenced for abusing hospital patients', *BBC News*, 19 January.

[96] Needham and Hall (2024), p 126.

[97] Needham and Hall (2024), p 132. See also discussion in Chapter 2 on co-production.

such as shopping and for social connection.[98] There were also formal calls for an NHS volunteer force during this period, though as Hudson comments, 'the tasks required to be undertaken more resembled the functions of adult social care'.[99] As it transpired, very few of the hundreds of thousands who signed up to help were assigned tasks.[100]

It was predictable that this combination of complexity and pressure would be sharply amplified in the extraordinary circumstances of a global pandemic and, as we will see in Chapter 4, this was factored into some extent into government-level pandemic planning and resilience strategy. In the event, the Westminster Government did introduce specific continuity measures through the Coronavirus Act 2020, which would allow local authorities to depart from certain adult social care powers and duties under the Care Act 2014 if workforce capacity was under too much strain. As noted, the changes in the 2020 Act proved controversial and only a very small number of local authorities decided to formally activate the Care Act easements provisions for a fleeting period of time. Nonetheless, the impacts of the pandemic on the delivery of adult social care services from 2020 onwards have proved considerable.

III. Research design

This book draws upon work undertaken during our research project 'Removing rights from the vulnerable: the impact of COVID-19 Social Care "easements"', funded by the Economic and Social Research Council (ESRC) COVID-19 Rapid Response Grant No. ES/V015486/1. We gratefully acknowledge the funding support of the ESRC for this project. Running from November 2020 to July 2022, our research was given ethical approval by the University of Birmingham Research Ethics Committee. In addition, we applied for and were given endorsement by the Association of Directors of Adult Social Services (ADASS) through their ethical approval process. Finally, some, although not all, of the local authorities which were approached for interview also required us to obtain formal approval through

---

[98] G. Mao et al (2021) 'What have we learned about COVID-19 volunteering in the UK? A rapid review of the literature', *BMC Public Health*, 21(1470).

[99] B. Hudson (2021) p 123. He cites as examples 'community response volunteers who would collect shopping medication or other essential supplies for someone self-isolating and deliver these to their home'; and also 'check in and chat volunteers, who would provide regular support calls to elderly people living in isolation and at risk of loneliness'.

[100] J. Moritz (2020) 'COVID-19 volunteers "not being called upon" to help NHS', *BBC News*, 24 April.

their respective research governance processes. In those instances, we sought and obtained the relevant clearance before undertaking any interviews with their staff.

The book takes a sociolegal approach to the issues raised. Our focus is on the impacts of the pandemic on adult social care law and policy in England, its legacy, and the lessons that can be drawn from the pandemic experience. The different approaches to health and social care and indeed some of the legal and policy choices made during the COVID-19 pandemic across the devolved jurisdictions go beyond the scope of this book.[101] As will be seen later we examine the provision and regulatory context of adult social care and of the pandemic across historical, ethical, and legal perspectives in the first three chapters of this book. We then provide a case study of one area in England – the West Midlands – which has a highly diverse population, with notable pockets of socio-economic deprivation in both rural and urban areas. The West Midlands is selected as a case study in which to examine the impacts of the Coronavirus Act 2020 and the associated Care Act easements as this was the part of the country where the largest number of local authorities chose to formally operate the easements. These five local authorities appeared to form a 'cluster' and we were curious to understand why they had implemented easements, what happened when these were implemented, why they were withdrawn, what happened after their withdrawal, and more broadly what lessons can be drawn for adult social care and pandemic planning can be drawn from these events.

Our approach comprised a literature review and analysis and an intensive period of qualitative empirical research involving semi-structured interviews. The literature examined included primary and secondary legal sources and published academic work from the fields of legal scholarship, history, social policy, health and social care, ethics, and politics. We also drew upon a range of grey literature, including minutes of meetings (at national, regional, and local government level – particularly the West Midlands local authorities – along with those of relevant professional networks and committees), professional letters and notifications, and formal reports in the public domain.

As part of our West Midlands case study, we undertook a series of semi-structured interviews with a broad range of stakeholders to build up a fuller and more nuanced picture of what had actually happened. The latter included DASSs, PSWs, and community assurance and resilience leads employed in local authorities. We also undertook interviews with individuals from organizations representing people who use social care services, social

---

[101] For an excellent recent comparative analysis, see C. Needham and P. Hall (2024).

care advocates, legal experts, local Healthwatch leads, and managers of care providers. All the interviews in this main group of interviewees were anonymized. Two other interviewees, neither of whom worked as local government employees, expressly provided that their transcripts should not be anonymized and that any quotes would be directly attributable to them or their role.

Given the parameters of the project, we used purposive sampling, seeking to recruit interviewees who would have professional knowledge of and involvement in the operation of social care delivery systems, and in most cases we specifically sought those who would have held some responsibility for the decision-making around the use or not of Care Act easements during the first year of the pandemic. We also contacted a range of professionals working in third-sector organizations and campaign groups to try to elicit a range of views on how these processes were being experienced and reported within professional networks and the wider media. We aimed to achieve some snowballing in this way, and we were fortunate that this was successful in several cases. Having initially identified those local authorities which had formally activated easements, we chose a sample of neighbouring authorities which had not, for comparison. We contacted potential interviewees directly via email.

Between March and October 2021, we conducted over 40 interviews, primarily using Zoom and Teams video calls, which were recorded, professionally transcribed, and then anonymized prior to analysis. These included interviews with employees of local authorities which had formally notified the Department of Health and Social Care (DHSC) that they had implemented easements (the DASS and PSW from two local authorities, the DASS from one authority, and the PSW from another). We also interviewed five other local authority employees directly engaged in managing the community pandemic response, including one working in community resilience. In relation to those local authorities which had not formally operated easements, we interviewed the PSWs from two local authorities, four other employees, of whom two were working on pandemic-related community support and resilience. In addition, we undertook five interviews with senior staff at Healthwatch branches across the West Midlands, and one with the West Midlands team at the national office.

There were also nine interviewees from national level bodies and ten interviewees from local or regional third-sector organizations. A final grouping of five interviews was drawn from the Local Government and Social Care Ombudsman Office, the DHSC regional assurance team, and representatives or associates of the Association of Directors of Adult Social Services (ADASS) and the British Association of Social Workers (BASW).

We devised two sets of interview schedules, one for local authority employees and one for those working in third-sector organizations, including charities, community organizations, social enterprises, and others. The interviews generally lasted between 60 and 90 minutes, and covered, among other things, issues such as the process by which individuals and organizations learned of the legislative and operational changes; the level of understanding of these in their organization; an examination of decision-making processes and consultation; an assessment of the impacts of any changes; and whether the Care Act easements had been useful for streamlining resources and prioritizing care or detrimental to service users or staff. We also asked interviewees what they felt would improve services, provision, and working conditions in the sector. The Care Act easements provision, under the Coronavirus Act 2020 and the related guidance, was expired on 16 July 2021, midway through our interview period. The last Care Act easements to be formally operated in the West Midlands were ceased on 30 June 2020. Despite the fact that they were still working amid pandemic conditions in 2021, our interviewees gave very detailed recollections of the situation and decisions made in the early months of 2020.

In addition to these individual interviews, we also participated in one collective Q&A session with the wider adult social services team of one of the West Midlands' local authorities that had formally activated easements, alongside other research teams from the University of Manchester[102] and from King's College London.[103] This was not therefore an 'interview' as such. The research teams had collated a set of core questions, and these were delivered in advance as requested to the local authority representative. Those in the adult social services team who had been involved in the decision-making around and operation of Care Act easements presented an account of their rationale and experience in response to the core questions, alongside a tranche of written materials. So, although we were provided with a notably thorough and systematic account, there was relatively little time for more exploratory questions or spontaneous discussion during the Zoom meeting.

The data from all the interviews was analysed thematically, using a reflexive thematic analysis approach.[104] Key excerpts were selected to capture the

---

[102] An NIHR-funded project, J. Astbury, D. Price, P. Drake and N. Allen (2020) 'The impact of Care Easements under the Coronavirus Act 2020 on the carers of partners with dementia' at https://www.opfpru.nihr.ac.uk/projects/past-projects/the-impact-of-care-act-easements/, accessed 10 July 2024.

[103] Another NIHR-funded project, M. Baginsky 'The operation of easements under the Coronavirus Act 2020 to England's Care Act 2014', at https://www.kcl.ac.uk/research/easements-to-the-care-act, accessed 10 July 2012.

[104] See V. Braun and V. Clarke (2021) 'One size fits all? What counts as quality practice in (reflexive) thematic analysis?', *Qualitative Research in Psychology*, 18(3): 328–52; and V. Braun, V. Clarke et al (2022) 'Doing reflexive thematic analysis', in S. Bager-Charleson and A. McBeath (eds) *Supporting Research in Counselling and Psychotherapy*, Cham: Palgrave Macmillan.

'voices' of some of those working at the frontline of the pandemic response, to illustrate interpretations and decision-making processes, and to explicate particular points of factual interest or divergence from the national-level narrative.[105] In all cases we requested permission to cite selected excerpts, and this was granted in the majority of cases. Only material that was given express documented consent has been used and published. We draw upon the voices of these research participants particularly in Chapters 5 and 6 of this book.

One of the limitations of our approach was that, given the timescales and the fact that we were a research team of two, we were unable to explore directly how people drawing on care and support services experienced the operational changes to delivery at different stages through the pandemic. While mindful of the call for 'Nothing about us without us',[106] the parameters of the initial rapid-response project were set to examine the decision-making processes and experiences specifically of (mostly quite senior) stakeholders working in local authorities and the wider sector. Our broader research for the book focused on the historical, theoretical, ethical, legislative, and policy backdrop to the provision of adult social care and the development of emergency legislation. Our analysis was supplemented by published research undertaken by third sector organizations and other academic research teams whose focus was on the experiences of people who draw on support and services and of carers. It then examines the impacts of the pandemic on social care delivery in the light of this emergency legislation and its aftermath.

There was a level of challenge in achieving access and candid responses from key individuals in certain local authorities and government departments, particularly given the fact that COVID-19 mitigation work was still 'live' and our research focus was considered sensitive by some. We remain very grateful that so many gave of their time and invaluable insights during the interviews.

IV. Conclusions and framework of the book

In this book we explore how adult social care law and policy in England was adapted in the face of the extraordinary challenges of the pandemic, the impact this had on the delivery of care and support services, and the lessons

---

[105] The key themes and a selection of illustrative interview excerpts comprise a substantial section of our report on initial findings: J.V. McHale and L. Noszlopy (2021) *Adult social care provision under pressure: lessons from the pandemic*, Initial report, Birmingham: University of Birmingham.

[106] UN Enable – International Day of Disabled Persons, 2004 – New York: United Nations.

that can be drawn from this experience. The book argues that there was a basic disconnect between adult social care pandemic planning introduced at national level and what happened in spring 2020 in practice. Moreover we argue that the events of 2020 and beyond sharply exposed the weaknesses in existing social care law as well as pandemic planning processes. We argue that lessons need to be learned for pandemic law and policy in particular but also more broadly for social care law and policy. In the next six chapters of this book we aim to set out why these conclusions have been reached. In Chapter 2, 'Foundational Paradigms in Adult Social Care Law and Policy', we examine what is meant by 'care' from a range of perspectives, with a particular focus on the ethic of care and the notion of 'nested realities' of relationality. The chapter explores concepts of fundamental rights and autonomy and suggests that a capabilities approach can provide a helpful framing for adult social care law and policy. It then examines the nature of 'vulnerability' – which remains a contested, but frequently invoked, concept. The links between these foundational paradigms and the ways in which they underpin key pieces of legislation are explored as we seek to understand and critically evaluate how adult social care law and policy operates today.

Chapter 3, 'Legal Regulation of Adult Social Care Provision in England', picks up from the introductory issues raised in the current chapter and takes a closer look at the legislation. It begins by examining the Care Act 2014 and the powers and duties it provides in relation to adults and carers with 'eligible needs', and other related provisions. It interrogates the 'well-being principle' that forms the heart of the legislation and examines how this may be seen as a means of supporting individual capabilities. It explores related statutory provisions concerning care and support under the NHS Continuing Health Care and section 117 of the Mental Health Act 1983. The chapter concludes by analysing the operation of the oversight and monitoring mechanisms that exist in relation to social care provision, and the scrutiny provided of local authorities by the Care Quality Commission (CQC) and the Local Government and Social Care Ombudsman (LGSCO).

Chapter 4, 'Pandemic Preparedness Planning and the Development of Emergency Legislation', explores the legislative powers concerning public health and their interface with civil contingencies frameworks and other emergency protocols. It then examines pre-2020 pandemic preparedness planning exercises in the UK, such as Winter Willow and Cygnus, and the discussions with stakeholders regarding appropriate emergency approaches to social care law and policy in the event they are needed. It interrogates those provisions of the Coronavirus Act 2020 and associated guidance which relate to adult social care, and which allow for changes to the exercise of Care Act powers and duties – the 'Care Act easements'. The chapter concludes with a discussion of how the easements were operated in practice, the controversies around their implementation, and the reasons for their withdrawal.

Chapter 5, '"Easing" the Care Act: Responding to COVID-19 in the West Midlands', provides a regional case study examining local authority responses to adult social care provision during the pandemic. We consider the implications of the Coronavirus Act 2020 and the emergency public health legislation on service delivery across these local authorities. The chapter draws upon the findings of our qualitative interviews with stakeholders, describing their perceptions of the application of the emergency legislation, and the extent to which Care Act easements were or were not operated in the West Midlands during this period. We explore the differences and similarities between the various approaches across the local authorities, and the extent to which the rhetoric of position statements made in public-facing documentation was reflected both in the available council minutes and in the post-hoc, and perhaps more candid, views of our interviewees across the region.

Chapter 6, 'Pandemic Legacies: "Living with COVID-19" in Adult Social Care', considers some of the lingering impacts of COVID-19 on adult social care provision. It begins by examining the legacy of the Care Act easements at national level. It then moves on to consider the lingering impacts felt across the sector from the winter of 2020/21 onwards. These include changes to the delivery of social care on a day-to-day basis; the accelerated drive towards digitization of working practices and service delivery; and the impact on day centres and non-residential support. Finally, Chapter 7 'Adult Social Care Law and Policy: Learning Lessons from the Pandemic' draws upon the findings in earlier chapters to highlight specific lessons which can be learned from the COVID-19 pandemic experience for future pandemic preparedness planning in particular and for adult social care law and policy in general.

2

Foundational Paradigms in Adult Social Care Law and Policy

I. Introduction

Our system of adult social care is built on certain paradigms and assumptions – some explicit, others implicit – and these have evolved significantly over time.[1] Many have been adopted by advocacy and other campaigning organizations, and some have subsequently found their way into policy, legislation, and social work practice. In this chapter we explore these key foundational paradigms and examine the extent to which these do and indeed should underpin adult social care law, policy, and practice in England today. The chapter begins by examining what is meant by 'care' and an ethic of care, its diverse connotations from psychological and ethical perspectives, and in terms of professional practice. We highlight how important it is to understand the 'nested realities' of relationality in care when examining legal and policy positions. Section two examines how discourse around adult social care, particularly where it concerns disability, has engaged with the concepts of fundamental rights and autonomy, and the important potential of the capabilities approach. Third, we consider the conceptualisation and utilisation of the language of 'vulnerability' and how this may inform the way in which we view adult social care. The chapter explores the links between these foundational paradigms and theoretical approaches, and shows how they are critically important for understanding adult social care law and policy in general as well as providing a framework for our subsequent examination of the efficacy of the legal and policy responses to the COVID-19 pandemic in later chapters.

---

[1] See further discussion in M.D. Fine (2007) *A Caring Society? Care and the Dilemmas of Human Service in the 21st Century*, New York: Palgrave Macmillan.

II. A question of 'care'

Some of the vocabulary used in community care law and social care law has an aspect of benign fluidity about it. As Clements et al comment: 'Ambiguity is the lubricant of public policy and social care is littered with soft beguiling labels masking harder intentions.'[2] The language of care underpins the formal provision, assessment, and delivery of adult social care services in England and shapes the ethics and values of professionals who work in the sector. To understand adult social care, we need to unpick our assumptions about what in fact we mean by 'care'. Care, while it might seem to some to be an integral element of human life, can also be viewed as an ambiguous notion. Rummery and Fine suggest that these are two main approaches to understanding its meaning.[3] The first of these approaches, following Folbre, views care in terms of defined tasks undertaken by a set group; namely, women in a 'care economy'.[4] The second is the approach identified by Fisher and Tronto, who state that:

> On the most general level, we suggest that caring be viewed as a species activity that includes everything that we do to maintain, continue and repair our 'world' so that we can live in it as well as possible. That world includes our bodies, ourselves and our environment, all of which we seek to interweave in a complex life sustaining web.[5]

Viewing activity and policy through a 'care' lens may inform the approach ultimately taken in practice by those delivering services. Over the last few decades there has been increasing interest in the idea of an 'ethic of care', which has been influenced particularly by the work of psychologist Carol Gilligan. In her book *In a Different Voice: Psychological Theory and Women's Development*, Gilligan suggested that women and girls have a different approach or 'voice' to males in terms of how they address relationships and issues in context. Females, she claimed, tended to place greater emphasis on

---

[2] L. Clements et al (2019) *Community Care and the Law* (7th edn), London: Legal Action Group.
[3] See further discussion in K. Rummery and M. Fine (2012) 'Care: a critical review of theory, policy and practice', *Social Policy & Administration*, 46(3): 321–43. and see also further discussion in M. Fine (2007), ch 2.
[4] See N. Folbre (2006) 'Measuring care: gender, empowerment and the care economy', *Journal of Human Development*, 7(2): 183.
[5] B. Fisher and J. Tronto (2013) 'Towards a feminist theory of care', in E.K. Abel and M.K. Nelson (eds) *Circles of Care: Work and Identity in Women's Lives*, New York: State University of New York Press. Generally on the interface between care and law, see J. Herring (2013) *Caring and the Law*, London: Bloomsbury Publishing.

empathy and compassion towards others rather than employing conscience- and rule-based morality.[6] While Gilligan's conclusions about gender differences have subsequently been criticized, she is often credited with prompting the 'justice perspective' that continues to inform contemporary policies regarding the provision of care and support. As Held comments, Gilligan's work is valued for

> its suggestion of alternative perspectives through which moral problems can be interpreted: a 'justice perspective' that emphasizes universal moral principles and how they can be applied to particular cases and values rational argument about these; and a 'care perspective' that pays more attention to people's needs to how actual relations between people can be maintained or repaired, and that values narrative and sensitivity to context in arriving at moral judgments.[7]

Considerable academic engagement with the ethic of care has developed over time. Tronto, for example, contests the association of care with women and their emotional labour, and favours instead a more intersectional approach that considers other factors such as class and ethnic background within the wider socio-economic and political contexts of caregiving. She argues that there are four principles which are to be linked together to achieve what is called 'integrity of care', a quality which needs to be maintained, particularly given that the delivery of care inevitably takes place within a political context. These principles are attentiveness, responsibility, competence, and responsiveness.[8] Attentiveness refers to the fact that there is both awareness and recognition of the need for care.[9] Responsibility means that the action of caring willingly flows from the anticipated need. This is deliberately distinguished from obligation by Tronto, who frames it not as a political concept, but rather as 'a term that is embedded in a series of implicit cultural practices rather than in a set of formal rules or series of promises'.[10] But, as Barnes notes, the inclusion of the responsibility principle inevitably raises questions about how such responsibility is handled when it placed upon a state in this context.[11]

---

[6] C. Gilligan (2003) *In a Different Voice: Psychological Theory and Women's Development*, Cambridge, MA: Harvard University Press (originally printed in 1982).

[7] V. Held (2006) *The Ethics of Care: Personal, Political and Global*, Oxford: Oxford University Press, p 28.

[8] J. Tronto (1993) *Moral Boundaries: A Political Argument for an Ethics of Care*, London and New York: Routledge.

[9] J. Tronto (1993), p 128.

[10] J. Tronto (1993), pp 131–2.

[11] M. Barnes (2012) *Care in Everyday Life: An Ethic of Care in Practice*, Bristol: Policy Press, p 22.

The principle of 'competence' is more self-evident, but it is by no means a given that caregiving is always undertaken competently. The principle of 'responsiveness' relates to how the care itself is experienced, from the perspective of the person who receives it.[12] An additional principle – the principle of trust – has been suggested by Sevenhuijsen, in recognition of the imbalance of power and vulnerability in a caring relationship and the possible consequent need for negotiation of the related caring responsibilities.[13] A further principle proposed by Engster[14] is that of respect, meaning: 'the recognition that others are worthy of our attention and responsiveness, are presumed capable of understanding and expressing their needs, and are not lesser beings just because they have needs that they cannot meet on their own'.[15] Barnes also suggests that another aspect of care can be derived from the broader recognition of human interconnectedness as seen in more communitarian approaches such as in the African philosophical concept of Ubuntu, where notions of kinship and mutuality are merged within social and biological categories.[16]

It has also been argued that the ethic of care is related to virtue ethics, and indeed writers such as Halwani would argue that virtue ethics itself embodies an ethic of care.[17] While the philosophical interest in virtue as a concept has a long and diverse history[18] rooted in Aristotelian philosophy, virtue ethics and the more generally growing interest in 'virtue' and 'character' are a relatively modern development in a field long dominated by utilitarian and deontological thought.[19] Slote suggests that the ethics of care is rooted in the notion and moral practice of empathy.[20] However, Held has argued that there is a distinction between the concepts: 'Virtue ethics focuses especially

---

[12] J. Tronto (1993), p 135.
[13] M. Barnes (2012), p 16.
[14] D. Engster (2007) *The Heart of Justice: Care Ethics and Political Theory*, Oxford: Oxford University Press.
[15] D. Engster (2007), p 31.
[16] M. Barnes (2012) A. Gouws and M. Van Zyl (2015) 'Towards a feminist ethics of ubuntu: bridging rights and ubuntu', in D. Engster and M. Harrington (eds) *Care Ethics and Political Theory*, Oxford: Oxford University Press, and Y. Waghid and P. Smeyers (2012) 'Reconsidering *Ubuntu*: on the educational potential of a particular ethic of care', *Educational Philosophy and Theory*, 44(2): 6–20.
[17] R. Halwani (2003) 'Care ethics and virtue ethics', *Hypatia*, 18(3): 161.
[18] See, for example, D. Friede (2013) 'The historical decline of virtue ethics', in D.C. Russell (ed) *The Cambridge Companion to Virtue Ethics*, Cambridge: Cambridge University Press.
[19] See further R. Hursthouse (2001) *On Virtue Ethics*, Oxford: Oxford University Press, pp 1–5; see also P. Simpson (1992) 'Contemporary virtue ethics and Aristotle', *Review of Metaphysics*, 45(3): 503 and D. Clifford (2014) 'Limitations of virtue ethics in the social professions', *Ethics and Social Welfare*, 8(1): 2 for a critical discussion of its application in the caring professions.
[20] M. Slote (2007) *The Ethics of Care and Empathy*, London: Routledge, pp 172–3.

on the state of character of individuals, whereas the ethics of care concerns itself especially with caring relations. Caring relations have primary value.'[21]

Recognizing the importance of caring and an ethic of care has led to calls for greater respect to be given for that caring by society more generally. Fineman sees this in terms of a duty to support carers.

> If infants or ill persons are not cared for, nurtured, nourished, and perhaps loved, they will perish. We can say, therefore, that they owe an individual debt to their individual caretakers. But the obligation is not theirs alone – nor is their obligation confined only to their own caretakers. A sense of social justice demands a broader sense of obligation. Without aggregate caretaking, there could be no society, so we might say that it is caretaking labour that produces and reproduces society. Caretaking labour provides the citizens, the workers, the voters, the consumers, the students, and others who populate society and its institutions. The uncompensated labour of caretakers is an unrecognized subsidy, not only to individuals who directly receive it, but more significantly, to the entire society.[22]

Fineman here raises important questions as to how as a society we view the value of care. In the context of social care, a major role is played by unpaid carers whose work – or what they may view themselves as a 'labour of love' – can often lack public visibility, recognition, or support.

While the concept of the ethic of care has been supported by some feminist writers, others are critical, arguing instead that this gendered characterization of care and caring roles sits in tension with feminist principles. Others regard the ethic of care as aligned with the principles of benevolence, familial relationships, and duty presented in Confucian ethical framework, which is itself regarded as fundamentally paternalist and at odds with feminist thought.[23] Allmark has commented that the theorization and terminology underpinning an ethic of care approach can be regarded as 'hopelessly vague'.[24] It has been argued that it is problematic and inaccurate to view care as inherently 'good' and caring itself as a moral quality. As Allmark states:

> The ethics of care says that we should care that caring is a moral quality and that we should encourage conditions that create care. What it

---

[21] V. Held (1996) *The Ethics of Care*, Oxford: Oxford University Press, p 20.
[22] M. Fineman (2000) 'Cracking the foundational myths: independence, autonomy, and self-sufficiency', *American University Journal of Gender, Social Policy and the Law*, 8(13): 12.
[23] See discussion in V. Held (2006).
[24] P. Allmark (1995) 'Can there be an ethic of care?', *Journal of Medical Ethics*, 21(19): 19.

means is that we should care about the right things in the right way and that we should encourage the required qualities. But by focusing on caring as a moral quality in itself, something it is not, the ethics of care can tell us nothing of what those right things are.[25]

The importance of supporting carers themselves is something which, as we shall see in our discussion in Chapter 3 of this volume, is recognized in the Care Act 2014 through the obligations placed on local authorities to assess and provide support for the needs of carers.

One of the most challenging aspects of an ethic of care approach is its relationship with questions of autonomy and of fundamental human rights. As social care law and policy has developed in an era in which human rights are a key consideration, increasing emphasis has been placed on the status of the autonomous individual receiving care, but at the same time there is consideration of the needs of the carers. This tension between feminist models of the relational ethics of care and more universalist notions of justice and individual rights is also illustrated in the juxtaposition of these priorities in the work of Gilligan, which Held characterizes as an either-or choice:

> An ethic of justice focuses on questions of fairness, equality, individual rights, abstract principles, and the consistent application of them. An ethic of care focuses on attentiveness, trust, responsiveness to need, narrative nuance, and cultivating caring relations. Whereas an ethic of justice seeks a fair solution between competing individual interests and rights, an ethic of care sees the interests of carers and cared-for as importantly intertwined rather than as simply competing. Whereas justice protects equality and freedom, care fosters social bonds and cooperation.[26]

While the primacy of the individual can be seen as necessary from a justice and human rights perspective this positioning is more complex in the context of the evolution of social care law and policy. Even when the individual and their individual well-being is seen as paramount it can be difficult to untangle the individual from their community, whether that is family members or other carers, in relation to decision-making processes. Held argues that:

> From a perspective of care, persons are relational and interdependent, not the individualistic autonomous rational agents of the perspective

---

[25] V. Held (2006), p 23.
[26] V. Held (2006), p 15.

of justice and rights. This relational view is the better view of human beings, of persons engaged in developing human morality. We can decide to treat such persons as individuals, to be the bearers of individual rights, for the sake of constructing just political and legal and other institutions. But we should not forget the reality and the morality this view obscures. Persons are relational and interdependent. We can and should value autonomy, but it must be developed and sustained within a framework of relations of trust.[27]

The importance and complexities of theoretical approaches to relationality are highlighted by Harding through her 'axis' of relational self, life and law.[28] Drawing upon the literature in this area, Harding suggests that there are distinct approaches to relationality. First, there is relationality 'as care ethics', as seen in the context of the previous discussion and in relation to autonomy of decision-making. She suggests that

> an ethics of care seeks to undermine the idea of individual, rational decision-making within an interpersonal vacuum. Instead an ethics of care approach seeks to embed an understanding of relationality into legal and political theory.[29]

Second, Harding identifies the category of 'relationality as constraint'.[30] This is the approach to relational analysis which suggests that the concept of autonomy needs to be reframed in the light of the way in which individuals undertake their day-to-day lives, complete with social interaction. Harding comments that:

> Where these relational approaches to autonomy have developed through practical application, however, theorists of relational autonomy seem more focused on uncovering the fact that choices are made within constraints, than focusing on the inherent relationality of the human experience.[31]

---

[27] V. Held (2006), p 72.
[28] R. Harding (2017) *Duties to Care: Dementia, Relationality and the Law*, Cambridge: Cambridge University Press.
[29] R. Harding (2017), p 23.
[30] Here drawing upon C. Mackenzie and N. Stoljar 'Introduction: autonomy refigured', in C. Mackenzie and N. Stoljar (eds) *Relational Autonomy: Feminist Perspectives on Autonomy, Agency and the Social Self*, Oxford: Oxford University Press, pp 3–31, and N. Priaulx (2007) *The Harm Paradox: Tort Law and the Unwanted Child in an Era of Choice*, Abingdon: Routledge.
[31] R. Harding (2017), pp 23–4.

Third, Harding cites the category of 'relationality as interpersonal contact',[32] which is to recognize it as 'an inevitable aspect of human life, such that legal actors should consider the relational *context* of decisions'.[33] She suggests that

> relationality helps to highlight the ways that everyday forms of regulation that consider an individual on her own divorced from her relational context necessarily omit various dimensions of subjectivity and experience. So it is not that without our relational context we 'cease to exist' or become a 'non-entity', rather that it is we lose important dimensions of ourselves. Being attentive to relationality can, instead, provide a richer and more complete legal subject.[34]

Nonetheless, while such relationality is seen as fundamental, Harding recognizes that relationships may not necessarily facilitate autonomy or be viewed as positive. She suggests, drawing on the work of Leckey, that there is a need to recognize the normative dimension and support the 'capacity for relational autonomy and ... promoting constructive relationships conducive to it'.[35] Finally, Harding incisively develops another approach in her examination of the position of people living with dementia and familial and informal carers building on the work of Nedelsky.[36] Here she views 'relationality as a lens, focused on interwoven dynamics of everyday life'.[37] Regarding relationality in law and in life, Nedelsky has argued that 'autonomy is made possible by constructive relationship not by independence. Dependence and independence are inherent parts of human life'.[38]

Nedelsky argues that her approach prompts shifts in legal thinking at normative, conceptual, and institutional levels. She proposes that we move beyond the 'traditionally individualistic conception of the self into a relational one, without subsuming the individual into the collective'[39] Instead, she

---

[32] Here drawing upon J. Herring and C. Foster (2012) 'Welfare means relationality, virtue and altruism', *Legal Studies*, 32(3): 480–98; J. Herring (2013) *Caring and the Law*, London: Bloomsbury Publishing; J. Herring (1999) 'The Human Rights Act and the welfare principle in family law – conflicting or complementary?', *Child and Family Law Quarterly*, 11(3): 223–35.

[33] R. Harding (2017), p 25.

[34] R. Harding (2017), p 25.

[35] R. Leckey (2008) *Contextual Subjects: Family, State and Relational Theory*, Toronto: University of Toronto Press, p 19.

[36] J. Nedelsky (2011) *Law's Relations: A Relational Theory of Self, Autonomy and Law*, Oxford: Oxford University Press.

[37] R. Harding (2017), p 22.

[38] J. Nedelsky (2011), p 152.

[39] J. Nedelsky (2011), p 19.

proposes that relationships and interactions be viewed in terms of 'nested' relations, as we impact upon one another and where:

> Each set of relations is nested in the next, and all interact with each other. Relational selves shape and are shaped by all our interactions.[40]

Nedelsky's work here also can be seen as connected with that of another ethical principle which came to the fore during the pandemic, that of solidarity.[41] Solidarity in relation to sharing and supportive action, as we will see in subsequent chapters, was exemplified during the first year of the pandemic when not only families and friends but also neighbours and volunteers across communities came together to offer support for those who had particular needs.[42]

Harding has suggested that law is also relational as she demonstrates in her analysis of the judicial determination of cases concerning dementia patients under the Mental Capacity Act 2005.[43] If an adult has decision-making capacity, they have the ability in law to make decisions for themselves, regardless of the wishes and views of others.[44] Where they are assessed as lacking such capacity then there is a requirement under section 4 of the Mental Capacity Act 2005 for decisions to be made where it is in their best interest to do so. Section 4(7) goes onto provide an obligation to consult other persons 'if practicable and appropriate' including those who the individual has identified should be consulted and persons 'engaged with caring for them or interested in their welfare'.[45]

However, this is simply a consultation requirement which is discretionary in nature and family members are not expressly included in the statute as having rights, although there is direct reference to carers. Nonetheless, as Harding illustrates, in making best interests determinations for persons who lack mental capacity there is judicial engagement with the relational aspects of such decision-making processes.[46]

---

[40] J. Nedelsky (2011), p 31.
[41] See further discussion in the context of the NHS, care and the pandemic, C.A.B. Redhead et al (2022) 'Relationships, rights and responsibilities: (re)viewing the NHS constitution for the post-pandemic "new normal"', *Medical Law Review*, 31(1): 83–108.
[42] Chapters 5 and 6, and see generally I. Hardhill, J. Grotz and L. Crawford (eds) (2022) *Mobilising Voluntary Action in the UK: Learning from the Pandemic*, Bristol: Policy Press.
[43] Harding (2007), p 16.
[44] See further ss 1, 2, and 3 of the Mental Capacity Act 2005 and also *King's College NHS Foundation Trust v C* [2015] EWCOP 80.
[45] Mental Capacity Act 2005, s 4(7).
[46] Mental Capacity Act 2005, Pt 1, s 4.

The approach here thus enables us to break away from the juxtaposition of care ethics and rights and justice arguments to see the interrelationship between these concepts. The approach of nested relationships may also be reflected as Chua and Engel note through perceptions of 'legal consciousness', which can manifest differently in different cultures that may not share certain normative Western legal assumptions about the nature of the individual.[47] As they point out,

> a more relational approach to legal consciousness has been evident in recent sociolegal research conducted in Asia, Africa, and other settings outside Europe and North America, where the influence of Enlightenment philosophy was uneven and popular understandings of atomistic individualism had shallow roots, if they existed at all. In those settings, legal consciousness researchers have discovered that worldviews, perceptions, and decisions develop relationally, and it is often impossible to disentangle the consciousness of any one person from those of her family members, fellow villagers, or other intimate associates ... if the self is essentially relational, it follows that an overly individualistic framework will fail to capture the essence of her legal consciousness.[48]

Harding's notion of 'law as relational law' is particularly important when considering the Care Act 2014 itself. We can see layers of relationality embedded into the decision-making aspects of the Care Act. As we shall see in Chapter 3, while the legislation sets out powers and duties upon the local authority to consider the need for care and support of specific individuals, it is also expressly concerned with the role and well-being of carers, with specific provisions applicable where carers themselves have need of support.[49] As such, the statute does acknowledge the relational nature of the caring process and recognizes the needs of the people involved, beyond those of the person needing care; and this recognition is built directly into the legislation. Furthermore, in considering the concept of 'well-being', section 1(3)(7) of the Act provides that:

> Section 1 (3) In exercising a function under this Part in the case of an individual, a local authority must have regard to the following matters in particular—

---

[47] L.J. Chua and D.M. Engel (2021) 'Legal consciousness reconsidered', *Annual Review of Law and Social Science*, 15: 335–53.
[48] L.J. Chua and D.M. Engel (2021) 'Legal consciousness reconsidered', 335–53.
[49] Care Act 2014, Pt 1, discussed in detail in Chapter 3.

(f) the importance of achieving a balance between the individual's well-being and that of any friends or relatives who are involved in caring for the individual

This provision is interesting and is again expressly building relationality into decision-making; it thus stands in contrast to the approach taken under the Mental Capacity Act 2005 in situations in which adults are held to possess mental capacity. If an adult possesses mental capacity, this means in English law that they have the right to make what others may view as fundamentally 'unwise' decisions and to have those decisions respected even if the consequence of such a choice is that they may come to harm or even die.[50]

Aspects of the Care Act 2014, as we shall see later in Chapter 3, reflect what Barnes has described as

> a real tension between the apparently progressive campaigns of social movements of service users and the arguments of care ethicists … The promotion of the human and civil rights of disabled people has emphasised an unhelpful contrast between rights and care. This has served to reinforce the moral boundaries between care and justice that Tronto and other care ethicists have sought to dismantle.[51]

As Humphries notes, we can differentiate between the notion of 'caring for' someone, with its assumptions of a 'traditional mindset that sees them as dependent and vulnerable, as passive recipients of traditional services in which power sits with professional organizations',[52] and 'caring about someone', which he suggests instead 'involves an individual and collective commitment to upholding their rights as equal citizens. This includes offering people real choices in how the support they need is tailored to their particular circumstances rather than "one size fits all"'.[53]

As Fine states, there has been 'rethinking of the carer-dependant paradigm affecting both informal and formal forms of care'.[54] He argues that care

> needs to be seen not simply as a one-directional service undertaken by the caregiver, but, as the outcome of a relationship between the

---

[50] See, for example, *King's College Hospital NHS Foundation Trust v C* [2016] COPLR 50.
[51] M. Barnes (2012) *Care in Everyday Life: An Ethic of Care in Practice*, Bristol: Policy Press, p 33.
[52] R. Humphries (2022) *Ending the Social Care Crisis: A New Road to Reform*, Bristol: Policy Press, p 173.
[53] R. Humphries (2022), p 174.
[54] See further M.D. Fine (2007), p 191.

different parties in which mutual respect and the fostering of the capabilities and sense of autonomy of the recipients are foremost. The emergence of concepts such as 'self-care' and 'co-production of care' which need to be respected and fostered ... are suggestive of the sorts of changes required.[55]

This is a clear recognition of the relational aspects of caring, combined with support for and a strengthening of the kinds of capabilities approach we discuss in the next section of this chapter. The tensions which may develop between the theoretical framing of ethics of care and the position in law, through human rights and capabilities approaches, and needs and mental capacity assessments, are thus quite evident. We examine these tensions further in the next section of the chapter.

III. From paternalism to autonomy and empowerment through rights and capabilities

The tensions between the language of care (in its various iterations) and autonomous decision-making are, as we have seen in the previous section, very evident. Social care policy and practice has a long history of paternalistic approaches to supporting individuals' well-being; this is a legacy of the Poor Laws and the Workhouse.[56] However, since World War Two, international human rights structures have been gradually embedded in UK policy following the establishment of the United Nations Declaration of Human Rights, and at European level the European Convention on Human Rights (ECHR). This was accompanied at UK domestic level by the passage of the Human Rights Act 1998. This piece of legislation enables domestic courts to interpret existing law in the light of the provisions of the ECHR incorporated into the legislation.[57] While it does not give the English courts the power to strike down legislation as incompatible with the Convention, a court does have the power to issue what is known as a declaration of incompatibility which, as its name suggests, indicates that the court has held that the legislation is incompatible with the ECHR.[58] If such a declaration is made it is then for Parliament to determine whether legislative changes are to be introduced. A further limitation with the legislation is that it is applicable to public bodies, it does not extend to private actors as

---

[55] See M.D. Fine (2007), p 191.
[56] M.A. Crowther (2016) *The Workhouse System 1834–1929: The History of an English Social Institution*, London: Routledge.
[57] Human Rights 1998, ss 2 and 3.
[58] Human Rights Act 1998, s 4.

such.[59] Another important but more recent international treaty relevant in this area is that of the United Nations Convention which we discuss below.[60]

The rise of the global disability rights movement has been crucial in campaigning for equal rights and opportunities for people with disabilities; it also fosters respect for individual rights and the empowerment of those seeking social care support.[61] The terminology and conceptualization of 'disability' is itself contested, with different assumptions and models underpinning successive reforms of the social care policy landscape. In the past, and indeed in some parts of the world today, disability was viewed within what might be termed a 'religious model' insomuch that certain conditions or disabilities were regarded as 'an act of God or a curse inflicted on an individual by an external supernatural force'.[62] Alternatively, the early 'medical model' of disability sought to examine the health of the individual to determine whether their 'functional limitations' were amenable to cure. The medical model has been criticized for its stigmatizing potential and, as Brisenden notes, for its 'debilitating emphasis on physical limitations and low expectations'.[63] As Barnes comments, there is evidence in Western culture of widespread oppression and prejudice against those with disabilities, which translated in time into extensive use of institutionalisation.[64] After the horrors of World War Two, there was a distinct policy shift – informed by the sense of the moral obligation to injured and disabled war veterans, along with the increased visibility of disabled and elderly people as life expectancy gradually increased – and the default of residential placements[65]

Change, however, took time, energy, and collective action. In 1965, two women in Surrey – Megan du Boisson and Berit Moore – formed the Disablement Incomes Group, which was the first UK pressure group to campaign for a full income through social security for all disabled people,

---

[59] *Callin, Heather and Ward v Leonard Cheshire* [2002] EWCA Civ 366.

[60] United Nations Convention on the Rights of Persons with Disabilities, at www.ohchr.org/en/instruments-mechanisms/instruments/convention-rights-persons-disabilities, drafted December 2006 and effective May 2008.

[61] See de Beco (2021) supra.

[62] See G. Henderson and W.V. Bryan (2011) *Psychosocial Aspects of Disability* (4th edn), Springfield: Charles C. Thomas, pp 7 and 18; and see further A. Broderick (2019) *International and European Disability Law and Policy*, Cambridge: Cambridge University Press, p 18.

[63] S. Brisenden (1986) 'Independent living and the medical model of disability', *Disability and Society*, 1(2): 173 at 177.

[64] C. Barnes (2019) 'Understanding the social model of disability: past, present and future', in N. Watson, A. Roulstone, and C. Thomas (eds) *Routledge Handbook of Disability Studies*, London: Taylor & Francis, p 15.

[65] C. Barnes (2019), p 15.

regardless of whether they were war veterans or 'civilian' disabled (where previously the former had received significantly more financial support than the latter).[66] This led to the development of the Disability Alliance which also campaigned for comprehensive disability rights and income.[67] This was followed by the establishment of the Union of the Physically Impaired Against Segregation (UPIAS) in 1974, which differentiated between an individual having an impairment (such as the loss or lack of all or part of a limb, for example) and the 'disability', which was defined contextually as 'the disadvantage or restriction of activity caused by contemporary organisation which takes no or little account of people who have physical impairments and thus excludes them from the mainstream of social activities'.[68] Thus, the 'social model' of disability was born, and this basic understanding of structural disadvantage and social exclusion continues to inform social care policy and practice today. As Broderick notes: 'The social model essentially means that responsibility lies with national governments and society as a whole to remedy the disadvantage and inequalities faced by persons with disabilities.'[69]

Oliver, who formally coined the term in the academic discourse on disability, distinguishes the social model from earlier approaches which he called the 'individual model of disability' (rather than a 'medical model' despite similarities of approach).[70] He suggests that the individual model locates

> the 'problem' of disability within the individual and ... see the causes of this problem as stemming from the functional limitations or psychological losses which are assumed to arise from disability.[71]

This highlights a fundamental clash in perceptions as to whether the 'problem' lies within the non-normative individual or with the non-inclusive, non-accessible society. The social model errs towards the latter, and therefore presents policy makers and society more broadly with a collective responsibility. As Lawson and Beckett comment: '[F]rom a social model

---

[66] J. Hampton (2016) *Disability and the Welfare State in Britain: Changes in Perception and Policy 1948–79*, Bristol: Policy Press, ch 4.
[67] J. Hampton (2016), ch 4.
[68] UPIAS (1976) 'What is a disability? Definition', at http://hcdg.org/definition.htm
[69] A. Broderick (2019), p 20.
[70] M. Oliver (1990) 'The individual and social models of disability', Paper presented at Joint Workshop of the Living Options Group and the Research Unit of the Royal College of Physicians on People with established Locomotor Disabilities in Hospitals, 23 July.
[71] M. Oliver (1990).

perspective disability is therefore viewed as a socially produced injustice which it is possible to challenge and eliminate through radical social change.'[72]

Approaches to the social model evolved over time, leading to 'significant inconsistencies in its articulation and usage'.[73] Broderick sets out key features of the various approaches to the social model. First is the 'rejection of impairment as a "personal tragedy" and the shifting of accountability to national governments to rectify disabling barriers as a matter of social justice'.[74] Second, is the distinction between the concepts of impairment and disability in the form of social exclusion. Third, that those who are disabled 'are an oppressed group in society and are systematically discriminated against'. Fourth, that societal barriers mean that those with disabilities are stopped from obtaining equal access to education, housing, recreation, and so on. Finally, Broderick notes that this model gives precedence to the importance of 'politics, empowerment, citizenship and choice'.[75] In short, it allows and calls for the possibility of change.

The social model of disability has also been criticized, however. One main criticism is that it can downplay the extent to which an impairment or condition may impact upon individual experiences and well-being – the bodily reality of the situation. Shakespeare has critiqued what he refers to as the 'strong social model'.[76] He argues that the social model of disability has now become an obstacle to the development of both disability studies and the wider disability rights movement.[77] Its activist ambition to target the political arena sometimes led to the use of simplified campaign slogans which, while they had some contextual utility, were problematic on closer scrutiny and failed to represent the heterogeneous identities of disabled people. He argues that the model was too aligned with identity politics, which he argues 'may cause more problems than it solves'. Third, he argues that the social model had hardly evolved since it was developed in the 1970s. Shakespeare takes a novel view of the distinction between impairment and disability: 'Impairment is defined in individual and biological terms. Disability is defined as a social creation. Disability is what makes impairment a problem. For social modellists, social barriers and social oppression constitute disability, and this is the area where research, analysis, campaigning and change must occur.'[78]

---

[72] A. Lawson and A.E. Beckett (2021) 'The social and human rights model of disability: towards a complementarity thesis', *International Journal of Human Rights*, 25(2): 349.
[73] A. Lawson and A.E. Beckett (2021), p 349.
[74] A. Broderick (2019), p 21.
[75] A. Broderick (2019), p 21.
[76] T. Shakespeare (2013) *Disability Rights and Wrongs Revisited*, London: Taylor & Francis.
[77] T. Shakespeare (2013), p 20.
[78] T. Shakespeare (2013), p 21.

Shakespeare argues that in fact impairment and disability are not necessarily linked: 'If you can walk, steps generally are not a problem.'[79] Arguing that impairment should be viewed as a spectrum, he calls for a more nuanced and robust empirical and conceptual debate: 'are the problems to be defined as a socially imposed restriction of activity or impairment effects?'[80] He questions the notion of a 'barrier free utopia', given that the natural environment itself throws up geographical barriers, limits, and obstacles.[81] Shakespeare suggests that:

> Rather than defining disability as a deficit or a structural disadvantage or alternatively a product of cultural discourse a holistic understanding is required. Put simply the experience of a disabled person results from the relationship between factors intrinsic to the individual and extrinsic factors arising from the wider context in which she finds herself.[82]

He includes under the umbrella of intrinsic factors, the nature and degree of the impairment, the individual's attitude to this, alongside contextual factors such as the attitudes of others and broader societal, economic responses to disability.[83]

In recent years there has been a strong movement to emphasize the human rights model of disability, which 'focuses on the inherent dignity of the human being and subsequently, but only if necessary, on the person's medical characteristics. It places the individual centre stage in all decisions affecting him/her and, most importantly, locates the main "problem" outside the person and in society.'[84]

Article 1 of the Universal Declaration of Human Rights provides that 'all human beings are born free and equal in dignity and rights'. It has been argued by Kayess and French that the social model was an 'enormous influence' upon the development of the UN CRPD.[85] However, the definition in Article 1 of the UN CRPD is notably broad: 'Persons with

---

[79] T. Shakespeare (2013), p 22.
[80] T. Shakespeare (2013), p 22.
[81] T. Shakespeare (2013), p 36.
[82] T. Shakespeare (2013), p 74.
[83] T. Shakespeare (2013), p 75.
[84] G. Quinn and T. Degener (2002) 'The moral authority for change: human rights values and the worldwide process of disability reform', in G. Quinn and T. Degener (eds) *Human Rights and Disability: The Current Use and Future Potential of UN Human Rights Instruments in the Context of Disability*, Geneva: United Nations, pp 13–14. And see also T. Denger (2016) 'A human rights model of disability', in P. Blanck and E. Flynn (eds) *Routledge Handbook of Disability Law and Human Rights*, London: Routledge.
[85] R. Kayess and P. French (2008) 'Out of darkness into light: introducing the United Nations Convention on the Rights of Persons with Disabilities', *Human Rights Law Review*, 8(1): 7.

disabilities include those who have long-term physical, mental, intellectual or sensory impairments which in interaction with various barriers may hinder their full and effective participation in society on an equal basis with others.' As Series comments, the extent to which this definition can be said to reflect 'any particular approach to disability is a matter of debate'.[86] Policy conversations and decisions made in the context of the UN CRPD often rely on the International Classification of Functioning, Disability and Health (ICF), a framework devised by the World Health Organization (WHO) for measuring statistics and indicators at individual and population levels. The ICF definition of disability is similarly broad and inclusive:

> an umbrella term for impairments, activity limitations and participation restrictions. It denotes the negative aspects of the interaction between an individual (with a health condition) and that individual's contextual factors (environmental and personal factors).[87]

Lawson and Beckett argue that the human rights and social models of disability can be viewed both distinct and complementary:

> The human rights model is important as a model of disability policy. It provides a detailed road map for the development of human-rights-consistent law and policy, as well as systems and frameworks for monitoring progress. The more open-textured social model operates to support emancipatory disability politics in contexts which are not framed by reference to human rights: and continues to be pivotal to the formation, amongst people who have impairments of a resistant subjectivity based upon shared experience of a disabling society. To operate effectively the human rights model must work alongside the social model.[88]

As Broderick notes, the human rights approach to disability is broad, simultaneously covering civil, political, economic, social, and cultural rights.[89] Yet as a theoretical approach it to a large degree assumes and is constructed from paradigms and social realities typical of the Global North, and these may not be applicable or relevant across large parts of the world.[90]

---

[86] L. Series (2019) 'Disability and human rights', in N. Watson, A. Roulstone, and C. Thomas (eds) *Routledge Handbook of Disability Studies*, London: Taylor & Francis.
[87] World Health Organization (2001) *International Classification of Functioning, Disability and Health*. Geneva: WHO.
[88] A. Lawson and A.E. Beckett (2021), p 371.
[89] A. Broderick (2019), p 25.
[90] See further S. Grech (2009) 'Disability, poverty and development: critical reflections on the Majority World debate', *Disability and Society*, 24(6): 771.

As noted previously, the UN CRPD came into effect on 3 May 2008.[91] The Convention was notable for the direct involvement of people with disabilities in its development and drafting, an exercise in co-production. The Convention does not include a definition of what constitutes disability, but the Preamble to the Convention states in paragraph (a) that: '*Recognising* that disability is an evolving concept and that disability results from the interaction between persons with impairments and attitudinal and environmental barriers that hinder their full and effective participation in society on an equal basis with others.'

In addition, Article 1 of the Convention 'Purpose' states that:

> The purpose of the present Convention is to promote, protect and ensure the full and equal enjoyment of all human rights and fundamental freedoms by all persons with disabilities, and to promote respect for their inherent dignity.
>
> Persons with disabilities include those who have long-term physical, mental, intellectual, or sensory impairments which in interaction with various barriers may hinder their full and effective participation in society on an equal basis with others.

The Convention includes traditional civil and political rights such as the right to life,[92] and equality and non-discrimination,[93] the right to the best possible health and access to health services,[94] and to habilitation and rehabilitation, in terms of building independence and participation.[95] At the same time, elements of the Convention can be seen as problematic or as liberating in relation to current norms and legal provisions. For example, Article 12(2), in relation to equal recognition before the law, provides that: 'States Parties shall recognize that persons with disabilities enjoy legal capacity on an equal basis with others in all aspects of life.'

The CRPD Committee, in its 'General Comment on Article 12: Equal Recognition before the Law', states that if a person has an impairment, including mental or psychosocial impairments, this is not to be a basis for the denial of legal capacity or for imposing substitute decision-making:

> Respecting the right to legal capacity of persons with disabilities on an equal basis includes respecting the rights of persons with disabilities to

---

[91] P. Bartlett (2012) 'The United Nations Convention on the Rights of Persons with Disabilities and the future of mental health law', *Modern Law Review*, 75(5): 752.
[92] Article 10.
[93] Article 5.
[94] Article 25.
[95] Article 26.

liberty and security of the person. The denial of the legal capacity of persons with disabilities and their detention in institutions against their will, either without their consent or with the consent of a substitute decision maker is an ongoing problem. This practice constitutes arbitrary deprivation of liberty and violates Article 12 and 14 of the Convention.[96]

The Convention also requires provision of support in order to exercise their legal capacity.[97] In relation to decision-making, the passage of the Mental Capacity Act 2005 was built upon existing common law principles, but the fact that the legislation provides for a statutory presumption that individuals have decision-making capacity (see Section 1) is an important signal regarding the need to respect autonomy. Concerns have been raised as to the extent to which the safeguards which have been provided by the UK in relation to those persons with disabilities are satisfactory leading to a major report by the UN Committee on the Rights of Persons with Disabililites.[98] This controversy remains ongoing.

It is unsurprising then that these fundamental principles of human rights which flow from the UN Declaration of Human Rights, the ECHR, and the UN CRPD also inform the ethical frameworks that underpin the work of the caring professions. Those social work professionals who are members of the British Association of Social Workers (BASW) have had a Code of Ethics since 1975.[99] The current version states that: 'Social work is based on respect for the inherent worth and dignity of all people as expressed in the United Nations Universal Declaration of Human Rights (1948), other related UN declarations and the European Convention on Human Rights and the conventions derived from those declarations.'[100]

Social workers in England are regulated by Social Work England, an organization which sets professional standards, holds a register of qualified social workers, quality assures education, and investigates complaints. It was established under the Children and Social Work Act 2017, and it took over the regulation of social workers in England from the Health and

---

[96] See further G. Szmukler (2017) 'The UN Convention on the Rights of Persons with Disabilities: "Rights, will and preferences" in relation to mental disabilities', *International Journal of Law and Psychiatry*, 54: 90.
[97] Article 12(3).
[98] UN Committee on the Rights of Persons with Disabilities (2016) *Inquiry Concerning the United Kingdom of Great Britain and Northern Ireland Carried Out by the Committee under Article 6 of the Optional Protocol to the Convention Report of the Committee*, 6 October.
[99] Though long-standing, this code is regularly updated. British Association of Social Workers Code of Ethics (updated 2021), at www.basw.co.uk/about-basw/code-ethics
[100] British Association of Social Workers (2021) Code of Ethics (updated 2021).

Care Professions Council in 2019.[101] The Professional Standards for Social Workers produced by Social Work England present the key values that social workers should:

1.1 Value each person as an individual, recognising their strengths and abilities.
1.2 Respect and promote the human rights, views, wishes and feelings of the people I work with, balancing rights and risks and enabling access to advice, advocacy, support and services.
1.3 Work in partnership with people to promote their well-being and achieve best outcomes, recognising them as experts in their own lives.[102]

These values demonstrate the emphasis on individual rights and autonomy, while also recognizing the need to 'respect and maintain people's dignity and privacy'.[103] In addition to the initial list of values, the British Association of Social Workers, in conjunction with other professional social work organizations, maintain the Professional Capabilities Framework (PCF) programme, which identifies nine levels of social work practitioner and provides guidance and goals for the required skillset associated with each level – from student social worker to the most senior strategic social worker.[104] The PCF underpins the evidence required to demonstrate continuing professional development (CPD) required of social workers, which is in turn required for the annual renewal of registration with Social Work England. As such, practitioners should keep professional values, ethics, and indeed the relevant legal and policy knowledge at the forefront of their awareness. The importance of ethical values in the professional decisions by social workers and others involved in social care is highlighted in the COVID-19 Ethical Framework for Adult Social Care documents, which we consider in Chapter 4.

The language of 'capabilities' is also used in relation to those who require some form of care and support. The 'capabilities approach' has proven particularly important over the last few decades as a means of engaging with and re-framing the complexities of contemporary human rights discourses in modern society. It is, however, rooted in the principles of classic philosophical

---

[101] See the related Social Workers Regulations 2018 (SI 2018/893).
[102] Social Work England (2019) *Professional Standards*.
[103] Social Work England (2019), para 2.2.
[104] British Association of Social Workers The Professional Capabilities Framework, https://new.basw.co.uk/training-cpd/professional-capabilities-framework/about-professional-capabilities-framework-pcf, accessed 10 July 2024.

thought in the form of Aristotle's views on equity and distributive justice,[105] and further in the Marxist argument that 'in the place of the wealth and the poverty of political economy come the rich human being and the rich human need … the human being in need of a totality of life activities, the man in whom his own realisation exists as an inner necessity as need'.[106]

When moral philosopher Amartya Sen delivered his Tanner Lecture on Human Values at Stanford in 1979, he sought to find a new response to the question 'Equality of What?'[107] Having critiqued various existing approaches as incoherent or ethically unjust, he instead suggested that a culturally specific model of 'basic capability equality' is more adequate than models based on notions of utility or access to resources. His emphasis on 'capabilities to achieve functionings' goes beyond more standard economic welfare models of resource allocation and looks instead at how people can undertake 'doings' and to interrogate barriers to fully 'being'.[108] In order to mitigate societal inequalities, he argues that policies and social actions should seek to provide capability equality and the freedom to choose.

Nussbaum regards human capabilities as inseparable from human dignity.[109] Human rights for both Sen and Nussbaum relate to basic capabilities, but Nussbaum's baseline also introduces a threshold for human dignity, and the need for political liberation.[110] She incorporates a list of 'central capabilities', which focus 'on the protection of areas of freedom so central that their removal makes a life not worthy of human dignity'.[111] In Nussbaum's view, 'every person is struggling for a life that is fully human, a life worthy of human dignity',[112] and such would require, as a 'bare minimum' a threshold of ten capabilities.[113] The first of these is life itself. This is the idea that

---

[105] See also Nussbaum, who initially drew upon Aristotle's work but demonstrated movement away from aspects of this over time. See further D. Weinstein (2020) 'Intellectual history and defending the capabilities approach', in E. Chiappero-Martinetti, S. Osmani and M. Qizilbash (eds) *The Cambridge Handbook of the Capability Approach*, Cambridge: Cambridge University Press.

[106] K. Marx, as cited in Sen (1990), and discussed in M. Qizilbash (2020) 'Historical antecedents and philosophical debates', in E. Chiappero-Martinetti, S. Osmani, and M. Qizilbash (eds) *The Cambridge Handbook of the Capability Approach*, Cambridge: Cambridge University Press.

[107] A. Sen (1979) 'Equality of What?, Tanner Lecture on Human Values, Stanford University', 22 May 1979.

[108] A. Sen (1979).

[109] M.C. Nussbaum (2011) *Creating Capabilities: The Human Development Approach*, Cambridge, MA: Harvard University Press.

[110] M.C. Nussbaum (2011), p 19.

[111] M.C. Nussbaum (2011), p 32.

[112] M.C. Nussbaum (2011), p 1.

[113] M.C. Nussbaum (2011), p 33.

someone is able to live for their natural lifespan. The second is the ability to have good 'bodily health'. Third, bodily integrity, including being 'secure against violent assault'. Fourth, the capability of senses, imagination, and thought. This is the ability to utilize and engage with those senses, the imagination and 'being able to use one's mind in ways protected by guarantees of freedom of expression with respect to both political and artistic speech and freedom of religious exercise'.[114] Fifth, the capability of emotion – this includes the ability to have attachments to people and things, to love, and also 'not having one's emotional development blighted by fear and anxiety'.[115] Sixth, practical reason, which Nussbaum defines as 'being able to form a conception of the good and to engage in critical reflection about the planning of one's life', including liberty of conscience and religious observance.[116] The seventh capability is that of affiliation, being able to live alongside others, and 'being treated as a dignified being whose worth is equal to that of others'. The eighth capability relates to other species, namely 'being able to live with concern for and in relation to animals, plants and the world of nature'.[117] And the ninth is that of play, and the enjoyment of recreational activities. The final capability is control over one's environment. This includes political control, such as participation in political choices and decision-making, and also material control, in relation to both property and employment. The aim of this approach, according to Nussbaum, is that these are predominantly individual, personal capabilities and thus would only be applicable 'derivatively' to groups. She argues that 'respect for human dignity requires that citizens be placed above an ample (specified) threshold of capability, in all ten of those areas'.[118]

As Mitra comments of Sen's approach:

> capability does not constitute the presence of a physical or mental ability; rather it is understood as a practical opportunity. Functioning is the actual achievement of the individual, what he or she actually achieves through being or doing. Here disability can be understood as a deprivation in terms of capabilities or functionings that result from the interaction of an individual's (a) personal characteristics (e.g. age, impairment) and (b) basket of available goods (assets, income) and (c) environment (social, economic, political, cultural).[119]

---

[114] M.C. Nussbaum (2011), p 33.
[115] M.C. Nussbaum (2011), pp 33–4.
[116] M.C. Nussbaum (2011), p 34.
[117] M.C. Nussbaum (2011), p 34.
[118] She does go on to expressly state that while she begins with citizens 'I do not wish to deny that resident aliens, legal or illegal, have a variety of entitlements, I simply begin with the core case'.
[119] S. Mitra (2006) 'The capability approach and disability', *Journal of Disability Policy Studies*, 16(4): 236.

How then could this be utilized in relation to the social care requirements of people with disabilities in society? Many such people may have multiple or complex disabilities. Mitra suggests that utilizing a capability approach to classification allows researchers and policy makers to view disability at a capability level; in terms of potential disability; and at the functioning level, namely actual disability.[120] Further she argues that a capability approach recognizes a range of personal characteristics such as gender, race, and impairment, as well as access to resources, and wider environmental factors. Mitra notes that:

> In general Sen has argued public policy should deal with capabilities rather than functionings ... However in practice a person's capabilities are difficult to observe and data are usually available for functionings. Therefore policymakers may have to settle for functionings.[121]

Trani et al have argued that the capabilities of persons with disabilities are impacted by 'conversion factors'; that is to say a lack of or reduced opportunities to participate in life due to social stigma. They argue that a capabilities approach provides an effective normative framework within which to comprehend and formulate more appropriate policies.[122]

> Theoretically the CA [Capabilities Approach] framework helps to overcome some of the limits and reduce the potential of contrasting results of the disability models. The CA shifts the focus from the specificities of the disabling situation to look at establishing equality in terms of possibilities and choices. This in turn helps to assess the wellbeing situation in a more comprehensive manner. The framework can be used as an operational tool to identify important dimensions of wellbeing and look at constraints that limit expansion of wellbeing, as well as resources that are available within the community to expand these.[123]

On its face, the framing of the Care Act 2014 seems to reflect such a capabilities approach, underpinned by the broad strokes of the well-being

---

[120] S. Mitra (2006), p 242.
[121] S. Mitra (2006), p 243.
[122] J.F. Trani, P. Bakhshi, N. Bellanca, M.Biggeri, and F. Marchetta (2011) 'Disabilities through the capability approach lens: implications for public policies', *European Journal for Disability Research*, 5(3): 143.
[123] Trani et al (2011), p 156.

principle in Section 1". A relatively recent development in social work practice is the 'three conversations' approach to undertaking Care Act assessments of needs, which refocuses the assessment process as a means of facilitating and maximizing capabilities. However, as we shall see in the following chapter, this approach can be regarded as aspirational, whereas the reality of its operation in day-to-day practice can be complex and at times problematic.

All this needs to be seen in the light of campaigners' and rights groups' calls to centre what people need and desire to enable them to live fulfilled lives on their own terms. Alongside the pandemic-related debates, organizations such as #socialcarefuture have long been arguing for what they see as the '5 key changes to unlock an equal life'. These are:

1. Communities where everyone belongs.
2. Living in the place we call home.
3. Leading the lives we want to lead.
4. More resources better used.
5. Sharing power as equals.[124]

These are important, far-reaching aims, all underpinned by an ambition to transform systemic health and socio-economic inequalities. This agenda is not, however, explicitly cast in terms of fundamental human rights. As part of the work of #socialcarefuture, the Social Care Innovation Network has facilitated meetings between those who commissioned services, progressive providers, and people with lived experience, with the aim of 'moving us on towards co-production, shifting power and using all local resources to improve lives and communities co-commissioning'.[125]

We have focused thus far mostly on the situation of people with disabilities, a substantial proportion of those who currently draw on adult social care services and support are older people. While ageing does not necessarily equate to poor health or disability, it does in many cases result in increased frailty and the onset of additional needs. The capability approach has also been applied in the context of the concept of 'ageing in place', or staying in your own home or community as you age.[126] As Grove has illustrated it is important to have:

---

[124] See #socialcarefuture (2022) *Towards an Equal Life; from here to there: What next for social care future?* Strategy briefing.

[125] #socialcarefuture (2021) *Whose Social Care is it Anyway? From permanent lockdown to an equal life*, p 21, at https://socialcarefuture.org.uk, accessed 10 July 2024.

[126] H. Grove (2021) 'Ageing as well as you can in place: applying a geographical lens to the capability approach', *Social Science and Medicine*, 228.

both a supportive environment and social supports in helping older people with compromised physical and cognitive capacities to realise their most valued functioning and capabilities. These typically revolve around being able to get out and about, engage and connect with others, carry out daily tasks and errands and remain independent.[127]

However as we saw in chapter 1 there is a danger in social care policy making assumptions that social care needs to be viewed through the prism of an increasingly ageing population. In fact social care is provided to people across the life-course with estimates of some 30% of those receiving care and support being between the ages of 18-64.[128] For this group too application of the capabilities approach can provide an important way in which individuals' rights can be both highlighted and safeguarded.

Framing a human rights response in terms of capabilities provides a more expansive approach which, when engaged with direct accounts of peoples' own experiences, could form a good basis for developing adult social care strategy and fresh legal approaches in the future. At the same time, integrating a capabilities approach is challenging given the polycentric nature of the kinds of experiences and decisions in question. It also raises the issue of how to align respect for one person's capabilities and rights with those of others, including those of carers. Nor can we ignore the matter of finite resources; in any socio-economic climate, certain choices maximize capabilities for one person but may have a consequent impact of the resources available to others. While there has been a movement from the language of paternalism in policy making, discriminatory societal attitudes towards disabled and older people remain commonplace and were brought to the fore in the prioritization and policy decisions made during the COVID-19 pandemic.[129]

Recognising capabilities and supporting human rights may potentially also be facilitated through the utilisation of 'co-production' in developing social care law and policy. The inclusive language and practice of 'co-production' is increasingly often employed in health and social care research and policy development, albeit with varying degrees of perceived success.[130] The UK Government has to some extent engaged with co-production initiatives, both

---

[127] H. Grove (2021), p 8.

[128] L. Allen and H. Alderwick (2020) *Social care for adults aged 18–64 in England*, Health Foundation.

[129] See, for example, discussion in House of Commons House of Lords *Joint Committee on Human Rights – The Government's response to COVID-19: human rights implications*, Seventh Report of Session 2019–21. We discuss this further in Chapter 4.

[130] It has a long history in relation to discussions concerning social care – see, for example, G. Wilson (1994) 'Co-production and self-care: new approaches to managing community care services for older people', *Social Policy and Administration*, 28(3): 236–50.

in a broad sense and specifically in relation to pandemic preparedness planning work and during the COVID-19 pandemic as we shall see in chapter 4 below. Local authorities are also increasingly engaging with elements of co-production, or at least public engagement, during consultations and more responsive local planning. While the term 'co-production' emerged in the 1970s in relation to industry,[131] it is now used in a range of situations, particularly in the public sector. In ideal form it might include an element of 'co-creation', suggestive of a far greater role in policy making:

> Co-production is generally associated with services citizens receive during the implementation phase of the production cycle, whereas co-creation concerns services at a strategic level. In other words, when citizens are involved in the general planning of a service—perhaps even initiating it—then this is co-creation, whereas if they shape the service during later phases of the cycle it is co-production. Input in the design of a service can be both individual or collective, depending on the level at which a service is addressed.[132]

The rallying call of 'Nothing about us without us' can be seen as important from the perspective of the disability rights movement globally and the United Nations Convention on the Rights of Persons with Disabilities (UN CRPD).[133] In the UK there is a national partnership organization Think Local Act Personal (TLAP) which 'spans central and local government, social care providers, the NHS, and the voluntary and community sector as well as people with lived experience'.[134] It lists co-production as one of its priorities and main work programmes, and its aim is that the work of the National Co-Production Advisory Group – 'made up of people who access services, carers, and family members' – is involved in TLAP's efforts to promote personalized care and support services.[135] Many of TLAP's partner organizations, and some other third-sector organizations, may have a seat in strategic planning exercises for the Department of Health and Social Care (DHSC) and other areas of government, sitting on committees, sharing views, and providing and assessing evidence. The involvement of representatives of these organizations, and

---

[131] E. Ostrom (1996) 'Crossing the great divide: coproduction, synergy, and development', *World Development*, 24(6): 1073.

[132] T. Brandsen and M. Honingh (2018) 'Definitions of co-production and co-creation', in T. Brandsen, B. Verschuere and T. Steen (eds) *Co-Production and Co-Creation: Engaging Citizens in Public Services*, London: Routledge.

[133] G. de Beco (2021) *Disability in International Human Rights Law* (online edn), Oxford: Oxford Academic, ch 9.

[134] TLAP 'About us', at www.thinklocalactpersonal.org.uk/About-us/

[135] See also Chapter 4.

especially those with lived experience of accessing services, is absolutely crucial to decision-making and for lending legitimacy to policies. The University of Birmingham IMPACT Centre for implementing evidence in adult social care defines co-production as 'people who draw on care and support and carers working with professionals in equal partnerships towards shared goals'.[136] The Centre aims to ensure that 'people who draw on care and support and carers will be meaningfully involved': 'Firstly, this will lead to better decisions that are closer to the realities of people's lives. Secondly, it will also help to readdress traditional power imbalances between people who draw on care and support, carers and professionals.'[137]

Jaspers and Steen have argued, however, that co-production, while widening participation, may also pose challenges in relation to inclusion, efficiency, freedom, and reciprocity.[138] Brandsen et al identify seven potential 'evils' which need to be taken into account when using co-production methods to reach decisions or policy positions. These 'evils' are 'the deliberate rejection of responsibility, failing accountability, rising transaction costs, loss of democracy, reinforced inequalities, implicit demands and co-destruction'.[139] While they recognize that wider public engagement can facilitate collective action on key issues, they also warn that 'it can also be a cover for minimising governments' responsibilities and accountability in a context of scarcity of financial resources in the public sector in general and in social and healthcare services more specifically'.[140]

In such instances, there can be problems regarding accountability where boundaries and consequent responsibilities between actors may have become blurred.[141] We return in later chapters of this book to the utilization of co-production in pandemic planning and its potential to help shape future social policy.

While the integration of these theoretical approaches into policy and practice may be seen as part of a natural synergy, or at least well-intentioned, 'care' is not always or necessarily mutual, reciprocal, or even desired. To

---

[136] IMPACT (2024) 'IMPACT's co-production approach,' webpage. https://impact.bham.ac.uk/our-mission/co-production/#:~:text=IMPACT%27s%20co%2Dproduction%20approach%20means,inclusive%20and%20accessible%20as%20possible.

[137] IMPACT (2024) 'IMPACT's co-production approach'.

[138] See S. Jaspers and T. Steen (2019) 'Realizing public values: enhancement or obstruction? Exploring value tensions and coping strategies in the co-production of social care', *Public Management Review*, 21(4): 606.

[139] T. Brandsen, B. Verschuere and T. Steen (2018) 'The dark side of co-creation and co-production: seven evils', in T. Brandsen, B. Verschuere and T. Steen (eds) *Co-Production and Co-Creation: Engaging Citizens in Public Services*, London: Routledge.

[140] T. Brandsen, B. Verschuere and T. Steen (2018), p 285. They use the example of the Big Society scheme launched under former Prime Minister David Cameron.

[141] T. Brandsen, B. Verschuere and T. Steen (2018), p 285.

return to England of the early noughties, the idea of individual service commissioning, also known as the personalization agenda,[142] marked a major shift in social policy. In 2007, the New Labour Government's landmark protocol, *Putting People First*, aimed to give choice and control to people who use care and support services. Personalization has implications for how we frame our collective responsibilities towards others, and Barnes argues that although the language of personalization is rooted in reciprocity and dignity,[143] there is an inherent power imbalance in this policy position, and an undermining of the relational nature of care.

Human rights themselves can be expressly delimited by broader policy considerations which may themselves be directed to safeguard the rights and freedoms of others. Safeguarding human rights can be seen as challenging as we shall see further in the discussion in chapter 3 below when set against the fact that at international human rights level considerable degrees of discretion are left to individual states in determining matters of expenditure on health and social care. Moreover as was graphically illustrated in the context of the COVID-19 pandemic, autonomy was constrained through what were extraordinary limitations imposed on personal choice in daily life, such as freedom of movement.[144] These rules were based on a utilitarian analysis of the public health situation, and as such can be seen as respecting the fundamental principle of the right to life.[145] We discuss the further development of law and policy regarding the COVID-19 pandemic in Chapter 4 below.

IV. Vulnerability

The paradigm of an adult as an autonomous entity able to make their own decisions, safeguarded and bolstered by fundamental human rights principles, is a basic tenet of international law. A capabilities approach ameliorates and adds texture to what otherwise might be seen as a blunt and consequently less effective series of norms, by recognizing and responding to individual needs. We have also seen the complex, reality of the relational nature of the nested relationship of care.

---

[142] HMG (2007) *Putting People First: A shared vision and commitment to the transformation of Adult Social Care*, at https://webarchive.nationalarchives.gov.uk/ukgwa/20130104175839/http://www.dh.gov.uk/en/Publicationsandstatistics/Publications/PublicationsPolicyAndGuidance/DH_081118

[143] M. Barnes (2011) 'Abandoning care? A critical perspective on personalisation from an ethic of care', *Ethics and Social Welfare*, 5(2): 153.

[144] See further discussion in A. Wagner (2022) *Emergency State: How We Lost Our Freedoms in the Pandemic and Why It Matters*, London: Bodley Head, ch 4.

[145] See further Chapter 1.

As we saw above the notion of autonomy is also subject to other limitations by reference to the rights and freedoms of others. In addition to limitations to safeguard the life of the individual, and to protect others from communicable diseases, in the context of health and social care policy and provision there are additional limitations placed upon individual decision-making when those individuals may be classed as being 'vulnerable'. But what does it mean to be 'vulnerable'? Who is a 'vulnerable person'? And 'when are they vulnerable'?

'Vulnerability' is a term fraught with contested meanings. For Goodin, writing in 1985, vulnerability was something which is inherently relational, and which necessarily gives rise to responsibilities.[146] Perhaps the best-known theorist of vulnerability is Martha Albertson Fineman. She argues that 'vulnerability' is 'universal and constant, a quality inherent in the human condition'.[147] She rejects the application of homogenizing notions of equality, in the sense of 'sameness of treatment' as these are deemed 'under exclusive' in the context of differing needs.[148] Fineman does not conceive of vulnerability in terms of 'vulnerable populations', but rather argues that:

> I claim the term 'vulnerable' for its potential in describing a universal, inevitable, enduring aspect of the human condition that must be at the heart of our concept of social and state responsibility. Vulnerability freed from its limited and negative associations is a powerful conceptual tool with the potential to define an obligation for the state to ensure a richer, more robust guarantee of equality than is afforded under the equal protection model.[149]

It is, she states, the very ambiguity in the concept of vulnerability which enables us to 'examine hidden assumptions and biases that shaped its original social and cultural meaning'.[150] Her analysis critiques the idea of the liberal subject, favouring instead 'the vulnerable subject', which she locates in the context of wider legal and philosophical debates around human autonomy and which she argues 'is a more accurate and complete universal figure to place at the heart of social policy'.[151]

---

[146] R.E. Goodin (1985) *Protecting the Vulnerable: A Re-analysis of our Social Responsibilities*, Chicago, IL: University of Chicago Press.

[147] M.A. Fineman (2020) 'The vulnerable subject: anchoring equality in the human condition', in M.A. Fineman (ed) *Transcending the Boundaries of Law: Generations of Feminism and Legal Theory*, New York: Routledge, p 161.

[148] M.A. Fineman (2020), p 162.

[149] M.A. Fineman (2020), p 166.

[150] M.A. Fineman (2020), p 167.

[151] M.A. Fineman (2020), p 168.

Fineman's critique aligns with other feminist writing which has criticized the policy emphasis on notions of autonomy and self-sufficiency.[152] Instead she argues that individuals are to be seen as having experienced

> a wide range of differing and inter-dependent abilities over a lifetime. The vulnerability approach recognises that individuals are anchored at each end of their lives by dependency and the absence of capacity. Of course between these ends, loss of capacity and dependence may also occur, temporarily for many and permanently for some. Constant and variable throughout life, individual vulnerability encompasses not only damage that has been done in the past and speculative harms of the distant future, but also the possibility of immediate harm. Humans live with the ever-present possibility that their needs and circumstances will change. On an individual level the concept of vulnerability captures this present potential for dependency based upon our persistent susceptibility to misfortune and catastrophe.[153]

She concludes that 'focusing on shared vulnerabilities and building a political movement around unequal institutional arrangements is a more promising and powerful approach in addressing the disadvantage that persists in society'.[154]

Cole, however, criticizes the approach taken by Fineman and others working on vulnerability analysis, arguing that

> the field as a whole seems more invested in presenting vulnerability as being foremost universal, always ambivalent and ambiguous, at a distance from questions of power and politics. The concept has been rendered so broad as to obscure the needs of specific groups and individuals, undermining its promise as a conceptual frame to understand and challenge systemic inequalities.[155]

As a result of this, Cole suggests that: 'Broadly speaking, the literature endeavours to transvalue, even normalize, vulnerability as a shared, constitutive and connective feature of our existence that encompasses

---

[152] M.A. Fineman (2020), p 167.
[153] M.A. Fineman (2020), p 168.
[154] M.A. Fineman (2020), p 172.
[155] A. Cole (2016) 'All of us are vulnerable, but some are more vulnerable than others: the political ambiguity of vulnerability studies, an ambivalent critique', *Critical Horizons: A Journal of Philosophy and Social Theory*, 17(2): 267.

not merely susceptibility to harm but also receptivity to positive forms of intersubjectivity'.[156]

She maintains, however, that 'the fundamentally negative connotations of vulnerability cannot be simply inverted':

> as these scholars ask us to embrace a more expansive understanding of vulnerability, they still preserve and frequently employ the conventional and narrower use of the term 'vulnerable' as a designation of harm and oppression. Such ambiguity is not incidental but intrinsic to their project. Retaining the now-double meaning of the term, scholars insist on basic, inescapable principles that are shared by all permutations of vulnerability. They semantically re-situate vulnerability-as-harm in a significantly richer range of human interactivity, thereby naturalizing its presence and disarming the potential threat that intensifies social divisions and propels the pursuit of invulnerability. Upholding vulnerability-as-harm and the more inclusive vulnerability-as-interconnectivity under a single designation, however, exacerbates the risk of conflating the two.[157]

The extent to which autonomy may be undermined by a classification of vulnerability is a point of debate. However, the two concepts can be seen as intertwined, having each evolved over time and through different sociopolitical contexts. Mackenzie has suggested that it is a mistake to see autonomy and vulnerability in opposition, and rather that:

> Autonomy – understood as both the *capacity* to lead a self-determining life and the *status* of being recognized as an autonomous agent by others – is crucial for a flourishing life in contemporary liberal democratic societies. It is thus a mistake for an ethics of vulnerability to reject either the concept of autonomy or its importance for achieving democratic equality.[158]

She argues that a relational approach to autonomy would have the effect of removing the perceived tension between recognizing and reacting to vulnerability and respect for autonomy of decision-making. Rather than adopting Fineman's approach, Mackenzie favours a model of relational

---

[156] A. Cole (2016), p 260.
[157] A. Cole (2016), pp 265–6.
[158] C. Mackenzie (2013) 'The importance of relational autonomy and capabilities for an ethics of vulnerability', in C. Mackenzie, W. Rogers and S. Dodds (eds) *Vulnerability: New Essays in Ethics and Feminist Philosophy*, Oxford: Oxford University Press.

autonomy as seen in Elizabeth Anderson's capability-based theory of democratic autonomy.[159]

The concepts of vulnerability, autonomy, and choice are by no means abstract concepts. The shifting ways in which they are viewed and interpreted inform policies that in turn impact very directly upon people's lives in the context of adult social care. As Munro and Scoular have argued: 'the dangers of any uncritical adoption of a discourse of vulnerability, without an interrogation of who is recognised to be vulnerable, under what conditions and why, as well as of the broader socio-economic and state agendas that are served by the responses imposed'.[160]

These conditions and agendas, and the intersectional nature of the resultant health inequalities, have perhaps never been more apparent than they were during the COVID-19 pandemic. The relative and unequal impacts of the virus and the efforts to mitigate its reach laid bare the underlying socio-economic and health inequalities in our society. As the work of Marmot and his team has shown, life expectancy in the UK has been declining since 2010, in contrast to many other economically developed countries, and poverty in childhood compounds health inequalities in later life.[161] There is ample evidence that mortality from COVID-19 was higher in less socio-economically advantaged areas, and that those who lived in areas of high deprivation often faced multiple points of vulnerability, in terms of underlying health conditions, residential circumstances, and type of employment, to name but a few.[162] Moreover, as stated in a 2020 Editorial in *The Lancet*, the parameters of what might constitute 'vulnerability' shifted and broadened as the virus spread: 'Certainly, amid the COVID-19 pandemic, vulnerable groups are not only elderly people, those with ill health and comorbidities, or homeless or underhoused people, but also people from a gradient of socioeconomic groups that might struggle to cope financially, mentally, or physically with the crisis.'[163]

---

[159] C. Mackenzie (2013), p 41. See also C. Mackenzie (2021) 'Relational autonomy', in K.Q. Hall and Ásta (eds) *The Oxford Handbook of Feminist Philosophy*, Oxford: Oxford University Press.

[160] V. Munro and J. Scoular (2012) 'Abusing vulnerability? Contemporary law and policy responses to sex work in the UK', *Feminist Legal Studies* 20(3): 189–206.

[161] M. Marmot et al (2020) *Build Back Fairer: The COVID-19 Marmot Review*, Health Foundation (December), see discussion, pp 13–17.

[162] V.J. McGowan and C. Bambra (2022) 'COVID-19 mortality and deprivation: pandemic, syndemic, and endemic health inequalities', *Lancet Public Health*, e-966-75; see also Office for National Statistics (2020) 'Deaths involving COVID-19 by local area and socioeconomic deprivation: deaths occurring between 1 March and 17 April 2020', 1 May, at ons.gov.uk

[163] Lancet (2020) 'Editorial: Redefining vulnerability in the era of COVID-19', *The Lancet*, 395(10230): 1089.

As previously discussed, the ability and freedom to make effective choices and to access resources in health and social care can be constrained and compounded by various factors for those living with a disability, or those who draw on social care services for any other reason, or indeed carers. These stresses and limitations were exacerbated during the pandemic. For example, access to information, contact with local authority and many care agency staff, and even Care Act assessments and reviews were shifted to a primarily digital approach to delivery. While this approach helped to limit face-to-face contact with the concurrent risk of infection, it also deepened existing inequalities as not everyone is able to access digital services effectively unless they have IT knowledge and skills, up-to-date technology and reliable broadband, and so on. For others, the support of a carer or other intermediary would be required in order to achieve any level of communication via digital or telephonic means.[164]

Dodds suggests that dependence is a specific form of vulnerability, and that this factor should inform the nature and practice of caregiving: 'The particular vulnerabilities associated with dependency are such that they are best met or supported by a specific person (or small number of people) due to the intimacy, immediacy or subtlety of the needs, support and protections that are involved.'[165]

There is a scale of dependency, from what is total, as in the case of an infant, or partial, as with an adult who has some degree or combination of physical or mental impairment and requires some support to maintain their autonomy. These nuances are part of her model of situational vulnerability. So, for example, as she suggests:

> An adult who experiences mobility impairment is situationally vulnerable because of his mobility limitations. He may not be dependant however, if his needs can be met without relying on the specific assistance of another person. For example, his workplace and home may have been designed or modified so that he can live and work independently, and the public transport systems that he uses may allow him to move readily between work, home and his other activities.[166]

Dodds re-considers Goodin's argument that vulnerability necessitates a wider social and moral protective responsibility in the light of Walker's criticism that

---

[164] M. Madianou (2020) 'A second-order disaster? Digital technologies during the COVID-19 pandemic', *Social Media + Society*, 6(3).

[165] S. Dodds (2013) 'Dependence, care and vulnerability', in C. Mackenzie, W. Rogers and S. Dodds (eds) *Vulnerability: New Essays in Ethics and Feminist Philosophy*, Oxford: Oxford University Press, at p 184.

[166] Dodds (2013), p 186.

the assignation of certain responsibilities may in turn precipitate consequent vulnerabilities.[167] Dodds goes on to explore how certain policy frameworks can result in what she terms 'pathogenic' vulnerability and dependency:

> Pathogenic vulnerability is generated or exacerbated by morally dysfunctional social or interpersonal relationships or expectations. Social and legal institutions designed to reduce dependency or to promote self-responsibility may pathogenically exacerbate the vulnerability of the dependent or his care provider if those institutional arrangements fail to address the complex relationships between dependency and vulnerability.[168]

One example is drawn from the Australian process of de-institutionalization in the context of mental health care, whereby people were moved from often dehumanizing institutional care placements into community settings was not supported sufficiently, which in turn exacerbated the situational vulnerabilities (and mental illness) of those people.[169]

The relational nature of vulnerability in people's everyday lives was writ large during the pandemic experience. The restrictions enacted in order to keep the virus from clinically vulnerable individuals, alongside the vulnerability of those caring for them, eroded individual autonomy for everyone, but this was especially felt among those who had to 'shield' for long periods. Psychological pressures caused by lockdown inevitably deepened existing vulnerabilities. For example, vital sources for support, such as day centres, were closed from the start of the pandemic, and this was often also the case with centres for respite care. This inevitably placed those caring for others under excessive strain. The pandemic also graphically demonstrated the extent of the relational vulnerabilities experienced by those living and working in residential care homes, particularly during 2020.[170] A study by Bell et al found that between 2020 and 2021 in England there was a 79 per cent increase in deaths of care home residents.[171]

Thus, the theoretical analysis of vulnerability and its impacts must remain ever conscious of the lived experiences and practical realities of those who

---

[167] Dodds (2013), s 2.0, p 189.
[168] Dodds (2013), s 4.0, p 197.
[169] Dodds (2013), s 4.0, p 199. A similar process happened in the UK with 'Care in the Community' during the 1990s (see further Chapter 1).
[170] See further M. Morciano et al (2021) 'Excess mortality for care home residents during the first 23 weeks of the COVID-19 pandemic in England: a national cohort study', *BMC Medicine*, at www.biomedcentral.com
[171] D. Bell et al (2020) 'COVID-19 mortality and long-term care: a UK comparison', *International Long Term Care Policy Network*, 29 August, at https://ltccovid.org

may be labelled as such. There are real-world and unwelcome consequences for individuals classified in this way. Some people object to the use of the term at all. In social care practice and law 'vulnerability' has a very specific meaning, distinct from these broader theoretical paradigms through the concept of the 'vulnerable person'. The Office for Health Improvement and Disparities states that 'being vulnerable is defined as in need of special care, support, or protection because of age, disability, risk of abuse or neglect', and that the NHS 'defines vulnerable adults as any adult (person over the age of 18) unable to take care of themselves or protect themselves from exploitation'.[172] There are number of notable statutory measures that exist in relation to protection for vulnerable adults. Sections 42 to 46 of the Care Act 2014, for example, contain safeguarding provisions for adults who are at risk of abuse and neglect. We consider these, along with the wider detail of the Care Act and related legislation, in Chapter 3.

V. Conclusions

As we have seen in this chapter, the very concept of 'care' itself remains contested. An understanding of the nested relationships of care as scholars such as Nedeslsky and Harding have developed is also critically important to understand how social care law, policy and day-to-day provision operate. The recognition of these nested relationships in turn, however, does not always provide us with straightforward solutions in relation to specific situations. Nonetheless it is vital to engage with this complexity, to understand the current situation as well as to develop and implement future law and policy.

Respect for fundamental human rights is also critical both as a fundamental ethical and policy paradigm, but also as a principle which should underpin the development of social care law and policy, in general and in the context of a pandemic. The promotion of well-being and the maximization of capabilities are embedded in aspects of the Care Act 2014 and in the language of social work practice. Yet as we have seen, engaging with human rights can involve at times difficult policy choices. This may arise due to financial constraints through public sector social care provision on a day-to-day basis, and in exceptional circumstances such as, for example, a major global pandemic. We will explore these issues further in Chapters 3 and 4. Involving those with lived experience in the development of law and policy choices through mechanisms such as co-production may indeed facilitate better engagement and understanding of individual human rights, but this in turn needs to be seen in the context of the political realities at the time those choices are made.

---

[172] Department of Health and Social Care (2022) 'Vulnerabilities: applying All Our Health', March.

An understanding of vulnerability as a concept and its disputed terminology utilized in practice is also crucial to inform our understanding of the way in which law and policy is constructed to address and engage with care and support needs. At the same time, while we recognize the real value of this as an important concept in understanding the inherent nature of human relationships, we also remain cautious as to its application when translated from a theoretical level to a practical dimension in policy terms, given its very loaded dimensions.

The foundational paradigms explored in this chapter provide us with important insights which will enable us to contextualize and better understand the contemporary adult social care law and policy landscape, the impacts of emergency provisions brought in during the pandemic, and their legacy in subsequent chapters. Nonetheless, as we have seen, they do not necessarily provide us with easy solutions. This does not mean that we should not engage with, understand or indeed attempt to apply them. Respect for fundamental human rights and maximisation of capabilities while at the same time recognising the complexity of the care process, relationships and inherent vulnerability is critical for developing effective social care and pandemic law and policy development and operation.

3

Legal Regulation of Adult Social Care Provision in England

I. Introduction

Adult social care law covers a vast area, as illustrated by its comprehensive examination in the classic text by Luke Clements and his colleagues.[1] As this chapter demonstrates, social care is an area characterized by legislation that, while placing certain duties and powers upon local authorities and NHS bodies, is underpinned by challenging and ongoing policy choices. As it explores the existing legal structures concerning adult social care the chapter highlights how these may be seen to address individual needs and vulnerabilities of those seeking care and support, and the extent to which local authorities can be held accountable for the provision of care. This analysis provides us with the structure to enable us to understand and interrogate in Chapters 4, 5, and 6 the nature and practical implications of the pandemic planning, legislative and policy decisions regarding Care Act powers, and duties made prior to and during the COVID-19 pandemic and their specific impacts on the provision of adult social care during and following that period.

The chapter is divided into three main sections following the Introduction. Section II considers the role of local authorities in relation to social care provision, considering the organizational structures under the Local Authorities Act 1970 and the Care Act 2014 concerning its duties and powers in relation to adults and their carers with eligible needs, and other related provisions. Section III examines related provisions concerning adult

---

[1] See further L. Clements with K. Ashton, S. Garlick, C. Goodhall, E. Mitchell, and A. Pickup (2019) *Community Care and the Law* (7th edn), London: Legal Action Group. Adult social care law relates to other important areas such as housing law but these go beyond the scope of this present volume. See further in relation to Housing Law, A. Arden and A. Dymond (2022) *Manual of Housing Law*, Legal Action Group; D. Astin (2022) *Housing Law Handbook* (5th edn), Legal Action Group; and Clements et al (2019), ch 15.

social care and support, separate from those under the 2014 Act, including in relation to NHS Continuing Healthcare and under the Mental Health Act 1983. Section IV considers the operation of the oversight mechanisms that exist in relation to social care provision, the scrutiny provided by local authorities, by the Care Quality Commission (CQC), and the Local Government and Social Care Ombudsman (LGSCO).

II. The Care Act 2014 and local authority duties and powers in relation to adult social care

As we saw in Chapter 1 the organization of social care at local authority level is derived from the Local Authority Social Services Act 1970.[2] The 1970 Act extends to local authority social services functions which include provisions in relation to the duties and powers under the Care Act 2014, and those in relation to assessment of needs for community care services under section 47 of the National Health Service and Community Care Act 1990 (see further discussion to follow).[3] Section 6 of the 1970 Act requires those local authorities to appoint a director of adult social services.[4] In addition, the Localism Act 2011 gives local authorities a 'general power of competence',[5] which means that they have the power to act as otherwise individuals (that is, persons with full mental capacity) may do.[6] The Explanatory Notes on the Act provide that there are no limits as to the way in which a local authority exercises these powers[7]. As Clements et al comment, 'in the social care context it can also act as a safety net; enabling local authorities to support individuals who, for one reason or another, are not entitled to support under the CA 2014'.[8]

Nonetheless, as they highlight, there are some limitations in relation to situations which there are preexisting restrictions in legislation enacted prior to the 2011 Act or where subsequent legislation which has been enacted provides for specific limitations (for these purposes, 'legislation' refers to both primary and secondary legislation).[9] The courts have held that where

---

[2] Local Authority Social Services Act 1970, s 1 defines local authorities as: 'The local authorities for the purposes of this Act shall be the councils of non-metropolitan counties and non-metropolitan districts in England, the councils of London boroughs and the Common Council of the City of London.'
[3] Local Authority Social Services Act 1970, Sch 1.
[4] Local Authority Social Services Act 1970, s 6(1).
[5] Localism Act 2011, s 1.
[6] Localism Act 2011, Explanatory Notes, para 10.
[7] Localism Act 2011, Explanatory Notes, para 10.
[8] Clements et al (2019), para 1.62.
[9] Clements et al (2019), para 1.63.

a claimant is unable to bring the claim within a specific provision of the Care Act, but that failure to provide a particular service would constitute a violation of the European Convention on Human Rights (ECHR), then the local authority may be required to consider exercising section 1(1) of the Localism Act 2011.[10] We explore below the implications of the Human Rights Act 1998 with regard to the powers and duties of local authorities.[11] There is also one further human rights provision which is relevant in this context. Local authorities must act in accordance with section 149 of the Equality Act 2010 which sets out the public sector duty to ensure equality and protection from discrimination. This places on public authorities the duty to have regard to the elimination of conduct including discrimination, harassment, and victimization, and to advance equality of opportunity and the fostering of 'good relations between persons who share a relevant protected characteristic and persons who do not share it'.[12]

As we saw in Chapter 1 the Care Act 2014 provided a major reform of the law pertaining to social care. It sets out a series of powers and duties regarding the provision of care and support for adults and support for carers, as well as a number of other regulations concerning safeguarding, care standards, and a range of health-related matters including integrated services.[13] Section 78 of the 2014 Act also provides for the production of statutory Guidance. The impact of statutory guidance on local authorities was considered in *R (X) v Tower Hamlets LBC*.[14] This approach is relevant when considering the application of the Care Act guidance. Here the Court of Appeal cited the approach taken by Males J at first instance that

> the guidance does not have the binding effect of secondary legislation, and a local authority is free to depart from it, even 'substantially'. But a departure from the guidance would be unlawful unless there is cogent reason for it, and the greater the departure the more compelling must that reason be. Conversely a minor departure from the letter of the guidance, while remaining true to its spirit may well be easy to justify or may not even be regarded as a departure at all.[15]

---

[10] *R (GS) v LB Camden* [2016] EWHC 1762 and see discussion in Clements et al (2019), para 1.66.

[11] See also A. Brammer (2020) *Social Work Law* (5th edn), London: Pearson, chapter 5.

[12] Equality Act 2010, s 149(1)(c). See further discussion in Clements et al (2019), paras 2.65–2.69.

[13] Care Act 2014. See also Feldon P. (2023) *The Social Worker's Guide to the Care Act 2014* (2nd edn), on its application by social work teams.

[14] [2013] EWCA 482 (Admin).

[15] [2013] EWHC 482 (Admin), para 35 *R(Munjaz) v Mersey Care NHS Trust* [2006] 2 AC 146.

Sections 1–7 of the Care Act 2014 place general duties upon local authorities, which, as Spencer-Lane notes, are also referred to as 'target duties'.[16] The relevant duties are first: the duty to promote well-being.[17] Second: the duty to provide or arrange provision of services, resources, or facilities that contribute to delaying or stopping adults or carers developing needs for care and support or for care or to the reduction of those needs.[18] Third: the requirement to take various measures which will promote integration of care and support services with health services. Fourth, there is a requirement for local authorities to establish and maintain information and advice services about the provision of care and support for adults and carers. Fifth, the Act requires local authorities to 'promote the efficient and effective operation of a market in services for meeting care and support needs';[19] they must ensure that those who want to access services will have available a range of providers,[20] 'high quality services',[21] and information which is sufficient to 'make an informed decision as to how to meet those needs in question'.[22] Sixth, there is a duty to cooperate in general with relevant partners (which include, for example, other local authorities, NHS bodies, government ministers, and police chiefs),[23] and this duty likewise applies to those relevant partners,[24] as well as a duty to cooperate in relation to specific cases.[25] We now examine these key aspects of the legislation in turn.

(a) The well-being principle

The Care Act 2014 is rooted in the well-being principle, which underpins all the provisions therein.[26] Section 1 of the Act sets out the well-being principle. This provides that:

---

[16] T. Spencer-Lane (2020) 'Overview of the Care Act 2014', in S. Braye and M. Preston-Shoot (eds) *The Care Act 2014: Wellbeing in Practice*, London: Sage (2020) and T. Spencer-Lane (2020) The Care Act Manual (3rd edn), London: Sweet & Maxwell at p 15.

[17] Care Act 2014, s 1.

[18] Care Act 2014, s 2; see further Clements et al (2019), ch 10.

[19] Care Act 2014, s 5(1); see further on the interpretation of this duty *R (on the application of Care England) v Essex CC* [2017] EWHC 3035 (Admin).

[20] Care Act 2014, s 5(1)(a).

[21] Care Act 2014, s 5(1)(b).

[22] Care Act 2014, s 5(1)(c).

[23] Care Act 2014, s 6(7).

[24] Care Act 2014, s 6.

[25] Care Act 2014, s 7.

[26] The original Law Commission consultation paper initially contained discussion of a series of principles, including: choice and control (paras 3.16–3.19); person-centred planning (paras 3.20–3.24); needs to be viewed broadly (paras 3.25–3.29); the need to reduce or remove future need (para 3.31); the need for independent living (paras 3.32–3.37); an assumption of home based care (paras 3.38–3.42); dignity in care (paras 3.43–3.48);

(1) The general duty of a local authority, in exercising a function under this Part in the case of an individual, is to promote that individual's well-being.

Clements et al suggest that 'wellbeing is a fashionable and politically favoured concept', at that time but was also rooted in related academic literature.[27] The 2014 Act expands upon what is meant by well-being:

Section 1(2)
'Well-being', in relation to an individual, means that individual's well-being so far as relating to any of the following—
(a) personal dignity (including treatment of the individual with respect);
(b) physical and mental health and emotional well-being;
(c) protection from abuse and neglect;
(d) control by the individual over day-to-day life (including over care and support, or support, provided to the individual and the way in which it is provided);
(e) participation in work, education, training or recreation;
(f) social and economic well-being;
(g) domestic, family and personal relationships;
(h) suitability of living accommodation;
(i) the individual's contribution to society.[28]

As Crossland comments, these aims are all to be seen as equal in weighting and that there is no hierarchy of well-being criteria.[29] There is, however, scope for disparate readings of these aims. For example, the nature and scope of 'dignity' as a concept inherent in respect for fundamental human rights has long been the subject of debate.[30] The active promotion of human rights and dignity is, however, considered a tenet of social work values and

---

and finally the need to safeguard adults at risk from abuse or neglect (paras 3.49–3.51). However, this approach was not ultimately included in the legislation Law Commission Consultation Paper, *Adult Social Care*, 2010, Pt 3.

[27] Clements et al (2019), para 2.9. See also Cabinet Office 2010, Prime Ministers Office, 10 Downing Street and the Rt Hon Lord Cameron 'PM's speech on wellbeing', 25 November 2010.

[28] Care Act 2014, s 1(2).

[29] See J. Crossland (2020) 'Implementing the Care Act: assessing need and providing care and support', in S. Braye and M. Preston-Shoot (eds) *The Care Act 2014: Wellbeing in Practice*, London: Sage p27.

[30] See, for example, discussion of the concept of dignity in D. Beyleveld and R. Brownsword (2001) *Human Dignity in Bioethics and Biolaw*, Oxford: Oxford. University Press;

practice, as inculcated in social work training and demonstrated in the British Association of Social Workers (BASW) professional capabilities framework.[31]

Borowski suggests that while the term 'dignity' is used frequently in social work and upholding it is indeed a core professional value, it has in practice been utilized 'without precision'.[32] Control and choice as rights in relation to independent living can be seen as derived from the approach taken in Article 19 of the United Nations Convention on the Human Rights of Persons with Disabilities (UN CRPD) with the aim that individuals have the right and ability to make choices and to 'choose their place of residence and where and with whom they live on an equal basis with others' as stated in the Guidance to the Act.[33] Clements et al note that choice in terms of 'preference' only arises in the legislation through the application of section 30 which provides for regulations regarding individual adults to express a preference for certain accommodation.[34] Thus while preference is to be taken into account, it is nonetheless but one factor considered in the wider determination of needs. Notably, the statutory Guidance does not explicate its interpretation of the well-being principle.[35]

When a local authority exercises its powers and duties under the Care Act 2014 it must have regard to a range of factors.[36] The first of these is that the person themselves is in the best position to determine the factors that contribute to their own well-being.[37] As Clements et al comment, there is a similar approach taken under the Mental Capacity Act 2005 which provides for a presumption of decision-making capacity; namely, that evidence would need to be given to rebut this presumption.[38] Second, the local authority must have regard to a person's 'views, wishes, feelings and beliefs.'[39] Third, the local authority must have regard to 'the importance of preventing or delaying the development of needs for care

---

J.R. May and E. Daly (2020) *Advanced Introduction to Human Dignity and Law*, Cheltenham: Edward Elgar.

[31] See BASW PFC at https://new.basw.co.uk/training-cpd/professional-capabilities-framework/social-worker-pcf. See also D. Tanner et al (2024) *Social Work with Older People: SWOP Project Final Report*.

[32] A. Borowski (2022) 'On human dignity and social work', *British Journal of Social Work*, 52(2): 609–23.

[33] Department of Health and Social Care (2024) *Care and Support Statutory Guidance*, updated 24 March 2024, para 1.19.

[34] Clements et al (2019), para 2.35.

[35] Clements et al (2019), para 2.23.

[36] Care Act 2014, s 1(3).

[37] Care Act 2014, s 1(3)(a).

[38] Clements et al (2019), para 2.19.

[39] Care Act 2014, s 1(3)(b).

and support or needs for support and the importance of reducing needs of either kind that already exist'; that is to say, it needs to act proactively and pre-emptively to promote well-being.[40] In addition, the local authority must ensure that decisions regarding that person relate to 'all the individual's circumstances', rather than what are 'unjustified assumptions about the individual's well-being', which may be derived solely from age or appearance.[41] The importance of the person themselves being able to participate in decision-making and having the necessary information to do so is also emphasized.[42]

This approach to well-being draws upon the similar approach under section 1 of the Mental Capacity Act 2005. It can be seen in terms of maximizing an individual's decision-making autonomy. However, there is one notable difference and extension of scope contained in section 1(3)(f) of the Care Act 2014, which states that:

> (f) the importance of achieving a balance between the individual's well-being and that of any friends or relatives who are involved in caring for the individual.[43]

Here the focus of the Act is not simply upon one person who needs care services or support; it also crucially takes into account the needs of (often unpaid or informal) carers and significant others.[44] There is an inbuilt relationality of approach in the legislation. Yes, there is recognition of individual rights and entitlements – but these are of both the individual who may need care and that of the person(s) who may be providing it. It aims to balance their respective need for well-being in a wider, relational context. This is a different emphasis to that under the Mental Capacity Act 2005 where, although there is, for example, consultation with family members in situations where a person lacks mental capacity, the focus is still upon the best interests of the individual person for such decisions are being made. Finally, in ascertaining well-being, there is a built-in safeguarding duty, phrased in terms of the 'need to provide protection from abuse and neglect'.[45] All the

---

[40] Care Act 2014, s 1(3)(c).
[41] Care Act 2014, s 1(3)(d).
[42] Care Act 2014, s 1(3)(e).
[43] Care Act 2014, s 1(3)(f).
[44] Though it is often claimed that the 2014 Act has put carers on an equal footing with adults in need of care and support, this appears not to have played out in practice; see J. Marczak et al (2022) 'How have the Care Act 2014 ambitions to support carers translated into local practice? Findings from a process evaluation study of local stakeholders' perceptions of Care Act implementation', *Health and Social Care in the Community*, 30(5): e1711–20.
[45] Care Act 2014, s 1(3)(g).

above, and any interventions taken with regard to promoting a person's well-being, must be proportionate and with any limitations on rights and freedoms being the 'minimum necessary for achieving the purpose for which the function is being exercised'.[46]

The concept of 'meeting needs' is of paramount importance here. As the Guidance to the Care Act maintains:

> 1.9 The Act therefore signifies a shift from existing duties on local authorities to provide particular services, to the concept of 'meeting needs' (set out in sections 8 and 18 to 20 of the Act). This is the core legal entitlement for adults to care and support, establishing one clear and consistent set of duties and power for all people who need care and support.
>
> 1.10 The concept of meeting needs recognises that everyone's needs are different and personal to them. Local authorities must consider how to meet each person's specific needs rather than simply considering what service they will fit into. The concept of meeting needs also recognises that modern care and support can be provided in any number of ways, with new models emerging all the time, rather than the previous legislation which focuses primarily on traditional models of residential and domiciliary care.[47]

Although this 'meeting needs' approach appears to be person-centred and well-intentioned, the application of the personalization agenda in English social care provision has been far from straightforward.[48] In practice, the assessments and reviews that social workers are required undertake as a central part of their role[49] are necessarily contingent on the resources available to the local authority – and so the well-being principle can sometimes remain but a best intention and a noble aim.

Right from the outset, commentators highlighted the perceived inconsistencies and tensions in approach between the legislation and its

---

[46] Care Act 2014, s 1(3)(h); see also the Deprivation of Liberty Safeguards (DoLS) 2019 amendments to the Mental Capacity Act 2005, and related Guidance for local authorities, at www.gov.uk/government/publications/deprivation-of-liberty-safeguards-forms-and-guidance. These all seek to ensure that a person's liberty and autonomy are safeguarded as far as possible while they lack the capacity to consent to treatment or care they may need.

[47] Department of Health and Social Care (2024) GOV.UK

[48] C. Needham and J. Glasby (eds) (2014) *Debates in Personalisation*, Bristol: Policy Press.

[49] J. Symonds et al (2018) 'The social care practitioner as assessor: people, relationships and professional judgement', *British Journal of Social Work*, 48(7): 1910.

related Guidance and the realities of care delivery. Writing in 2014, Slasberg and Beresford argued that:

> The reality is that the future will continue to be needs, not choice, based and that councils will continue to have the power to define needs and have to do so within limited budgets. Experience to date has shown that this has proven to have a seriously deleterious impact on service users for all but the small number who have the ability to escape the system and are given the resource to employ and manage their own supports.[50]

Writing in 2016 Whittington was also critical of the approach taken in relation to the drafting of the legislation. He argued that, in light of the reality of the political and socio-economic situation into which the Care Act was being introduced, and the broader impacts of austerity, 'the promise to promote people's well-being looks like a false prospectus at the heart of the Care Act itself'.[51] Beresford and Slasberg have commented that

> the Act does not attempt to define the extent to which wellbeing should be promoted. Until that is known, no vision can be said to exist. A person may be a mile away from having the level of wellbeing that is right for them. If a council provides resources that moves them a mere inch along that path, the council can say it has satisfied the Care Act.[52]

One problematic issue was the extent to which the well-being principle requires that the local authority would need to take into account an individual's wishes and feelings when assessing and offering a package of care, including, for example, the wish of a person with a disability to be able to live independently in accordance with Article 19 of the United Nations Convention on the Rights of Persons with Disabilities. This formed the basis of what ultimately was an unsuccessful challenge in *Davey v Oxfordshire County Council* in 2017.[53] Luke Davey, the claimant in this case challenged the decision of the Local Authority to reduce his own personal budget from £1,651 per week to £950 per week and in addition the Council revised his care and support plan. Here at first instance Mr Justice Morris stated that:

---

[50] See C. Slasberg and P. Beresford (2014) 'Government guidance for the Care Act: undermining ambitions for change?', *Disability and Society*, 29(1): 1677.

[51] C. Whittington (2016) 'The promised liberation of adult social work under England's 2014 Care Act: genuine prospector false prospectus?', *British Journal of Social Work*, 46(7): 1942.

[52] P. Beresford and C. Slasberg (2020) 'The Care Act: the service user's experience', in S. Braye and M. Preston-Shoot (eds) *The Care Act 2014: Wellbeing in Practice*, London: Sage, p 44.

[53] [2017] EWCA Civ 1308.

The importance of the wishes of the service user is fully addressed in the provisions of the Act itself. The relative balance between those wishes and the assessment of the local authority is struck in the provisions of the Act themselves. In my judgment, and in the light of the principles set out above, there is no warrant for a conclusion that, by dint of the application or consideration of Article 19 itself and the concept of independent living therein, that balance is weighted more in favour of the service user, than it would otherwise be under the Act, to the extent that the service user can have the final say on his own needs and personal budget or dislodge the principle that, under the Act, the decisions are ultimately to be taken by the local authority. The wishes of the disabled person may be a primary influence, but they do not amount to an overriding consideration.[54]

As the Court of Appeal noted at first instance, the judge 'held that no specific ambiguity in the 2014 Act had been identified in respect of which Article 19 might serve as an interpretative tool'.[55] It remains uncertain as to how Article 19 might be utilized in litigation in this area in the future. not least given the in relation to the difficult balancing tests pertaining to proportionality and availability of resources which can arise in such situations.

In undertaking assessment of well-being, or indeed any other relevant provisions under the Act, there are two specific pieces of legislation which also need to be taken into account. These are the Autism Act 2009 and Down Syndrome Act 2022. These are notable as they each make specific reference to a particular form of disability in a bespoke piece of legislation. The structure of both pieces of legislation is similar, albeit not identical. The Autism Act 2009 provides in section 1(1) for the preparation of an 'Autism Strategy' for 'meeting the needs of adults in England with autistic spectrum conditions by improving the provision of relevant services to such adults by local authorities, NHS bodies and NHS foundation trusts'.[56] Section 2(1) of the Act then places an obligation on the Secretary of State to produce guidance for local authorities and relevant NHS bodies for 'the purpose of securing the implementation of the autism strategy', with the aim of improving services. Obligations are placed on local authorities and

---

[54] [2017] EWHC 354 (Admin) 6.

[55] [2017] EWHC 354 (Admin) 6. Further analysis of the ramifications of this care are laid out by A. Sharland, 11KBW Community Care Blog, at https://communitycare11kbw.com/2017/09/07/r-davey-v-oxfordshire-cc-court-appeal/

[56] Autism Act 2009, s 1. See further discussion in Clements et al (2019), paras 16.27–16.34; and for background discussion in relation to social care and autism, see V. D'Astous et al (2016) 'Retracing the historical social care context of autism: a narrative overview', *British Journal of Social Work*, 46: 789–807.

the relevant NHS bodies to act in accordance with this guidance.[57] The latest version of the Autism Strategy was published in 2021.[58] There are also concerns regarding the number of deaths of persons with learning disabilities which could be avoided, resulting in the Government producing draft guidance for training health and social care staff in relation to people on the autism spectrum; this piece of work was influenced by the tragic death of Oliver McGowan.[59]

In relation to the Down Syndrome Act 2022 the Explanatory Notes refer to the fact that persons with Down Syndrome 'face specific challenges', which may relate to particular health needs concerning development and co-morbidities, as well as problems in accessing services and social care support.[60] In contrast to the 2009 Act there is no reference to a 'strategy' which needs to be produced. Rather section 1 of the Act simply provides that guidance is to be given to relevant authorities on steps it would be appropriate for them to take in order to meet the needs of persons with Down Syndrome in the exercise of their relevant functions. These authorities 'must have due regard to the guidance in the exercise of their relevant functions'.[61] Here 'relevant authorities' include county councils, district councils where a particular area in England has no county council, and London Borough Councils.[62] The Guidance will be applicable to legislative provisions, including section 117 of the Mental Health Act 1983 and the provisions under Part I of the Care Act 2014.[63] The Down Syndrome Act 2022 was brought into force on 18 March 2024.[64] Consultation was undertaken in 2022–23, and it has been announced that draft statutory Guidance will be produced later in 2024.[65] While both these pieces of legislation highlight the undoubted importance of services being provided for these groups there remains a question as to whether taking a separate legislative approach to two specific forms

---

[57] Autism Act 2009, s 3.

[58] H.M. Government (2021) 'The national strategy for autistic children, young people and adults: 2021 to 2026'.

[59] Department of Health and Social Care (2019) *'Right to be heard': The Government's response to the consultation on learning disability and autism training for health and care staff*; See also in relation to the need for health and social care provision which is safe and responsive for those with disabilities, including autism, S. Ryan (2017) *Justice for Laughing Boy: Connor Sparrowhawk – A Death by Indifference*, London: Jessica Kingsley.

[60] See discussion in the Explanatory Notes, paras 6–11.

[61] Down Syndrome Act 2022, s 1(1)(2).

[62] Down Syndrome Act 2022, schedule s 3(1).

[63] Including the well-being principle. See later for more detailed discussion of powers and duties under the Care Act 2014.

[64] Down Syndrome Act 2022 Commencement Regulations 2024 (SI 2024/373).

[65] Department of Health and Social Care (2024) Written statement Update on Implementation of the Down Syndrome Act 2022, 21 March 2024.

of disability in this way is in itself appropriate rather than recognising the importance of meeting the needs of individuals regardless of the specific disability which they have.

(b) Assessment of an adult's needs for care and support

The Care Act 2014 sets out a series of duties and powers in relation to assessment and support needs. Section 8 provides examples as to those things which may be provided to meet needs including care home accommodation,[66] care and support being provided to the person at home or in a community setting,[67] counselling,[68] other 'goods and facilities',[69] and 'information, advice and advocacy'.[70] It goes on to provide further examples as to the manner in which such needs can be met by the local authority, such as arranging for others to attend to these needs, for local authority staff to do so directly, or for direct payments be given to the individual to arrange the provision of services themselves.[71]

In a situation in which it appears to a local authority that an adult has care and support needs then section 9(1) provides that – whether via self-referral, the concern of another, or a referral from another public or voluntary sector agency – the local authority has an obligation to assess those needs, along with the support needed by any associated carer:[72]

> Section 9(1)
> Where it appears to a local authority that an adult may have needs for care and support, the authority must assess—
> (a) whether the adult does have needs for care and support, and
> (b) if the adult does, what those needs are.

Local authorities are obliged to carry out a Care Act assessment of needs, regardless of the perceived extent of the individual's needs, and regardless of that individual's financial situation.[73] There should be no assumption made that family members will provide care to the individual in need. The obligation applies to the local authority and thus would apply once the

---

[66] Care Act 2014, s 8(1)(a).
[67] Care Act 2014, s 8(1)(b); see further in relation to provision of domiciliary services Clements et al (2019), paras 8.29–8.38.
[68] Care Act 2014, s 8(1)(c).
[69] Care Act 2014, s 8(1)(d).
[70] Care Act 2014, s 8(1)(e).
[71] Care Act 2014, s 8(2).
[72] Care Act 2014, s 9.
[73] Care Act 2014, s 9(3).

person becomes known to the local authority, rather than specifically to the social services department.[74] The local authority does have power to delegate certain functions, which include social care assessments.[75] However, the extent of a person's needs is not a relevant factor in the undertaking of assessment duties; all local authority residents have the right to a needs assessment under the Care Act.[76]

Under the well-being principle, the scope of 'needs' goes beyond the basic functional essentials to include the goals and aspirations of the individual, and their wider quality of life. As far as assessing the needs for care and support of an individual, section 9(4) provides that this must include assessing:

(a) the impact of the adult's needs for care and support on the matters specified in section 1(2),
(b) the outcomes that the adult wishes to achieve in day-to-day life, and
(c) whether, and if so to what extent, the provision of care and support could contribute to the achievement of those outcomes.

It is the case that the assessment should be 'appropriate and proportionate'.[77] There is no duty to achieve the outcomes an individual wishes to achieve; rather, the local authority must simply give them consideration.[78]

In undertaking the assessment of the individual adult, a carer, or someone else the person has asked the local authority to involve, or – if it is a situation in which the person lacks (specifically focused) decision-making capacity and section 9 (5) applies – a person who 'appears to the authority to be interested in the adult's welfare' shall also be involved. This is often a relative, a close friend, or a neighbour. The Act goes on to provide other factors which are to be considered by the local authority, notably in determining eligibility for funded care if the individual's needs cannot be met through signposting or referral to other services available in the local area including:

> s 9(6)(a) whether, and if so to what extent, matters other than the provision of care and support could contribute to the achievement of the outcomes that the adult wishes to achieve in day-to-day life, and

---

[74] See further *R (Patrick) v Newham LBC* (2008) CCLR 48.
[75] Care Act 2014, s 79.
[76] See further Statutory Guidance at para 6.6 and discussion in Clements et al (2019), paras 3.49–3.51.
[77] Care and Support (Assessment) Regulations 2014 (SI 2014/2827), reg 3(1).
[78] *Davey v Oxfordshire* [2017] EWCA Civ 1308.

(b) whether the adult would benefit from the provision of anything under section 2 or 4 or of anything which might be available in the community.[79]

Section 10 of the Act requires local authorities to ascertain whether carers have or are likely in the future to have their own needs for support, and what these might be.[80] Carers are defined in section 10(3) as being 'an adult who provides or intends to provide care for another adult (an "adult needing care")'. Section 10(9) excludes someone as a carer if this care is given under a contract or as part of voluntary work, except in a situation in which 'the local authority considers that the relationship between the adult needing care and the adult providing or intending to provide care is such that it would be appropriate for the latter to be regarded as a carer.'[81] In this situation 'care' also includes providing practical and emotional support.[82] The provisions of the legislation, including support for carers, can be seen as an important step towards ensuring the fulfilment of fundamental rights and supporting well-being. The reality of obtaining such support can prove challenging due to budgetary constraints and lack of available support services, and it has been suggested that greater access to support has not resulted.[83]

Other matters the local authority is required to consider are whether the carer is working or wishes to work,[84] and likewise participation in education, training, or recreation.[85] The carer must be directly involved in any carer assessment, along with any person the carer requests to be involved.[86] As with the obligation to consider the wider circumstances of a person participating in a needs assessment, the local authority should also consider whether matters or things other than provision of support might assist a person in achieving the outcomes they would value in their day-to-day life.[87]

In terms of who undertakes the various assessments under the legislation, while reference is made to the local authority, and by extension the social workers it employs, in practice the task of assessment can be delegated to

---

[79] Care Act 2014, s 9(6); it should be noted that third-sector provision has suffered severe cutbacks through austerity and consecutive Conservative administrations, thus limiting the options indicated in this section.
[80] Care Act 2014, s 10.
[81] Care Act 2014, s 10(9).
[82] Care Act 2014, s10(11).
[83] See further discussion in J. Fernandez (et al) (2020) *Supporting Carers Following the Implementation of the Care Act 2014: Eligibility, Support and Prevention. The Carers in Adult Social Care (CASC) Study*, CPEC and NIHR.
[84] Care Act 2014, s 9(6)(a).
[85] Care Act 2014, s 9(6)(b).
[86] Care Act 2014, s 9(7).
[87] Care Act 2014, s 9(8)(b).

other bodies under section 79 of the Care Act. Although not specified, this type of work, particularly in situations where outcomes are deemed likely to be 'straightforward', is increasingly often outsourced to 'trusted assessor' organizations under a scheme initiated by the NHS in an effort to 'reduce the number of delayed discharges'.[88] However, the legislation still provides that the legal obligation for fulfilling this role is placed upon the local authority as:

> Anything done or omitted to be done by or in relation to a person authorised under this section in, or in connection with the exercise or purported exercise of the functions to which this authorisation relates is to be treated for all purposes as done or omitted to be done by, or in relation to the local authority.[89]

Part 1 of the Care Act does not define 'needs'. In *R (on the application of) Antoniak v Westminster City Council* in 2019[90] Vice President of the Upper Tribunal Ockelton J. stated that the assessment of needs should be undertaken without taking into account how at that time those needs were being met. He noted that this was also the approach taken in the Regulations.[91] He went on to say that

> Part 1 of the Care Act makes the individual, and the individual's wellbeing, the starting point of the delivery of such services as are required. In this context it would be surprising if a needs assessment were not also intended to be primarily about the individual, rather than merely about some residuary part of an individual's needs that were not currently being met.[92]

Information regarding the process of the assessment must be given to the person whose needs are being assessed and this is to be given 'wherever practicable' before that assessment was given and in addition 'in a format which is accessible to the individual to whom is given'. The Care and Support (Assessment) Regulations provide that this must be both appropriate and proportionate 'to the individual's needs and circumstances such that the

---

[88] These schemes are usually established in collaboration with ICBs, and the requisite training is available from various private and third-sector providers. See Care Quality Commission (2018), *Guidance on Trusted Assessors*. See also Care Provider Alliance (2017), 'Developing Trusted Assessments Schemes: essential elements', July.
[89] Care Act 2014, s 79(6). See further discussion in Clements et al (2019), paras 3.152–3.156.
[90] [2019] EWHC 3465 (Admin).
[91] Care and Support (Assessment) Regulations 2014 (SI 2014/2827).
[92] [2019] EWHC 3465 (Admin), para 29.

individual will be able to participate in this process as effectively as possible'. The Regulations go on to provide that:

3(2) In seeking to ensure that an assessment is carried out in an appropriate and proportionate manner, a local authority must have regard to—
(a) the wishes and preferences of the individual to whom it related;
(b) the outcome the individual seeks from the assessment; and
(c) the severity and overall extent of the individual's needs.

Where needs are fluctuating over time, as is often the case, the Regulations state in section 3(3) that 'the local authority must take into account the individual's circumstances over such period as *it considers necessary* [our emphasis] to establish accurately the individual's level of needs'.[93]

What is notable is that the Regulations take a relational approach to the assessment of needs in that the local authority is required to take into account the impact of the needs of the person being assessed on someone who is caring for them[94] or upon 'any person the local authority considers to be relevant'.[95] The Guidance states that practitioners should take a 'whole-family approach': 'The intention of the whole-family approach is for local authorities to take a holistic view of the person's needs and to identify how the adult's needs for care and support impact on family members or others in their support network.'[96] The Guidance goes onto provide that: 'People should be considered in the context of their families and support networks, not just as isolated individuals with needs. Local authorities should take into account the impact of an individual's need on those who support them and take steps to help others access information or support.'[97]

The importance of family and personal support networks, as we shall see later in this book, was even more keenly felt during the pandemic as people were required to minimize or cease face-to-face contact under social-distancing rules. These restrictions disproportionately affected people who rely on care and support to engage with the wider world, or indeed those anyway largely restricted to the confines of their homes or other residential settings.

---

[93] SI 2014/2827.
[94] SI 2014/2827, reg 4(1)(a).
[95] SI 2014/2827, reg 4(1)(b).
[96] Department of Health (2024) *Care and Support Statutory Guidance. Issued under the Care Act*, para 6.65; and see further discussion in Association of Directors of Adult Social Services et al (2015) *The Care Act and Whole-Family Approaches*.
[97] Department of Health (2024) *Care and Support Statutory Guidance*, para 1.14(f).

Whether or not the person who is undertaking the assessment is employed by the local authority or an external provider, they should have 'the skills, knowledge and competence to carry out the assessment in question' and to have been trained appropriately.[98] As noted, since 2005, a Trusted Assessors scheme has been introduced to expedite hospital discharge and reduce pressure on social workers.[99]

Where an individual refuses an assessment there is no continuing duty, subject to the exception where the individual lacks capacity to refuse and where the assessment is deemed to be in their best interests.[100] The duty also remains in a situation where an individual is either currently experiencing, or is at risk of, abuse.[101] Finally, the question of delays in initiating or actually undertaking assessments is particularly relevant to our discussion in Chapters 5 and 6, where we discuss how such delays and 'pauses' became an issue during the early months of the pandemic. Clements et al highlight that to delay undertaking a statutory duty can constitute a breach of duty or may mean that the local authority is acting unreasonably.[102]

In current social work practice, the exercise of the statutory powers and duties under the Care Act 2014 needs to be viewed through the lens of a strengths-based approach.[103] The Department of Health and Social Care (DHSC) Strengths-Based Approach Handbook states that a strengths-based approach

> explores, in a collaborative way, the entire individual's abilities and their circumstances rather than making the deficit the focus of the intervention. We should gather a holistic picture of the individual's life; therefore it is important to engage and work with others (i.e. health professionals, providers, the individuals own network, etc., with appropriate consent).[104]

It states that the aim is to 'enable better outcomes and/or lives for people'.[105] Furthermore, it provides that 'it is important to clarify that "reduction of packages of support" is generally a collateral benefit of a strengths-based

---

[98] SI 2014/2827, reg 5(1).
[99] See Care Quality Commission (2017) *Guidance: Trusted Assessors*; and Care Quality Commission (2020) *COVID-19 Trusted Assessor Guidance* for pandemic era guidance.
[100] Care Act 2014, s 11(2)(a).
[101] Care Act 2014, s 11(2)(b).
[102] Clements et al (2019), paras 3.65–3.67.
[103] See further Department of Health and Social Care (2019), *Strengths-based Approach: Practice Framework and Practice Handbook* (February). The strengths-based approach practice framework was authored by S. Baron and T. Stanley, and the practice handbook was authored by C. Colomina and T. Pereira.
[104] Department of Health and Social Care (2019), p 24.
[105] Department of Health and Social Care (2019), p 25.

approach. A reduction in provision of services should not be the outcome we are seeking and this is not what the application of a strengths-based approach is.'

Working from a strengths-based position, is not about

> giving people less support and services but working with people to identify together, the best next step for them utilizing all the strengths and resources they currently have or may have access to. Moreover, working in this way is not about 'not providing help' but rather it is about ensuring that as practitioners we are providing the right help, advice, and support at the same time.[106]

The Framework emphasizes that the individual is to play an 'active part' in this process and, where the person 'lacks capacity' or 'may be overwhelmed', the social worker 'should look at what is getting in the way of the individual to "fully participate" and take the necessary steps to overcome as many barriers as possible'.[107] As per the Care Act Guidance, the social worker must ensure that any interventions 'are proportionate to the circumstances'.[108] It notes that the Care Act makes no explicit reference to a strengths-based approach but argues that the well-being principle requires social workers to consider 'well-being' in a broad, holistic sense, beyond those needs that may require direct provision of services.[109] The guidance goes on to state that:

> The assessment must be person centred throughout. Local authorities must find out the extent to which the person being assessed wants to be involved in the assessment and should meet those wishes as far as is practicable do so [sic], as the person is best placed to understand the impact of their condition(s) on their outcomes and well being.[110]

A recent National Institute for Health and Care Research (NIHR)-funded qualitative evaluation of strengths-based approaches suggested that understanding and implementation tend to be 'adopted in a fluid, flexible way', with the Three Conversations model being that most commonly used.[111] The Partners4Change management consultancy developed the

---

[106] Department of Health and Social Care (2019), p 25.
[107] Department of Health and Social Care (2019), p 27.
[108] Department of Health and Social Care (2024) Care and Support Guidance, para 6.42, p 27.
[109] Department of Health and Social Care (2019), pp 32–42.
[110] Department of Health (2024), para 6.35.
[111] See J. Caiels et al (2022) *Perspectives on Strengths-based Approaches: Social Workers, Commissioners and Managers*, NIHR Policy research unit in adult social care discussion paper 2021–22. Other strengths-based approaches include Collaborative Networks; Co-design and Co-production; Social value in contracts; Making it Real (MIR); Person-centred approach; Proud conversations; Good conversations; Multi-agency Working, Motivational

'Three Conversations' (3Cs) strengths-based model for assessment and care planning, which has been tested with and adopted by a growing number of local authorities across England. According to Sam Newman, the Director of Partners4Change, the aim of this model is to

> dynamically and intensively replace our 'assessment for services' culture with a commitment to proper conversations, we can really listen and begin to deliver the holy grail of better lives for people and families, and a reduction in the consumption of health and social care resources, matched with a liberated, productive and inspired workforce.[112]

Typically, Conversation 1 happens at initial contact and is a strengths- and assets-focused discussion to explore the person's aims and what their existing family, friends, and the local community can offer in terms of care and support; the focus is on signposting. Conversation 2 takes place where a person is considered at risk and is used to explore what resources that person requires to be safe, and to help make an emergency plan. Conversation 3 explores options where longer-term support may be needed and what form the person would like that to take.

This model is designed to help practitioners move away from the traditional 'checklist' style needs assessment processes towards a more discursive, informal approach 'led by the person rather than by following a form'.[113] Done well, these conversations are thorough, and are used to gather the information necessary for practitioners to complete assessment, review, and package of care forms away from the immediate interaction. While the majority of social work practitioners surveyed in a 2022 study by Caiels et al 'seemed to embrace strengths-based approaches', they also suggested that these

> may not be suitable for people with severe mental health problems or severe learning or intellectual disabilities and/or people in crisis. Most importantly, strengths-based approaches were not seen as suitable for people where the services they need are not available and/or need immediate or urgent support.[114]

Interviewing; the Think Family approach; and others (at 5.1.1). In relation to social workers understanding of the Care Act, also see A.J. Jenkinson and J. Chamberlain, J. (2019) 'Social workers' knowledge and skills and the Care Act: Practice Advice Note', November, NIHR Policy Research Unit in Health and Social Care Workforce, The Policy Institute, King's College London.

[112] DHSC (2016) 'Three Conversations, Multiple Benefits', Blog post (26 September), L. Romeo and S. Newman (Partners4Change).

[113] See Skills for Care (in partnership with TLAP) (2018) *Using Conversations to Assess and Plan People's Care and Support. The Principles of Conversational Assessment*.

[114] J. Caiels et al (2022), p 19.

The strengths-based approach can be seen as an illustration of the fluidity, flexibility, and discretion inherent in undertaking assessments under the Care Act 2014. This in turn illustrates the notable challenges in interpretation concerning the nature and scope of the legislative powers and duties and their 'easing' during the pandemic, which we discuss in Chapters 5 and 6.

(c) Eligibility criteria

Section 13 of the Care Act concerns the eligibility criteria used to determine whether a person is in need of, or entitled to, the provision of care and support services. The use of this type of criteria has a legacy pre-dating the 2014 Act.[115] As was noted in *R v Gloucestershire CC ex parte Barry* in 1997 in the House of Lords by Lord Clyde when considering the application of section 2 of the Chronically Sick and Disabled Persons Act 1970:[116]

> in determining the question whether in a given case the making of particular arrangements is necessary in order to meet the needs of a given individual it seems to me that a mere list of disabling conditions graded in order of severity will still leave unanswered the question at what level of disability is the stage of necessity reached. The determination of eligibility for the purposes of the statutory provision requires guidance not only on the assessment of the severity of the condition or the seriousness of the need but also on the level at which there is to be satisfaction of the necessity to make arrangements. In the framing of the criteria to be applied it seems to me that the severity of a condition may have to be to be matched against the availability of resources. Such an exercise indeed accords with everyday domestic experience in relation to things which we do not have.[117]

Thus eligibility for services is rooted itself in issues of resource allocation.

The Care Act 2014 provides for national statutory minimum eligibility criteria. These are set out in the Care and Support (Eligibility Criteria) Regulations 2015, which replaced the Fair Access to Care Services (FACS) guidelines in which eligibility thresholds were determined by individual local authorities.[118] This has the aim of facilitating standardization and certainty regarding who is eligible for services. As Spencer-Lane notes: 'Local authorities are no longer permitted to vary the upper threshold for services

---

[115] See discussion in Clements et al (2019), paras 4.2–4.7.
[116] [1997] 2 WLR 459.
[117] [1997] 2 WLR 459.
[118] SI 2015/313.

(which had previously led to accusations of a "postcode lottery" for service provision).'[119]

The Regulations set out lists of eligible needs for adults needing care and support, and for carers. These needs will be considered eligible where:

(a) the adult's needs arise from or are related to a physical or mental impairment or illness;
(b) as a result of the adult's needs the adult is unable to achieve two or more of the outcomes specified in paragraph (2); and
(c) as a consequence there is, or is likely to be, a significant impact on the adult's well-being.[120]

The outcomes listed in paragraph 2 include things such as nutrition management, maintaining personal hygiene and toilet needs, suitable clothing, being able to live safely at home, being able to both develop and maintain family and other relationships, access to work and education, being able to utilize local community services such as public transport and recreation, and undertaking any caring responsibilities for a child.[121] A person will be held to be unable to achieve an outcome under the Regulations where that individual:

(a) is unable to achieve it without assistance;
(b) is able to achieve it without assistance but doing so causes the adult significant pain, distress or anxiety;
(c) is able to achieve it without assistance but doing so endangers or is likely to endanger the health or safety of the adult, or of others; or
(d) is able to achieve it without assistance but takes significantly longer than would normally be expected.[122]

Paragraph 3 of the Regulations relates to the needs of carers and sets out essentially the same criteria. The statutory Guidance[123] states that the range of services provided may also include adaptations to a person's home or equipment, such as handrails, telecare, ramps, alarms, and so on.[124] Provision of holidays and carer respite support may be included in the categories of needs met.[125]

---

[119] Spencer-Lane (2020), p 21.
[120] Care and Support (Eligibility Criteria) Regulations 2015 No. 313, s 2(1).
[121] Care and Support (Eligibility Criteria) Regulations 2015, s 2(2).
[122] Care and Support (Eligibility Criteria) Regulations 2015, s 2(3).
[123] Department of Health (2024), paras 6.25, 10.12 and 15.62.
[124] See, for example, further discussion in Clements et al (2019), paras 8.73–8.87.
[125] See further discussion Clements et al (2019), paras 8.82–8.83 and paras 8.96–8.100.

The local authority must, once a decision has been made regarding eligibility, provide the adult needing care and support or the carer needing support with a written record of reasons for the decision under section 13(2) of the Care Act 2014. If these needs are not to be met, information is to be given as to what can be done to meet needs in the future or reduce the need for future needs developing.[126] In a situation in which the criteria is met then section 13(3) states that:

(3) Where at least some of an adult's needs for care and support meet the eligibility criteria, the local authority must—
   (a) consider what could be done to meet those needs that do,
   (b) ascertain whether the adult wants to have those needs met by the local authority in accordance with this Part, and
   (c) establish whether the adult is ordinarily resident in the local authority's area.

A similar provision is applicable in relation to carer's support needs under section 13(4). Crucially, section 3(4) of the Care and Support (Eligibility Criteria) Regulations 2014. provides that where a person's needs may fluctuate (as indeed they often do), the local authority 'must take into account the carer's circumstances over such period as it considers necessary to establish accurately the carer's level of need' before reaching a decision.

We now turn to examine the statutory duties in relation to meeting needs and their application in relation to financial criteria.

(d) Duties and powers to meet needs for care and support

In a situation in which the local authority decides that an adult meets the eligibility criteria, and where the adult concerned is either ordinarily resident in that local authority or present there but of... of no settled residence, then section 18 of the Care Act 2014 sets out duties to meet that person's needs for care and support. Section 14(1) of the statute provides that the local authority does have power to make charges for care provided under section 18.

Section 19 sets out the power to meet needs for care and support. This applies in a situation in which the requirement to meet needs in section 18 is not satisfied, where the person is ordinarily resident or in the area but of no settled residence. The local authority is also able to meet care and support needs in certain situations where the adult is ordinarily resident in another local authority.[127] Section 19(3) provides that where care and support needs

---

[126] Care Act 2014, s 13(5).
[127] Care Act 2014, s 19(2).

are urgent those needs may be met by the local authority, whether or not the person is ordinarily resident, and without having to have undertaken a needs or financial assessment or make any determination under section 13. There is also a specific provision to meet needs where a person is terminally ill.[128]

Section 20 concerns the duty and power of a local authority to meet carer's needs for support. This provision very much mirrors the provision under section 18. The carer's needs are to be met where they are ordinarily resident in the particular local authority in question or where they are present but of no settled residence, and the needs can be met either if there is no charge under section 14 in meeting them, or if certain conditions are met.[129] The conditions operate as follows. Condition 1 is that the local authority is satisfied that the financial resources of the carer are below the limit. Condition 2 is met if the carer's resources exceed the limit but the carer asks the local authority to meet the needs. Condition 3 concerns situations where the financial resources of the persons needing care are at or below the financial limit, and in addition they agree that the local authority provides care and support to them. Condition 4 applies in a situation in which the resources of the person needing care are above the financial limit, but the person who needs care has asked the local authority to meet the needs by provision of care and support. A local authority may also decide to meet carers' needs, although they are not required to do so if this involves the provision of care and support to the person needing care.[130] If the local authority is required to meet a carer's needs for support and it isn't actually feasible to meet those needs by providing care and support to that person, then it should ascertain if there are other ways in which it can do so.[131] Further express exclusions from meeting needs include persons subject to immigration control where needs relate solely to destitution or because of 'physical effects, or anticipated physical effects, of being destitute'.[132] Local authorities are also prohibited from providing NHS or nursing services except if this is ancillary to the provision of needs or otherwise provided in regulations.[133] However, section 22(4) does make provision in some cases for arranging care along with nursing care in a situation in which consent has been obtained from the local NHS Integrated Care Board which has the task of commissioning local NHS services[134] or if this is undertaken as an urgent temporary arrangement.[135]

---

[128] Care Act 2014, s 19(4).
[129] This means that there is no charge but either they are prohibited by regulations from making the charge or they decide not to do so. See s 20(2-9).
[130] Care Act 2014, s 20(7).
[131] Care Act 2014, s 20(8).
[132] Care Act 2014, s 21(1)(b).
[133] Care Act 2014, s 22.
[134] Care Act 2014, s 22(4)(a).
[135] Care Act 2014, s 22(4)(b).

The difficulty of challenging such local authority decisions is rooted in the fact that these are administrative choices made by professionals concerning resource allocation, an area in which historically the courts have been circumspect in their involvement. The advent of the Human Rights Act in 1998, as noted earlier, raised the prospect of challenges brought on those grounds. As we will see, aspects of these statutory provisions allow for a notable degree of discretion. While, as with NHS care, social care decisions and other decisions made by public bodies can be challenged via judicial review on the basis that they are irrational, ultra vires, or that that they infringe the rules of procedural propriety, this remains solely judicial review and not appeal. When a decision is quashed, it will be simply sent back to the decision-making body to redetermine. Since the Human Rights Act 1998 came into force in October 2000, domestic law, such as the Care Act 2014, needs to be interpreted in the light of the ECHR provisions incorporated in that legislation. However, as we shall see, successfully bringing human rights challenges is by no means straightforward.

This is to be expected. First, while the Human Rights Act 1998 utilizes the provisions of the ECHR, these are broad statements in what is a very traditional civil and political rights declaration. It does not contain the more modern social economic rights provisions, such as the right to health, contained in more recent international rights statements. This means that in challenging social care decisions the existing law needs to be interpreted in the light of ECHR provisions which mado not neatly fit this particular situation. Second, the Act needs to be interpreted in the context of ECHR jurisprudence. This, as we shall see below, is somewhat problematic in relation to attempts to challenge social care resource allocation decisions and other operational-level choices, not least due to the wide margin of appreciation given to member states on some of these issues.

The difficulty of bringing litigation with regard to the determination of needs is shown by *R (McDonald) v Kensington and Chelsea RLBC*, a case decided under the pre-Care Act legislation but still important in considering the approach and ability to scrutinize the determination of needs at a high level.[136]

Ms McDonald had been the prima ballerina of the Scottish Ballet. She suffered a stroke at the age of 56, which resulted in limited mobility. Due to bladder problems she needed to urinate several times during the night. Originally her care package had enabled her to have a night-time assistant

---

[136] [2011] UKSC 33; and see H. Carr (2011) 'Rational men and difficult women – *R (on the application of McDonald) v. Royal Borough of Kensington and Chelsea* [2011] UKSC 33', *Journal of Social Welfare and Family Law*, 34(2): 219–30.

to enable her to use a commode. However, her needs were then reclassified as requiring 'assistance with toileting' and that this would be addressed through ensuring that incontinence pads would be made available – a cheaper option for the council. This decision was subject to judicial review to determine whether the reviews undertaken were a reassessment of her care needs, whether it was the case that the decision constituted a violation of her rights under Article 8 of the ECHR to privacy of home and family life, and whether there was a violation of the Disability Discrimination Act 1995 (this legislation was replaced by the Equality Act 2010). All the grounds pleaded were unsuccessful.

In the Supreme Court, in the *McDonald* case, the majority held that the decision of the council was lawful. On the needs assessment Lord Kerr stated that:

> If needs are defined as the issues and problems that the particular individual presents, that would appear to open the way to taking a rather broader view of what needs means and includes not only the narrow connotation of needs but also how those needs may be met. On that basis, it can be said that the reviews in 2009 and 2010, although it was not their purpose, in fact involved a re-assessment of the appellant's needs and that they may now be regarded as the need to avoid having to go to the lavatory during the night. Viewed thus, the needs can be met by the provision of incontinence pads and suitable bedding. Not without misgivings, I have therefore concluded that it was open to the respondent to re-assess the appellant's needs, to re-categorise them as a need to avoid leaving bed during the night and to conclude that that need could be met by providing the appellant with the materials that would obviate the requirement to leave her bed.[137]

This again can be seen as a more traditional approach to engaging with the scope of needs, allowing a wide margin of discretion to the local authority. In relation to the human rights argument and the application of Article 8 of the ECHR which is the provision of the ECHR which relates to respect for privacy of home and family life, Lord Brown stated that

> the clear and consistent jurisprudence of the Strasbourg Court establishes 'the wide margin of appreciation enjoyed by states' in striking 'the fair balance ... between the competing interests of the individual and of the community as a whole' and 'in determining the steps to be taken to ensure compliance with the Convention',

---

[137] [2011] UKSC 33, para 40.

and indeed that 'this margin of appreciation is even wider when ... the issues involve an assessment of the priorities in the context of the allocation of limited state resources' – *Sentges*, at p 405, *Pentiacova v Moldova* (Application No 14462/03 (unreported) 4 January 2005, p 13) and *Molka v Poland* (Application No 56550/00 (unreported) 11 April 2006, p 17).[138]

In contrast, Lady Hale was critical of the decision of the local authority and concluded by saying:

> As Lord Lloyd put it in *Barry* 'in every case, simple or complex, the need of the individual will be assessed against the standards of civilised society as we know them in the United Kingdom' (p 598F). In the United Kingdom we do not oblige people who can control their bodily functions to behave as if they cannot do so, unless they themselves find this the more convenient course. We are, I still believe, a civilised society. I would have allowed this appeal.[139]

The *McDonald* case was then heard at the European Court of Human Rights (ECtHR) in Strasbourg.[140] Here, on the facts of the case, because the care had been withdrawn initially without the full care plan review having taken place, the Court held that this constituted a violation of Article 8 of the ECHR. In relation to the rest of her claim, while the ECtHR held that Ms McDonald's rights under Article 8 were engaged, there was no violation as the actions of the local authority were held to be lawful under Article 8(2). Emphasis was placed on the wide margin of appreciation given to member states in cases concerning resource allocation:

> In the present case the Supreme Court primarily considered the applicant's Article 8 complaint within the sphere of positive obligations. It therefore had to consider whether or not a fair balance had been struck between the interests of the applicant and those of the wider community and it would have been impossible to do so without addressing one of the fundamental principles underpinning the Court's jurisprudence in such cases: namely, that States are afforded a wide margin of appreciation in issues of general policy, and that margin is

---

[138] [2011] UKSC 33, para 16.
[139] [2011] UKSC 33, para 79.
[140] *McDonald v United Kingdom* [2014] ECHR 492 and see also L. Pritchard-Jones (2015) 'Night-time care, Article 8 and the European Court of Human Rights: a missed opportunity?', *Journal of Social Welfare and Family Law*, 37(1): 108.

particularly wide when the issues involve an assessment of the priorities in the context of the allocation of limited State resources.[141]

The approach taken to the question of resource allocation and the margin of appreciation here is in line with earlier decisions of the ECtHR.[142] Pritchard-Jones has persuasively argued that: 'The ECHR's disinclination to engage with substantive discussions of dignity and autonomy, and with the CRPD, can be seen as a failure to take "disability rights" seriously.'[143]

Clements et al have also suggested that:

> However the *McDonald* case pre-dated the CA 2014. The CA 2014 focuses on the ability to achieve a more clearly prescribed set of outcomes. One of those outcomes is being 'able to make use of the adults home safely'. This includes accessing the bathroom (as the statutory guidance acknowledges). The local authority's response in the *McDonald* case left Ms McDonald unable to achieve the very outcome (accessing the toilet) that was having a significant impact on her dignity – an essential aspect of well being. Her need (in order to be able to achieve this outcome) would be for some form of care and support so that she could mobilise in her home safely.[144]

This then raised the question of whether post the Care Act 2014 the courts might be able to interpret what may be seen as a fundamental rights issue and provide support for it through the wellbeing concept. A broader approach to well-being was taken in *R (BG) v Suffolk County Council*.[145] The case concerned two brothers BG, 37 and KG, 38. Both brothers are autistic and have epilepsy and learning disabilities. BG is also incontinent and needs support with eating, washing, and toileting. KG has fibromyalgia, which leads to pain. He also needs support with all aspects of daily living and is incontinent at night-time. After experiencing abuse at a day centre in the past, BG and KG cannot attend day centres. The lack of trust of persons outside the family resulted in their care being provided by their mother, SQ. SQ receives support from her husband and from other members of the family. Previously Suffolk County Council had funded holidays for the brothers. However, in 2020 it stated that it was no longer including this funding in the care and support package provided through personalized budgets. The brothers' challenge was successful at first

---

[141] [2014] ECHR 492, para 55.
[142] See, for example, *Louisa Watts v UK* [2010] ECHR 793.
[143] L. Pritchard-Jones (2015), p 110.
[144] Clements et al (2019), para 4.76.
[145] [2022] EWCA Civ 1047.

instance.¹⁴⁶ The Judge, Lang J, was notably critical of the approach taken by the council's eligibility statements, commenting that they were

> deliberately drafted so as to reflect the Council's restrictive stance on eligible needs, with the focus on any need for care, and the exclusion of financial support for goods and facilities, in this case, the cost of accessing recreational facilities.¹⁴⁷

Commenting on the decision at first instance Diver and Schwehr noted that:

> In sum, if the professional view was that the Claimants' assessed needs (arising from their disabilities) could be met through 'a holiday or other recreational activities, then the cost of the holiday to the disabled person is a need which can be met under CA 2014.' ... For the Council to attempt to argue otherwise – for example, as here, that they lacked any power to somehow support the meeting of relevant, related, eligible needs – suggests a quite disingenuous disregard for Parliament's legislative intentions, and an extremely limited grasp of the daily realities facing disabled persons and their carers.¹⁴⁸

The Court of Appeal upheld the judgment at first instance. Davies LJ, giving the leading judgment in the case, stated that:

> As identified in the assessments, the respondents' well-being is assisted by the taking of holidays, visiting nature reserves and similar activities, which is no doubt the reason why the appellant previously provided financial support for the same. I accept that the needs of the respondents to take part in recreational activities, which include holidays, arises from their physical and mental impairment (regulation 2(1)(a)). The financial support, previously provided by the appellant, is not simply a means of paying for the respondents to take part in such activities and to go on holiday, it is a means of meeting their needs which arise from and are related to the physical and mental disability from which each suffers. It is a need which cannot be met without financial support from the appellant.¹⁴⁹

---

[146] See further [2021] EWHC 3368 (Admin); see also L. Clements (2022) 'Holidays and Poor Law Commissioners', Blog (21 January) and A. Diver and B. Schwehr (2022) 'The significance of *R (BG and Anor) v Suffolk CC* (2021): meeting "eligible need[s]" in social care?', *Liverpool Law Review*, 43: 539.

[147] [2021] EWHC 3368 (Admin), para 135.

[148] Diver and Schwehr (2022), p 547.

[149] [2022] EWCA Civ 1047), para 75.

The *R (BG)* case represented only the third time that a Care Act 2014 case had reached the Court of Appeal.[150] These arguments may be effectively applicable in relation to the question of well-being through a judicial review lens. However, it remains to be seen how extensively the courts will be prepared to interpret the question of human rights itself in the context of social care and resource allocation decisions in the future. It is certainly possible that the courts in this area will still be likely to accord a wide margin of appreciation.[151]

Where the local authority is required to, or decides to, meet needs, then the Care Act requires it to provide a care and support or a support plan for the person concerned.[152] The local authority must then inform them as to whether these needs will be met via direct payment[153] and in addition must assist them in deciding how these needs are to be met.[154] Where it is not required to, and decides not to, meet needs for care and support for a person or a carer then the local authority must provide written reasons for not doing so[155] – save where they have already been given information and advice[156] regarding what could be done in relation to meeting those needs,[157] or to stopping or delaying development of care and support needs in the future.[158] Local authorities are required to involve the individual and their family in the decision-making process. As Judge Pievsky commented in *P, R (on the application of) v London Borough of Croydon*:[159]

> an outcome decision, made about a person who is entitled to care and support under the 2014 Act, which fails to involve her or her family in a meaningful way so as to provide the sort of autonomy and control expressly anticipated by that Act is itself 'substantially different' from one which does.[160]

---

[150] M. Samuel (2022) 'Council adopted "restrictive and wrong interpretation" of Care Act in cutting brothers' care, finds court', *Community Care*, 5 August.

[151] See also in relation to NHS resource allocation in general: see, for example, *R v Northwest Lancashire Health Authority ex parte A D and G* [2000] 1 WLR 97; *R (on the application of Alexander Thomas Condliff) v North Staffordshire PCT* [2011] EWCA Civ 910.

[152] Care Act 2014, s 24(1)(a).

[153] Care Act 2014, s 24(1)(b).

[154] Care Act 2014, s 24(1)(c).

[155] Care Act 2014, s 24(2)(a).

[156] Care Act 2014 s 24(2)(b).

[157] Care Act 2014, s 24(2)(b)(i).

[158] Care Act 2014, s 24(2)(b)(ii).

[159] *P, R (on the application of) v London Borough of Croydon* [2022] EWHC 2886 (Admin).

[160] [2022] EWHC 2886 (Admin), para 60.

Finally, there is an obligation placed on the local authority where it is not going to meet care and support needs to prepare an independent personal budget (as described in s 28) where those needs do meet the eligibility criteria,[161] where some of those needs at least are not currently being met by a carer,[162] and where the person is either ordinarily resident in the area or although present is of no settled residence.[163]

Information in relation to the needs assessment or carer's assessment must be included in the care and support plan or the support plan, respectively.[164] Other relevant information included should concern the individual's personal budget and information as to what may be done to meet or reduce their needs and to stop or delay development of such needs in the future.[165] If these needs are to be met in whole or in part by direct payments then this must be included, along with how much those direct payments will be and how often they will be paid.[166] As noted, care and support plans are to be drawn up involving the adult who it is being cared for,[167] carers they may have,[168] and a person who the adult asks to be involved or, in the case of a care and support plan where the person lacks mental capacity, 'any person who appears to the authority to be interested in the adult's welfare'.[169] Support plans are to be drawn up with the involvement of the carer it is being prepared for, and also if requested, the person who needs care, as well as any other person the carer has asked the authority to involve.[170] There is an obligation placed on the local authority in drawing these plans up of taking 'all reasonable steps to reach agreement with the adult or carer for whom the plan is being prepared about how the authority should meet the needs in question'.[171] One critical issue is that the plan is to be 'proportionate to the needs to be met'.[172] These plans do not have to be prepared by the local authority, and they may authorize others to do this.[173]

---

[161] Care Act 2014, s 24(3)(a).
[162] Care Act 2014, s 24(3)(b).
[163] Care Act 2014, s 24(3)(c).
[164] Care Act 2014, s 25(1)(a).
[165] Care Act 2014, s 25(1)(e) and (f).
[166] Care Act 2014, s 25(2).
[167] Care Act 2014, s 25(3)(a).
[168] Care Act 2014, s 25(3)(b).
[169] Care Act 2014, s 25(3)(c).
[170] Care Act 2014, s 25(4).
[171] Care Act 2014, s 25(5).
[172] Care Act 2014, s 25(6).
[173] Care Act 2014, s 25(7).

When a care and support plan is prepared then it must be given to the person for whom it has been prepared[174] and, on their request, to a carer[175] or another person.[176] Support plans should be given to the carer[177] and, if the carer requests it, to the person needing care[178] or another.[179] Provision is also made for the local authority to keep these plans under review, and also for it to provide a review when a reasonable request for such is made by the person in receipt of the plan.[180] Finally, the Care Act provides for the situation in which an individual needing care and support moves to another local authority area, and the transfer of information and provision of accommodation, care, and support is facilitated.[181]

(e) Financial assessment, paying for services, and personal budgets

An important part of ascertaining whether and what care and support will be provided is the financial assessment. As we saw in Chapter 1 in contrast to NHS healthcare which, other than some limited charges for example for prescriptions for eligible groups, adult social care provision is means tested. Once the assessment for care and support is undertaken the local authority then has discretion under section 14 of the Care Act 2014, which states that it can charge in relation to provision of care and support under sections 18 and 20 of the Act. In some situations, it is prohibited from charging under the Care and Support (Charging and Assessment of Resources) Regulations 2014.[182] In undertaking the financial assessment under section 17 the local authority will take into account the person's financial resources and the 'amount (if any) the person would be likely to pay towards the cost of meeting the needs for care and/or support'.[183] The details and operation of the charging regime process and the questions for reform as we noted in Chapter 1 have been under consideration for a number of years with changes originally envisaged to be introduced in the Care Act 2014.[184] Notably, however, there is currently an upper capital limit of £23,250, and if individuals have resources – including cash savings and investments,

---

[174] Care Act 2014, s 25(9)(a).
[175] Care Act 2014, s 25(9)(b).
[176] Care Act 2014, s 25(9)(c).
[177] Care Act 2014, s 25(10)(a).
[178] Care Act 2014, s 25(10)(b).
[179] Care Act 2014, s 25(10)(c).
[180] Care Act 2014, s 27.
[181] Care Act 2014, s 37.
[182] SI 2014/2672.
[183] Care Act 2014, s 17(1)
[184] See further Chapter 1.

land, property, or business assets – totalling more than that amount, they will be charged for the full cost of a care home placement.[185] This figure then proportionately reduces until it reaches the lower capital level which is currently £14,250. In the case of, for example, a person who moves into a care home but with their partner still living in the family home, the value of the family home will not be taken into account for the purposes of that assessment, whereas it would be taken into account were they to be a single person. In calculating resources support, as in the case of an older person, their pension will be taken into account, but adults are to be left with a sum, their personal expense allowance. Where a person is not living in a care home a 'minimum income guarantee' (MIG) is applied, which is a weekly amount applicable as follows:

> People receiving local authority-arranged care and support other than in a care home need to retain a certain level of income to cover their living costs. Under the Care Act 2014, charges must not reduce people's income below a certain amount, but local authorities can allow people to keep more of their income if they wish.[186]

In some situations, what is known as a 'light touch' financial assessment may be undertaken, typically if a person with substantial resources would not want a full assessment.[187] The Act still requires the local authority to make a financial assessment and also to ascertain that this person is both able and willing to pay any charges incurred. Some individuals may choose, rather than having to sell their home to pay for care costs during their lifetime, to enter into what is known as a 'deferred payment agreement' in which the local authority defers a payment, as the name suggests, until a specified date.[188] So the Act allows for a range of potential means of paying for care and support services.

The Care Act also makes provision for personal budgets to be included in personal care plans.[189] The statutory Guidance states that:

> The personal budget is the mechanism that, in conjunction with the care and support plan, or support plan, enables the person, and their advocate

---

[185] Department of Health and Social Care (2022) Social Care – Charging for Care and Support: local authority circular – LAC(DHSC)(2022)1. See also K. Baxter, E. Heavey and Y. Birks (2020) 'Choice and control in social care: experiences of older self-funders in England', *Social Policy & Administration*, 54: 460–74.
[186] Department of Health and Social Care (2024).
[187] Department of Health and Social Care (2022).
[188] Care Act 2014, ss 34–6.
[189] Care Act 2014, s 25(1)(e); see further discussion of personal budgets in Clements et al (2019), ch 11.

if they have one, to exercise greater choice and take control over how their care and support needs are met.[190]

The Guidance goes on to provide that:

> This allows the person, and anybody else the person wishes, to make informed decisions about how to meet their care and support needs. The person can choose for the personal budget allocation to remain with the local authority to arrange care and support on the person's behalf, and in line with their wishes. Alternatively, if available locally, it can be placed with a third-party provider on the same basis, often called an individual service fund (ISF). Where an ISF-type arrangement is not available locally, the local authority should explore arrangements to develop this offer and should be receptive to requests from personal budget recipients to create these arrangements with specified providers.[191]

The budget may also take the form of some direct payments to the person to be used for some services, while other money is retained by the local authority to provide other services under a 'mixed package of care and support'.[192] Obligations are placed on the authority to maintain a 'care account'; namely, an 'up-to-date record of accrued costs' and if these exceed the care cap then the individual must be informed.[193] Individuals seeking support themselves or carers can also request direct payments be made to them so that they can commission their own care and support.[194]

The introduction of personalized budgets might be seen as transformative. Tarrant notes that that the language of choice and control, which was used from their inception, can be seen as related to ongoing discussions regarding disability rights such as Article 19 of the UN CRPD which concerns the right to live independently and be included in the community.[195] However, the operation of personal budgets has come under criticism. Clements et al argue that they can be seen as 'an ideological construct – the basis of which is that commodification is a good thing'.[196] Beresford and Slasberg have

---

[190] Department of Health and Social Care (2024), para 11.3.
[191] Department of Health and Social Care (2024), para 11.8.
[192] Department of Health and Social Care (2024), para 11.9.
[193] Care Act 2014, s 29(1).
[194] Care Act 2014, s 31 and see also s 32 for the position where an adult lacks mental capacity.
[195] A. Tarrant (2020) 'Personal budgets in adult social care: the fact and the fiction of the Care Act 2014', *Journal of Social Welfare and Family Law*, 42(3): 381.
[196] Clements et al (2019), at para 11.4. See also L. Series and L. Clements (2013) 'Putting the cart before the horse: resource allocation systems and community care', *Journal of Social Welfare and Family Law*, 32(2): 207–26.

argued that this 'policy has proven be undeliverable in practice'.[197] Research by Slasberg et al published in 2015 demonstrated large inconsistencies between the upfront allocation indicated and the amount of money ultimately received.[198] Tarrant has also highlighted the realities of austerity and argued that 'there is a considerable and critical discrepancy between the policy rhetoric and the legal reality of personal budgets and the link between the terminology of choice and control which comes from disability activists'.[199] This in turn links into the further broader question regarding the approaches taken to funding social care which were discussed in Chapter 1 of this book.

(f) Safeguarding

The Care Act 2014 also contains safeguarding provisions to protect adults who may be at risk of abuse or neglect.[200] The approach taken in the legislation, as Clements et al note, was to align domestic law with Article 16(1) of the UN CRPD, which places an obligation on states to 'protect persons with disabilities, both within and outside the home, from exploitation, violence and abuse'.

The 2014 legislation does not use the term 'vulnerable'.[201] Section 1(2)(c) of the well-being principle provides that part of that duty is 'protection from abuse and neglect';[202] what constitutes abuse and neglect is not fully defined, though Section 42(3) states it does include financial abuse. Section 42 of the 2014 Act provides that:

(1) This section applies where a local authority has reasonable cause to suspect that an adult in its area (whether or not ordinarily resident there)—
    (a) has needs for care and support (whether or not the authority is meeting any of those needs),
    (b) is experiencing, or is at risk of, abuse or neglect, and
    (c) as a result of those needs is unable to protect himself or herself against the abuse or neglect or the risk of it.
(2) The local authority must make (or cause to be made) whatever enquiries it thinks necessary to enable it to decide whether any

---

[197] P. Beresford and C. Slasberg (2020) 'The Care Act: the service user's experience', in S. Braye and M. Preston-Shoot (eds) *The Care Act 2014: Wellbeing in Practice*, London: Sage, p 45.
[198] C. Slasberg, P. Beresford and P. Schofield (2015) 'Further lessons from the continuing failure of personal budgets', *Research Policy and Planning*, 31(1): 43.
[199] See Tarrant (2020), p 269.
[200] See generally A. Bramner and L. Pritchard-Jones (2019) *Safeguarding Adults* (2nd edn), Basingstoke: Palgrave Macmillan; Clements et al (2019), ch 19.
[201] Clements et al (2019), para 19.19.
[202] Care Act 2014, s 42(3).

action should be taken in the adult's case (whether under this Part or otherwise) and, if so, what and by whom.

This covers a wide range of abuse and neglect. The extent to which self-neglect may fall in this category is subject of debate, given the tensions that arise between a position of paternalism, though this may potentially be seen to be justified, and respect for individual decision-making autonomy. The Care Act 2014 Guidance states that self-neglect

> covers a wide range of behaviour neglecting to care for one's personal hygiene, health or surroundings and includes behaviour such as hoarding. It should be noted that self-neglect may not prompt a section 42 enquiry. An assessment should be made on a case by case basis. A decision on whether a response is required under safeguarding will depend on the adult's ability to protect themselves by controlling their own behaviour. There may come a point when they are no longer able to do this, without external support.[203]

The duty to investigate which arises under section 42 may take a range of forms, determined at the discretion of the social work team:

> An enquiry is the action taken or instigated by the local authority in response to a concern that abuse or neglect may be taking place. An enquiry could range from a conversation with the adult, or if they lack capacity, or have substantial difficulty in understanding the enquiry their representative or advocate, prior to initiating a formal enquiry under section 42, right through to a much more formal multi-agency plan or course of action. Whatever the course of subsequent action, the professional concerned should record the concern, the adult's views, wishes, and any immediate action has taken and the reasons for those actions.[204]

In addition, section 68(2) of the Care Act 2014 provides that there is an obligation on local authorities to provide the person who may be subject to such an enquiry with a independent advocate.[205] Where the enquiry has taken place, and if action is needed, then the local authority is required to

---

[203] Department of Health and Social Care (2024). See further discussion in S. Braye and M. Preston-Shoot (2019) 'Adult safeguarding', in S. Braye and M. Preston-Shoot (eds) *The Care Act 2014: Wellbeing in Practice*, London: Sage, p 82.

[204] Department of Health and Social Care (2024), para 14.77.

[205] In *R (SG) v Haringey Council* [2015] EWHC 2579 (Admin) one of the successful grounds in that case was that a failure to provide an advocate led to the initial decision being quashed and the needs assessment having to be undertaken again.

take this, which is likely to include the production of an agreed course of action to be included in the individual's care plan, setting out future steps to ensure continuing safety and provide support, and so on.[206]

Section 6 places an obligation on local authorities to cooperate with other bodies when undertaking their statutory functions. The duty applies to the local authority but, as Bramner and Pritchard-Jones comment, both the legislation and statutory Guidance are premised on the notion of cooperation between organizations.[207] Section 6(3) provides that:

> (3) The following are examples of persons with whom a local authority may consider it appropriate to co-operate for the purposes of subsection (2)—
> (a) a person who provides services to meet adults' needs for care and support, services to meet carers' needs for support or services, facilities or resources of the kind referred to in section 2(1);
> (b) a person who provides primary medical services, primary dental services, primary ophthalmic services, pharmaceutical services or local pharmaceutical services under the National Health Service Act 2006;
> (c) a person in whom a hospital in England is vested which is not a health service hospital as defined by that Act;
> (d) a private registered provider of social housing.

In undertaking their work today, local authorities are required to take safeguarding into account at all times; this is framed by policy principles such as Making Safeguarding Personal.[208] This is part of the Care and Health Programme developed by the Local Government Association and the Association of Directors of Adult Social Services, funded by the Government.[209] It is informed by a Toolkit of principles which are those of Empowerment, Prevention, Proportionality, Protection, Partnership, and Accountability and transparency in delivering safeguarding.[210] While

---

[206] Department of Health and Social Care (2024), para 14.111.
[207] Bramner and Pritchard-Jones (2019), p 68.
[208] See J. Lawson (2017) (on behalf of ADASS and the LGA), *Making Safeguarding Personal. For safeguarding adults boards*, at https://www.local.gov.uk/our-support/partners-care-and-health/care-and-health-improvement/safeguarding-resources/making-safeguarding-personal, accessed 8 August 2024.
[209] Local Government Association Care and Health Improvement | Programme, at https://www.local.gov.uk/our-support/partners-care-and-health/care-and-health-improvement, accessed 10 July 2024.
[210] Local Government Association Making Safeguarding Personal Toolkit Practice Tool 5: Six core principles – 'I' statements, at https://www.local.gov.uk/msp-toolkit, accessed 10 July 2024.

frontline social workers attend to the first level of response and investigation of safeguarding concerns, local authorities are required to establish a Safeguarding Adults Board (SAB) to oversee and coordinate a multi-agency approach.[211] SABs have the power to undertake a Safeguarding Adults Review where it is suspected that individuals have suffered abuse and neglect. This power concerns both living adults and those who were suspected to have suffered such abuse or neglect leading to their death and, in this situation, where there is some cause for concern regarding the way in which agencies have undertaken their work.[212] The aim of these exercises is that of learning lessons for the future.[213] Under Section 45 of the Act the Boards have powers to require the provision of information to enable them to undertake reviews. The statutory powers concerning information do not provide easily effective sanctions where there is resistance to the provision of information. As Braye and Preston-Shoot note: 'If the person or agency is providing a regulated service then that breach of duty could be reported to the regulator. Seeking a judicial review would be an option but would be time-consuming, expensive and ultimately a blunt instrument in terms of improving local relationships.'[214]

Safeguarding may also give rise to related proceedings under criminal law, but such actions are beyond the scope of this book.[215] The impact of the COVID-19 pandemic on safeguarding practice and outcomes remains a matter of concern and is discussed further in Chapter 5.[216]

(g) Supporting decision-making: the role of the advocate

As with the Mental Capacity Act 2005, section 67 of the Care Act 2014 makes provision for a statutory advocacy scheme. This more general advocacy role is distinct from the safeguarding-specific role of the section 68 advocate discussed in the previous section. An advocate should be provided if the criteria in section 67(4) are applicable; namely, that:

> The condition is that the local authority considers that, were an independent advocate not to be available, the individual would experience substantial difficulty in doing one or more of the following—

---

[211] Care Act 2014, s 43.
[212] Care Act 2014, s 44(1)–(3) and see also Bramner and Pritchard-Jones (2019), ch 7.
[213] Care Act 2014, s 44(5).
[214] See Braye and Preston-Shoot (2019), p 92.
[215] See further discussion in Bramner and Pritchard-Jones (2019), ch 3.
[216] See further L. Pritchard-Jones et al (2022) 'Exploring the changes and challenges of COVID-19 in adult safeguarding practice: qualitative findings from a mixed-methods project', *Journal of Adult Protection*, 132.

(a) understanding relevant information;
(b) retaining that information;
(c) using or weighing that information as part of the process of being involved;
(d) communicating the individual's views, wishes or feelings (whether by talking, using sign language or any other means).

While subsections (a)–(d) seem very much drawn from section 3 of the Mental Capacity Act, the test in the Care Act 2014 is not the same as the capacity test under the 2005 legislation – which relates to both section 2 (determining whether a person has a disorder or disturbance of the mind or the brain), and section 3 (the capacity to understand/weigh up specific information). Rather, the Care Act is concerned with whether the person would 'experience substantial difficulty' if an advocate were not available to them. The local authority will not, however, be required to provide an independent advocate if it is satisfied that there is 'an appropriate person to represent and support the individual for the purpose of facilitating the individual's involvement' and that this person is not a professional paid carer.[217] The advocate will be providing support in relation to needs assessments for an individual or a carer and preparing or revising care and support plans or support plans, respectively.[218]

(h) Oversight over the provision of the care market

As we noted previously, section 5 places statutory duties upon local authorities in relation to market efficiency and effectiveness. The statutory Guidance provides that:

> When considering the quality of services, local authorities should be mindful of the capacity, capability, timeliness, continuity, reliability and flexibility of services delivered to support wellbeing, where appropriate, using the definitions that underpin the CQC's fundamental standards of care as a minimum, and having regard to the ASCOF of population outcomes.[219]

---

[217] Care Act 2014, s 67(5)(a).
[218] Care Act 2014, s 67(3).
[219] Department of Health and Social Care (2024), para 4.22. ASCOF refers to the Adult Social Care Outcomes Framework, at https://www.gov.uk/government/publications/adult-social-care-outcomes-framework-handbook-of-definitions, accessed 13 August 2024.

Moreover, the Guidance notes that local authorities should encourage the availability of a wide range of provision options so 'that people have a choice of appropriate services; appropriateness is a fundamental part of quality' and in recognition of the fact that the needs of working-age people, for example, are likely be different to those of older people.[220]

The Guidance states that in commissioning services the local authorities should also take note of the cost effectiveness and value of money that services offer for public funds.[221] It is therefore an increasingly challenging balancing act. One very real problem in this area is the marketization of care and particularly the danger of the failure of providers.[222] Should providers fail, individuals may be left homeless, but homeless in a very specific way because they may still need care and support from highly specialized sources. The Care Act 2014 contains provisions relating to measures which can be taken in case of provider failure.[223] In such a situation:

> A local authority must for so long as it considers necessary (and in so far as it is not already required to do so) meet those of an adult's needs for care and support and those of a carer's needs for support which were, immediately before the registered care provider became unable to carry on the regulated activity, being met by the carrying on of that activity in the authority's area by the provider.[224]

This is a broad duty to meet needs and it applies whether or not the person is ordinarily resident in the local authority area, or whether any needs, carer, or financial assessment has gone ahead, or indeed whether such needs meet the eligibility criteria.[225] In addition, if section 48(2) applies then such needs, carer, financial or eligibility assessments are not required.[226] The CQC is also required to inform the local authority if a provider is unlikely to be able to continue to provide services due to business failure.[227] There is a default power in section 72A of the Care Act 2014, as amended by the Health and Care Act 2022, which provides that the Secretary of State can, in a situation in which a local authority has failed or is deemed to be failing to discharge its functions to an 'acceptable standard', issue directions to them.

---

[220] Department of Health and Social Care (2024), para 4.24.
[221] Department of Health and Social Care (2024), para 4.27.
[222] S. Lewis (2023) 'Care homes closing at twice rate of openings, study finds Care Home Professional', 27 February.
[223] Care Act 2014, s 48.
[224] Care Act 2014, s 48(2).
[225] Care Act 2014, s 48(3).
[226] Care Act 2014, s 48(4).
[227] Care Act 2014, s 56.

These directions can include requiring them to comply with the advice of the Secretary of State or to require certain local authority functions to be undertaken by a nominee of the Secretary of State.[228]

(i) Challenging the decisions of local authorities

While various duties are set out under the 2014 Act, challenging these can in practice prove problematic. Local authorities operate their own complaints processes.[229] If, however, something is not amenable to local resolution, and the local authority maintains that it has 'taken all reasonable steps to address the situation',[230] then the individual may complain to the Local Government and Social Care Ombudsman (see following section). The Guidance emphasizes that the local authority should, through person-centred planning and seeking to reach agreement with the individual in question, seek to avoid such disputes.[231]

Actions may also be brought, as we have seen, through the means of judicial review, but the scope of judicial review is inevitably limited and critically there is no free-standing appeals system. As we saw in Chapter 1, the Law Commission proposals, which led to the development of the Care Act 2014, highlighted the problems with the existing system.[232] Ultimately section 72 of the Care Act 2014 enables the Secretary of State to issue regulations concerning appeals. However, in a December 2021 policy paper, the DHSC stated that:

> The Care Act 2014 includes a provision to introduce a new system to allow the public to appeal certain social care decisions made by local authorities. While we do not intend to introduce such a system immediately, we are keeping it under ongoing review as the new reforms are implemented and will continue to gather evidence to inform future thinking. [233]

The failure to introduce legislation led to litigation in the case of *HL, R (on the application of) v Secretary of State for Health and Social Care* in 2023.[234] Here the claimant asserted that she had had problems in obtaining social care

---

[228] Care Act 2014, s72(2)A.
[229] Local Authority Social Services and National Health Service Complaints (England) Regulations 2009 (SI 2009/309).
[230] Department of Health and Social Care (2024), updated 5 October, para 10.86.
[231] Department of Health and Social Care (2024), paras 10.83–10.86.
[232] Law Commission (2011) *Adult Social Care*, Law Com No 326, HC 941.
[233] Department of Health and Social Care (2021) *People at the Heart of Care: adult social care reform*, Policy paper, 1 December, p 56.
[234] [2023] EWHC 866 (Admin).

support and in challenging the decisions made and also provided evidence of problems also experienced by others in challenging decisions. It was stated that the Secretary of State had failed to consult before deciding not to implement the Regulations; second, that the lack of an appeal system impacted individual's rights of access to justice and there was a 'real risk' that they would be left without an appropriate legal remedy; and, finally, that there was a violation of the guarantee of a right to an effective remedy under Article 8 of the ECHR. The Court, however, rejected the claims. They found that while there had been previous consultations – for example, prior to the Care Act – this did not mean that there was an automatic obligation that future consultations needed to take place. In relation to the other claims the Court held that this was a different situation than where an individual was denied access to a court or a tribunal. Here there was no statutory duty to create an appeals system and in addition other legal remedies were available to use. Finally, on the issue of human rights and Article 8 the Court again recognized that although an obligation arose under Article 8 this was an area where member states of the Council of Europe were accorded a margin of appreciation and that, as noted previously, other remedies were available. It thus appears to be the case that the law in this area is unlikely to be reformed in the near future.

III. Relationship with NHS care and the role of NHS Continuing Healthcare and obligations under section 117 of the Mental Health Act 1983

While NHS care is subject to a separate funding regime than social care, there are two notable instances in which care for individuals which has a social care element may be exempt from means testing and be provided free of charge. The first of these is that of the NHS Continuing Healthcare assessments and the second is that of aftercare provided under section 117 of the Mental Health Act 1983. We consider these in turn.

(a) NHS Continuing Healthcare assessments

In addition to the Care Act 2014, there are further statutory provisions which enable the provision of NHS care and support without charge following discharge from hospital in the form of NHS Continuing Healthcare (CHC).[235] This scheme was introduced by the NHS and Community Care Act 1990.

---

[235] National Health Service Commissioning Board and Clinical Commissioning Groups (Responsibilities and Standing Rules) Regulations 2012 (SI 2012/2996), Pt 6. See further discussion in Clements et al (2019), ch 13.

The CHC system was developed in the context of a movement away from 'indefinite' long stays in hospital for (particularly older) patients and towards the provision of more 'personalised care'.[236] If an individual falls within the category that qualifies for such care and treatment (which is classified as NHS care) then, in contrast to adult social care services, the patient is not charged for this care. Inevitably, were such a scheme to be very generous then it would have a substantial impact on the budgets of NHS Commissioners. Over time the eligibility criteria for CHC have been significantly tightened.[237] In the period leading up to the pandemic there was media controversy about how the scheme was operating, with reports that thousands of patients had died while waiting for funding to be provided.[238]

Today NHS CHC[239] applies to individuals who have a 'primary health need'.[240] This is ascertained with reference to a 'checklist' assessment known as the 'National Decision Support Tool' which is used to assess specific health and care needs and rate these in terms of severity.[241] These assessments can be undertaken by a nurse, doctor, or other NHS health professional, or by a social worker, though they are usually undertaken by a small multi-agency team to ensure input from both health and social care perspectives. A special expedited procedure operates where patients who are, for example, in the last stages of a terminal illness wish to spend their final days at home. If a person is assessed to have such a primary health need, then the NHS will have the responsibility to undertake the commissioning of that patient's care package, to address both health and social care needs. The duties in relation to CHC are imposed on NHS England, the body which leads the NHS in England, Integrated Care Boards (ICBs), which are now the primary commissioners of healthcare at local level,[242] and also upon local authorities.

---

[236] See further D. Oliver (2016) 'NHS continuing care is a mess', *British Medical Journal Online*, 354.

[237] See, for example, the discussion in National Audit Office Report by the Controller and Auditor General *Investigation into NHS continuing healthcare funding*, HC 239, Session 2017–2019, 5 July 2017.

[238] E. Unia and D. Rhodes (2014) 'Thousands died while waiting for NHS Funding decisions', *BBC News*, 24 August; see also D. Oliver (2019) 'NHS continuing care confusion', *British Medical Journal*, 366(14): 720; see also Parliamentary and Health Service Ombudsman (2020) News 'NHS continuing healthcare failing to provide care for most vulnerable, says Ombudsman', webpage.

[239] See further DHSC (2022) Guidance, *National Framework for NHS Continuing Healthcare and NHS-funded Nursing Care*, published 28 November 2012, updated 31 October 2022.

[240] Where, once all a person's needs are taken into account, their primary needs, or the majority of their needs, require care that is focused on addressing or preventing health needs. DHSC (2022) Guidance, *National Framework*, para 4.

[241] See further J.V. McHale (2023) 'Choosing home: discharge to assess and the Health and Care Act 2022', *Northern Ireland Legal Quarterly*, 74(4): 713–38.

[242] Established under the Health and Care Act 2022.

In addition, as the National Framework for NHS Continuing Healthcare and NHS-funded Nursing Care notes:

> If a person does not qualify for NHS Continuing Healthcare, the NHS may still have a responsibility to contribute to that individual's health needs – either by directly commissioning services or by part-funding the package of support. Where a package of support is commissioned or funded by both a local authority and an ICB, this is known as a 'joint package of care'.[243]

ICBs have obligations to comply with and deliver the National Framework for NHS Continuing Healthcare and the governance arrangements for determining eligibility, for promotion of and commissioning of packages, and decisions on eligibility.[244] They have the task of consulting 'so far as is reasonably practicable, with the relevant social services authority before making a decision on a person's eligibility for NHS Continuing Healthcare (the Care and support statutory guidance should be used to identify the relevant social services authority)'.[245]

Other obligations relate to the implementation of good practice and of quality standards.[246] There is oversight from NHS England, including the appointing of chairs of independent review panels.[247] Specific obligations are also placed on local authorities to refer persons who may be eligible for NHS CHC to their local ICB.[248]

It is recognized that the CHC assessment process can be complex, not least because they tend to take place under already difficult circumstances of ill health and significant personal challenges. While the statutory advocacy provisions which apply in relation to Care Act assessments do not directly extend to this category of provision, the Care Act statutory Guidance states that:

> These processes and arrangements have historically been difficult for individuals, their carers, family or friends, to understand and be involved in. Local authorities (with CCGs) will therefore want to consider the benefits of providing access to independent advice or independent advocacy for those who do not have substantial

---

[243] DHSC (2022) Guidance, *National Framework for Continuing Health Care*, para 20.
[244] DHSC (2022) Guidance, *National Framework*, para 22(a)–(c) and (e).
[245] DHSC (2022) Guidance, *National Framework*, para 22(d).
[246] DHSC (2022) Guidance, *National Framework*, para 22 (i) and (j).
[247] Department of Health and Social Care (2012), para 23.
[248] Department of Health and Social Care (2012) Guidance, *National Framework*, para 26.

difficulty and/or those who have an appropriate person to support their involvement.[249]

It is envisaged this will involve joint commissioning arrangements. Thus, local authorities have statutory obligations to assess individual needs for care and support both under the Care Act 2014 and in relation to NHS CHC. Historically in the case of hospital patients this assessment was taken prior to discharge from hospital. The need for an effective, responsive hospital discharge system has been an issue for several decades.[250] If patients remain unduly long in hospital after they are clinically fit to leave, this can have a deleterious impact on their health. However, ensuring appropriate discharge requires that an appropriate place of discharge is available, along with the requisite availability of nursing and social care support. There was widespread concern about patients waiting for months for discharge long after they were medically fit. Conversely, there were also concerns that at times rapid discharge policy could lead, for example, to patients being discharged home too soon, leading to a further rapid readmission to hospital, and/or being discharged unsafely. During the early months of the pandemic, rapid hospital discharge was linked to the transmission of COVID-19 into care homes with often devastating consequences.[251]

The discharge to assess (D2A) approach was promoted as a means to conduct formal statutory assessments of patients' needs largely after they had been discharged from hospital. Aspects of this approach were subsequently followed in the reforms of the hospital discharge provisions contained in the Care Act 2014 introduced under the Health and Care Act 2022.[252] NHS CHC assessments were paused in the early months of the COVID-19 pandemic, while many hospital and social work staff focused on the work of rapid discharge to clear beds for acute surges. How effective the new statutory provisions ultimately will be in facilitating rapid discharge from hospital while facilitating patient dignity and choice remains to be seen but the early evidence has not been encouraging.[253]

---

[249] Department of Health and Social Care (2024) *Care and Support Statutory Guidance*, para 7.22, updated March 2024.

[250] See further J.V. McHale (2023) 'Choosing home: discharge to assess and the Health and Care Act 2022', *Northern Ireland Legal Quarterly*, 74(4): 713–38.

[251] See M. Daly (2020) 'COVID-19 and care homes in England: what happened and why?', *Social Policy and Administration*, 54(7): 985–98; and S. Rajan, A. Comas-Herrera and M. McKee (2020) 'Did the UK government really throw a protective ring around care homes in the COVID-19 pandemic?', *Journal of Long-Term Care*, 185–95.

[252] See further discussion in J.V. McHale (2023).

[253] See further J.V. McHale (2023) 'Choosing home: discharge to assess and the Health and Care Act 2022'.

(b) Provision of aftercare services under section 117 of the Mental Health Act 1983

Section 117 of the Mental Health Act 1983 provides for the free provision of care to patients after discharge from care under the 1983 Act.[254] The Mental Health Act 1983 is an extensive piece of legislation which governs the detention and treatment of patients with mental illness. Section 117 concerns those persons who were detained for treatment under section 3 of the Act or directions under section 45A, which refer to persons who are removed to hospital following a criminal conviction or patients who have been serving sentences following conviction who are then transferred to hospital.[255] Section 117(2) imposes a duty on the relevant NHS body known as the Integrated Care Board and the local authority social services team to provide or to arrange in cooperation with 'relevant voluntary agencies' for the provision of aftercare[256] until they are satisfied that the person is 'no longer in need of such services'. The section defines 'aftercare services' as being services which have both of the following purposes:

(a) meeting a need arising from or related to the person's mental disorder; and
(b) reducing the risk of a deterioration of the person's mental condition (and, accordingly, reducing the risk of the person requiring admission to a hospital again for treatment for mental disorder).[257]

Section 117 also needs to be read in conjunction with section 47 of the National Health Service and Community Care Act 1990. Section 47 provides that where a local authority believes that a person is in need of those services then section 47(1) provides that they:

(a) shall carry out an assessment of his needs for those services; and
(b) having regard to the results of that assessment, shall then decide whether his needs call for the provision by them of any such services.

The Mental Health Act Code of Practice provides that NHS bodies and local authorities:

---

[254] See further discussion in S. Abbott (2019) 'Navigating practice at the interface between mental health and social care law', in S. Braye and M. Preston-Shoot (eds) *The Care Act 2014: Wellbeing in Practice*, London: Sage.
[255] Mental Health Act 1983, ss 47 and 48.
[256] Mental Health Act 1983, s 117(2).
[257] Mental Health Act 1983, s 117(6).

should interpret the definition of after-care services broadly. For example, after-care can encompass healthcare, social care and employment services, supported accommodation and services to meet the person's wider social, cultural and spiritual needs, if these services meet a need that arises directly from or is related to the particular patient's mental disorder, and help to reduce the risk of a deterioration in the patient's mental condition.[258]

Payments in relation to the provision of aftercare services can be made to the individual for whom those services will be provided should they have capacity or, if that is not the case, then payments are to be made to 'an authorised or suitable person'.[259] Where aftercare services are provided under section 117, these are not to be charged for.[260] However, as with services under the Care Act 2014, it is the case that should an individual prefer accommodation where its cost falls outside that which is considered reasonable by the NHS or the relevant local authority body then the funding can be supplemented through the provision of 'top up fees'.[261] Finally, the individual who has capacity is not compelled to receive this aftercare unless this comes under the category of 'supervised aftercare'.[262] As with CHC assessments provision in relation to the section 117 duties was also included in the statutory "easements" in the Coronavirus Act 2020 we discuss in Chapter 4.

IV. Oversight bodies for social care

Adult social care services are subject to the oversight of the Secretary of State of Health and Social Care and the oversight of the Care Quality Commission (CQC) and the Local Government and Social Care Ombudsman (LGSCO). There is regulation of both local authority and private providers. Further oversight is provided by local and regional Health and Well-being Boards.

---

[258] Department of Health and Social Care (2015) *Code of Practice Mental Health Act 1983*, para 33.4.

[259] Department of Health and Social Care (2015) *Code of Practice Mental Health Act 1983*, para 33.17.

[260] *R v Manchester City Council ex parte Stennett; R v Redcar and Cleveland Borough Council ex parte Armstrong; R v Harrow London Borough Council ex parte Cobham* [2002] UKHL 34 and see further N. Priaulx (2002) 'Charging for after-care services under section 117 of the Mental Health Act 1983 – the final word?', *Journal of Mental Health Law*, 313–22.

[261] Care and Support and After-care (Choice of Accommodation) Regulations 2014 (SI 2014/2670), para 4.

[262] See further discussion in B. Andoh (2005) 'An analysis of aftercare under section 117 of the Mental Health Act 1983', *Medicine Science and the Law*, 45(1): 7.

We begin to consider the structures and roles of these various bodies in relation to scrutiny of adult social care during the pandemic and its aftermath.

(a) Local authorities' obligations regarding the scrutiny of health and care services

Local authorities are required to make arrangements to support and promote the engagement of local people in the commissioning, providing, and scrutinizing of care services in their area.[263] They are also obliged to put in place measures so that local people can monitor and scrutinize standards of local care services and how these may be improved and should be improved.[264] The Secretary of State, where satisfied that the local authority has failed in relation to its functions under the Local Authority Social Services Act 1970, can, for example, give directions as to how the local authority should take action.[265]

Health and Well-being Boards are local authority committees established under the Health and Social Care Act 2012.[266] This legislation moved responsibility for public health, which was originally situated within the NHS, to sit with local authorities. Health and Well-being Boards have a statutory duty to encourage integrated working practices in health and social care.[267] Each board should include at least one councillor from the local authority; the directors of adult social services, children's services, and public health of that local authority; along with a local Healthwatch representative (see further regarding discussion of Healthwatch to follow), a representative from each ICB that relates to services provided by that local authority;[268] and representatives from other bodies such as they deem appropriate.[269] It also has the obligation of ensuring that the local authority is complying with its statutory obligations under section 116 and section 116A of the Local Government and Public Involvement in Health Act 2007.

Section 116 requires the local authority to work with the ICB to develop an integrated needs assessment involving local Healthwatch representatives and people of the local area. Section 116ZA provides that the ICBs and 'each responsible local authority whose area coincides with or falls wholly

---

[263] Local Government and Public Involvement in Health Act 2007, s 221(2)(a).
[264] Local Government and Public Involvement in Health Act 2007, s 221(2)(b)(3).
[265] Local Authority Social Services Act 1970, s 7D, inserted by Health and Care Act 2022, s 164.
[266] Health and Social Care Act 2012, s 194.
[267] Health and Social Care Act 2012, s 195.
[268] Place-based partnership groupings of organizations that evolved from the sustainability and transformation planning/partnerships or STP model in 2016.
[269] Health and Social Care Act 2012, s 194(2).

or partly within the board's area' shall establish a joint committee for that area known as an Integrated Care Partnership. These are supposed to bring local bodies and agencies together to work collaboratively towards finding ways to improve the health and well-being of local people, and to agree priorities and strategies for achieving this. There is also a statutory obligation under section 116ZB to establish an integrated care strategy to establish how assessed needs will be provided for by the ICB, NHS England, or the relevant responsible local authority falling in this area.[270]

A 2019 report by the Local Government Association was quite positive regarding the operation of Health and Well-being boards and optimistic about their potential impact for local communities and public health.[271] It characterized them as 'effective vehicles for strategic planning in the new landscape',[272] with a role in 'driving health and care integration'. However, other research has suggested that the full potential of these bodies has not yet been achieved. Hunter et al, in a report for the National Institute for Health Research published in 2018, noted that in practice there was considerable variation between the operation of Health and Well-being boards.[273] These variations related to a range of matters, such as size, governance models, and workload. In addition, it suggested that the role of many Health and Well-being boards was more focused on ratifying decisions as opposed to being decision-making bodies in their own right.[274] As we will see in our review of the provision of adult social care in the West Midlands during the pandemic – which we discuss in Chapter 5 – the variation identified by Hunter et al was regularly reflected in the minutes of Health and Well-being Boards.

(b) The Care Quality Commission

The Care Quality Commission (CQC) was established under the Health and Social Care Act 2008 and its powers in relation to local authorities were amended by the Health and Care Act 2022.[275] It is the independent

---

[270] Local Government and Public Involvement in Health Act 2007, s 116ZB(1).
[271] Local Government Association (2019) *What a Difference a Place Makes: The Growing Impact of Health and Wellbeing Boards*, Report.
[272] Local Government Association (2019), p 6.
[273] D.J. Hunter (et al) (2018) 'Evaluating the leadership role of health and wellbeing boards as drivers of health improvement and integrated care across England', Report, at https://whiterose.ac.uk/. This research reflects earlier findings of the House of Commons Health Committee (2016) report, para 76, p 37 – see discussion in D.J. Hunter (2020) 'Strictly come partnering: are health and wellbeing boards the answer?', in A. Bonner (ed) *Local Authorities and the Social Determinants of Health*, Bristol: Policy Press.
[274] Ibid, D.J. Hunter et al (2018).
[275] Health and Care Act 2022, s 165.

regulator of health and adult social care in England.[276] Section 3 of the Health and Social Care Act 2008 provides that the Act has the 'role to protect and promote the health, safety and welfare of people who use health and social care services'.

The Commission has a Chair and a board of directors, and other members appointed by the Secretary of State, including persons who have 'knowledge and experience which concerns health care, social care and the Mental Health Act 1983'.[277] Health[278] and social care service providers and managers are required to be registered with the CQC.[279] The CQC regularly inspects services and premises and its findings and ratings are published and accessible to the public on their website.[280] The effectiveness of the CQC has over time come under critical scrutiny.[281] While some changes were made in their approach to healthcare regulation in the lead up to the COVID-19 pandemic they still remained subject to considerable criticism.[282] Problems included the assessment of risk by the CQC; the standards set and how these are applied; extent and quality of data collection; and the frequency and announcement of inspections. It was argued that current inspections remain as 'tick box' exercises and that their findings are unduly simplistic, while the Commission's responses to serious matters, such as abuse, remain inadequate.[283] During the early stages of the pandemic, the CQC was designated with the role of tracking and publishing information regarding the activation and operation of Care Act easements by local authorities. Yet the CQC itself had paused its routine inspections and site visits between March and September 2020.[284]

---

[276] Health and Social Care Act 2008, s 1.
[277] Health and Social Care Act 2008, Sch 1, para 3(1) and (2).
[278] Health and Social Care Act 2008, s 9(2). 'Health care' as defined in this context may be similar to but distinct from medical or surgical care 'but are not provided in connection with a medical condition'.
[279] Health and Social Care Act 2008, ss 10–19.
[280] www.cqc.org.uk
[281] See further discussion in R. Baldwin and J. Black (2016) 'Driving priorities in risk-based regulation: what's the problem?', *Journal of Law and Society*, 43(4): 565.
[282] Care Quality Commission (2018) *Our Updated Approach to Regulating Independent Healthcare Services*, June.
[283] See G. Iacobucci (2018) 'New CQC-style inspections don't raise standards or improve patient safety, say RCGP members', *British Medical Journal*, 363. The CQC was criticized for failing to publish a condemning report on Whorlton Hall in 2015 A. Harwood (2019) 'Whorlton Hall: advisers quit government review in protest at CQC's handling of abuse scandal', *British Medical Journal*, 365. Abuse of patients at Whorlton Hall was subsequently exposed by a BBC investigation: BBC (2019) 'Whorlton Hall abuse: Watchdog defends inspection', *BBC News*, 12 June.
[284] Care Quality Commission (2020) 'Routine inspections suspended in response to Coronavirus outbreak' (16 March), updated 12 May 2022.

The CQC was given new powers under the Health and Care Act 2022 which introduced provisions into the Health and Social Care Act 2008 to undertake reviews of the ways in which local authorities undertake their regulated care functions and to assess performance. These assessments are then followed by a report produced by the CQC.[285] Objectives and priorities are to be set by the Secretary of State as to the performance of local authorities and these are to be reviewed over time.[286] The CQC also has the task of producing a statement as to how frequently it will be reviewing local authorities and related methodology concerning assessments and evaluation.[287] The CQC is also required to publish its objectives and priorities regarding making assessments of local authorities, related quality indicators, and also the statement as to how it is undertaking its functions under section 46A(8).[288] This process began with a small number of pilots 'looking at how well they [local authorities] meet their duties under the Care Act 2014'; these assessments make use of the same single-assessment framework as used for providers, albeit 'tailored carefully to their specific context'.[289]

The CQC is also required to establish as one of its committees the body called Healthwatch England.[290] This body is required to provide the CQC or 'other persons' with related information, advice, and assistance regarding specified functions under the Health and Social Care Act 2008.[291] Its role is to assist local Healthwatch organizations with advice and assistance concerning the statutory arrangements concerning the provision of local care services and their operation under section 211 of the Local Government and Public Involvement in Health Act 2007.[292] Healthwatch activities are required at local level to ensure scrutiny of publicly funded health and social care services including personal budgets under section 9 of the Care Act 2014.[293] The legislation provides that local authorities are required to put contractual arrangements in place to ensure the provision of activities for

---

[285] Health and Care Act 2022, s 163(3), which inserts a new s 46A(1) into the Health and Social Care Act 2008.
[286] Health and Social Care Act 2008, s 46A(4).
[287] Health and Social Care Act 2008, s 46A(8).
[288] Health and Social Care Act 2008, s 46A(11).
[289] Care Quality Commission (2023) 'Our approach to assessing local authorities'.
[290] Health and Social Care Act 2008, Sch 1, para 1A.
[291] Health and Social Care Act 2008, Sch 1, para 1B.
[292] Health and Social Care Act 2008, s 45A.
[293] See further Local Government and Public Involvement in Health Act 2007, s 221(6) and for a discussion of the historical backdrop to local Healthwatch organizations, see further E. Stewart, A. Desia, and G. Zoccatelli (2023) 'Our NHS? The changing involvement of patients and the public in England's health and care system', in M. Exworthy, R. Mannion, and M. Powell (eds) *The NHS at 75: The State of UK Health Policy*, Bristol: Policy Press.

the promotion and support of local people in 'commissioning, provision and scrutiny of local care services',[294] the monitoring and review of such care services,[295] and to obtain the views of local people as to how those services operate.[296] Each local Healthwatch is required to be provided by social enterprise organizations.[297] A body is defined as a social enterprise 'if a person might reasonably consider that it acts for the benefit of the community in England', and in addition complies with any criteria set out by the Secretary of State.[298] Some of the challenges identified regarding the operation of local Healthwatch organizations by Carter and Martin include the diverse forms they can take (for example, being part of voluntary sector or hybrid public–private organizations, some have charitable status), the extent to which they can reconcile their involvement in existing governmental structures of the local authority while at the same time needing to act on behalf of local people, and the extent to which they have access to sufficient resources to undertake their role.[299] As Stewart et al also note the considerable variation in fundings from some £50,000 to £500,000 and the larger funding enables greater flexibility such as the appointment of staff with knowledge of areas such as academic research and co-design.[300] An ethnographic study of local Healthwatch teams found that despite pivoting to online working practices during the pandemic, most of the local Healthwatch teams that Zoccatelli et al observed 'remained committed to resisting and ultimately overcoming the potential for the pandemic to change to change their organisation into one that primarily conveyed the voice of the system *to* the people, rather than fulfilling their mandate to deliver the voice *of* the people to the system'.[301]

---

[294] Local Government and Public Involvement in Health Act 2007, s 221(2)(a).
[295] Local Government and Public Involvement in Health Act 2007, s 221(2)(b).
[296] Local Government and Public Involvement in Health Act 2007, s 221(2)(c).
[297] Local Government and Public Involvement in Health Act 2007, s 222(2).
[298] Local Government and Public Involvement in Health Act 2007, s 222(8); such organizations must either be Community Interest Companies, Charitable Incorporated Organizations, or where they have a constitution which has requirements which include that over 50 per cent of their distributable profits per year are to be used for Healthwatch tasks and also that they are undertaking role for the benefit of the local community and there are specific statements as to the distribution of the assets of the organization in a situation where it is wound up or dissolved. See further discussion in Healthwatch Network (2020) *A Guide to Running Healthwatch*, p 5.
[299] See further discussion in P. Carter and G. Martin (2016) 'Challenges facing Healthwatch, a new consumer champion in England', *International Journal of Health Policy Management*, 5(4): 259.
[300] Stewart et al (2023), p 241.
[301] G. Zoccatelli et al (2021) 'Finding the voice of the people in the pandemic: an ethnographic account of the work of local Healthwatch in the first weeks of England's COVID-19 crisis', in

Stewart et al maintain that during the pandemic Healthwatch was of particular value to local NHS and social services where normal channels of information gathering were unable to operate.[302] At the same time, they suggested that this changing role during the pandemic could be problematic since

> an enhanced role in managerial accountability (providing much needed intelligence for managers to evaluate services and make decisions) risked crowding out scope for the more outward-facing work of Healthwatch as a potential space for more political forms of accountability. These tensions, are at the time of writing, unresolved; the long-term effects of the transformation wreaked by COVID-19, particularly when framed in the broader shifts of health and care commissioning and provision through ICSs, remain unclear.[303]

We return to examine the involvement and oversight undertaken by Healthwatch in relation to the provision of social care services during the pandemic in subsequent chapters.

(c) The Local Government and Social Care Ombudsman

Scrutiny of adult social care is also provided through the work of the Commissioner for Local Administration, more commonly known as the Local Government and Social Care Ombudsman (LGSCO), a body set up under the Local Government Act 1974.[304] The LGSCO must lay an annual report before Parliament.[305] They have powers to investigate complaints relating to actions taken by a local authority.[306] Section 26(1) of the 1974 Act provides that the matters which can be investigated concern:

(a) alleged or apparent maladministration in connection with the exercise of the authority's administrative functions;
(b) an alleged or apparent failure in a service which it was the authority's function to provide;

P. Beresford (et al) *COVID-19 and Co-production in Health and Social Care Research, Policy, and Practice, Volume 1: The Challenges and Necessity of Co-production*, Bristol: Bristol University Press.

[302] Stewart et al (2023), p 242.
[303] Stewart et al (2023), p 242.
[304] Local Government Act 1974, s 23. See further on the work of the Local Government and Social Care Ombudsman, R. Thomas (2022) 'The English Local Government and Social Care Ombudsman: systemic administrative justice and bureaucratisation. Part 1', *Public Law*; and R. Thomas (2023) 'The English Local Government and Social Care Ombudsman: systemic administrative justice and bureaucratisation. Part 2', *Public Law*, 424.
[305] Local Government Act 1974, s 23A.
[306] Local Government Act 1974, s 24A(1).

(c) an alleged or apparent failure to provide such a service.

The jurisdiction of the LGSCO covers services provided by or commissioned via local authorities, privately funded providers, and there is also a service for complaints regarding services provided to private payers and persons who fund care through personal budgets. Complaints can be brought by the individual who has suffered injustice or another who is authorized by them in writing to do so. What constitutes maladministration in the area of local authority complaints was given by Lord Donaldson in *R v Commissioner for Local Administration ex parte Eastleigh BC* where he stated that:

> Maladministration is not defined in the 1974 Act, but its meaning was considered in *R v Local Cmr for Administration for the North and East Area of England ex parte Bradford MCC* [1979] 2 All ER 881. All three judges (Lord Denning MR, Eveleigh LJ and Sir David Cairns) expressed themselves differently but in substance each was saying the same thing, namely that administration and maladministration in the context of a local authority is concerned with the manner in which decisions of the local authority are reached and the manner in which they are or are not implemented.[307]

Complaints must be referred for consideration by the local authority before they can be brought to the Ombudsman, who only then will be able to examine these and have the opportunity to investigate and respond to those who have brought the complaint.[308] There is a discretion for the Ombudsman to investigate directly where it isn't reasonable for the matter to be taken to the local authority or for them to investigate the matter in the first instance.[309] The Ombudsman cannot investigate if in the situation it will be reasonable to expect the complainant to seek an alternative remedy; for example, to go to a tribunal.[310] The Ombudsman has been recently notably critical in relation to some aspects of adult social care provision during the pandemic and we return to this issue in Chapter 6 below.

V. Conclusions

The Care Act 2014 provides a legal basis for safeguarding the social care needs of adults. Nonetheless, as we have seen, there is considerable discretion

---

[307] [1988] 3 WLR 113 CA.
[308] Local Government Act 1974, s 26(5).
[309] Local Government Act 1974, s 26(5)(b).
[310] Local Government Act 1974, s 26(6).

and flexibility facilitated by the statutory provisions, which may result in fluidity of interpretation and potentially some differences in perspective and operational practices across England's local authorities. The well-being principle, while clearly well intentioned, is a principle, not a right.

Human rights law provides a safeguard but, as we have seen, bringing human rights challenges can be far from straightforward. The approach taken by the legislation is underpinned by an understanding of individual rights – those of a person with care and support needs and those of carers. As such, fundamental considerations of relational autonomy are also applicable. The implementation of the legislation is strained, as is the social care sector as a whole, by the challenging situation of social care resource allocation at local authority level in the context of long-standing economic cuts and scarcity. Adult social care provision, while subject to separate funding strands to the NHS, is nonetheless interwoven with the provision of NHS care in some respects, as seen in relation to the operation of NHS CHC assessments and care under section 177 of the Mental Health Act 1983. The tensions between NHS and social care priorities were thrown into sharp relief during the COVID-19 pandemic. Local authorities are subject to scrutiny both in terms of judicial review and through the operation of bodies such as Healthwatch and the Care Quality Commission, as we will see in later chapters these bodies were involved in providing oversight and insights into the way in which social care services were provided during the pandemic itself. In Chapter 4, we will explore the extent to which the UK was prepared for the impact of a pandemic, and how the resilience of the health and social care sectors was tested to the extreme.

4

Pandemic Preparedness Planning and the Development of Emergency Legislation

I. Introduction

The enactment of the Coronavirus Act 2020, with its extensive powers and ramifications, caused considerable consternation among legal professionals, third-sector organizations, and the wider public. However, although a pandemic on the scale of COVID-19 is often presented as 'unprecedented', and many of its challenges 'unforeseeable', a substantial body of multi-agency, cross-government pandemic preparedness planning work had in fact been undertaken over many years. This work was devised to identify, test, and consolidate crisis-mitigation strategies, operational resilience and contingencies, and to maintain business continuity across adult social care and related services. Indeed, the threat of a pandemic on the scale of COVID-19 had been identified as a 'highest priority "tier-1" security risk' in national security risk assessments since 2010.[1] Yet there remains a paradox. Despite this extensive engagement, it has been suggested that there was a lack of appreciation of the potential impact of a lethal pandemic on social care by the Government and the NHS. The House of Commons Health and Social Care Select Committee and Science and Technology Select Committee in their 2021 Report stated that

> 13. The Government and the NHS both failed adequately to recognise the significant risks to the social care sector at the beginning of the

---

[1] House of Commons & House of Lords, Joint Committee on the National Security Strategy (2020) *Biosecurity and national security*. First Report of Session 2019–21, HC 611 and HL 95 p 3.

pandemic. Until the social care working group was established in May 2020, SAGE [Scientific Advisory Group for Emergencies] either did not have sufficient representation from social care or did not give enough weight to the impact on the social care sector. Without such input and broader expertise, Ministers lacked important advice when making crucial decisions.[2]

The subsequent report from the first module of the UK COVID-19 Inquiry published in July 2024 took a similar approach.[3] Given the late establishment of the Social Care Working Group in May 2020, it has been suggested that neither the Government nor its advisory body the Scientific Advisory Group for Emergencies (SAGE-discussed below) initially gave sufficient weight to adult social care. Nonetheless, as we will see later, there was in fact a substantial history of direct input from social care policy actors into national- and regional-level pandemic planning. While aspects of input from social care may not have been sufficiently efficacious or timely in the drafting of policy and legislation, or indeed in guiding its eventual implementation, a blueprint did exist prior to the start of the COVID-19 pandemic, and this did, to varying degrees, inform the policy choices made in the early months of 2020.

This chapter begins by exploring the nature of public health powers and their operation in relation to pandemic planning. Secondly, it examines related pre-2020 pandemic planning exercises, and the range, roles, and level of accountability of governmental and various professional bodies involved with these exercises.[4] It interrogates the interface with NHS care and emergency response, public health policy and legislation, and civil contingencies legislation. The parts of the Coronavirus Act 2020 which impacted on social care are then scrutinized. The chapter also examines the operational framework in which this legislation was interpreted, and why the national approach to policy drafting and dissemination led to

---

[2] House of Commons Health and Social Care, and Science and Technology Committees (2021) *Coronavirus: lessons learned to date*. Sixth Report of the Health and Social Care Committee and Third Report of the Science and Technology Committee of Session 2021–22, HC 92, pp 7–8.

[3] UK COVID-19 Inquiry (2024) *Module 1: The resilience and preparedness of the United Kingdom: A Report by the Rt Hon the Baroness Hallett, DBE Chair of the UK Covid-19 Inquiry*, 18 July 2024, HC 18.

[4] See further Joint Select Committee on the National Security Strategy Biosecurity and National Security (2020) which highlighted the lack of sharing of information in relation to various Pandemic Planning exercises.

such variation in implementation at local level.⁵ Crucially, it also explores the extent to which these policies reflected recognition and respect for those with social care needs and those who care for them; appropriate consideration and comprehension of 'vulnerabilities'; and the necessity of safeguarding fundamental rights when drafting emergency legislation for adult social care.

II. The backdrop: public health and emergency powers

Charles-Edward Amory Winslow, in his classic definition, stated that:

> Public Health is the science and art of preventing disease, prolonging life and promoting physical health and efficiency through organised community efforts for the sanitation of the environment, the control of community infections, the education of the individual in principles of personal hygiene, the organisation of medical and nursing service for the early diagnosis and preventative treatment of disease, and the development of social machinery which will ensure to every individual in the community a standard of living adequate for the maintenance of health.⁶

The precise extent to which the state should be involved in directing the behaviour of individuals and populations with the aim of improving public health has long been debated.⁷ Infectious diseases, as the COVID-19 pandemic so tragically demonstrated, are no respecter of borders. The coordination of international responses to such situations is critically important and the international community and its institutions were found wanting in the early months of 2020. Legal mechanisms at international level facilitate public health actions. The starting point for these initiatives were the cholera epidemics in Europe in the 1800s, which led to the International Sanitary Conference in Paris in 1851 and subsequent conferences aimed

---

[5] Section III of this chapter draws upon our ESRC project Report 'Adult social care provision under pressure, lessons from the pandemic'; see J.V. McHale and L. Noszlopy (2021) *Adult social care provision under pressure: lessons from the pandemic*. Initial report, University of Birmingham.

[6] C. Winslow (1920) 'The untilled fields of public health', *Science*, 51(1306): 23. at p30 See further in relation to the meanings of 'public health' J. Coggon (2012) *What Makes Health Public?*, Cambridge: Cambridge University Press; M. Rothstein (2002) 'Rethinking the meaning of public health', *Journal of Law, Medicine and Health*, 30(2): 144–9.

[7] See, for example, L.O. Gostin, L.F Wiley, and T.R.F. Frieden (2016) *Public Health Law: Power, Duty and Restraint* (3rd edn), Berkeley, CA: University of California Press, chs 1 and 2.

at standardizing approaches to contagion control.[8] These were followed by the establishment of the International Sanitary Regulations,[9] and the International Health Regulations which are applicable today and which were last updated in 2005 following the outbreak of Severe Acute Respiratory Syndrome (SARS) in China in 2002 which resulted in some 774 deaths across the world.[10] The stated aims of the Regulations are

> to prevent, protect against, control and provide a public health response to the international spread of disease in ways that are commensurate with and restricted to public health risks, and which avoid unnecessary interference with international traffic and trade.[11]

However, the operation of this legislation and the effectiveness of the international community in responding to global health challenges was a matter of concern and substantial criticism, not least in relation to the response to the cross-border spread of the Ebola virus in 2014.[12] Similar criticism can be seen in relation to the effectiveness of international responses to the COVID-19 pandemic, although the details of this debate is something which goes beyond the scope of this book.[13]

There is a long history in the UK of legislation which has enabled actions to be taken on the basis of public health. In the 1800s, the work of Edwin Chadwick, who also played an important role in the Poor Law reforms, was an important driver in addressing the harms of disease suffered

---

[8] For background see W.F. Bynum (1993) 'Policing hearts of darkness: aspects of the international sanitary conferences', *History and Philosophy of the Life Sciences*, 15(3): 421–34; and H. Valeska (2006) 'The unification of the globe by disease? The international sanitary conferences on cholera, 1851–1894', *Historical Journal*, 49(2): 453–76. For a history of the issue of pandemics see also UK COVID-19 Inquiry (2024) chapter 1.

[9] See further: L.O. Gostin (2014) *Global Health Law*, Cambridge, MA: Harvard University Press, pp 177–81; L.O. Gostin (2006) 'The international health regulations: a new paradigm for global health governance', in S. McLean (ed) *First Do No Harm: Law, Ethics and Healthcare*, Farnham: Ashgate; and L.O. Gostin (2004) 'International infectious disease law: revision of the World Health Organization's international health regulations', *Journal of the American Medical Association*, 291(21): 2623; M. Livrani and R. Coker (2012) 'Protecting Europe from diseases: from the international sanitary conferences to the ECDC', *Journal of Health Politics, Policy and Law*, 37(6): 915.

[10] WHO (2005) *International Health Regulations* (3rd edn); L.O. Gostin (2014) ch 6.

[11] WHO (2005) 'International Health Regulations', Article 2.

[12] See further L.O. Gostin and R. Katz (2016) 'The international health regulations: the governing framework for global health security' *Milbank Quarterly*, 96(2): 264.

[13] See, for example, the discussion in A. Rendo and R. Castro (2020) 'Toward stronger EU governance of health threats after the COVID-19 pandemic', *European Journal of Risk Regulation*, 11(2): 273–82.

by the population.[14] There remain tensions between the aims of public health in terms of reducing disease across the population and what may be seen as legitimate concerns in relation to respect for individual personal liberty.[15] This was controversially illustrated by the introduction of powers to compulsorily detain tuberculosis patients in the early part of the 20th century[16] through to the debates in the 1980s regarding the legitimacy of the use of powers to detain HIV-positive patients due to concerns about the risk of disease transmission.[17] The debates about the scope of public health powers over the next two decades led to the passage of the Public Health (Control of Disease) Act 1984, which dealt with the management and containment of notifiable diseases at local authority level. The Act was in turn amended to allow for the implementation of the International Health Regulations.[18] These amendments, including provision under section 45C, provided that:

> The appropriate Minister may by regulations make provision for the purpose of preventing, protecting against, controlling or providing a public health response to the incidence or spread of infection or contamination in England and Wales (whether from risks originating there or elsewhere.

The powers were subject to the requirement that they were to be proportionate.[19] They could also be implemented for a period of up to 28 days without the need for the scrutiny or authorization of Parliament,[20] and they were implemented to varying degrees at different points throughout the COVID-19 pandemic under policies such as the 'stay at home' orders, the restrictions placed upon movement and public gatherings, and ultimately through the guidance on 'social distancing'.

---

[14] See C. Hamlin and P. Sidley (1998) 'Revolutions in public health: 1848, and 1998', *British Medical Journal*, 317(7158): 587.

[15] See further J. Coggon, K. Syrett, and A. Viens (2017) *Public Health Law Ethics, Governance, and Regulation*, London: Routledge; Nuffield Council on Bioethics (2007), *Public Health: Ethical Issues*, London: Nuffield Council on Bioethics.

[16] See the discussion in R. Coker (2001) 'Civil liberties and the public good: detention of tuberculous patients and the Public Health Act 1984', *Medical History*, 45(3): 41.

[17] By our Legal Correspondent (1985) 'Detaining patients with HIV', *British Medical Journal*, 219: 1102 and see further discussion in A .Wagner (2022) *Emergency State: How We Lost Our Freedoms in the Pandemic and Why it Matters*, London: Bodley Head, pp 28–9.

[18] WHO (2005) *International Health Regulations* (3rd edn), as amended.

[19] Public Health (Control of Disease) 1984, s 45D.

[20] See s 45F(8) and A. Wagner (2022) *Emergency State: How we lost our freedom during the Pandemic and why it matters*, London: Vintage, p 31.

Alongside public health powers, the other major statutory provision immediately available in 2020 to address the challenges of the pandemic was the Civil Contingencies Act 2004. To understand this fully we need to look back to the 2000s, when the then Labour government led by Prime Minister Tony Blair sought to develop robust strategies to address business continuity, prompted by the weaknesses highlighted by the tanker drivers' dispute – which nearly brought the UK to its knees.[21] The Government also suffered compound pressures from the foot and mouth crisis,[22] which led to the recognition that contingency plans for contending with emergencies needed to be carefully considered and tested, and the relevant agencies readied and properly resourced for their roles. A review of the handling of risk and uncertainty undertaken by the Government Strategy Unit was published by the Cabinet Office in 2002.[23] This itself could be seen as a response to Lord Phillips' report into the BSE (or 'mad cow disease') crisis.[24] The Strategy Unit review noted that 'risk management has been found wanting in recent policy failures and crisis',[25] and that there was need for a more 'developed approach'.[26] The review proposed embedding risk-management approaches in the planning and delivery of policy, along with contingency and consequence planning and mainstreaming of resilience.[27] There should be quality standards for Government-level risk management,[28] which should follow principles of openness and transparency, engagement, proportionality and precaution, and evidence and responsibility.[29] Public trust was seen as important, as was the need for ministers and senior civil servants to 'take a clear lead in, improving risk handling'.[30] This work led to the Civil Contingencies Act 2004. This 2004 legislation replaces earlier legislation in the form of the Emergency Powers Act 1920, the Emergency Powers Act (Northern Ireland) 1920, the Civil Defence Act 1948, and the Civil Defence Act (Northern Ireland) 1950. The Emergency Powers Act 1920 Section 1 applied in circumstances in which:

---

[21] A. Campbell (2007) *The Blair Years: Extracts from the Alastair Campbell Diaries*, London: Hutchinson, pp 469–73.
[22] Campbell (2007), pp 508–22.
[23] Cabinet Office (November 2002) *Risk: Improving government's capability to handle risk and uncertainty*. Strategy Unit Report.
[24] Lord Philips (2000) *The BSE Inquiry: Volume 1 Findings and Conclusions*, London: HMSO.
[25] Cabinet Office (2002), para 3.5.
[26] Cabinet Office (2002), para 3.44
[27] Cabinet Office (2002), para 4.2.63.
[28] Cabinet Office (2002), para 4.5.
[29] Cabinet Office (2002), p 91.
[30] Cabinet Office (2002), p 108.

any action has been taken or is immediately threatened by any person or body of persons of such a nature and on so extensive a scale as to be calculated, by interfering with the supply and distribution of food, water, fuel, or light, or with the means of locomotion to deprive the community or any substantial portion of the community, of the essentials of life.

Then a state of emergency could be declared. It was in fact, as Ewing notes, only used in relation to emergencies due to major industrial action in key industries.[31] Its replacement, the Civil Contingencies Act 2004, is rooted in the definition introduced in the legislation of what constitutes an 'emergency'.[32] The Act sets out the respective roles and responsibilities of various agencies and bodies, as well as protocols to be followed, in the event of various types of emergency situation. Events which threaten serious damage to human welfare,[33] environment,[34] or security in the UK can all fall within the definition of an emergency.[35] Situations impacting on human welfare include those which will cause or may cause loss of human life,[36] illness or injury,[37] or disruption of services relating to health.[38] As Greene comments, this legislation would be clearly suited to the situation of the pandemic.[39] Para 1 relates to local arrangements, Para 2 to national arrangements. These emergencies, as defined in Part 1 of the Act in section 1(1)(a) and for Part 2 of the Act in section 19(1)(a), differ in their geographical extent. Part 1 relates to 'a place in the United Kingdom', while in Part 2 this concerns 'the United Kingdom in a Part or region'.[40] As Anderson and Adey comment:

> Rather than replace the word 'serious' with 'severe' or some other term indicating intensity, geographical extent is used as a measure

---

[31] K. Ewing (2020) 'COVID-19: government by decree', *King's Law Journal*, 31(1): 1–24.

[32] Section1 of the 2004 Act sets out the definition of emergency in relation to local arrangements for Civil Protection in Pt I of the Act. Section 19 sets out the definition of emergency in relation to the application of emergency powers under Pt II of the Act.

[33] For Pt 1 of the Act s 1(1)(a) and for Pt 2 of the Act s 19(1)(a) Civil Contingencies Act 2004.

[34] For Pt 1 of the Act s 1(1)(b) and for Pt 2 of the Act s 19(1)(b) Civil Contingencies Act 2004.

[35] For Pt 1 of the Act s 1(1)(a) and or Pt 2 of the Act s 19(1)(c) Civil Contingencies Act 2004.

[36] For Pt 1 of the Act s 1(1)(b) and for Pt 2 of the Act s 19(2)(a) Civil Contingencies Act 2004.

[37] For Pt 1 of the Act s 1(1)(h) and for Pt 2 of the Act s 19(2)(b) Civil Contingencies Act 2004.

[38] For Pt 2 of the Act s 19(2)(h) Civil Contingencies Act 2004.

[39] See discussion in A. Greene (2020) *Emergency Powers in a Time of Pandemic*, Bristol: Bristol University Press, p 98.

[40] Civil Contingencies Act 2004, s 19(1)(a).

of the seriousness of an event. For Part 2 emergency powers to be triggered, an emergency must have a minimum geographical extent. The emphasis in Part 1 is on a 'place', a word that is not defined in the Act and does not have a standard legal meaning but is used to emphasise 'more localised events or situations whereas the scale of an event or situation must be greater before emergency powers may be used' (Cabinet Office, 2004c: 5).[41]

Part 1 of the Act focuses on the local arrangements for Civil Protection. Duties are placed on Category 1 responders (such as police, fire and rescue, NHS bodies and local authorities) to assess the risk level as to whether an emergency will arise and to produce and maintain plans in response.[42] They are also to publish such plans to the extent to which this is 'necessary or desirable to deal with the emergency'.[43] Provisions also exist concerning the advice and assistance provided to the public regarding whether commercial or voluntary activities will continue to operate during an emergency.[44]

In addition, the legislation provides for the establishment of what are known as Local Resilience Forums,[45] which operate across England and correspond to police areas. They comprise Category 1 responders along with Category 2 responders or 'co-operating bodies' which include organizations such as transport, Health and Safety Executive and utility companies. The statutory duty in relation to the assessment of risks and preparation of a Community Risk Register for local resilience areas is placed on Category 1 responders but the Guidance states that the duties are to be provided through the Local Resilience Forums.[46] The precise composition of these bodies in terms of involvement of local authorities and NHS Integrated Care Boards varies.[47] McClelland and Shaw suggest that these can be seen as hybrid bodies, operating primarily as regional 'soft spaces' where they act as an arena for the involvement of a range of partners operating more informally, and as a harder space where they respond to disaster management through the prism

---

[41] B. Anderson and P. Adley (2012) 'Governing events and life: emergency in UK civil contingencies', *Political Geography*, 31(24): 29; also quoting from the Cabinet Office 2004, p 5.
[42] Civil Contingencies Act 2004, s 2(1)(c)(d).
[43] Civil Contingencies Act 2004, s 2(1)(f)(g).
[44] Civil Contingencies Act 2004, s 4.
[45] Civil Contingencies Act 2004, s 2(5). See further: Cabinet Office (July 2013) *The role of Local Resilience Forums: A reference document*, Civil Contingencies Secretariat.
[46] Cabinet Office (2013), Guidance, Preparation and Planning for Emergencies para 44.
[47] A.G. McClelland and D. Shaw (2023) 'Resilience to disruptions: the role of regional soft spaces', *Regional Studies*, [online], 19 October, p 6.

of command and control.[48] Oversight of the Forums was undertaken by the Ministry of Housing, Communities and Local Government which had a Resilience and Emergencies Division (subsequently known as the Resilience and Recovery Directorate) and the Cabinet Office.[49]

The local authorities we examine in the West Midlands in Chapter 5 are grouped into separate Local Resilience Forums. The relevant groupings are the Staffordshire Forum (comprising Stoke-on-Trent and Staffordshire); West Mercia Forum (with Herefordshire, Shropshire, Worcestershire, and Telford and Wrekin), and the West Midlands Conurbation Resilience Forum (with Birmingham, Coventry, Dudley, Sandwell, Solihull, Walsall, and Wolverhampton). Under the umbrella of these Forums, there are also operational groupings; for example, the Coventry, Solihull, and Warwickshire Resilience Team.[50] The Local Resilience Forums, in both their formal and informal aspects, came into their own during the pandemic.[51]

The UK COVID-19 Inquiry Module 1 Report published in July 2024 criticised the lack of alignment between Resilience Forums' geographical areas, which reflected police areas rather than those of local health resilience partnerships[52] which are organisations that relate to NHS structures through integrated care boards.[53] A further issue highlighted in the Inquiry Report was the fact that local Directors of Public Health did not 'typically' sit on Local Resilience Forums as they were not invited to do so.[54] The Report recommended that there needed to be greater involvement of Directors of Public Health at local level in pandemic planning development.[55]

Part 2 of the Civil Contingencies Act concerns the nature and operation of emergency powers. Section 20(1) gives extensive powers to the King to make emergency regulations by Order in Council if conditions set out in section 21 are complied with or under section 20(2) by a Senior Minister to make such regulations if there is not sufficient time to make an Order in Council and the criteria under section 21 are complied with. Section 21 out the conditions for such an Order in Council which are first 'that an emergency has occurred, is occurring or is about to occur',[56] and 'second that it is necessary to make provision for the purpose of preventing, controlling or mitigating an aspect of effect of the emergency',[57] and finally 'that the need

---

[48] McClelland and Shaw (2023), p 8.
[49] UK COVID-19 Inquiry (2024), para 2.41.
[50] CSW Resilience Team (cswprepared.org.uk).
[51] See further discussion in Chapter 5.
[52] UK COVID-19 Inquiry (2024), para 2.44.
[53] See further discussion in Chapter 3.
[54] UK COVID-19 Inquiry (2024), para 2.45.
[55] UK COVID-19 Inquiry (2024), para 2.45.
[56] Civil Contingencies Act 2004, s 21(2).
[57] Civil Contingencies Act 2004, s 21(3).

for the Order is urgent'.⁵⁸ Section 22 of the legislation enables regulations to make provision covering a wide range of issues including protecting life and health and safety.

In relation to emergency planning, the Guidance issued by the Cabinet Office states that risk assessments to add or to modify emergency plans are to be collectively considered by Category 1 responders through the Local Resilience Forums, and that the Forums themselves are to address local issues and 'collectively exercise plans and must learn and implement lessons from exercises, emergencies and emerging policy'.⁵⁹ Collaboration with other neighbouring Local Resilience Forums is anticipated.⁶⁰ Good-practice indicators for emergency planning include such things as regularly undertaking processes that enable them to identify where modifications to plans are necessary or expedient'.⁶¹

The legislation was followed by the establishment of a Civil Contingencies Secretariat to provide a horizon-scanning function to coordinate national- and local-level responses to possible future crises and worst-case scenarios. The Secretariat manages the Resilience Capabilities programme. The stated aim of this programme is

> to increase our capability to respond to and recover from civil emergencies. It does this by understanding what capabilities we need to deal with the consequences of emergencies, regardless of whether those emergencies are caused by accidents, natural hazards or man-made threats. The programme then coordinates cross-government efforts to build capabilities.⁶²

The Secretariat also provides support for the Civil Contingencies Committee, more commonly known as COBR or COBRA, as its meetings are held in the Cabinet Office Briefing Rooms at 70 Whitehall.⁶³ The UK COVID-19 Inquiry first Module 1 report in July 2024 commented that

> Katharine Hammond, Director of the Civil Contingencies Secretariat from August 2016 to August 2020, told the Inquiry that it was principally a 'co-ordinating' body for whole-system civil emergency

---

[58] Civil Contingencies Act 2004, s 21(4).
[59] Cabinet Office (2013), p 20.
[60] Cabinet Office (2013), p 20.
[61] Cabinet Office (2013), p 22.
[62] H.M. Government (2013) *Guidance Preparation and planning for emergencies* (last updated May 2018).
[63] COBR was developed from an emergency situation centre that was responding to the miners' strikes of the 1970s.

planning, response and recovery ... Although it was located at the centre of government, it did not lead and was not in charge of the preparedness and resilience of other government departments. Each government department was in charge of managing the risks that fell within its remit.[64]

The UK COVID-19 Inquiry Module 1 Report noted that: 'The issues of constant reorganisation and rebranding go to the top of the institutions responsible for preparedness and resilience in the UK.'[65] It gave as an illustration how the Secretariat was later divided into two divisions: a 'Resilience Directorate' and a 'COBRA' unit.[66] From 2008 the Secretariat produced a National Risk Register and from 2009, a National Security Risk Assessment which is a classified document.[67]

In 2020 the Conservative–Liberal Coalition Government established the National Security Council, a body chaired by the Prime Minister, which discusses the national security objectives of the UK Government and the delivery of those objectives.[68] This body also had a National Security Council (Threats, Hazards, Resilience and Contingencies) sub-committee whose focus included preparedness planning.[69] The UK COVID-19 Inquiry Module 1 Report commented on the importance of this sub committee in relation to the implementation of the UK Influenza Pandemic Preparedness Strategy 2011 discussed later in the chapter.[70] The last formal meeting of this sub-committee was in 2017 and the subcommittee was disbanded from 2019.[71] In 2017 the sub-committee had established a Pandemic Flu Readiness Board.[72]

But although certain measures undertaken during the early years of the COVID-19 pandemic were rooted in Public Health powers, such as restrictions on movement and gathering, the powers under the Civil Contingencies Act 2004 were not utilized. It would initially appear that the crisis of the COVID-19 pandemic would fall into the category of circumstances

---

[64] UK COVID-19 Inquiry (2024), para 2.19.
[65] UK COVID-19 Inquiry (2024), para 2.46.
[66] UK COVID-19 Inquiry (2024), para 2.46.
[67] UK COVID-19 Inquiry (2024), para 3.8.
[68] National Security Council, https://www.gov.uk/government/groups/national-security-council, accessed 10 July 2024, and see further for background: J. Devanney and J. Harris (2014) *The National Security Council: National security at the centre of government*, Institute for Government and discussion in the UK COVID-19 Inquiry Module 1 Report, para 2.21.
[69] UK COVID-19 Inquiry (2024), para 2.22.
[70] UK COVID-19 Inquiry (2024), para 2.24.
[71] UK COVID-19 Inquiry (2024), para 2.25.
[72] UK COVID-19 Inquiry (2024), para 2.28.

covered by the 2004 legislation. Nonetheless the UK COVID-19 Inquiry Module 1 Report states that

> At the time of the coronavirus (COVID-19) pandemic, the legislative framework and associated national guidance was 'widely acknowledged [by public health specialists and practitioners] as being outdated and did not relate to contemporary structures, roles and responsibilities'. As is being examined in subsequent modules of the Inquiry, it was not utilized.[73]

However a different justification for the reason why it was not used was provided in the House of Commons debates of March 2020 by the then Leader of the House, Jacob Rees-Mogg, who stated that

> Unfortunately the Civil Contingencies Act would not have worked in these circumstances because the problem was known about early enough for it not to qualify as an emergency under the terms of that Act. The legal experts say that if we can introduce emergency legislation, we should do so rather than using the Civil Contingencies Act, because if we have time to introduce emergency legislation, we obviously knew about it long enough in advance for the Act not to apply. That is why that Act could not be used.[74]

This approach has, however, been criticized by Moosavian, Walker and Blick, who argue that: 'This assertion appears to be mistaken because it automatically rules out the CCA 2004's application to any pandemic or other emergency where the danger emerges and grows. There is no rule in the CCA 2004 against the foreseeability of a crisis.'[75]

Beyond Rees-Mogg's assertion, one other suggestion as to why this legislation was not used is the enhanced level of parliamentary review which would have been required regarding the initiation and subsequent operation of its powers.[76] The Civil Contingencies Act requires these powers to be laid before Parliament 'as soon as is reasonably practicable',[77] and they will lapse after seven days unless both of the Houses of Parliament has passed a resolution approving them.[78] Once enacted, the legislation requires that

---

[73] UK COVID-19 Inquiry (2024), para 2.14.
[74] HC Debates, 19 March 2020, vol 673, col 1188.
[75] R. Moosavian, C. Walker and A. Blick (2021) 'Coronavirus legislative responses in the UK: regression to panic and disdain of constitutionalism', *Northern Ireland Legal Quarterly*, 72(1): 16.
[76] See Greene (2020), p 98 and Wagner (2022), p 50.
[77] Civil Contingencies Act 2004, s 27(1)(a).
[78] Civil Contingencies Act 2004, s 27(1)(b).

they would lapse after 30 days,[79] or 'at such earlier time as may be specified in the regulations'.[80] In addition, section 29 places an obligation on the UK Government to consult with the devolved governments, unless they were prevented from doing so by the urgency of the situation.

In short, there were self-regulating strictures (a 'triple lock' mechanism) built into the legislation to ensure that it would only be used where no alternative, appropriate legislation was available. It could be argued that there was alternative legislation in existence in the form of the Public Health Act 1984. However, Moosavian, Walker and Blick argue that the triple lock

> should not be seen as automatically demanding or justifying a shift to any alternative legislation such as the PHA [Public Health Act] 1984. That legislation can cover some of the same ground but patently contains shortcomings which could have been avoided or minimised through use of the CCA 2004.[81]

The decision not to use the Civil Contingencies Act was subject to very heavy criticism by the Public Administration Committee in its Report on the Parliamentary Scrutiny of the Government's handling of COVID-19.[82] Government ministers argued before the Select Committee that the fact that there was time to develop legislation illustrated that this was not a sufficient emergency to utilize the legislation.[83] The Committee stated that

> 34. the Committee is not convinced that the Civil Contingencies Act could not have been used for COVID-19 and believes there was a potential role for the Civil Contingencies Act in providing a 'stop-gap' for more detailed scrutiny of the Coronavirus Bill to take place. … Furthermore, the Coronavirus Act does not have the same safeguards as the Civil Contingencies Act. … Any separate legislation to deal with civil contingencies—and particularly legislation that needs to be passed very quickly—should include safeguards and scrutiny provisions that are equivalent to those in the CCA, with regular renewal of powers allowing for more detailed Parliamentary scrutiny that, due to expediency, cannot be given during the passing of emergency legislation.[84]

---

[79] Civil Contingencies Act 2004, s 26(1)(a).
[80] Civil Contingencies Act 2004, s 26(1)(b).
[81] Moosavian, Walker and Blick (2021), p 16.
[82] Public Administration Committee (2020) *Parliamentary Scrutiny of the Government's handling of COVID-19*, 10 September.
[83] Public Administration Committee (2020), at para 27.
[84] Public Administration Committee (2020), paras 34–5.

The Committee concluded by stating that: 'The Government's reticence to use the Civil Contingencies Act in response to a genuine national emergency calls into question how fit for purpose that legislation is'.[85]

Ultimately the powers which operated to limit and structure behaviour during the pandemic were a combination of public health legislation and bespoke new legislation in the form of the Coronavirus Act 2020. Nonetheless the whole process of planning for a pandemic can be seen as integrally linked to these civil contingency powers and the ongoing development, updating, and maintenance of national emergency planning strategies. We shall explore the rationales which led to this approach, leading ultimately to the 2020 Act, in the next section of this chapter.[86]

III. Planning for a pandemic

The need to address the risk of new infectious diseases was highlighted by the then Chief Medical Officer in the document 'Getting Ahead of the Curve: A strategy for combating infectious diseases' back in 2002.[87] This states that: 'A key component of any infectious diseases strategy must address the ever-present threat arising from new diseases, newly discovered diseases or old diseases posing a new or different threat.'[88]

It stated that in relation to a 'healthcare protection service' that 'a modernised service would be expected to protect our population against a wide range of eventualities' and that one of these possible future eventualities was identified as being 'the next influenza pandemic' or 'a major animal epidemic with implications for human health'.[89] In December 2005, the first meeting of the Ministerial Committee on Pandemic Influenza Planning (MISC32) was held 'to guide the preparations for a potential influenza pandemic and related international activity'.[90] The Committee was supported by the cross-departmental Pandemic Flu Implementation Group and the

---

[85] Public Administration Committee (2020), paras 34–5.
[86] On the background to the Civil Contingencies Act 2004, see further B. Anderson and P. Adley (2012) 'Governing events and life: emergency in UK civil contingencies', *Political Geography*, 31(1): 24–33.
[87] Department of Health (2002) *Getting Ahead of the Curve: A strategy for combating infectious diseases.*
[88] Department of Health (2002), para 3.2.
[89] Department of Health (2002), p 132.
[90] See discussion on this at para 1.12 of the independent review into the response to the 2009 swine flu pandemic D. Hine (2010) *The 2009 Influenza Pandemic: An Independent Review into the Response to the 2009 Swine Flu Pandemic,* Cabinet Office, July.

devolved administrations were involved at every level, despite not having official membership of the group.

From 2007 onwards, a series of multi-agency preparedness exercises took place. In the opening months of 2007, Exercise Winter Willow[91] was undertaken with the aim of checking 'preparation for the major disruptive challenges that an influenza pandemic might bring'.[92] It involved nine Regional Civil Contingencies Committees in England and related committees in the devolved governments.[93] In addition, some 51 local Strategic Co-ordination Groups from across the UK were involved, as were the then existing Strategic Health Authorities (SHAs) and local Health Community Groups for each of the SHA areas.[94] Prescient to the legislative easements later enacted in relation to COVID-19, Winter Willow stated that: 'As part of the current planning for a pandemic, government departments have identified possible regulations that may need to be relaxed. The Cabinet Office will lead on work to identify appropriate legislative vehicles'.[95]

The work of this exercise was to be fed into the revision of the UK National Framework for Responding to an Influenza Pandemic, which was published in November 2007.[96] This document set out a broad strategy for dealing with decisions consequent upon a pandemic. It recognized that there would be difficult ethical decisions and that the Department of Health had requested the establishment of an independent committee to develop an ethical framework to inform policy development and implementation.[97] The importance of multi-agency planning was highlighted.[98] It also specifically stated that: 'Planning and response at regional and local government level will focus on wider aspects, including support of the health response, the *maintenance of social care* and other essential local services and managing potentially large numbers of deaths.'[99]

---

[91] Department of Health (2007) *Winter Willow Exercises Identified*, Cabinet Office and Health Protection Agency.
[92] Department of Health (2007).
[93] Department of Health (2007), p 4.
[94] Department of Health (2007), p 4.
[95] Department of Health (2007), p 17.
[96] Department of Health (2007), p 5. A National Framework for Responding to an Influenza pandemic.
[97] Department of Health (2007) A National Framework for Responding to an Influenza Pandemic, p 14.
[98] Department of Health (2007) A National Framework for responding to an Influenza Pandemic, para 4.1.
[99] Department of Health (2007) A National Framework for responding to an Influenza Pandemic, para 4.10, emphasis added.

Local Resilience Forums were seen as 'the principal mechanism for the coordination of multi-agency planning at local level'.[100] The document addressed different alert levels. Level 1 was where the virus or cases were only outside the UK. In relation to Alert Level 2, where the virus was isolated in the UK, efforts were to concentrate on managing surge capacity, ensuring business continuity, and communications. Measures included investigation of cases, relevant care and mitigations to slow spread.[101]

At Alert Level 3, which applied where the pandemic had become established, the health priorities would include:

- ensuring that patients have access to appropriate assessment, treatment and care, including rapid access to antiviral medicines for those with symptoms compatible with pandemic influenza
- adapting health and social care services to ensure that the maximum amount of surge capacity is available in primary and secondary care in anticipation of additional demand
- implementing and maintaining staffing contingency plans
- ensuring that infection control measures are strengthened in all health and social care settings.[102]

At Alert level 4, which related to 'widespread activity across the UK,' it was stated that:

It is anticipated that activity will rise to a peak across the UK about seven weeks from the first recognition of cases, following the pattern described. Initially, all organisations should monitor the impact on their service or business against planned expectations in order to modify responses appropriately, if necessary.[103]

Priorities regarding health and social care included:

- surveillance – the HPA [Health Protection Agency] will have moved from detailed to aggregate reporting of cases by geographic region together with assessment of the efficacy of antiviral medicines (and, if relevant, vaccine), monitoring of the cause and antimicrobial

---

[100] Department of Health (2007) A National Framework for Responding to an Influenza Pandemic, para 4.10.2.
[101] Department of Health (2007) National Framework for Responding to an Influenza Pandemic, para 5.2.
[102] Department of Health (2007) National Framework for Responding to an Influenza Pandemic, para 6.5.2.
[103] Department of Health (2007) National Framework for Responding to an Influenza Pandemic, para 6.6.

susceptibility of bacterial complications, and reviewing the clinical effectiveness of the response
- providing health and social care advice and information
- monitoring antiviral consumption against expected use and adapting policies accordingly
- monitoring and responding to pressures on health and social care services, maximising the effective use of the capacity available, supplementing staffing, maintaining essential care for those who are suffering from other emergencies or illness, conserving essential supplies and maintaining services
- developing a specific vaccine and securing UK supply.[104]

It recognized the fact that a 'pandemic will result in intense and sustained pressure on all parts of the health and social care system, limiting the scope for mutual aid and threatening to overwhelm services at its peak'.[105] Services would consequently need to adapt. It went on to recognize potential demands on health care, noting that if the pandemic was short in duration, it would have a more intense strain on services; services would also be under pressure and deaths rates higher if the virus was particularly dangerous for older persons.[106] The impact of pressures on hospitals was noted, with some estimates suggesting that 'existing hospital capacity may only meet 20% to 25% of the expected demand at the peak,' thus prompting the need for strategies to deal with demand, such as fast discharge from hospital wards and alternative arrangements for care.[107]

The document mentioned the importance of adult social care and noted that integrated contingency arrangements would be crucial to managing the impact of a pandemic:

> Effective contingency arrangements developed jointly by health and social care agencies will be critical to the relief of suffering and to achieving the wider public health aims of keeping symptomatic patients at home, caring for them in a community setting and reducing the burden on healthcare facilities.[108]

---

[104] Department of Health (2007) A National Framework for Responding to an Influenza Pandemic, para 6.6.2.

[105] Department of Health (2007) A National Framework for Responding to an Influenza Pandemic, para 9.

[106] Department of Health (2007) A National Framework for Responding to an Influenza Pandemic, para 9.3.2.

[107] Department of Health (2007) A National Framework for Responding to an Influenza Pandemic, para 9.11.

[108] Department of Health (2007) A National Framework for Responding to an Influenza Pandemic, para 9.24.

The document also highlighted the large number of informal carers who would be affected, as well as the potential impacts on social care providers working with individuals in the community who might be particularly vulnerable to the virus. It recognized that, in addition to those with existing care needs, a pandemic could give rise to others developing new short-term and long-term additional care needs, and that 'all forms of care provision' including 'voluntary, private or independent sector' would need to be factored into planning.[109]

It went on to list the key challenges in maintaining social care services:

- sustaining indirect care services that form an essential lifeline for some people, e.g. meals on wheels, provision of community equipment, community alarm services, with reduced staff
- meeting the additional burden on already overstretched local social care services and intermediate care services due to the additional pressures on acute hospital beds
- ensuring that the necessary lines of communication exist to relay essential national, regional and local messages to the diverse range of social care services across all sectors (statutory, voluntary, independent and private)
- relieving additional pressures on caring time to support care home residents and people cared for in their own homes when they have influenza
- sustaining people with complex disabilities who are currently supported with intensive care packages in the community
- providing emergency respite care for vulnerable people looked after at home by informal carers for the period their carer is ill
- maintaining a balance between appropriate safety and infection control measures and ensuring that the quality of life of vulnerable adults is maintained as far as possible.[110]

The document also identified the likely impacts of pressures on staff and staffing, in health and social care, including compound ethical dilemmas:

> An influenza pandemic will put staff under considerable pressure and there are likely to be conflicts between staff members' professional and/or contractual obligations, personal or family responsibilities and

---

[109] Department of Health (2007) A National Framework for Responding to an Influenza Pandemic, para 9.24.

[110] Department of Health (2007) A National Framework for Responding to an Influenza Pandemic, para 9.24.

concerns about risks. The forthcoming guidance on human resource issues will have relevance to the ethical and professional obligations of staff. When this guidance is available, trusts will need to work with staff to explain what will be considered appropriate professional practice mechanisms to support them in resolving any ethical dilemmas that may arise out of their work.[111]

While it was stated that the Department of Health was undertaking work with NHS employers to develop a human resources management plan for the pandemic, there was no reference in this document to this being developed for the social care sector.[112] The emphasis was on the ethical dilemmas that would be faced by NHS staff[113] but, as we shall see later in this book, there would also be ethical and operational dilemmas for social care.

Despite measures being taken to provide for 'high level preparedness for Pandemic Flu' in the mid-2000s, their effectiveness remained unclear. The preparedness for residential and nursing homes for an influenza pandemic was criticized by Fell in a 2008 article published in the *Journal of Public Health*.[114] He undertook a survey of care homes in West Yorkshire, both local authority and privately owned, which revealed that 'none of the homes surveyed had undertaken any contingency planning for pandemic flu,' nor had there been any planning for clinical management or business continuity in a pandemic.[115]

In 2009 there was a global H1N1 Swine Flu pandemic. In the UK this led to some 457 deaths. Subsequently, in 2010, an independent review of the H1N1 Swine Flu pandemic was undertaken by Dame Deidre Hine.[116] This concluded that the pandemic response had been 'proportionate and effective'.[117] It did not address the question of legislative easements, but it did note weaknesses in crucial communications regarding workforce capacity and redeployment in the pathways between national policy level and local operational levels. In terms that would later be echoed during the COVID-19 pandemic, the Hine Review commented that:

---

[111] Department of Health (2007) A National Framework for Responding to an Influenza Pandemic, para 9.25.
[112] Department of Health (2007) A National Framework for Responding to an Influenza Pandemic, para 9.25.
[113] Department of Health (2007) A National Framework for Responding to an Influenza Pandemic, para 9.25.
[114] G. Fell (2008) 'Preparedness of residential and nursing homes for pandemic flu', *Journal of Public Health*, 30(1): 99–102.
[115] Fell (2008).
[116] Dame Deidre Hine (2010) *The 2009 Influenza Pandemic: An independent review of the UK response to the 2009 influenza pandemic*, July, p 3, para 2.
[117] Dame Deidre Hine (2010), p 3.

I heard, anecdotally, that the flow of information to front-line health workers could have been improved. Some heard key information first through the media rather than from the authorities, and others felt inundated with information and guidance. I heard that some freelance and locum staff did not receive any information but could have played a role in augmenting services if asked. While I did not explore this element of the response in detail, I would suggest that the four health departments ensure that a clear gateway system is in place to make sure that the information and documentation reaching staff is timely and co-ordinated and takes account of the overall burden it places upon them.[118]

The Department of Health produced its Influenza Pandemic Preparedness Strategy in 2011.[119] This evolved from the 2007 National Framework and the Hine Report, and the changes included ambitions to

Develop better plans for the initial response to a new influenza pandemic when the focus should be on rapid and accurate assessment of the nature of the influenza virus and its effects, both clinically and in relation to wider public health implications.

Put in place plans to ensure a response that is proportionate to meet the differing demands of pandemic influenza viruses of milder or more severe impact, rather than just focusing on the 'worst case' planning assumptions.[120]

As the subsequent UK COVID-19 Inquiry Module 1 Report in 2024 noted, its objectives were those of the minimisation of the impacts of a future influenza pandemic on health, and also on society and the economy while also being able to 'instill and maintain trust and confidence'.[121]

The 2011 Strategy recognized that in the case of a situation in which there is 'widespread disease in the UK' there would be pressure on primary care, social care provision, and the voluntary sector which would, in turn, have an impact on secondary care.[122] The 2011 strategy entailed moving between five phases of activity. Those these would not necessarily follow in the same order. The first phase was 'detection' that a pandemic has

---

[118] Dame Deidre Hine (2010), para 8.50.
[119] Department of Health (2011) *UK Influenza Pandemic Preparedness Strategy*, see also discussion in chapter 4 of the UK COVID-19 Inquiry Module 1 Report, UK COVID-19 Inquiry (2024).
[120] Department of Health (2011), pp 7–8.
[121] UK COVID-19 Inquiry (2024), para 4.6.
[122] Department of Health (2011), p 25.

emerged; for example, by declaration by the World Health Organization (WHO) of a 'Public Health Emergency of International Concern'.[123] This would be followed by an assessment phase, ascertaining the impact, severity, and reduction of risk of transmission of infection at local level through locating cases, self-isolation, and treatment of cases and suspected cases. The next stage is that of 'treatment' which, as the name suggests, is concerned with treating specific individuals but also includes other public health measures to reduce transmission and, depending on the progress of the pandemic, the prospect of targeted vaccinations. There is then an 'escalation' phase which comes into play in situations in which demand exceeds capacity. This involves measures such as escalating surge provisions, triage, and contingency plans, and de-escalation steps where the situation has 'improved significantly'.[124] Finally, there would be a 'recovery' phase, restoring 'business as usual services', further pandemic planning, addressing 'staff exhaustion', and, interestingly, reference to 'normalisation of services, perhaps to a new definition of what constitutes normal service'.[125] Reference was made to the Ethical Framework which was produced in 2007 and it was stated that this remained 'appropriate and fit for purpose in planning for a further pandemic'.[126] It stated that coordination of activities at central Government level would be managed through the National Security Council, along with COBR, and with the involvement of SAGE to provide scientific advice.[127]

The 2011 Strategy echoes the 2007 Guidance in rooting the initial health and social care responses in 'detection' and 'assessment' phases.[128] In the treatment phase, some of the challenges of service delivery and workforce capacity are highlighted. It is stated that:

> In a moderate or more severe influenza pandemic, all health and social care services will be stretched and will need to reduce or cease non-urgent activity in order to make the maximum capacity available to meet the health care needs of those who are severely ill as a result of the influenza virus.[129]

---

[123] Department of Health (2011), para 3.13.
[124] Department of Health (2011), p 28.
[125] Department of Health (2011), p 29.
[126] Department of Health (2011), para 3.20.
[127] Department of Health (2011), para 3.28.
[128] Department of Health (2011), para 6.6.
[129] Department of Health (2011), para 6.18.

The Strategy then goes on to state that:

> The majority of patients will be cared for in their own homes, which may lead to increased pressure in primary and community services, social care, voluntary agencies and the private sector companies that support these services. In a severe pandemic where most age groups are affected, and many severely affected, it is likely that many sectors will be affected with high rates of sickness and absence.[130]

In the 'escalation phase', statements are made in relation to delivery of services which, as we will see later, subsequently transpired during the COVID-19 pandemic. The Strategy states that:

> Maximising the use of capacity remains the responsibility of local health organisations. In severe circumstances, it will not be possible to continue 'business as usual' activities and an escalating series of actions to reduce non-essential activity will be required in order to prevent service failures.[131]

It then goes on to say that:

> In more severe circumstances, it may be necessary to prioritise access to some services in an ethically appropriate way. The provision of the best available alternative care in situations of extreme demand will be an important part of the response, as will professional support and close discussion with families.[132]

The Strategy also contains prescient commentary on expectations around the 'recovery phase':

> Although the objective is to return to inter-pandemic levels of functioning as soon as possible, the pace of recovery will depend on the residual impact of the pandemic, ongoing demands, backlogs, staff and organisational fatigue, and continuing supply difficulties in most organisations. Therefore a gradual return to normality is to be expected.[133]

---

[130] Department of Health (2011), para 6.19.
[131] Department of Health (2011), para 6.33.
[132] Department of Health (2011), para 6.34.
[133] Department of Health (2011), para 6.38.

Moreover it was recognized that there would be compounded challenges such as the ongoing health complications due to illness, seasonal flu and staff shortages

> Although recovery is characterised as a move back to normality, it is not possible to predict further waves of the pandemic or the same and impact of the pandemic virus as it becomes a future seasonal influenza virus, which will emerge and which will again require organisations to regroup and respond. In this sense expectations around the performance of health and social care services should be tempered with a recognition of the experience of dealing with the influenza pandemic.[134]

In terms of legislative response, the presumption was to be that of voluntary compliance, with other measures not being introduced unless these were deemed necessary; there was no intention of compulsion in relation to treatment or vaccination.[135] It mentioned the existing powers under the Public Health Act 1984 and the scope for regulations to be made to address serious and imminent threats. Reference is also made to the powers of the Civil Contingencies Act 2004. The Strategy does highlight the fact that:

> Departments have identified a series of legislative measures that will or could be required in anticipation of, or during a pandemic in order to enable some of the response measures aimed at mitigating its impact on the UK. In the majority of cases provision for such amendments is included in existing legislation.[136]

As we shall see later, such statutory powers were eventually enacted in 2020. Alongside this Strategy, specific planning guidance was also issued to Local Resilience Forums in relation to local operational matters and pandemic planning.[137]

The 2011 Strategy was considered by the UK COVID-19 Inquiry Module 1 Report in 2024.[138] The Report stated that:

---

[134] Department of Health (2011), para 6.42.
[135] Department of Health (2011), para 7.5.
[136] Department of Health (2011), para 7.28.
[137] See further: Cabinet Office (July 2013) *Preparing for Pandemic Influenza. Guidance for Local Planners*. There had also been earlier guidance produced for Local Resilience Forums by the Civil Contingencies Secretariat (2007) *Preparing for Pandemic Influenza. Guidance to Local Planners*; Civil Contingencies Secretariat (2008) *Preparing for Pandemic Influenza: Supplementary Guidance for Local Resilience Forum Planners*.
[138] UK COVID-19 Inquiry (2024), ch 4.

The 2011 Strategy correctly identified that the impact a pandemic would have on the population and wider society would be determined by three factors:

- the characteristics of the disease (which it recognised as only being possible to assess once sufficient data were available);
- the capacity of healthcare services, other public services, utilities and businesses; and
- the behavioural response of the population to public health advice, antiviral medicines, vaccination and the use of healthcare services.[139]

However, the Inquiry Report suggested that there were four major flaws in the Strategy.[140] These were, first, that the Strategy had failed to adequately consider prevention and how, if there were no vaccines or other clinical therapeutics available, the disease spread could be stopped.[141] Second, it had only considered one type of pandemic, influenza.[142] The Report noted that the 2011 Strategy enabled the plans to be adapted and used for other infectious diseases and went on to say that: 'There should have been sufficient flexibility and adaptability to cope with the pandemic that struck, but there was not. This is evident from the virtual abandonment of the 2011 Strategy in the response to the Covid-19 pandemic.'[143] Third, it did not 'adequately' consider proportionality of response.[144] Finally the Report stated that there was a 'lack of an effective economic and social strategy'.[145]

A further issue which the Inquiry Report highlighted was that the Pandemic Flu strategy was not amended after 2011, which meant that it did not reflect any learning from, for example, international pandemics of other illnesses in the intervening period.[146]

Two further exercises followed examining the impacts internationally of the Ebola outbreak in the period 2013–16[147] and MERS, the Middle East respiratory syndrome coronavirus.[148] An Ebola Preparedness Surge Capacity

---

[139] UK COVID-19 Inquiry (2024), para 4.10
[140] UK COVID-19 Inquiry (2024), para 4.12.
[141] UK COVID-19 Inquiry (2024), paras 4.13–4.22.
[142] UK COVID-19 Inquiry (2024), paras 4.23–4.30.
[143] UK COVID-19 Inquiry (2024), para 4.26.
[144] UK COVID-19 Inquiry (2024), paras 4.31–4.41.
[145] UK COVID-19 Inquiry (2024), para 4.12.
[146] UK COVID-19 Inquiry (2024), paras 4.48-4.53.
[147] UK Health Security Agency (January 2023) *Guidance Ebola: overview, history, origins and transmission.*
[148] Middle East respiratory syndrome coronavirus (MERS-CoV).

Exercise was undertaken in 2015, followed by an exercise known as 'Exercise Alice' in 2016 which focused on contingencies for a MERS outbreak, but neither of these exercises provided a detailed examination of the need to maintain adult social care provision during a pandemic.[149] 'Exercise Cygnet' was an initial tabletop simulation which fed into the much broader 'Exercise Cygnus' command post exercise (CPX). Cygnus was undertaken in 2016 by then Public Health England (PHE) on behalf of the Department of Health to test multi-agency preparedness at national, regional, and local levels.[150] It was conducted, as far as possible, by professionals in their usual work locations, in real time, based around the timing of simulated COBR meetings in the Cabinet Office.

The Exercise Cygnus Report recommended that the voluntary sector should be mobilized at the local level to support the social care sector; that the Department of Health should work with social care partners to map out 'a strategic approach to prioritising local authority social care services during a pandemic with consideration given to the role of the Association of Directors of Adult Social Services (ADASS)'.[151] It also recommended that there should be proper risk assessments of patients prior to discharge (something which as we have seen in Chapter 1 was not in fact the case), highlighted the possibility of support from military command and control structures, and the option to relax the Care Quality Commission (CQC) registration of premises.[152]

Although the overall focus was on the maintenance of public health and supply chains, the Report emphasized that legislative and operational flexibility would be required to enable 'capability and capacity to surge resources into key areas, which in some areas is currently lacking'.[153] It was deemed necessary to consider 'the *introduction of legislative easements* and regulatory changes to assist with the implementation of the response to a worst case scenario pandemic' and to 'assist with the operationalisation of health care surge arrangements and keeping essential services running'.[154] These would 'form part of pandemic influenza planning assumptions,'[155] and they do indeed appear to be the blueprints for the Care Act easements, and indeed for the other legislative easements utilized during COVID-19. This part of Exercise Cygnus

---

[149] Public Health England (2016) *Report Exercise Alice Middle East Respiratory Syndrome Coronavirus. (MERS-Cov)*, 15 February.

[150] Public Health England (2017) Annex B. *Exercise Cygnus Report*. Tier One Command Post Exercise Pandemic Influenza – 18 to 20 October 2016 (13 July).

[151] Public Health England (2017).

[152] Public Health England (2017), p 31.

[153] Public Health England (2017), p 8, point 4.

[154] Public Health England (2017), pp 7–8, point 2, emphasis added.

[155] Public Health England (2017), pp 7–8, point 2.

highlighted the importance of a large number of statutory restrictions that, if lifted, would be of significant assistance to local and national government departments and agencies in responding to a pandemic. This legislation could be quickly tailored and amended to suit the live situation and could be prepared with input from all departments to include the most important variations and additions to existing legislation that may be needed during an event of this nature.[156]

The Report went on to say that a methodology for assessing social care requirements and surge capacity during a Pandemic be needed to be developed by the then Department of Communities and Local Government, the Department of Health, and the Directors of Adult Social Services and with the devolved administrations. The notion of 'lifting' the 'statutory restrictions' contained within the very legislation that was originally designed to protect the rights and wellbeing of citizens is notable and unusual. In the absence of such, the Report argued, 'there might be 100s of vulnerable people who won't get the help that they want or need and won't be identified'.[157] The very use of the term 'easement' is striking. This is a technical legal term in English Land Law concerning certain specific rights benefiting one piece of land over another piece of land; for example, a right of way.[158] Its introduction into adult social care policy is something which may be viewed as 'novel' – it can also be viewed as incongruous and inappropriate given that the intention was ultimately the introduction of legal change.

In February 2018 there was a meeting of the National Security Council, chaired by the then Prime Minister Theresa May. Those attending included the then Secretary of State for Health, Jeremy Hunt, along with Boris Johnson as Foreign Secretary, Amber Rudd as Home Secretary, Katherine Hammond, the Director of the Civil Contingencies Secretariat, and Dame Sally Davies, the Chief Medical Officer.[159] The meeting had followed a discussion by the Cabinet of the National Risk Assessment. The minutes of this meeting note that:

> The purpose was to consider the highest priority risks faced by the UK and the general level of preparedness for them. Pandemic influenza was the greatest risk, and it was right to focus on this in light of the lessons from a major exercise in 2016.[160]

---

[156] Public Health England (2017), pp 7–8, point 2.
[157] Public Health England (2017), A.5, p 24.
[158] See *Re Ellenborough Park* [1955] EWCA Civ 4.
[159] NSC (THRC)(17)01 Meeting – this document appears in the bundle of documents disclosed to and made publicly available by the UK COVID-19 Inquiry NO INQ 00012805.
[160] NSC (THRC)(17)01 Meeting.

In the minutes, Jeremy Hunt is quoted as saying that:

> Exercise Cygnus had been a significant test of the country's readiness for a severe pandemic influenza strain, and there were three important lessons to learn. First, the plans for responding to an influenza pandemic should reflect the need for decisions to be taken at the right level. For example, it was not appropriate for the Government to interfere with local clinical decision-making concerning access to hospital care. Second, the preparation of a Pandemic Flu Bill would help to take the various legislative measures to streamline and augment capacity in health and other services. Third, the country's capacity to manage excess deaths needed to be improved.[161]

Actions from this meeting included that both the Department of Health and the Civil Contingencies Secretariat would take forward a programme of work, alongside the relevant departments, which would include:

> a draft Pandemic Flu Bill; scalable options for dealing with excess deaths; work on the implications (including legal) of differential decision-making across the UK; consideration of what more radical measures to control transmission might be effective and support departments in fulfilling their responsibility for the resilience of the sectors they represent to the risk of pandemic influenza.[162]

The subsequent cross-government multi-sectoral Pandemic Flu work programme was undertaken with the intention to develop draft legislation to be used in the event of a future pandemic.[163] A specific workstream focused on 'the improvement of health and care sector plans to flex systems and resources to expand beyond normal capacity levels'.[164] A further Pandemic Influenza briefing paper, focused on 'adult social care and community health care', was released in June 2018; it contained planning recommendations for the Chief Medical Officer, Chief Scientific Advisor, Chief Nursing Officer, and the Chief Social Worker, including 'key options and considerations to maintain and augment the community health care and adult social care

---

[161] NSC (THRC)(17)01 Meeting.
[162] NSC (THRC)(17)01 Meeting.
[163] Written evidence provided by H.M. Government (20 July 2020), at https://committees.parliament.uk/writtenevidence/10701/html. At the time of writing, only a table of contents has been made publicly available through the UK COVID-19 Inquiry: UK COVID 19 Inquiry - INQ000023118_0001-0003 – Extract of Draft Pandemic Influenza (Emergency) Bill, dated 21/01/2020.
[164] H.M. Government (20 July 2020).

sectors' response to an extreme influenza pandemic'.¹⁶⁵ ADASS, among other professional representatives from the sector, was asked by the Department of Health to support its pandemic planning work through the provision of strategic adult social care expertise.¹⁶⁶ (ADASS had already been involved in a several of contingency planning exercises involving the Department of Health and Social Care.¹⁶⁷) A number of briefing papers were produced by ADASS for the Department of Health and Social Care.¹⁶⁸ One of these papers identified the types of 'regulatory and standards easements' that Directors of Adult Social Services might require in order to manage the reprioritization of needs and the delivery of services, in 'implementing the least worst options and decisions'.¹⁶⁹ Such planned easements were to include briefer needs assessments for determining eligibility for services, 'followed by reviews as 'where necessary' (rather than according to the standard schedule).¹⁷⁰ Similar suggestions for easements were also made by the Care Providers Alliance and the Home Care Association UK (UKHCA).¹⁷¹ The crucial monitoring and quality assurance role of the CQC, alongside DASSs and local authority commissioners, was emphasized throughout as 'vital to manage any easements and monitor care quality in a controlled and

---

[165] 'Pandemic Influenza briefing paper: Adult social care and community health care' (2018), p 5, at www.leighday.co.uk/media/gilfgpwy/pandemic-influenza-briefing-paper-adult-social-care-and-community-health-care.pdf, accessed 2 July 2024.

[166] ADASS (2018) 'Proposals to support Directors of Adult Social Care and local areas to prepare now for a future flu pandemic'; see also Williams, C. (2022) 'First Witness Statement of Cathie Williams Chief Executive of the Director of Adult Social Services Local Government Association, In The Matter of Module 1 of The UK COVID-19 Public Inquiry14 December 2022'.

[167] See further Williams (2022) who cites the following at p 6:
- 'Exercise Mercury June 2016 – examined the failure of a large domiciliary care provider – ADASS involved
- Exercise Thorne 2018 – led by DHSC – explored the failure of a large social care provider. ADASS involved
- Exercise Fulcrum 2018 – explored the commercial failure of large adult social care providers. ADASS involved. The resulted in PHE publishing its report in February 2019'.

[168] See further Williams (2022).

[169] ADASS (2018) *A Report Identifying the Regulatory and Process Easements that DASSs Require to Manage the Reprioritisation of Needs and Delivery of Services in a Future Pandemic Flu Response*, April, p 4.

[170] ADASS (2018) *A Report Identifying the Regulatory and Process Easements that DASSs Require to Manage the Reprioritisation of Needs and Delivery of Services in a Future Pandemic Flu Response*, April, para 5.3 and recommendation 7.

[171] ADASS (2018) *A Report Identifying the Regulatory and Process Easements that DASSs Require to Manage the Reprioritisation of Needs and Delivery of Services in a Future Pandemic Flu Response*, April, p 10.

measured way'.[172] The need for a clear communication strategy transmitting from national through to local level, and utilizing social media channels, was emphasized.[173] While the importance of communication was stressed in this preparatory work, the transmission of information and messaging concerning legislative easements and other operational changes during the early stages of the COVID-19 pandemic was problematic in several areas, as will be shown in the following chapters. After this planning exercise, the ADASS documents were left as resource material to be drawn upon by DASSs amid post-EU-referendum fears of a No Deal Brexit, 'as much of the material was transferable in terms of service continuity'.[174]

While the National Security Council sub-committee met and considered the strategy after Exercise Cygnus it appears that that committee was not operational in the early stages of COVID-19. In December 2020, the House of Commons and House of Lords Joint Committee on the National Security Strategy stated in their report on biosecurity and national security that:

> There is a striking absence of leadership of the UK's biological security as a whole. Neither the National Security Council (NSC) nor the Cabinet Office provided strategic leadership in this area. The NSC sub-committee to which Government departments with responsibilities in this field are supposed to report was not re-established in this Parliament, and the auditing of departmental preparations is weak. There was only one 'tier-1' national health crisis exercise in the last decade ('Exercise Cygnus' in 2016), and this did not test important areas that were known to be critical (including Detection capabilities).[175]

They went on to state that:

> The lessons of exercises that do take place are not fully shared: the Biological Security Strategy made no mention of Cygnus, despite being published two years later. Frontline organisations – local authorities, emergency responders and Local Resilience Forums – have sometimes

---

[172] ADASS (2018) *A Report Identifying the Regulatory and Process Easements that DASSs Require to Manage the Reprioritisation of Needs and Delivery of Services in a Future Pandemic Flu Response*, April, p 10.

[173] ADASS (2018) *The Communications and Support Infrastructure Required by DASSs to Support Them Communicating Service Reprioritisation in a Future Pandemic Flu Response*, April.

[174] ADASS (2018) website guide for pandemic flu planning.

[175] House of Commons and House of Lords Joint Committee on the National Security Strategy (2020) *Biosecurity and national security*. First Report of Session 2019–21, HC 611, HL 195, 18 December, p 3.

lacked the intelligence information and support they need from central government to carry out their role effectively.[176]

A further issue highlighted in the UK COVID-19 Inquiry Module 1 Report in 2024 was that of vulnerability. In Chapter 2 we saw how vulnerability can be viewed as a contested paradigm in relation to adult social care. One issue highlighted subsequently in the Module I Inquiry Report in 2024 was the lack of engagement in the risk assessment process with people who were 'vulnerable'. The Report noted the National Risk Assessment which had been undertaken in 2019 and went on to state that

> The risk assessment system overseen by the Civil Contingencies Secretariat and the Department of Health and Social Care did not sufficiently take into account factors – beyond age and clinical vulnerability – that might make particular sections of the population especially susceptible to a pathogen outbreak. The full scenario assessment for an influenza-type disease pandemic included only a short section on the 'impact on vulnerable groups' ... It was too narrowly drawn and had too limited focus on the impact on public services and staff capacity.[177]

It went on to comment as to the limitations of other guidance documents produced since 2006, the way in which they addressed vulnerability issues and how: 'The definitions of vulnerability in both the statutory and non-statutory guidance produced by the Cabinet Office were too vague to have any utility.'[178] We return to examine issues of vulnerability and adult social care at the time of the pandemic in subsequent chapters.

In the period 2015–2019 alone, no fewer than 11 multi-agency pandemic simulation and preparedness tests were staged by the UK Government; this does not include smaller regional or sector-specific tests.[179] The resulting pre-pandemic preparedness structures have since been described as 'much more like a bowl of spaghetti than a clear and coordinated framework for a cogent national response'.[180] This complex structure was subsequently

---

[176] House of Commons and House of Lords Joint Committee on the National Security Strategy (2020), p 3.
[177] UK COVID-19 Inquiry (2024), para 3.57.
[178] UK COVID-19 Inquiry (2024), para 3.61.
[179] Leigh Day (2021), 'Eleven pandemic simulation exercises were staged between 2015–19', 10 June.
[180] Lawyer for the Trades Union Congress to Baroness Heather Hallett in the first week of the UK COVID-19 Inquiry, June 2023. Reported in R. Booth (2023) '"A bowl of spaghetti": COVID inquiry opens with flowchart on UK's pandemic planning', *The Guardian*, 13 June.

highlighted in the UK COVID-19 Inquiry Module 1 Report.[181] Notably, however, in the period prior to the Coronavirus Act 2020 there had been clear and substantial engagement with adult social care stakeholders regarding key pandemic planning issues, and this made subsequent claims about a lack of awareness among professionals across the sector somewhat puzzling.

III. The COVID-19 pandemic, the Coronavirus Act 2020, and Care Act 'easements'

(a) From Wuhan to the Coronavirus Act 2020

On 31 December 2019, the China Office of the WHO was informed by Chinese authorities of the detection of pneumonia from an 'unknown cause' in Wuhan City.[182] The genetic sequencing of the condition known as severe acute respiratory syndrome coronavirus was made available by the Chinese authorities on 12 January 2020, followed by notification of the first deaths in Wuhan, which by 27 January 2020 had grown to 80. On 30 January 2020 the WHO declared a Public Health Emergency of International Concern.[183] In early 2020, emergency pandemic planning proceeded apace, in the UK though it appeared that not everyone fully recognized the seriousness of the situation. On 12 February 'Exercise Nimbus' was held in COBR, as a ministerial exercise chaired by the then Secretary of State for Health and Social Care, Matt Hancock.[184] The written evidence of Dr Ben Warner to the COVID-19 Inquiry explains that Exercise Nimbus involved forward projection to envisage how this uncertain situation might progress in the coming months: 'The objective of the meeting was to expose ministers to decisions they might be expected to take during a Pandemic in the reasonably worst case scenario. The exercise was taking place on the 14th of April 2020.'[185]

Initially in the UK, the introduction of coronavirus regulations by Hancock in February 2020, gave the government powers, including Regulation 3 whereby it could issue a serious and imminent threat declaration in a situation

---

[181] UK COVID-19 Inquiry (2024), p 18.

[182] See discussion in J. Farrar with A. Ahuja (2021) *Spike: The Virus v the People: The Inside Story*, London: Profile Books; A. Wagner *Emergency State: How we lost our freedoms in the Pandemic and Why it Matters*.

[183] WHO (2023) Coronavirus Disease (COVID-19) Pandemic: Overview.

[184] As confirmed in Scottish Government. Exercise Nimbus: FOI reference FOI/202300362536, Information request and response under the Freedom of Information (Scotland) Act 2002. Published 25 July 2023.

[185] Evidence of Dr Ben Warner to the COVID-19 Inquiry (2023), para 33. See also Public Health England (2020) Summary Note on Exercise Nimbus Novel Coronavirus Preparation, 12 February, COVID-19 Inquiry paper INQ000273915_001.

in which the incidence or transmission of Coronavirus is at such a point that the measures outlined in the regulations may reasonably be considered as an effective means of preventing the further, significant transmission of Coronavirus.[186]

This was then superseded by the Coronavirus Act 2020.

By March 2020 the UK was in the shadow of the COVID-19 developments elsewhere in Europe; notably, the tragedy in the Italian city of Bergamo, which filled the news channels.[187] The first COVID-19 death in the UK was reported on 5 March, and on 11 March the WHO stated that COVID-19 was now a global pandemic.[188] The modelling in the UK demonstrated that the country faced the prospect of hundreds of thousands of deaths if the Government did not act.[189] On 3 March 2020 the Department of Health and Social Care (DHSC) published a policy paper, titled 'Coronavirus action plan: a guide to what you can expect across the UK'.[190] It stated that:

> There is similarity between COVID-19 and influenza (both are respiratory infections), but also some important differences. Consequently, contingency plans developed for pandemic influenza, and lessons learned from previous outbreaks, provide a useful starting point for the development of an effective response plan to COVID-19.
>
> That plan has been adapted, however, to take account of differences between the two diseases.[191]

The plan proposed measures to 'contain' the existing spread, to 'delay' the onset of an 'epidemic' where this was regarded as 'inevitable' to mitigate, and to engage in research, into confirmation of testing and into vaccines, and so on.[192] The UK COVID-19 Module 1 Inquiry Report in July 2024 stated that

> As is being examined in Module 2 of this Inquiry, the 2011 Strategy was never in fact properly tested. When the pandemic struck, the

---

[186] Health Protection (Coronavirus) Regulations 2020, s 3(1). See also Wagner (2022), p 39.
[187] J. Horovitz and F. Bucciarelli (2020) 'The Lost Days That Made Bergamo a Coronavirus Tragedy: Behind the Curve', *The New York Times*, 29 November.
[188] Wagner (2022), p 43; WHO (2020) 'WHO Director-General's opening remarks at the media briefing on COVID-19', 11 March.
[189] Wagner (2022), p 53.
[190] DHSC (2020) *Coronavirus action plan: a guide to what you can expect across the UK*, 3 March.
[191] DHSC (2020) *Coronavirus action plan: a guide to what you can expect across the UK*.
[192] DHSC (2020), *Coronavirus action plan: a guide to what you can expect across the UK*, s 4.

UK government did not adapt the 2011 Strategy. The doctrine that underpinned it (ie to respond to the emergency as opposed to prevent it from happening) was effectively abandoned, as was the 2011 Strategy itself. Mr Hancock explained this was because it was, in his words, 'woefully inadequate'.[193]

Instead a lockdown approach was subsequently instituted and Local Resilience Forums were alerted. On 10 March 2020 it was reported that then Housing and Communities Secretary Robert Jenrick had established a task force with the aim of reviewing Resilience Plans. There were reports in the *Sunday Times* on 15 March 2020 that 'Local Resilience Forums were screaming for help'.[194] By 16 March 2020, 38 members of non-uniform military personnel had been deployed, one to each Local Resilience Forum, in order to assist local areas in strategic planning.[195] On 23 March 2020, using an 'urgent power' in the Public Health (Control of Diseases) Act 1984, the first UK lockdown came into force.[196]

As noted previously, the intention following the National Security Committee meeting had been to produce a draft Pandemic Influenza Bill. This was developed, it is believed, in the period between 2016 and 2020 by the Westminster Government and those in the devolved administrations, along with other stakeholders, 'to be used in the event of a future influenza pandemic, set out the legislative easements required to support local and national response activities, as recommended in one of the 4 key learnings from Exercise Cygnus'.[197] This appears to have formed the basis of the Coronavirus Act 2020.

This Bill has not – at the time of writing, in summer 2024 – been published in full. However, a table of contents was published as part of the tranche of documents released by the UK COVID-19 Inquiry in 2023.[198] This table of contents follows the same approach as was taken in the Coronavirus Act 2020. Interestingly there is some evidence of scrutiny of the Bill in February 2020. A news report on 27 February 2020 stated that the Education Committee of the devolved Stormont Government in Northern Ireland had

---

[193] UK COVID-19 Inquiry (2024), para 4.54.
[194] J. Hill (2020) 'Military planners tasked with assisting local virus response', *Local Government Chronicle*, 16 March.
[195] J. Hill (2020).
[196] J. Brown and E. Kirk-Wade (2022) *A History of Lockdown Laws in England*, House of Commons Library, 22 December.
[197] DHSC (2020) UK Pandemic Preparedness Policy Paper (updated 5 November); see also Wagner (2022), p 50.
[198] See H.M. Government (2020) Pandemic Influenza (Emergency) Bill, 1–3. Draft issued to UK COVID-19 Inquiry, dated 21 January 2020. INQ000023118_1-3.

been due to receive a briefing on the draft Pandemic Influenza Bill, which was then cancelled at short notice.[199] Subsequently, on 17 March 2020, the 'Coronavirus Bill' itself was published in draft form. The provisions of the eventual legislation, the Coronavirus Act 2020, built upon the approach taken in the cumulative recommendations of the preparedness exercises as previously discussed.

The Coronavirus Act 2020 was given Royal Assent on 25 March 2020 and came into force on 31 March 2020. The focus here is the approach taken in England; different legislation was applicable across the devolved jurisdictions.[200] As initially drafted, the Coronavirus Act would have been in force for a period of two years before it could have been reviewed by Parliament.[201] This was criticized by parliamentarians and civil society bodies, and the Bill was consequently amended to require that the Coronavirus Act 2020 needed to be authorized every six months by Parliament.[202] There was a 'sunset clause' by which the provisions of the Act would automatically expire after two years of the Act's passing, though under sections 89 and 90, certain provisions could be expired by ministers, following debate in Parliament during the week following the end of a six-monthly review.[203]

The emergency legislation was rushed through in haste.[204] Hidalgo et al undertook a review of Hansard debates on the Act and found that in relation to the Westminster Parliament there had only been 19 hours and 40 minutes of debate in total on the Coronavirus Bill during its passage through the House of Commons and House of Lords.[205] The legislation was discussed through what are known as 'Legislative Consent Motions' in the legislative assemblies of the devolved jurisdictions.[206]

There was no formal risk or impact assessment carried out in advance of the Coronavirus Act 2020. Instead, there was only a brief summary of

---

[199] S. McBride (2020) 'Government stays silent on draft coronavirus pandemic emergency bill after Belfast meeting cancelled', *The Independent*, 27 February.

[200] J. Sargeant (2020) *Co-ordination and divergence. Devolution and coronavirus*, Institute for Government, IfG Insight, October.

[201] See discussion in A. Greene (2020) *Emergency Powers in a Time of Pandemic*, Bristol: Bristol University Press, p 98.

[202] Coronavirus Act 2020, ss 89–90. See further discussion of the appropriateness of this as a time frame in Greene (2020) pp 99–101.

[203] See further F. Davis and G. Cowie (2020) *Coronavirus Bill: what is the sunset clause provision?*, House of Commons Library Insight (20 March).

[204] See further Greene (2020) *Emergency Powers in a Time of Pandemic*, p 99.

[205] P.G. Hidalgo, F. de Londras and D. Lock (2022) 'Parliament, the pandemic and the constitutional principle in the United Kingdom: a study of the Coronavirus Act 2020', *Modern Law Review*, 85(6): 1463–503, p 1467.

[206] See further P.G. Hidalgo et al (2022), pp 1481–8.

possible impacts and policy alternatives associated with the Act: 'As this is temporary, emergency legislation, a formal impact assessment is not required for Better Regulation purposes.'[207]

In a rare direct reference to the rationale behind the provision of the Care Act easements the Coronavirus Bill 'Summary of Impacts' published in March 2020 stated that:

> Without these provisions, LAs would be constrained by existing assessments, which could result in them maintaining these at the expense of new, more urgent needs, or prevent them from allocating scarce support purely on the basis of severity of need. Such decisions could be inhibited by the fear of legal challenge under the Care Act or, once taken, could become subject to such challenge, consuming resources at a critical time. Concerns around legal challenge could cause LAs to delay the prioritisation process beyond the point of viability, resulting in poor decision making and worse outcomes than if they were given the legal space to take strategic decisions around prioritisation ... these clauses should not in themselves cause LAs to reduce their adult social care offer as (at the point of triggering) this would be an imminent risk regardless of any legislative easements made by the government. However, the policy intent of these clauses is to give LAs cover to make this reduction in the most planned, prioritised way possible.[208]

A number of the provisions of the Coronavirus Act 2020 enabled local authorities to depart from various provisions of the Care Act 2014, under the direction of the Secretary of State.[209] Returning to the parts of the Coronavirus Act 2020 which altered existing social care laws, section 15 concerned provisions regarding local authority care and support. This needed to be read in conjunction with Schedule 12 of the Act, as well as the supporting Guidance documents discussed previously. Schedule 12 set out a series of provisions which modified aspects of the Care Act 2014. Notably, while the term 'easement' had been extensively utilized in pre-COVID pandemic planning documentation, it did not ultimately appear

---

[207] Department of Health and Social Care (2020) *Impact Assessment. Coronavirus Bill: Summary of Impacts* (updated 23 March).

[208] DHSC (2020) *Impact Assessment. Coronavirus Bill: Summary of Impact* at NHS and local authority care and support: Key considerations.

[209] Note also that general emergency guidance was provided to local authorities at this time: Local Government Association (2020) 'Emergency response structures during the COVID-19 pandemic. Councillor guidance', May.

in the Coronavirus Act 2020; this was unsurprising given its very specific meaning in the context of Land Law.

Schedule 12 of the Act effectively eased some of the mandatory duties and obligation incumbent on local authorities, and their social services staff, under the Care Act 2014.[210] It provided that local authorities did not have to comply with duties in relation to assessing an adult's needs for care and support;[211] assessment of a carer's needs for support;[212] or duties to provide written records of those assessments.[213] In addition, the local authority was no longer required to comply with the duty to determine whether a person's needs met the eligibility criteria under section 13 of the Care Act 2014.[214] They were still able to undertake assessments/determinations if they thought this appropriate.[215] Local authorities were also not required to comply with the duties of notification and assessment under section 37 of the Care Act 2014 where a person moves to a new local authority area or under section 38 of the Care Act 2014 where assessments are not complete on the day of the move. This marked a radical revision of standard social work obligations and practices.

Local authorities were also not required to comply with duties under section 17 of the Care Act 2014 regarding the assessment of an individual's financial resources.[216] If the local authority provided services during the emergency period under sections 18, 19, 20, or 62 of the Care Act 2014, and would have been entitled to charge for those services but decided at that time not to undertake an assessment under section 17 of the Act, it would be able to subsequently undertake that assessment and make a retrospective charge for meeting those needs during that period.[217] As Sloan notes, 'some users may be surprised to be faced with charges after the event and the giving "reasonable information in advance" about this (as the Guidance puts it) is particularly important'.[218]

Another controversial aspect of the measures in the 2020 Act relates to the amendments made to section 18 of the Care Act 2014 which sets out the duties imposed upon local authorities to meet the needs for adult care

---

[210] Coronavirus Act 2020, Sch 12, para 2(1).
[211] Duty imposed by Care Act 2014, s 9.
[212] Duty imposed by Care Act 2014, s 10.
[213] Care Act 2014, s 12(3)(4) duties, and consequently the duty under s 11 of the Care Act 2014 relating to refusal of assessment also did not apply.
[214] Coronavirus Act 2020, Sch 12(2).
[215] Coronavirus Act 2020, Sch 12(4).
[216] Coronavirus Act 2020, Sch 12, para 3.
[217] Coronavirus Act 2020, Sch 12, para 10(2).
[218] B. Sloan (2021) '"Easing" duties and making dignity difficult: COVID-19 and the Care Act 2014', *Public Law*, 37.

and support if people meet the eligibility criteria. Schedule 12, paragraph 4 of the Coronavirus Act 2020 provided that:

> Section 18 of CA 2014 (duty to meet needs for care and support) has effect as if for subsection (1) there were substituted—
>
> (1) A local authority must meet an adult's needs for care and support if—
>   (a) the adult is ordinarily resident in the authority's area or is present in its area but of no settled residence,
>   (b) the authority considers that it is necessary to meet those needs for the purpose of avoiding a breach of the adult's Convention rights, and
>   (c) there is no charge under section 14 for meeting the needs or, in so far as there is, condition 1, 2 or 3 is met.
>
> In this subsection 'Convention rights' has the same meaning as in the Human Rights Act 1998.

Similar amendments were made to section 20 of the Care Act 2014, which sets out the obligation to meet carer's needs for support.[219] This meant that in relation to the obligation to meet needs for care and support, the existing provisions were amended to increase the level of discretion for local authorities.

The 2020 Act amendments to Sections 18 and 20 the Care Act provided that needs had to be met if this was necessary to avoid constituting a breach of a person's rights as stated under the European Convention on Human Rights (ECHR) provisions, which form part of domestic law under the Human Rights Act 1998.[220] Moreover, the statutory Guidance stated that once the period in which the easements were operational came to an end, a full needs assessment would need to be undertaken.[221] The legislation thus did not depart from the baseline human rights requirements. The Government could have decided to undertake a derogation from specific human rights provisions under Article 15 of the ECHR.[222] Indeed, it was suggested in 2020 that the COVID-19 pandemic would indeed constitute a 'public emergency' which might 'threaten the life of the nation' for the

---

[219] Coronavirus Act 2020, Sch 12, para 6.
[220] Human Rights Act 1998.
[221] B. Sloan (2021) '"Easing" duties and making dignity difficult: COVID-19 and the Care Act 2014', *Public Law*, 37 and Health and Social Care (2020) *Care Act Easements: Guidance to Local Authorities* (updated 29 June 2021), s 4.
[222] See further in relation to derogation powers and human rights the discussion in Greene (2020), ch 2 (concerning non-derogable rights) and ch 3 (concerning derogable rights).

purposes of a derogation under Article 15 but it did not take this course, opting instead to lower the thresholds for emergency action or the easing of standard protocols.[223] Greene has suggested that:

> Failure to declare a state of emergency – and instead attempting to accommodate emergency powers through the ordinary parameters of normalcy – risks normalising these exceptional powers. It risks permanently recalibrating human rights norms downwards without the quarantining effect of a de jure declaration of a state of emergency.[224]

He correctly goes on to highlight, however, that one of the challenges of the use of Article 15 is the question of whether it is an effective means of scrutiny; moreover, in the past the European Court of Human Rights (ECtHR) in general has been unwilling to override the approach taken in practice at national level in an emergency situation. At the same time, he notes that the courts have tended, regardless of a formal declaration of a state of emergency, to be deferential to states in such situations.[225] The use of a formal power of derogation may provide a better means of holding governments to account rather than the risk of leaving matters, as Greene suggests, to judicial scrutiny 'so light touch that it might as well be non-existent'.[226]

The supporting legislative Guidance produced for local authorities emphasized that these amendments to the Care Act provisions were temporary, and only to be used as a last resort 'where this is essential in order to maintain the highest possible level of services. They should comply with the pre-amendment Care Act provisions and related Care and Support Statutory Guidance for as long and as far as possible'.[227] As we shall see later, there are notable tensions between what was publicly declared as statutory amendments and what happened at local authority level. In addition, the 2020 Act provided that local authorities did not have to comply with a series of duties in relation to the preparation and review of care and support plans or of care plans under sections 24–5 and section 27(1), (4), (4A), and (5) of the 2014 Act.[228]

---

[223] See discussion in *BP v Surrey CC* [2020] EWCOP, and discussion in S. Vicary, K. Stone, P. McCusker, G. Davidson, and T. Spencer-Lane (2020) ' "It's about how much we can do and not how little we can get away with": coronavirus-related legislative changes for social care in the United Kingdom', *International Journal of Law and Psychiatry*, 72: 15–16.

[224] See Greene (2020), p 90.

[225] See, for example, A. Greene (2021) 'Falling at the first hurdle? *Terhes v Romania*: lockdowns and normalising the exception', *Strasbourg Observers*.

[226] Greene (2021).

[227] DHSC (2021) *Care Act Easements: Guidance to Local Authorities* (updated 29 June).

[228] See Sch 12, para 11.

During the debates on the Coronavirus Act 2020 in Westminster, as Hidalgo et al comment, members of both the House of Commons and House of Lords had raised concerns that the amendments to the Care Act 'would violate the rights of the elderly and those with disabilities'.[229] As they note, the Government did not support any amendments to the changes, although reassurances were given by Lord Bethell that the Westminster Government 'would "do everything" it could to "meet all needs". Notably Munira Wilson (Liberal Democrat) requested clarification as to the threshold for triggering the powers, and no response was given by the Government'.[230]

While the legislation incorporated specific reference to the ECHR in section 18 which can effectively be seen as a 'floor' beneath which services should not drop, the real-life utility of this provision has been questioned. First, as Sloan comments, the

> legal significance of this distinction is presumably limited, since a legal authority as a 'public authority' would remain bound by Convention rights as judicially and objectively determined through the Human Rights Act 1998. Its effect in practice may nevertheless be considerable in deterring challenges to local authority action or inaction.[231]

Sloan suggests that the applicability of the ECHR in this context may be limited, noting the case of *McDonald v UK*,[232] although, for example, failure to assess needs and provide requisite services in the case of *R (Bernard) v Enfield LBC* led to a successful challenge in relation to Article 8 of the ECHR, the right to privacy of home and family life.[233] The Coronavirus Act 2020 did retain the Care Act 2014's broad and far-reaching wellbeing principle,[234] though even during the implementation of the 2014 legislation 'the Government admitted that the principle was not designed to require a Local Authority to "undertake any particular action in ... itself"'.[235] In practice, responsiveness to the various facets of wellbeing were discretionary

---

[229] Hidalgo et al (2022) 'Parliament, the pandemic and the constitutional principle in the United Kingdom: a study of the Coronavirus Act 2020'.
[230] Hidalgo et al (2022), p 1477.
[231] B. Sloan (2021) '"Easing" duties and making dignity difficult: COVID-19 and the Care Act 2014', *Public Law*, 37.
[232] *McDonald v United Kingdom* (2015) 60 EHRR 1.
[233] *R (Bernard) v Enfield LBC* [2002] EWHC Admin; see further L. Clements, with K. Ashton, S. Garlick, C. Goodall, E. Mitchell and A. Pickup (2019) *Community Care and the Law*, London: Legal Action Group, ch 2.
[234] Department for Health and Social Care (2020) (2024) Care and Support Statutory Guidance at Chapter 1 'Promoting Wellbeing'.
[235] B. Sloan (2021); see also re the application of the ECHR, A. Ruck-Keene (2020) 'Capacity at the time of coronavirus', *International Journal of Law and Psychiatry*, 70: 101560.

and contingent on local context and allocation of limited resources.[236] Further, 'one of the ways in which the principle was invoked before the 2020 Act was as part of the needs assessment duty, which the Act disapplies in addition to the national eligibility threshold. So precious little comfort is likely to be gained from that principle either.'[237]

In any case, the specific reference to the ECHR threshold did not in practice mean that those rights would necessarily be understood or effectively safeguarded given uncertainties as to what such provisions mean. Harding and Taşcıoğlu's research indicates the limited understanding that care professionals may have of human rights law,[238] even at times when there is no extraordinary health crisis or emergency legislation to navigate. This concern was echoed by the British Institute of Human Rights, in a survey undertaken during 2020 which found that

- Over 82% of people working in health and care who responded to our call for evidence told us it has been harder to uphold human rights during COVID-19.
- Over 76% of people working in health and care who responded to our call for evidence told us that during COVID-19 they were not provided with legal training or clear information about upholding human rights law.
- Over 79% of people working in health and care who responded to our call for evidence told us that during COVID-19 they were not provided with legal training or clear information about the use of Emergency Powers under the Coronavirus Act (CVA).[239]

All qualified social workers registered to practice in the UK are required to know and understand the Care Act 2014, as well as other relevant legislation that protects the rights of citizens, though there are inevitable knowledge gaps in practice.[240] Legislative changes that directly affected the operation and person-centred values of social work practice contributed

---

[236] C. Slasberg and P. Beresford (2014) 'Government guidance for the Care Act: undermining ambitions for change?', *Disability & Society*, 29(10): 1677–82.

[237] Sloan (2021).

[238] R. Harding and E. Taşcıoğlu (2017), 'Everyday Decisions Project: Supporting Legal Capacity Through Care, Support and Encouragement', at www.legalcapacity.org.uk/research-findings, accessed 10 July 2024; see also R. Harding (2021) 'COVID-19 in adult social care', in D. Cowan and A. Mumford (eds) *Pandemic Legalities Legal Responses to COVID-19 Justice and Social Responsibility*, Bristol: Bristol University Press.

[239] BIHR (2020) Written evidence from the British Institute of Human Rights "COVO236 p 1 and pp 17–20.

[240] A.J. Jenkinson and J. Chamberlain (2019) 'Social workers' knowledge and skills and the Care Act: Practice Advice Note', November.

to the negative impacts on social workers' mental health and wellbeing experienced during the pandemic.²⁴¹ Antova queried whether the application of the Care Act easements was a proportionate response and argued that the emergency legislation undermined the core principles of social work and social care law:

> From a broader disability perspective the nature of the CA 2020 suggests that the Government has deviated from the person-centred approach evident in the Care Act 2014. Overall, the approach of the CA 2020 is to conceptualise disabled people's entitlement as collateral damage meaning the approach allows for disabled people's. rights to be rolled back to alleviate the social care system of the burden imposed by COVID-19.²⁴²

As we saw in Chapter 3, the implementation of adult social care law is often challenging and subject to varying interpretations, local variables, and financial limitations, even without the disruption of a public health crisis. Critically, there are inbuilt degrees of discretion in relation to aspects of the provision of care and support under section 8 of the Care Act 2014. Rather than specifying precisely the services which must be provided to meet needs, the section rather presents a list of examples. This format can in itself be seen to facilitate degrees of 'flexibilities' regarding the manner in which the legislation can be interpreted and implemented, according to context, suitability, and the availability of increasingly scarce resources. This is relevant when considering how local authority staff may have interpreted the various 'stages' of easement detailed in the DHSC Guidance concerning Care Act easements. We turn to this issue in the following section of the chapter.

(b) Implementing Care Act easements: guidance and ethical framework

The Care Act Easement Guidance provided four 'stages' or categories of easement in ascending order of seriousness and scope, with 'Stage 4' being the most extensive departure from Business as Usual. The first two stages involved some 'flexing' of pre-existing Care Act provisions and obligations. This meant that local authorities could, for example, alter the manner in

---

[241] J. MacLochlainn et al (2023) 'The COVID-19 pandemic's impact on UK older people's social workers: a mixed-methods study', *British Journal of Social Work*, BCAD139; see also M. Baginsky et al (2023) 'Changing English local authority duties by the adoption of easements in the COVID-19 pandemic: findings from an interview-based study', *British Journal of Social Work*, 53(2): 939.

[242] I. Antova (2020) 'Disability rights during COVID-19: emergency law and guidelines in England', *Medical Law Review*, 28(4): 804.

which some services were delivered by moving from face-to-face to online or telephone contacts, or by simplifying assessment or review protocols. If either of the higher two stages were reached, the local authority would be formally operating under Care Act easements. While the Guidance set out recommendations for the conditions under which local authority officers could or should activate an easement to their Care Act obligations, only actions taken under Stages 3 and 4 required formal notification to the DHSC.[243]

> **Stage 1:** 'Business as usual', with the directive to 'continue at this stage for as long as is feasible'
> **Stage 2:** 'Applying flexibilities' under the pre-amendment Care Act 'to prioritise short term allocation of care and support using current flexibilities within the Care Act … Where COVID-19-related absence means service types need to be changed, delayed or cancelled short term within that service type'
> **Stage 3:** 'Streamlining services under Care Act easements', whereby local authorities can cease formal Care Act assessments, applications of eligibility and reviews … though 'there is an expectation in the Act that local authorities will do everything they can to continue to meet need as was originally set out in the Care Act'
> **Stage 4:** Prioritisation under Care Act easements: 'Whole system prioritising care and support', which effectively meant rationing, re-allocation of resources across adult social care services and, as last resort, withdrawal of some services.[244]

As noted, Stages 3 and 4 were the formal Care Act easement stages. Data from the interviews we undertook for the Economic and Social Research Council (ESRC) COVID-19 rapid response project suggest that there was a sense of ambiguity around the boundaries of each stage, and scope for individual or contested interpretation about the thresholds for when activities and practices at operational level might tip from one stage into another. This sense of confusion and ambiguity about the Stages was echoed in related research elsewhere.[245]

---

[243] Department of Health and Social Care (2020) Care Act Easements: Guidance for Local Authorities Annex A, s 4.

[244] Department of Health and Social Care (2020) *Care Act Easements: Guidance for Local Authorities*, Annex A, s 4.

[245] See, for example, J.V. McHale and L. Noszlopy (2021) *Adult Social Care Provision under Pressure: Lessons from the Pandemic*, Research Report, Birmingham: University of Birmingham; M. Baginsky, E. Thomas and J. Manthorpe (2023) 'Reasons for not adopting COVID-19 permitted changes to legal duties: accounts from English local authorities',

As noted previously, the ECHR provisions provided a floor in relation to meeting the needs of service users and carers. The Guidance for local authorities stated that:

> Local authorities will remain under a duty to meet needs where failure to do so would breach an individual's human rights under the European Convention on Human Rights (ECHR). These include, for example, the right to life under Article 2 of the ECHR, the right to freedom from inhuman and degrading treatment under Article 3 and the right to private and family life under Article 8.[246]

And that 'sufficient care and support will have to remain in place at all times in order to ensure that the Convention rights of all those in need of care and support, and of carers, are respected'.[247]

From a reading of the Guidance, Stages 2 and Stage 3 appeared to be distinct: the former a 'flexibility' and the latter an 'easement'. In practice, as we shall see, the 'flexibilities' incorporated by some local authorities operating in Stage 2 were often referred to as 'easements' and did indeed bear a striking resemblance to Stage 3 changes. Nonetheless, there was a sense of gravity around decision-making at this stressful time, and the matter of formally activating easements was to be considered only in extremis and in response to pressing local conditions. The Guidance set out the steps which should be taken before easements were introduced:

> A local authority should only take a decision to begin exercising the Care Act easements when the workforce is significantly depleted, or demand on social care increased, to an extent that it is no longer reasonably practicable for it to comply with its Care Act duties (as they stand prior to amendment by the Coronavirus Act) and where to continue to try to do so is likely to result in urgent or acute needs not being met, potentially risking life. Any change resulting from such a decision should be proportionate to the circumstances in a particular local authority.[248]

Health & Social Care in the Community. This matter will be examined in detail, with interview excerpts from those who navigated such decisions, in Chapter 5.

[246] Department of Health and Social Care (2020) *Care Act Easements: Guidance to Local Authorities*, p 4.

[247] Department of Health and Social Care (2020) *Care Act Easements: Guidance to Local Authorities*, Annex A.

[248] Department of Health and Social Care (2020) *Care Act Easements: Guidance to Local Authorities*, p 6.

While the Guidance recognized that different local authorities have different internal structures and protocols, it made clear that the decision to activate and implement easements should nevertheless be undertaken by the Director of Adult Social Services along with the Principal Social Worker.[249] The decision should be recorded and monitored, along with the evidence taken into consideration in reaching that decision. It was suggested that:

> Where possible the record should include the following:
> The nature of the changes to demand or the workforce;
> The steps that have been taken to mitigate against the need for this to happen;
> The expected impact of the measures taken how the changes will help to avoid breaches of people's human rights at a population level;
> The individuals involved in the decision-making process; and
> The points at which this decision will be reviewed again.[250]

The DHSC Guidance included a checklist tool for assessing capacity and need,[251] though many local authorities developed their own R-A-G (Red-Amber-Green) rating systems to track the fast-changing situation, inform decision-making and, in rare cases, to trigger the use of formal easements. Many local authorities already had community resilience officers in post, working with the Local Resilience Forums, and these scrambled to assess the local situation, and sites and levels of need.

Shortly after this emergency legislation came into force, and as provided in Schedule 12, paragraph 18 of the Act itself, local authority staff received formal Guidance documents from the Department of Health and Social Care to help them interpret and implement the new protocols and specifically the Care Act easements.[252] This Guidance, although it was interpreted in a variety of ways, would prove crucial to such local level decision-making, and to local authorities' ability to balance pressures on their workforce capacity and responsiveness to strain in the NHS with the needs and rights of those they remained legally bound to support. A delicate balance was required between the exercise of centralized powers

---

[249] Department of Health and Social Care (2020) *Care Act Easements: Guidance to Local Authorities*.

[250] Department of Health and Social Care (2020) *Care Act Easements: Guidance to Local Authorities*, s 6.

[251] Department of Health and Social Care (2020) *Care Act Easements: Guidance to Local Authorities*.

[252] Department of Health and Social Care (2020) *Care Act Easements: Guidance to Local Authorities*.

and directives, and the operational expertise of local government. As the Impact Assessment Summary of the legislation stated:

> These provisions would also provide Secretary of State with a power to direct LAs to comply with Government guidance regarding the principles they should follow when prioritising care. These prioritisation decisions are complex and it is important that Local Authorities are able to use their expertise and knowledge of individuals' needs to make the right decision in each situation. However, Government guidance, and the power to direct LAs to follow this, will ensure that these decisions are underpinned by consistent principles.[253]

At national level, members of existing a social care crisis coordination committees were also mobilized to establish a National Adult Social Care (COVID-19) Group (NACG) to facilitate social care planning and determine 'how best to understand the impact of the easements'.[254] Various stakeholders in the social care sector were quickly recruited into adjunct working groups involved in drawing up the supporting Guidance with DHSC staff. These included the Association of Directors of Adult Services (ADASS), the British Association of Social Workers (BASW), Mark Harvey and Fran Leddra (who were then employed as joint-Chief Social Workers,[255] the Local Government Association (LGA), the Ministry of Housing, Communities and Local Government (MHCLG), and Think Local Act Personal (TLAP).[256] Two official Guidance documents on the Care Act easements were produced at the end of March 2020: (1) general Supporting

---

[253] Department of Health and Social Care (2020) *Impact Assessment. Coronavirus Bill: Summary of Impacts*.

[254] See Association of Directors of Adult Social Services (2020) *Themes and Learning from ADASS Members on the Local Response to COVID-19 in Spring and Early Summer 2020*, p 2; see also Institute for Government (2022) 'Timeline of UK Government coronavirus lockdowns and measures March 2020 to December 2021'.

[255] DHSC. The Report of the Chief Social Workers states that:
As CSW, we led on the development of guidance to ensure, where used, they were done so with clear decision making and oversight. Principal Social Workers were central to the decision-making process and as such ensuring that a social work perspective led local processes and had a clear voice in any decision. We ensured that the guidance was drafted with user-led, professional and sector organisations. (Chief Social Workers Annual Report 2020-21, para 3.3.1)

[256] TLAP, hosted by the Social Care Institute for Excellence, is a 'national partnership of more than 50 organisations committed to transforming health and care through personalisation and community-based support'. See www.thinklocalactpersonal.org.uk/About-us/

Guidance,²⁵⁷ and (2) Guidance for local authorities.²⁵⁸ These needed to be considered and applied in relation to existing professional codes of ethics and conduct,²⁵⁹ and the Ethical Framework for Adult Social Care, which was based on the existing Pandemic Flu Framework. The Ethical Framework was presented by the Chief Social Worker to the Moral and Ethical Advisory Group (MEAG), established in 2019, on 10 March 2020.²⁶⁰ The document was subsequently revised and published following MEAG's input.²⁶¹

The Ethical Framework for Adult Social Care could be seen as a way in which recognition of individual rights, vulnerabilities, and of fundamental issues concerning the ethics of care could be factored into social care decision-making processes, even under pressure. Through a list of eight points of principle – Respect; Reasonableness; Minimizing Harm; Inclusiveness; Accountability; Flexibility; Proportionality; and Community – the Ethical Framework sought to provide planning support and promote accountability as local authorities and the wider health and care workforce made 'difficult decisions under new and exceptional pressures with limited time, resources or information':

> Recognising increasing pressures and expected demand, it might become necessary to make challenging decisions on how to redirect resources where they are most needed and to prioritise individual care needs. This framework intends to serve as a guide for these types of decisions and reinforce that consideration of any potential harm that might be suffered, and the needs of all individuals, are always central to decision-making.²⁶²

The Ethical Framework for Social Care thus aimed to provide a principled rationale for decision-making, alongside existing regulations and professional

---

[257] www.gov.uk/government/publications/coronavirus-covid-19-changes-to-the-care-act-2014/care-act-easements-supporting-guidance

[258] Department of Health and Social Care (2021) Care Act easements: guidance for local authorities, withdrawn 22 July 2021.

[259] British Association for Social Workers (2014) *The Code of Ethics for Social Work. Statement of Principles.*

[260] Having previously been adapted from an earlier version initially developed by the Committee on Ethical Aspects of Pandemic Influenza in 2007, and later revised by the DHSC in 2017. See Department of Health and Social Care (2020) *Guidance COVID-19: ethical framework for adult social care* (withdrawn 1 April 2022) for the iteration used during the pandemic.

[261] Meeting of the Moral and Ethical Advisory Group (Meeting 1–10 March 2020), at 200310, MEAG meeting note – Moral and Ethical Advisory Group publications.

[262] Department of Health and Social Care (2020) 'Responding to COVID-19: the ethical framework for adult social care, 2020'.

codes of conduct.[263] It was developed to introduce 'a set of core ethical values and principles, which provide a structure to ensure rights and strengths-based social work values are embedded when organising and delivering adult social care'.[264] The principles of 'respect', reasonableness', and 'proportionality' are invoked in relation to the aim of 'minimising harm' and

> 'striving to reduce the amount of physical, psychological, social and economic harm that the outbreak might cause to individuals and communities. In turn, this involves ensuring that individual organisations and society as a whole cope with and recover from it to their best ability'.[265]

Decision-making must be 'inclusive', 'accountable', and 'flexible'. 'Community' (rather than 'solidarity') is also included as a principle, which seems prescient when one considers the extraordinary support role that would soon be played by third-sector organizations and volunteers, spontaneously developed mutual-aid support groups, and indeed by family, friends, and neighbours during the pandemic. It is readily acknowledged that local authorities would have faced far greater challenges without the support of the communities they serve. Consequently, the mobilization of community volunteers and groups was an integral part of the Government's post-pandemic resilience agenda.[266]

From the outset, however, there were tensions as to how this Ethical Framework might actually operate in such emergency conditions. To what extent could respect for rights, the need for care, and proper recognition of and safeguards for the elderly, disabled, or seriously unwell, be aligned with the urgent day-to-day decisions taken regarding social care provision during the pandemic? The Framework was criticized by Elves and Herring for its undue reliance on the principles of 'autonomy' and 'dignity' which they deemed to be 'at best unhelpful when it comes to aiding decision-makers deliberating on ethically fraught and practically complex care prioritisation decisions'.[267] Issues regarding the Guidance were also raised by

---

[263] Department of Health and Social Care (2020) 'Responding to COVID-19: the ethical framework for adult social care, 2020'.

[264] Department of Health and Social Care Chief Social Workers' *Annual Report 2020–2021*, para 3.1.1. See further C. Elves and J. Herring (2020) 'Ethical framework for adult social care in COVID-19', *Journal of Medical Ethics*, 46, 662.

[265] Department of Health and Social Care (2020) 'Responding to COVID-19: the ethical framework for adult social care, 2020', withdrawn 1 April 2022.

[266] Cabinet Office (2022) *The UK Government Resilience Framework*, Policy paper (updated 4 December 2023); and see also Locality (2020) *We Were Built for This: How community groups helped us through the coronavirus crisis – and how we can build a better future*. London, June.

[267] Elves and Herring (2020), p 665.

practitioners in the BASW Adults Social Work Group who were concerned about a lack of guidance on process, a lack of monitoring, and a lack of emphasis on the duty to work within the parameters of existing human rights legislation: 'there is arguably a need for further guidance to ensure operational consistency and transparency. In particular there is concern about the lack of guidance on the duty to apply the ECHR, and the lack of recognition that this is an issue'.[268] Both sets of Care Act easements Guidance were withdrawn in July 2021, and the Ethical Framework was withdrawn later, in April 2022, as the impacts of COVID-19 continued to be felt across the health and care sectors.

To return to the operationalization of the easements, and as previously noted, local authorities were required to directly inform the DHSC as and when they activated Stage 3 or 4 easements, via a dedicated email address. In a webinar hosted by the DHSC on 4 April 2020, Rhia Roy, then DHSC COVID-19 Team Leader and Policy Lead for Care Act Easements, stated that:

> There is no set format which should be used to present evidence of consideration of easements to DHSC. Any report to DHSC only needs to be brief and should explain why the decision to prioritise services under the easements has been taken and briefly provide any relevant detail.
>
> Appropriate evidence to back up the decision is expected as part of the internal process but does not need to be shared with DHSC. What is considered appropriate will vary locally, depending on local circumstances and the extent to which the easements are used. Some Local Authorities may wish to use their own template locally or to share this with their networks.[269]

The Guidance does make reference to the use of a notification form[270] to be used first, when the easements were established; second, if their use changed; and third, when they ceased to use the easements. In practice, however, it appears that a simple email was deemed to suffice. An Open Document format template of this notification form appeared later in a September 2020 update on the Government's COVID-19 webpages. This happened some months after the last formal easements were ceased by local authorities, so

---

[268] P. Feldon (2020) for BASW, 'Adults social work group response to Coronavirus Crisis', 20 April 2020, see especially p 5.

[269] See Department of Health and Social Care (2020) Adult Social Care COVID-19 Forum – weekly teleconferences 8 April 2020, 13:00–14:00: 'Care Act Easements'.

[270] Department of Health and Social Care (2020) *Care Act Easements: Guidance to Local Authorities* (updated 29 June 2021), p 6.

perhaps we can assume that it had been designed for potential future use in the second wave.

Recording and evidencing of decision-making processes appears to have been a weak spot. While the Guidance aims to set out thresholds and tipping points, it mostly places the onus on local authorities to manage and take responsibility for the inevitable 'difficult decisions', with monitoring and scrutiny formally delegated to the CQC, ADASS, and the LGO, rather than meriting detailed external scrutiny by the DHSC. Although information in relation to easements was to be provided to the DHSC, the responsibility of publishing the online record of which local authorities were operating under easements was given to the CQC rather than the DHSC and, even then, the publicly available list was rudimentary.[271]

Public-facing communications were also left to local authorities. There were calls from the National Care Forum for guidance on how best to communicate with service users and providers, as well as the wider public, but this too was left to the discretion of local authorities:

RR [Rhia Roy DHSC]:	Local Authorities are experienced at communicating with their key audiences and are best placed to decide how to communicate regarding the easements. The guidance emphasises the importance of appropriate communication.
JB [James Bullion, ADASS]:	Amending the guidance would only serve to re-emphasise that Local Authorities have pre-existing expectations on them to communicate. This is best practice and can be seen in TLAP 'I' statement.[272]

As it transpired, local authorities were not used to addressing the kinds of issues raised by operating in pandemic conditions, and some struggled to adapt their own systems, let alone communicate nuanced changes at a range of levels to a range of different people and organizations at pace. National-level communications were flawed and uneven, and this often had repercussions down the line. As we will see in Chapters 5 and 6, this absence

---

[271] Care Quality Commission (2022) 'The Care Act and the "easements" to it. Local authorities that have exercised the easements' (last updated 12 May 2022).

[272] See Department of Health and Social Care (2020) 'Care Act Easements', a Social Care COVID-19 Forum – weekly teleconferences 8 April 2020, 13:00–14:00: 'Care Act Easements'.

of clear guidance on communications coming from central Government may have contributed to the lack of consistency across local authorities and also to undermining public trust around the implementation of the easements from the outset. There were also issues in relation to accessibility of information for service users, and again national guidance was lacking in this area, leading to uneven coverage and quality. Not everyone was prepared for the move to digital services and communications when office phone lines and post rooms were suddenly off limits.

Nonetheless, there were some examples of good practice: Mencap produced an Easy Read Guide[273] to the easements, and basic information appeared on the websites of certain organizations supporting the care sector. Coventry City Council, one of the West Midlands local authorities which did formally enact Stage 3 easements which we discuss further in Chapter 5, produced a One Minute Guide for its citizens.[274] Wolverhampton Council stands out as a council which did not ultimately enact easements, but did undertake a considerable amount of preparatory work in relation to their potential implementation. Unlike other local authorities in the region, Wolverhampton Council produced and hosted a public consultation.[275] Moreover, the consultation was facilitated through the production of 'An Easy Read Guide to Care Act easements in Wolverhampton: How local services may change because of Coronavirus and how it may impact you', following best practice in accessible communications.[276] The guide set out the four stages outlined in the Government easement Guidance and explained how different stages would have consequent impacts upon service users. The consultation approach appears to have been well received in the local community.

> Local organisations and groups as well as carers and people with care and support needs and also employees participated. The vast majority agreed with the local approach to Care Act easements. Some comments included: 'I consider this to have been thorough and well thought-through'; 'The fact that Wolverhampton are consulting on this issue is exemplary. You put some of your near neighbours to shame'.[277]

---

[273] Mencap (2020) 'Easy Read Guide about the Care Act Easements', 3 April.
[274] www.coventry.gov.uk/downloads/file/32626/care_act_easement_one_minute_guide
[275] City of Wolverhampton Council (2020) Consultation on the proposed Care Act Easement Procedure.
[276] City of Wolverhampton Council (2020) 'An easy read guide to Care Act easements in Wolverhampton: How local services may change because of Coronavirus and how it may impact you', May.
[277] City of Wolverhampton Council (2021) *Principal Social Worker Annual Report 2020–2021*, 28 July, para 3.7.

In addition, Wolverhampton Council published a very detailed proposed Operating Model for Care Act easements in April 2020.[278] This included a prioritization tool and analysis of easements against the Ethical Framework in its appendices. But, overall, communication across different local authorities with local residents was another area where a clearer, more consistent and systematic approach would have been desirable.

(c) Relationship of adult social care and pandemic hospital discharge processes

From the outset of the pandemic, it was clear that patients would need to be rapidly discharged from hospitals due to concerns that capacity would very rapidly become overwhelmed. New discharge policies provided that individuals were to be discharged rapidly if they were deemed to be clinically ready,[279] on the basis that Government would fully fund 'new or extended out-of-hospital health and social care support packages'.[280] This was supported, by the inclusion in section 14 of the Coronavirus Act 2020 of further 'easements' of the existing provisions concerning the assessment process for NHS Continuing Health Care (CHC) (which provides NHS-funded care for those with very high medical care needs).[281] The decisions in relation to rapid discharge linked to lack of testing in the early stages of the pandemic led to tragic consequences as in some cases patients who had COVID-19 on discharge infected other care home residents.[282]

Specific obligations were placed on local authorities and Directors of Adult Social Services, Clinical Commissioning Groups, and the voluntary sector. Local authorities were asked to agree a single contact point for each hospital or NHS Trust, to collaborate and enable 'pool staffing' to facilitate resources and prioritization on discharge, and to coordinate with voluntary sector organizations so that certain tasks could be taken on by volunteers while

---

[278] City of Wolverhampton Council (2020) Care Act easements Temporary Operating Model procedures SEB v6.0.
[279] Department of Health and Social Care (2020) *Coronavirus (COVID-19): hospital discharge service requirements*, withdrawn 25 August 2020.
[280] Department of Health and Social Care, (2020) *Coronavirus (COVID-19): hospital discharge service requirements*.
[281] DHSC Guidance (July 2022) *National Framework for NHS Continuing Healthcare and NHS-funded nursing care* (last updated 2 June 2023).
[282] See further V. L. Moore and L.D. Graham (2022) '*R (Gardner and Harris) v Secretary of State for Health and Social care and Others* [2022] EWHC 967: scant regard for COVID-19 risk to care homes', *Medical Law Review*, 30(4): 734–43, and M. Morciano, J. Stokes, K. Kontopantelis, I. Hall and A.J. Turner (2021) 'Excess mortality for care home residents during the first 23 weeks of the COVID-19 pandemic in England: a national cohort study 2021', *BMC Medicine*, 19(71).

NHS staff and civil servants could be redeployed.[283] In addition, they were to have lead contracting responsibilities, drawing on the NHS COVID-19 budget, to increase domiciliary care, and care home and reablement service capacity.[284] Local authorities were also asked to prioritize and manage the redeployment of social work staff to support patients once discharged, to develop move 'robust mechanisms' to track care placements, to commission seven-day working rotas for community social care teams, and to 'deploy adult social care staff flexibly in order to avoid any immediate bottlenecks in arranging step down care and support in the community and at the same time focusing on maintaining and building capacity in local systems'.[285]

Patients would be discharged without the normal assessment processes being undertaken, and without the standard element of choice usually offered by local authorities regarding the place to which they would be discharged. Social care staff and other 'trusted assessors'[286] were also redeployed to undertake this work, which was usually completed by qualified social workers.[287] The NHS Capacity Tracker/Care Home live bed state portal, a web-based app designed to help minimize delay in transfers of care by enabling care homes to instantly share their live bed status,[288] was fully utilized, thus enabling hospital discharge teams to more rapidly identify available nursing and residential care beds. These expedited processes were operated by local authorities separately from the Care Act easements, but their very operation can also be seen as 'flexing' the provisions of the Care Act, which allows for an element of autonomous choice. Instead, individuals would be moved to whatever care beds were available, even if they were not the preferred destination. As previously discussed, choice of accommodation was not the only casualty of these emergency processes; in the absence of sufficient NHS capacity or COVID testing, many were discharged into nursing or residential care homes while they were still COVID-positive, while others were discharged into homes in the throes of a local outbreak.

---

[283] Department of Health and Social Care (2020) *Coronavirus (COVID-19): hospital discharge service requirements*, para 5.1.

[284] Department of Health and Social Care (2020) *Coronavirus (COVID-19): hospital discharge service requirements*, para 5.1.

[285] Department of Health and Social Care (2020) *Coronavirus (COVID-19): hospital discharge service requirements*, para 5.2.

[286] The trusted assessor model was a national initiative introduced before the pandemic in order to reduce delays to hospital discharge and avoid duplication of work. They were supposed to only undertake 'simple' assessments, while qualified social workers were tasked with more complex work. See Care Quality Commission (2018) *Guidance: Trusted Assessors*.

[287] See further Chapter 6 for discussion of hospital discharge in the context of COVID-19.

[288] Department of Health and Social Care (2020) *Coronavirus (COVID-19): hospital discharge service requirements*, para 8.1, at https://capacitytracker.com/

As noted, the Coronavirus Act 2020 also contained provisions which enabled easements to be enacted in relation to NHS Continuing Health Care[289] and the Mental Health Act 1983.[290] Section 14 of the Act enabled NHS bodies to halt Continuing Health Care Assessments. The Government initially paused these assessments nationally, though they were restarted from 1 September 2020.[291] Schedule 8 of the Coronavirus Act 2020 provided for alterations to the Mental Health Act 1983; these powers included detention under sections 2 or 3 of the legislation only requiring the recommendation of one doctor where to obtain this from a second would be impractical or would involve undesirable delay'.[292] In addition, time limits for detaining patients already in hospital could be extended from 6 to 12 hours pending a report from a practitioner or clinician under section 5(4) of the Mental Health Act 1983 or from 72 to 120 hours following a report from a practitioner of clinician under section 5(2) of the Act.[293] The powers of the police to detain persons in a place of safety under sections 135 and 136 were extended from 24 to 36 hours.[294] In fact these powers were never used in practice. Speaking in the House of Commons in October 2020 the then Secretary of State for Health and Care, Matt Hancock, stated that: 'These were always powers of last resort and I was not persuaded even in the peak that they were necessary because our mental health services have shown incredible resilience and ingenuity.'[295]

The Coronavirus Act did not impact on the deprivation of liberty safeguards (DoLS) procedures which as the name suggests are provisions that enable the restriction of the liberty of persons lacking lacking mental capacity under the Mental Capacity Act 2005.[296] However, non-statutory guidance was issued regarding contexts where DoLS authorizations would be undertaken and the utilization of adapted virtual assessments and reviews.[297]

---

[289] See further discussion of NHS Continuing Healthcare provisions in Chapter 3.
[290] See further discussion of s 117 duties in Chapter 3.
[291] Department of Health and Social Care Guidance (2020) *Reintroduction of NHS Continuing Healthcare (NHS CHC guidance)*, withdrawn 21 August 2020.
[292] Coronavirus Act 2020, Sch 8, para 3(1).
[293] Coronavirus Act 2020, Sch 8, para 4(2).
[294] Coronavirus Act 2020, Sch 8, para 10.
[295] C. Carter (2020) 'Government to drop Coronavirus Act provisions weakening Mental Health Act protections', *Community Care*, 2 October.
[296] See further in relation to these powers: Mental Capacity Act 2005, ss 4(3)(A) and 16(2).
[297] See further S. Vicary, K. Stone, P. McCusker, G. Davidson and T. Spencer-Lane (2020) '"It's about how much we can do, and not how little we can get away with": coronavirus-related legislative changes for social care in the United Kingdom', *International Journal of Law and Psychiatry*, 72(1).

As time passed, some formalized reporting systems were developed for roll-out at local government level. In May 2020, the DHSC announced that an important part of the COVID-19 Recovery strategy was to be the production of regularly updated Local Outbreak Management Plans (LOMPs)[298] by local authorities with the aim of identifying and breaking chains of transmission and managing outbreaks of infection at local level; these linked to the broader national work in areas such as the NHS Test and Trace Programme, the Joint Biosecurity Centre, and PHE. New Local COVID Outbreak Engagement Boards were also established, with a multi-agency approach.[299] Since the LOMPs followed a formulaic template, their completion and publication resulted in one of relatively few sources of easily comparable data regarding COVID-19 impacts and mitigation responses from local authority to local authority. As stated in the 'Shropshire COVID-19 Outbreak Control Plan: Prevent, Contain and Recover', for example, these Boards were intended to 'ensure oversight and assurance and foster a culture of collective responsibility and leadership to protect the population's health'.[300]

IV. Care Act easements: a controversial approach

From the outset, the introduction of Care Act easements was subject to heavy criticism from disability and civil rights groups.[301] There was concern about the pace at which the legislation had been drafted; concern about an apparent lack of consultation, scrutiny, and monitoring (both parliamentary and from external stakeholders); and indeed concern about the content and real-life implications of the legislation. As one of our interviewees later commented:

> The first thing we did was work with something called the Disability Charities Consortium, before the Act was passed, to write to parliamentarians basically saying that they shouldn't pass anything that diminished the rights of disabled people. (Policy lead at a national disabled people's organization)

---

[298] See UK Health Security Agency (2020) *COVID-19 contain framework: a guide for local decision makers*.

[299] See, for example, Shropshire Council (2020) 'COVID-19 Outbreak Control Plan: Prevent, Contain and Recover', V2.1, 22 June.

[300] Shropshire Council (2020) 'COVID-19 Outbreak Control Plan: Prevent, Contain and Recover.' V2.1, 22 June, at p 4.

[301] 'Liberty and Disability Charities Warn Councils not to Weaken Social Care During Coronavirus Pandemic', 7 May 2020, at www.libertyhumanrights.org.uk/issue/liberty-and-disability-charities-warn-councils-not-to- weaken-social-care-during-coronavirus-pandemic/

Liberty and Disability Rights UK both issued statements, supported by a large cohort of other third-sector organizations, opposing what they viewed as the 'suspension of Care Act rights' which 'risked being unlawful'.[302] Later in the year, the Equality and Human Rights Commission also called for the UK Government to

> urgently repeal the provisions in the Coronavirus Act which allow for the reduction in safeguards and level of provision in the delivery of social care, strengthen oversight of changes to social care provision at the local level beyond those implemented under the emergency legislation, and take immediate action to address reductions in care that disproportionately affect particular groups.[303]

Meanwhile, in this context, it was reported in April 2020 that: 'A leaked letter from the Association of Directors of Adult Social Services dated 11 April said the Care Act easements alongside the ethical framework "afford an opportunity to prioritise limited resources" and were "greatly appreciated" by councils.'[304]

After the legislation was enacted, however, only a small number of local authorities formally declared that they were operating under Care Act easements. These were Derbyshire County Council, Middlesbrough Council, and Sunderland City Council, and a cluster of local authorities in the West Midlands: Birmingham City Council, Coventry City Council, Solihull Metropolitan Borough Council, Staffordshire County Council, and Warwickshire County Council. These local authorities came under intense scrutiny, with Liberty and other groups warning that the eight councils known to have activated easements 'risk breaking the law'.[305] A number of organizations sent Freedom of Information (FoI) requests to local authorities which had implemented easements regarding decision-making and any impacts upon their citizens; press coverage of the legislative changes was also largely critical. Responses to these challenges are considered in the discussion of individual local authorities in the following chapter.

In early May 2020, a legal challenge was brought by Professor Katherine Runswick-Cole against Derbyshire County Council on behalf of her son

---

[302] See R. Booth (2020) 'Stop using coronavirus powers to neglect care duties, UK councils told', *The Guardian*, 7 May.

[303] Equality and Human Rights Commission (2020) *How Coronavirus has affected equality and human rights.* Report, October, p 38.

[304] J. Hill (2020) 'Exclusive: Five councils start bypassing Care Act duties amid COVID pressures', *Local Government Chronicle*, 24 April.

[305] Liberty (2020) 'Liberty and disability charities warn councils not to weaken social care during Coronavirus pandemic', 7 May.

William Runswick-Cole, who relied on support through direct payments from the local authority.[306] The challenge questioned the lack of evidence provided by the council that the criteria set out under the Guidance for the operation of easements had been met, and indeed a wider failure of communication.[307] This dispute was ultimately resolved out of court once Derbyshire County Council made a number of concessions in relation to the manner in which it operated easements and communicated with those drawing on services.[308]

The adverse publicity experienced by local authorities which utilized easements in the early stages had a perceptible 'chilling effect' on other local authorities. Although the operation of the emergency statutory framework could be seen as a means of conferring legitimacy upon what were clearly very tough policy and ethical choices, the formal activation of legislative easements from the outset in April 2020 came with very obvious costs for the local authorities concerned, as well as the potential to undermine the gradual gains made over years in securing the rights and autonomy of people who draw on services and support.

V. Conclusions

As we saw in this chapter, the Coronavirus Act 2020 followed years of contingency planning for pandemic flu. However the need for specific responses to public health crises had, as we have seen, a much longer history. While the Civil Contingencies Act 2004 provided a framework to address the challenges of a major public emergency this was never utilised; as we have seen a range of different rationales have been given for this choice. As we saw in our discussion earlier the UK COVID-19 Inquiry Module 1 report illustrated that pandemic planning was predicated upon an Influenza pandemic and that, rather than a seamless pivot of strategy rooted in detailed planning for alternative forms of pandemic responses, there was an abandonment of that approach. However in relation to adult social care and the disapplication of Care Act 2014 provisions the pre-existing pandemic planning was indeed followed. The work undertaken with organisations such as ADASS, the preparation of the draft Pandemic Influenza Bill all fed into the Coronavirus Act 2020 and related guidance documents.

---

[306] M. Samuel (2020) 'Council faces legal challenge for suspending Care Act duties', *Community Care*, 7 May.

[307] S. Broach, hosting K. Runswick-Cole (2020) 'COVID-19: banana bread, blankets, beans and the law', at https://rightsinreality.wordpress.com/2020/06/03/COVID-19-banana-bread-blankets-beans-and-the-law/, accessed 10 July 2024.

[308] M. Samuel (2020) 'Council says it has "learned lessons" after Care Act legal challenge dropped', *Community Care*, 5 June.

The enactment of the legislation with its specific provisions enabling departure from certain Care Act powers and duties could be seen as a pragmatic decision, recognizing that at times, in extreme or 'unprecedented' situations, unpalatable choices may arguably need to be made in the wider public interest. The provisions of the Coronavirus Act 2020 could be viewed as measures providing both legitimacy to the very difficult resource allocation choices that might need to be made and also legal protection for those local authorities where such choices were indeed made. They appear to have been constructed at least in part, in explict recognition of the situation utilitarian balancing exercises that might need to be undertaken in pandemic conditions while still maintaining human rights as the statutory boundary that should not be breached. As we saw from the outset, the extent to which these provisions could be seen as safeguarding individual human rights and persons who might be regarded as 'vulnerable' gave rise to major concern at national level. Yet the actual formal operation of easements by just eight local authorities nationwide only lasted a matter of weeks. Nonetheless, as we shall see in the next two chapters, substantive changes to the operation of Care Act provisions across a far larger number of local authorities took place over a much longer period and have had lingering consequences.

5

'Easing' the Care Act: Responding to COVID-19 in the West Midlands

I. Introduction

The Coronavirus Act 2020 provided a legal structure within which statutory duties could be 'eased' where workforce or other operational capacity was over-stretched, but very few local authorities in England formally took up the provisions. This apparent lack of uptake does not mean that there were not notable challenges to social care delivery at the height of the pandemic across all local authorities in England, with impacts on service provision and on the experiences of those who draw on them. Nor did it mean that local authorities did not make operational changes to address the pressures they faced.

In this chapter we explore some of these challenges and responses in the period between March 2020, when the Wuhan strain of SARS-CoV-2 was spreading rapidly, and the advent of the Delta variant in March 2021. It takes as a case study the experience of the adult social care sector in the West Midlands region, with a specific focus on the decision-making processes of and operational changes made by local authorities as found in the public record.[1] The majority of the information shared below was found on council websites or in the minutes of meetings logged therein; the material presented here makes no claim to be wholly comprehensive as it remains possible that not all documentation was made publicly available. In addition, sources that were initially uploaded later disappeared from the relevant Councils' websites.

The West Midlands is a part of the country which was very adversely impacted during the early stages of the pandemic. It is a region with notable

---

[1] This chapter draws upon our ESRC project initial report, see J.V. McHale and L. Noszlopy (2021) 'Adult social care provision under pressure: lessons from the pandemic', Birmingham: University of Birmingham.

pockets of socio-economic deprivation and a very diverse population, served by fourteen local authorities. These demographic factors, along with individuals being older, clinically vulnerable, and/or from certain Black, Asian, and Minority ethnic backgrounds, were identified as significant risk factors for COVID-related mortality.[2] The West Midlands region also had the largest concentration of local authorities – five in total, of the eight nationwide – to declare that they had implemented Stage 3 and/or 4 Care Act easements. All in this cluster decided to activate the easements in quick succession and all decided to stand down from Stages 3 or 4 after a short period of time. Some of these local authorities then indicated that they were going to operate at Stage 2 of the Guidance, while others simply stated that they had ceased the use of easements.

Although the contemporary vernacular described 'easement councils' and 'non-easement councils', this simple shorthand was misleading. There was a great deal of slippage and ambiguity around interpretations of the Guidance, and especially the tipping points or thresholds at which 'easements' would occur. There was, for example, a further group of West Midlands local authorities that stated that they were applying 'Stage 2 easements' starting in the early months of the pandemic. This was despite the fact that, as detailed in the previous chapter, Stage 2 did not refer to 'easements' as such but rather concerned the application of 'flexibilities' within the pre-amendment Care Act. However, many of these authorities undertook a formal internal process in reaching the decision to enact 'Stage 2 easements', with this process and information documented in the minutes of meetings and publicly available decisions. One local authority in this group, Dudley Metropolitan Borough Council, indicated in its official records both that it had and that it had not implemented Care Act easements – this is considered later. The final and smallest group were local authorities which stated that they did not implement easements at all. Comprised of only four councils: Shropshire, Stoke-on-Trent, Wolverhampton, and Worcestershire – these local authorities described the operation of flexibilities such as the movement to online working and simplified assessments but, in contrast to the previous group, the language of 'Care Act easements' was used only to explain the national-level provision and to state that they had not been enacted.[3]

This chapter begins by analysing the diverse approaches to maintaining social care provision taken across the three categories of West Midlands local authorities during the first period of the pandemic. We draw upon documentary evidence available in the public domain, including local

---

[2] Public Health England (2020) *Disparities in the risk and outcomes of COVID-19*, August.

[3] As we shall see, Wolverhampton undertook a consultation and much internal discussion to support its decision-making.

authority documents and the minutes of meetings, media coverage, and from Freedom of Information (FoI) requests issued by advocacy groups and others. First, we consider those local authorities which formally activated Stage 3 or Stage 4 easements. We then examine the self-reporting of 'Stage 2' councils, and finally those local authorities which stated that they did not implement easements, but which did implement flexibilities within the pre-amendment Care Act provisions, are examined.

The remainder of the chapter draws upon the findings of our empirical study and the anonymized voices of key stakeholders describing their perceptions of how easements operated or were not operated in the West Midlands during this period, which covered from spring 2020 to September 2021. We explore the differences and similarities between the various approaches, and the extent to which the rhetoric of position statements made in public-facing local authority documentation was reflected both in the available council minutes and in the post-hoc, and more candid, views of our interviewees across the West Midlands.

II. The formal operation of easements in the West Midlands 'cluster'

As with other local authorities which activated and/or implemented formal Stage 3 or 4 easements, our cluster of West Midlands local authorities did so very early in the pandemic. In very quick succession, all five 'switched on' the easements option. Then, in a matter of weeks, these same local authorities decided to 'switch off' the easements in similarly quick succession (Table 5.1).

As we will show, rationales for the decision to activate varied from council to council.

Table 5.1: Timeline of Care Act easements activities and cessation announcements

Local authority	Highest 'stage'	Activation date	Cessation date and rationale
Solihull	Stage 4	8 April 2020	30 June 2020 'returned to full compliance with CA 2014'
Warwickshire	Stage 3	9 April 2020	23 May 2020 'reverted to Stage 2'
Staffordshire	Stage 3	9 April 2020	26 May 2020 'notified DHSC of cessation'
Birmingham	Stage 3	14 April 2020	18 May 2020 'cease use of easements'
Coventry	Stage 3	28 April 2020	29 May 2020 'notified', but 'revoked' 2 June 2020

(a) Birmingham City Council

Birmingham City Council is Europe's largest local authority; it serves a diverse urban population. Its population according to the ONS 2022 estimate was 1,157,603 and rising.[4] During 2020 and 2021 COVID-19 cases remained very high across deprived areas of the city, in Asian and other minority ethnic communities, and among working-age adults.[5] The decision to activate easements was made under the Council's Emergency Plan,[6] which operated under the existing Gold-Silver-Bronze Command response model.[7] This model forms part of the broader national–local resilience structure derived from the Civil Contingencies Act 2004. While the powers of the 2004 Act were not utilized in response to the pandemic and were not therefore related to the operation of easements, the Gold-Silver-Bronze Command model and related guidance informed the practical day-to-day decision-making on the ground. In Birmingham, as elsewhere, the Command model incorporated Council leaders, Adult Services leaders, NHS leaders, Local Resilience Forum (LRF) leaders, and other senior strategic leads from across the emergency services. Birmingham's Director of Adult Social Services (DASS), then Interim Chief Executive, Graeme Betts CBE, led Gold Command throughout most of the pandemic.[8] It should also be noted that Birmingham City Council had been experiencing considerable financial pressures in the years before the pandemic.[9] Major re-organizations in adult social work in Birmingham took place in that period as part of a ten-year programme of transformation from 2008 to 2018.[10] In addition there was a move in 2013–14 to introduce new measures called *A Fair Deal in Times of Austerity*[11] which included, as Lotinga states, 'a so called new adult social care "offer" including a big push on increasing the number of people in receipt of direct payments'.[12] The changes were

---

[4] https://www.birmingham.gov.uk/downloads/file/29114/2022_mid-year_population_estimate, accessed 2 July 2024.
[5] Birmingham City Council (2021) Local Outbreak Management Plan, para 17.2.
[6] Birmingham City Council (2020) *Emergency Plan Decision Log*, item nos 77 and 78.
[7] See Local Government Association (2020) 'Emergency response structures during the COVID-19 pandemic. Councillor guidance', May.
[8] During the period that Graeme Betts stepped up as Acting Chief Executive of the Council, Louise Collett took up the role Interim DASS, and was advised on operational matters by the PSW Julie Parfitt. See Birmingham City Council (2021) *Annual Governance Statement 2020/2021*, pp 203–204.
[9] See discussion in A. Lotinga (2015) 'Context matters: general practice and social work – the Birmingham story', *Journal of Integrated Care*, 23(2): 88–95 at 89.
[10] Lotinga (2015), p 92.
[11] Birmingham City Council (2014) *Birmingham City Council Social Care for Adults in Birmingham: A Fair Deal in Times of Austerity*.
[12] Lotinga (2015), p 92.

directed to increase productivity and reduce costs, along with 'producing clearer roles and clearer pathways and setting the scene to help progress more effective integrated working with the NHS and other key partners'. This included multi-disciplinary primary care and community teams, and an independent social work pilot run with the Department of Health, which Lotinga describes as an attempt to run half of the social work services relating to people with physical disabilities independently through promotion of direct payments and also the testing of 'community development models'.[13] However he raises a note of caution regarding the developments at that time:

> Although these changes have been necessary and, so far, appear to be largely successful, we cannot overstate how much management and staff turmoil and extra pressures have been created by these initiatives, over the past year [Lotinga was writing in 2015] in particular. As we write some staff within the service are taking redundancy, some are lower pay grade and most jobs have changed in some respect. Therefore we need to be very careful before we embark upon another reorganisation of the adult social work service in Birmingham.[14]

These developments provide some contextual background to the events of 2020. Birmingham's decision to activate the easements almost immediately that they became available appears to reflect the need to make a pre-emptive response to speed up patient discharge, amid concerns about projected pressures on hospital and social care staffing capacity. The city was chosen as the site for one of the emergency Nightingale hospitals, close to the boundary with neighbouring Solihull,[15] and this awareness appears to have hastened the pace of decision-making. In a press interview, Shadow Cabinet Member for Health and Social Care, Councillor Matt Bennett (Edgbaston, Conservative) noted that he had raised concerns regarding the use of easements and while assured they were 'only being used to speed up discharge from hospital and ease the pressure on the NHS' went on to question 'the increase in power and weakening of accountability that this entails'.[16] He asked 'for assurances on safeguards, to make sure that what starts out as a well-intentioned and pragmatic easing of bureaucracy doesn't end up as a cost cutting reduction of provision which could have a real impact on vulnerable people'[17] and

---

[13] Lotinga (2015), p 93.
[14] Lotinga (2015), p 93.
[15] The hospital cost £65 million. See Birmingham Mail (2021) 'Birmingham Nightingale Hospital Closes without treating a single patient', *Birmingham Mail*, 1 April.
[16] T. Dare (2020) 'Concern for vulnerable as Birmingham no longer obliged to assess people over care needs', *Birmingham Mail*, 28 April.
[17] T. Dare (2020).

went on to say that: 'I am also concerned that this decision, its scope and the rationale behind it has not been communicated to service users and other partners, despite this being a requirement.'[18]

In response to written questions from Councillor Julien Pritchard, the Cabinet Member for Health and Social Care, Paulette Hamilton stated that:

> the situation in Birmingham was extremely serious, with hospitals reporting some of the highest death rates in the country. Over the Easter weekend, the Midlands was the worst affected region for COVID-19 deaths significantly higher than any other region including London. The Birmingham Nightingale Hospital was under construction, with Birmingham and Solihull Councils expected to provide social care support to the new hospital.
>
> The local decision to temporarily streamline some of processes required in the Care Act was made by officers at this time and in this context to ensure that we would be able to protect and support citizens at this period of unprecedented pressure on the health and social care system. We wanted to enable staff to focus on priority activities, to recognise the pressures on the care and hospital sectors and the practical difficulties of operating in the lockdown environment.[19]

The decision was not subject to broader public consultation, and practical and political concerns were raised, cross-party, by Council Members as to how the process had been undertaken and whether the relevant Committee members had been 'kept informed'.[20] The Council stressed that:

> This was not about cutting services and we continued to assess and provide services to those who had an eligible need for care and support. There was no change to the services received by existing service users as a result of this decision.[21]

---

[18] T. Dare (2020).

[19] Birmingham City Council (2020) 'Written Questions to Cabinet Members', 'Written questions focusing on the response to the COVID-19 Pandemic', Date of Publications, 18 May.

[20] Birmingham City Council (2020) 'Health and Social Care Overview and Scrutiny Committee', p 51. See also Birmingham City Council (2020) Meeting of the City Council. Written Questions for Cabinet Members. Question from Councillor Charlotte Hodivala at D3.

[21] T. Dare (2020).

What then did these Stage 3 easements mean in practice? Professor Graeme Betts, Birmingham's Gold Commander, reported to Cabinet that:

> The only easements agreed during this period related to streamlining assessments, including not providing hard copies of assessments/support plans and limiting the choice of providers, in recognition of the limited options due to pressures in the care provider sector. This decision was informed by dialogue with health partners and was kept under regular review, with information available on the City Council's website.[22]

Yet the use of Stage 3 easements was stepped down relatively rapidly, just over a month after they were activated. The reason given for this was that:

> The directorate subsequently took the decision that, given that the peak of COVID-19 deaths and infections now appears to have passed, and capacity in the health and care system has improved, to cease use of the easements with effect from 18th May 2020. We are now in the process of revisiting the assessments undertaken during this period, alongside continuing our ongoing work with providers and partners to ensure that citizens receive the care and support that they need. The provisions in the Coronavirus Act 2020 [are] in place should the situation deteriorate.[23]

In response to a question from Councillor Simon Morrall about what changes had actually been implemented as a result of the easements in Birmingham, the Leader of the Council reiterated that 'there was no change to the services received by existing service users as a result of this decision'.[24] It was also noted that the social work teams were revisiting committed to examining and completing the assessments made when the easements were implemented to 'ensure that citizens receive the care and support that they need'.[25] Social workers were 'working with Citizens that the easement impacted upon to ensure all their needs [were] met'.[26]

---

[22] Birmingham City Council (2020) *Birmingham City Council's response to COVID-19 Report of Cabinet Report author: Professor Graeme Betts, Gold Commander March to May 2020 & Director, Adult Social Care*, 9 June para 4.18.
[23] Birmingham City Council (2020) *Birmingham City Council's response to COVID-19 Report*, para 1.1.9.
[24] Birmingham City Council (2020) 'Minutes of meeting of the City Council,' 9 June at Q D2, p 4282.
[25] Birmingham City Council (2020) Birmingham City Council's response to *COVID-19 Report*, para 1.4.1.9.
[26] Birmingham City Council (2020) Minutes of meeting of the City Council, 9 June at Q D2, p 4282.

Notably, the NHS Nightingale Hospital, built on the NEC site near Solihull for a potential overspill of up to 2,000 patients at a cost of £66 million, was never used.[27] Information provided to Council meetings emphasized how Birmingham City Council's capacity to support its communities and meet citizens' needs was greatly bolstered by collaborative work in the voluntary sector. Birmingham Voluntary Services Council (BVSC) had been asked early on to refocus the existing Neighbourhood Networks programme across the city to form a #COVID19SupportBrum partnership[28] with local voluntary sector organizations designated to sub-groups focused on supporting specific groups of citizens, particularly those who draw on services.[29] The local response was described by the Council as 'a once in a lifetime display of community spirit'.[30]

Birmingham's use of Care Act easements remained contentious. At a Council meeting on 3 November 2020, some six questions were raised by councillors for the Cabinet Member for Health and Social Care regarding the potential reintroduction of easements in the event of future surges, with a focus on evidencing rationales for decision-making, accountability, and how any decisions would be communicated to peers and to citizens. It was stated that the Council 'do not anticipate using the Care Act easement powers in the future, but were they to do so, 'Would set out clearly the rationale for any changes and ensure that these are communicated to service users'.[31]

However, this intention did not mean that services totally resumed in a pre-COVID mode at that point. Day centres are one illustration. These were closed during the initial period of the pandemic due to concerns of risk of infection of both service users and also day centre staff.[32] Funded care

---

[27] Birmingham Mail (2021) 'Birmingham's Nightingale Hospital closes without treating a single patient", *Birmingham Mail*, 1 April; see also M. Day (2020) 'COVID-19 Nightingale hospitals set to shut down after seeing few patients', *BMJ*, 369.

[28] See Birmingham Voluntary Service Council (2020) 'COVID-19 Support Brum Partnership weekly briefing bulletins'.

[29] See Birmingham City Council (2020) Minutes of meeting of the City Council, 15 September; see also Birmingham City University and Birmingham Voluntary Service Council (2021) *Community-based Responses to COVID-19 in Birmingham: Insights and Experiences*, research report, 28 June.

[30] Birmingham City Council (2020) Birmingham City Council's response to COVID-19 Cabinet. Professor Graeme Betts (Gold Commander March to May 2020 & Director, Adult Social Care), 9 June, para 3.3.

[31] See Birmingham City Council (2020) 'Minutes of the meeting of the City Council', 3 November. Response to Written Question to the Cabinet Member for Health and Social Care from Councillor Peter Fowler.

[32] See Birmingham City Council (2020) 'Cabinet Meeting regarding Impact on Day Centres', 13 October, paras 3.8 and 3.9.

packages continued for this group and alternative provision was provided in the form of

> a range of alternative and creative therapeutic, educational outreach services. These have included the provision of phone and online services, supply of meals, safe and well-checks, home visits, support to carers, assistance with medical appointments and shopping deliveries.[33]

In November 2020 it was reported that the continued closure of day centres was still having a serious impact on service users and their families in Birmingham.[34] A consultation on the future of the city's adult social care day centres was launched on 7 May 2024, in the wake of the Council's section 114 notice announcement, with the aim to 'rationalise' the available offer.[35]

(b) Coventry City Council

Coventry is another substantial urban centre, with an estimated population of 379,387 in 2020, and diverse communities.[36] There are pockets of socio-economic deprivation in some areas, and notable health inequalities. Coventry City Council, along with a group of neighbouring local authorities – including Solihull Metropolitan Borough Council, Warwickshire County Council, and also Rugby Borough Council and Stratford-on-Avon District Council – participated in an exercise called 'Exercise Black Swan' on 8 January 2020, with the aim of testing 'our response to an outbreak of Pandemic Influenza'.[37] This process had begun in November 2019 – the aim being to provide communications 'to replicate the longevity of such an incident'.[38]

Coventry City Council at first indicated that it was 'operating at Stage 2 of the easements, prioritising services to ensure that care and support continues

---

[33] Birmingham City Council (2020) Cabinet meeting of 13th October 2020 'Cabinet Meeting regarding Impact on Day Centres', para 3.19.

[34] M. Cardwell (2020) 'Day centre closures in Birmingham having "terrible" impact on families due to COVID-19 pandemic', *Express & Star*, 7 December.

[35] Birmingham City Council (2024) 'Your day, your say – Adult social care day centre consultation', webpage, 7 May.

[36] See Coventry City Council (2020) *Coventry Adult Social Care Annual Report and Key Areas of Improvement 2019/20 (Local Account)*.

[37] Solihull Metropolitan Borough Council (2021) *Local Outbreak Management Plan, Revised 2021*, p 39. This exercise was discussed further in D. Irwin (2021) ' "Viruses are much cleverer than we are" – Solihull public health chief on why COVID battle has changed but isn't over', *Birmingham Mail*, 17 August.

[38] Solihull (2021) *Local Outbreak Management Plan, Revised 2021*, p 39.

to be delivered according to Care Act principles', but later announced that it was moving to formal Stage 3 easements from 24 April 2020.[39] The DASS and PSW, after consultation with the Adult Social Services Senior Management Board, the Lead Member of the City Council, and local NHS Leadership the Chief Executive, took the decision that this was an emergency and that there would be movement to implement initially Stage 3 easements. In addition authority was to be given to the DASS after consultation with the above parties to move 'when necessary' between Stages 3 and 4, stating that:

> This will ensure that so far as possible the City Council will continue to meet need as set out in the Care Act but where necessary will be able to move to prioritising service delivery so that urgent or acute needs are met, supporting the most vulnerable people in the City.[40]

The approach taken was in line with Department of Health and Social Care (DHSC) guidance by logging decisions in the public domain and communicating the situation to its citizens and care providers. It also produced a 'One Minute Guide' explaining easements in accessible format online[41] In response to a Freedom of Information Act request, it was stated on 28 May 2020 that 'the decision has been published on the Council's webpages and a stakeholder communication and engagement plan enacted'[42] In addition, it was stated that 'Coventry City Council is not operating at Stage 4, or reprioritising services and therefore are not acting in such a way as to risk breaching an individual's human rights'.[43] It was also confirmed that service users and their families and carers, service providers, advocacy organizations, and the voluntary sector had been informed of the Council's position on 28 April 2020.[44]

On 29 May, Coventry's DASS, Pete Fahy, emailed the DHSC to state that 'Coventry has moved back to level 2 and are therefore operating again under Care Act "normal"'.[45] However, although it remains within the bounds of Care Act compliance, Stage 2 does not formally constitute 'normal' under the Care Act easement Guidance (as Stage 1 is defined as 'business as usual').

---

[39] Coventry City Council (2020) 'Exercise of emergency functions – Use of the Care Act Easements, created under the Coronavirus Act 2020', 2 June.

[40] Coventry City Council (2020)' Exercise of Emergency Functions- Use of the Care Act easements created under the Coronavirus Act 2020', 24th April 2020.

[41] See Coventry City Council (2020) 'One Minute Guide. The Care Act Easements', Coventry Safeguarding Adults Board, April.

[42] Coventry City Council (2020) Response to Freedom of Information Act 2000 (FOIA) Request ID: REQ07114, 28 May.

[43] Coventry City Council (2020) Response to FoI REQ07114, 28 May.

[44] Coventry City Council (2020) Response to FoI REQ07114, 28 May.

[45] Coventry City Council (2020) Response to FoI from Liberty, 1 June.

Four days later, a document signed by the Chief Executive of Coventry Council, Martin Reeves, stated that it was no longer necessary to implement easements.[46] The rationale for the easements and decision to move down to Stage 2 was further set out in a document published following a FoI request from civil rights organization Liberty to the Council on 1 June. It stated that a review on 13 May had taken the approach that easements wouldn't be used for financial assessments because an existing digital adaption was already in place: these were 'undertaken remotely and via our on online assessment tool, this is happening without any delay and is now "business as usual"'.[47] The review on 27 May had indicated that there was not 'significant workforce depletion, rise in demand and/or market pressures', and that discharge pathway activity was comparable with the previous year, with demand and activity of waiting lists 'managed successfully.'[48] In addition, it stated that remote assessments were being undertaken, along with emergency reviews of care plans; and 'some scheduled reviews have commenced'. A new form of 'enhanced and detailed' risk assessment was put in place 'to enable face to face assessments to be undertaken as required'. The workforce was described as 'stable' with 'relatively low rates of absence'.[49]

The recommendation from the Principal Social Worker (PSW) to the DASS was therefore to cease the use of Stage 3 easements and 'operate under the "pre-amendment Care Act" including continuing to only take Stage 2 actions to suspend certain services such as Day Opportunities and Travel Training but retain the ability to use easements in the future as required due to any subsequent workforce depletion and/or surge in demand.'[50]

The Chief Executive of the Council announced that 'after careful review and consideration it is currently no longer necessary to operate under the Care Act easements and I am therefore making the decision to revoke the instigation of the Care Act easements by the City Council'.[51]

Retrospective information regarding the nature of the easements that had operated in Coventry was provided in a report by Pete Fahy on 27

---

[46] Coventry City Council (2020) Document signed by Chief Executive Coventry City Council on 2 June 2020, 'Exercise of emergency functions – Use of the Care Act Easements, created under the Coronavirus Act 2020'.
[47] Coventry City Council (2020) Response to FoI from Liberty, 1 June.
[48] Response to FoI request from Liberty.
[49] Response to FoI request from Liberty.
[50] Coventry City Council (2020) 'Adult Social Care – Care Act Decision Report – Care Act Easements, 27 May, from: Andrew Errington, Adults Principal Social Worker, Sally Caren, Head of Social Work, Mental Health and Sustainability to: Pete Fahy – Director of Adult Services' in response package to FoI request 07144.
[51] Coventry City Council (2020) 'Exercise of emergency functions – use of the Care Act Easements, created under the Coronavirus Act', 2 June.

July 2020 to a meeting of the Coventry Health and Wellbeing Board.[52] In addition to explaining the scope of the easements, Fahy notes that social work colleagues worked with those in the NHS in 'freeing up a significant number of hospital beds in the early stages of the pandemic'.[53] He commented that there was a greater reliance on remote working and use of technology while recognizing that:

> For some people with care and support needs and family carers the remote working approach has been extremely effective but for others it has not been as successful and as always Adult Social Care will not be a one size fits all service as we progress.[54]

> Where services did temporarily cease, including day opportunities, residential respite provision and travel training work is underway to bring these back where possible and in a COVID compliant way. This includes supporting independent sector providers to reinstate services safely as well as restarting City Council provision.[55]

In January 2021 in his Report to the Meeting of Coventry Health and Wellbeing Board Fahy stated that: 'Following wave one, services were re-opened or reinstated wherever this could be done in a COVID-19 compliant way, with the necessary infection prevention and control measures in place. Care Act easements had not been required beyond the first wave of the pandemic.'[56]

Nonetheless it was recognized that, 'Adult Social Care operations have been and continue to be significantly impacted in a number of key areas'.[57] He noted that support was provided by the Commissioning Team to the external provider market, and that despite 'numerous challenges throughout

---

[52] Coventry City Council (2020) Report to: Coventry Health and Wellbeing Board Date: 27 July 2020, from: Pete Fahy, Director of Adult Services; Title: 'Adult Social Care – Key programmes of work to support COVID-19 to date', at pp 79–84.

[53] Coventry City Council (2020) 'Adult Social Care – Key programmes of work to support COVID-19 to date', para 8.1.

[54] 'Adult Social Care – Key programmes of work to support COVID-19 to date', para 9.3.1.

[55] Coventry City Council (2020), para 9.3.1. Note: travel training is defined by Coventry as 'Independent Travel Training (ITT) provides people with the knowledge and skills they need to travel independently, whilst providing parents and carers with peace of mind that people are travelling safely'.

[56] Coventry City Council (2021) Report to Coventry Health and Wellbeing Board Date: 25 January 2021 from: Pete Fahy, Director Adult Services, 'COVID-19 – The impact on Adult Social Care', at coventry.gov.uk, para 3.1.2.

[57] Coventry City Council (2021) 'COVID-19 – The impact on Adult Social Care', para 3.1.3.

the pandemic to date there has only been one case of provider failure and this was not due to COVID-19'.[58]

As elsewhere, operational changes and adaptations were implemented long after the formal use of easements had ceased, not least in provision of day care opportunities and the resultant shift of responsibilities from providers to unpaid or informal carers.

> Maintaining Day Services and providing respite and carer support wherever possible has required changes to operating processes and reductions in numbers of those people accessing services to enable safe practices. The City Council has funded additional support for unpaid carers in order to help to sustain this resource and prevent carer breakdown and the need for formal support service provision.[59]

It was made clear in the documents for Council that by the start of December 2020 there was significant, growing pressure on the social care team at University Hospital Coventry and Warwickshire which was undertaking speedy discharge on a seven-day a week basis,[60] leading to a 40 per cent increase in the work of the Hospital Social Worker Team[61] with resources utilized to redeploy staff. It was recognized that 'this will inevitably mean focus on other, less critical but important, activity such as enablement and therapy will be impacted'.[62]

Referrals had declined since the first wave, with requests for support in line with 2019, but nonetheless restrictions and operational changes to social practice remained in place. As Fahy reported, social work staff 'continue to work from home and do as many of their duties from home as possible and only undertake face to face assessments where necessary using appropriate PPE and safety measures'.[63]

Although the Council maintained that there were 'no complaints or challenges were raised as a result of the easements',[64] there was some

---

[58] Coventry City Council (2021) 'COVID-19 – The impact on Adult Social Care', para 3.1.4.
[59] Coventry City Council (2021) 'COVID-19 – The impact on Adult Social Care', para 3.1.5.
[60] Coventry City Council (2021) 'COVID-19 – The impact on Adult Social Care', para 3.1.7.
[61] Coventry City Council (2021) 'COVID-19 – The impact on Adult Social Care', para 3.1.8.
[62] Coventry City Council (2021) 'COVID-19 – The impact on Adult Social Care', paras 3.1.8 and 3.1.9.
[63] Coventry City Council (2021) 'COVID-19 – The impact on Adult Social Care', paras 3.1.8 and 3.1.9.
[64] Coventry City Council (2020) 'Minutes of meeting of Coventry Health and Well-Being Board', 27 July, at point 8.

suggestion from elsewhere that certain citizens had been affected.[65] The Women's Budget Group COVID-19 Report stated that there were examples of adverse impacts of the pandemic on service users:

> Betty is 87 years old and lives alone. She has mobility and mental health problems and was assessed for care needs prior to the crisis, but only received partial care equipment in early June. Betty normally relies on neighbours in the community to help with shopping as well as on many services which are currently unavailable. She has no access to the internet, or family members nearby so has become very isolated. The Care Act easements, which have been implemented in Coventry, have meant that Betty is not seen as an essential care user and has not been offered the level of support needed, leaving her vulnerable and lonely.[66]

By the end of 2020, practice in Coventry had not fully returned to pre-pandemic models, with social workers continuing to work primarily from home, and face-to-face assessments only undertaken 'where necessary' rather than as standard, but operations were deemed to be fully Care Act compliant.

(c) Solihull Metropolitan Borough Council

Solihull is a relatively affluent borough, characterized by above-average levels of income and home ownership, and only limited pockets of socio-economic deprivation. As of 2019, it had a population of approximately 214,909 people, with a notable rise in the number of older citizens.[67] Solihull was the only West Midlands local authority which formally notified the DHSC that it had activated Stage 4 easements. Solihull's decision-making process was very clearly documented through council committee minutes, including recordings of online meetings and related documentation. Decisions pertaining to activating easements were ultimately the responsibility of the DASS, though here as elsewhere there was evidence of wider involvement and support at senior management level.[68] The activation decision was published on the Council website. Although this is a decision for local authority officers

---

[65] Women's Budget Group (2020) 'COVID-19 Report: The Impact on Women in Coventry', p 21. and Central England Law Centre, Rights in Peril report 2022, Rights in Peril Project, Central England Law Centre.

[66] Women's Budget Group (2020) 'COVID-19 Report: The Impact on Women in Coventry', p 21.

[67] Solihull Observatory on behalf of Solihull Metropolitan Borough Council (2019) *Solihull People and Place*, August.

[68] Solihull Metropolitan Borough Council (2020) 'CPH Adult Social Care and Health Decision Session', 6 April.

there appears to be clear acknowledgement of the importance of cross-party political buy-in as well as engagement with other stakeholders.[69]

The recommendation to move to Stage 4 was presented at the Cabinet Portfolio Holder (CPH) Adult Social Care and Health Decision Session on 6 April 2020.[70] It was stated that this decision related to service pressures including the vast majority of approaches to the Adult Care and Support services concerning COVID-19 which included '90% of calls coming through the Adult Care and Support Front Door related to COVID-19 impact[71]'. The role of Adult Social Care teams expanded beyond their normal remit to include highlighting Government guidance, facilitating emergency access to money and food, and responding to queries concerning personal protective equipment (PPE); there was also 'significant additional work associated with shielding and protecting those who are deemed as extremely vulnerable' with over 3,000 citizens on the shielding list.[72]

During this period staffing had been adversely hit. For example, some 25 per cent of the Council's Adult Care and Support staff were on sick leave, with a further 10 per cent of other staff self-isolating due to potential infections. Some staff were on compassionate leave due to COVID-19-related bereavement. Issues around staffing problems due to sickness and self-isolation, including in relation to care providers, were also felt in the contact centre. The result of the policy of home working where possible had led to assessments taking double the amount of time due to issues with information gathering.[73] There were extended working hours due to acting as part of the COVID-19 hospital discharge process and Discharge to Assess (D2A) pathway team. Overall, an additional level of mapping was introduced to prioritize the actions required.

> In line with the Care Act Easements guidance, operational teams have been mapping all existing known community packages for complexity and need and risk rating in order to establish the high priority cases

---

[69] Solihull Metropolitan Borough Council (2020) Report to: Health and Adult Social Care Scrutiny Board. Care Act Easements. 15 June. Report from: Jenny Wood, Director: Adult Care and Support Karen Murphy, Assistant Director: Adult Care and Support Lizzie Edwards, Acting Assistant Director: Adult Care and Support Beth Hutchinson, Principal Social Worker: Adult Care and Support; Report author/lead contact officer: Safina Mistry, Strategic Commissioner Safina Mistry, Beth Hutchinson, Principal Social Worker: Adult Care and Support, Laura Harwood, Acting Governance Lead: Adult Care and Support, para 3.8.

[70] Solihull Metropolitan Borough Council (2020) 'CPH Adult Social Care and Health Decision Session', 6 April.

[71] Solihull Metropolitan Borough Council (2020) 'CPH Adult Social Care and Health Decision Session', 6 April, p 11.

[72] Solihull Metropolitan Borough Council (2020) Solihull Metropolitan Borough Council (2020) 'CPH Adult Social Care and Health Decision Session', 6 April, p 11.

[73] Solihull Metropolitan Borough Council (2020) 'CPH Adult Social Care and Health Decision Session', 6 April.

for action and potential low priority cases for potential easement of Care Act duties. This is part of the approach recommended in national guidance but has impacted on usual service delivery and added to the backlog of work to be completed.[74]

Other factors included challenges facing providers, such as impact on care home staff due to sickness, self-isolation, some resignations due to COVID-19 risks, and recruitment problems, as well as the number of hospital discharge individuals with 'more complex needs' requiring community care. It was also noted that PPE supply chain issues were impacting on the provision of care, which therefore needed 'consideration and prioritisation'.[75]

Subsequently in the papers for the Council Health and Adult Social Care Scrutiny Board it was noted that:

> 3.4. [...] The main impacts of implementing easements on direct support have been changes to day opportunities access and changes to support for some people receiving low-level care and support.[76]

The documentation noted that local authority day centres had closed due to social distancing and the as staffing was impacted by COVID-19 they had not been able 'to provide alternative day opportunities'.[77] The Director for Public Health and the Director for Adult Social Care stated in the meeting documentation that as a consequence of operation of Stage 4 easements 'there have been 41 people who had their home care reduced or suspended. All of these people have now been offered the return of their original home care hours'.[78]

The report maintained that: 'The easements have supported teams to prioritise workload and ensure that those most in need receive a timely response, and teams are now allocating some non-urgent work as a result of previous prioritisation due to easements.'[79]

---

[74] Solihull Metropolitan Borough Council (2020) 'CPH Adult Social Care and Health Decision Session', 6 April.
[75] Solihull Metropolitan Borough Council (2020) 'CPH Adult Social Care and Health Decision Session', 6 April.
[76] Solihull Metropolitan Borough Council (2020) 'Report to: Health and Adult Social Care Scrutiny Board. Care Act Easements', 15 June para 3.4.
[77] Solihull Metropolitan Borough Council (2020) 'J. Wood, K. Murphy, L. Edwards, B. Hutchinson, S. Mistry, B. Hutchinson and L. Harwood, Adult Care and Support Meeting of 15 June 2020. Report to: Health and Adult Social Care Scrutiny Board. Care Act Easements Report', para 3.4.
[78] Solihull Metropolitan Borough Council (2020) 'Minutes: Meeting of the Health and Adult Social Care Scrutiny Board. Care Act Easements', 15 June, Agenda item 3.
[79] Solihull Metropolitan Borough Council (2020) 'Report to: Health and Adult Social Care Scrutiny Board. Care Act Easements', 15 June, para 5.3.

Overall, Solihull Council appears to have undertaken careful decision-making, closely aligned with the legislative Guidance provided by the DHSC. While it was an officer-led decision, adult social services also took legal advice, presumably from the in-house legal team, in order to check their interpretation. Solihull did provide information regarding the operational changes to service provision on its website. In relation to 'Equality Implications' it is stated that 'the duties outlined in the Equality Act 2010 remain in place'.[80] However, it is unclear whether a full Equality Impact Assessment had been undertaken at this stage. By 30 June 2020, Solihull Council reported that it had returned to full compliance with the Care Act 2014.[81]

(d) Staffordshire County Council

Staffordshire County Council provides services for approximately 870,800 citizens across a relatively affluent, largely rural area, with some pockets of high deprivation.[82] The Council decided to activate Stage 3 easements on 9 April 2020 on the basis that:

> One of the Council's strategic objectives for management of the immediate impact of the coronavirus COVID-19 epidemic is to: ensure sustainability of adult social care during the coronavirus COVID-19 epidemic, and that planning and actions to sustain adult social care link with planning and actions in the NHS. This is against a backdrop of increasing demand and reducing capacity due to staff absence as a result of sickness and self-isolation.[83]

The decision stated that approval had been given by the Council Leader and Deputy Leader, who was also the Cabinet Member for Health Care and Wellbeing Board, along with the DASS and the PSW.[84] A public-facing statement from the Deputy Leader, Alan White, published on the Council's

---

[80] Solihull Metropolitan Borough Council (2020) 'CPH Adult Social Care and Health Decision Session, Care Act Easements', 6 April, para 6.6.1.
[81] Solihull Metropolitan Borough Council (2020) 'News item: How COVID-19 is affecting care and support for adults', webpage.
[82] Staffordshire County Council (2020) 'Care for all Ages. Information for providers', webpage.
[83] Staffordshire County Council (2020) 'Executive Officer Delegated Decision Form Decision Title: Coronavirus COVID-19: implementation of Care Act easements', Decision Date 9 April.
[84] 'Staffordshire County Council (2020) 'Executive Officer Delegated Decision Form Decision Title: Coronavirus COVID-19: implementation of Care Act easements', Decision Date 9 April, para 28.

website indicated that the activation of easements was pre-emptive and precautionary, with an initial intention to use 'flexibilities', presumably at Stage 2:

> We have taken the decision to use these flexibilities if we have to — but we will only use them where absolutely necessary. This will enable us to maintain care for people at higher risk. This is us thinking ahead and planning to use the Care Act easements if and when they are needed, rather than whole scale implementation at this stage. This means that if we do have to use them we can do so in a managed way.[85]

The statement sought to reassure the public that any changes would be as sparing as possible, and that the Council would seek to ensure that citizens would continue to receive care.

> Decisions are being made on a case by case basis. The only easement we have had to enact so far is deferring a small number of people's full Care Act assessments. We are still assessing everyone to ensure that they are properly looked after.[86]

The recommendation to implement easements had been discussed with 'local NHS leadership including the Clinical Commissioning Groups'[87] and the co-chairs of the Health and Wellbeing Board and Healthwatch had also been informed of the position, presumably to assure and confirm buy-in.[88] On 17 April 2020, Richard Harling, the DASS, formally notified the DHSC of Staffordshire's decision to activate easements via the dedicated easements email address.[89]

Staffordshire shared substantial information about the decision-making and rationale for activation in the notification email. First, it outlined the COVID-19 Assessment Process, introduced because of insufficient capacity for normal Care Act assessments and reviews because of staff absence

---

[85] Staffordshire County Council (2020) 'Statement on Care Act easements', Newsroom item, 23 April.

[86] Staffordshire County Council (2020) 'Statement on Care Act easements', Newsroom item, Statement 23 April 2020.

[87] Staffordshire County Council (2020) 'Executive Officer Delegated Decision Form Decision Title: Coronavirus COVID-19: implementation of Care Act easements', Decision Date 9 April, para 29.

[88] Staffordshire County Council (2020) 'Executive Officer Delegated Decision Form Decision Title: Coronavirus COVID-19: implementation of Care Act easements', Decision Date 9 April, para 30.

[89] Email from R. Harling to DHSC, 17 April 2020, contained in FoI response sent to Liberty on 20 May 2020.

(approximately one third of staff were absent at that stage) and also due to the need to support the COVID-19 hospital discharge pathway. Second, the prioritization of home care was introduced where needed. It was recognized that due to the hospital discharge pathway there would be rise in home-based care demand. However, this too was problematic because home care staff were themselves experiencing high levels of staff sickness and absence. The home care provider situation was serious, with two thirds of home care providers being reported as having initiated business continuity plans. In the case of three other providers, the easement notification stated that these had 'declared a high risk to business continuity even with plans enacted and there is a sizeable backlog of people awaiting homecare'.[90] These problems in turn could result in delays in people being discharge from hospital if appropriate home care was not available. It was stated that: 'The Council is seeking to mitigate this by redeploying staff into home care and by recruiting additional home care workers through the iCare campaign. However this is expected to offer only a partial mitigation.'[91]

To augment formal service provision, the Council, with support from the LRF (a multi-agency body led by Harling and shared with Stoke-on-Trent), established a community support effort called 'iCare'. This crucial community volunteer force was typical of responses across the region, and indeed the country, in supplementing the efforts of professional staff.[92] Following the community impact assessment, the iCare scheme was stepped up immediately to 'safeguard the most vulnerable people' and

> ensure that the most serious and urgent needs of existing service users are always prioritised, so that they do not become unwell, not only because this is important in its own right but because it avoids placing an unnecessary additional demand on the NHS at this time of crisis.[93]

The broader intention was for social services teams to undertake the triage of new referrals and broker home care for high- and medium-risk individuals with home care for low-risk individuals to be deferred if required:

(a) Work with home care providers to triage existing home care packages, continue care for high and medium risk individuals and suspend care for low risk individuals if required.

---

[90] Email from R. Harling to the DHSC, 17 April 2020.
[91] Email from R. Harling to the DHSC, 17 April 2020.
[92] Staffordshire County Council (2020) Cabinet meeting, 15 April, 'Staffordshire County Council's Response to COVID-19'.
[93] Staffordshire County Council (2020) iCare Campaign report. Cabinet meeting, Agenda item 7, 15 April, p 29.

(b) Put in place a system of welfare checks for low risk individuals for whom home care has been deferred or suspended.[94]

The Director of Health and Care reported to a Cabinet meeting of 20 May 2020 that:

> We temporarily introduced a shortened COVID-19 assessment to determine whether people needed care and support and whether this was required immediately. People were informed that their full care act assessment would be completed at a later date. This has helped maintain staff capacity to support the COVID-19 hospital discharge pathway and ensure that everyone can be assessed in a timely way.[95]

The Council also indicated that it was putting in place preparations, if needed, to move to Stage 4 easements. This never happened and, by 27 May 2020, it was stated that 'the county council now has improved staffing capacity, and therefore it is no longer operating under "Care Act Easements" and is now providing full Care Act Assessments and annual reviews'.[96]

Later, in the Recovery Plan presented at a Cabinet meeting on 17 June 2020, certain aspects of the easements approach were revisited and commended, framed as 'transformational opportunities'. The team would continue to 'work to implement video and telephone social care assessments and reviews as routine and enable staff to work flexibly' to harness 'the improved ways of working'.[97] The Plan noted that the shortened COVID-19 assessment had been utilized for some 1,813 people, and that work had now begun to undertake full Care Act assessments and financial assessments for that group; suspended routine Care Act reviews were being taken up again and were to be completed by September 2020.

> In addition to dealing with the backlog, the recovery plan will also ensure that the services are able to respond to an anticipated increase in demand following the emergency response. In the event that demand exceeds this or staff capacity reduces it may be necessary to acquire additional temporary resource.

The COVID-19 pandemic has required implementation of streamlined assessments by telephone in the majority of cases. It has

---

[94] Staffordshire County Council (2020) Coronavirus/COVID-19 Update Executive Officer and Delegated Decision Form.
[95] Staffordshire County Council (2020) Cabinet meeting, 20 May.
[96] Staffordshire County Council (2020) Coronavirus/COVID-19 Update, 27 May.
[97] Staffordshire County Council (2020) Recovery Plan – Health & Care, 17 June, para 18.

been possible to arrange care for people more quickly than would have previously been possible.[98]

This also last point demonstrates how easements where appropriately implemented could indeed have provided councils with protection.

(e) Warwickshire County Council

Warwickshire County Council serves approximately 596,773 citizens across a mixture of historic towns and rural areas.[99] The decision to implement Stage 3 easements was signed on 9 April 2020 by the DASS, Nigel Minns.[100] The governance structure utilized in making the decision to activate the easements and the support given to this process is very clearly stated. It is noted that there were discussions with 'local NHS leadership', including the local Clinical Commissioning Groups (CCGs), which endorsed them, and that the decision was also supported by the PSW, Ian Redfern, who was to monitor their use.[101] It also stated that the Portfolio Holder for Adult Social Care and Health and Chair of the Health and Wellbeing Board, Councillor Caborn, had been 'briefed' and had supported the actions taken. Opposition members were also briefed, as were the chair and spokespersons from all parties on the Adult Social Care and Health Overview and Scrutiny Committee.[102]

The Care Act easements were also discussed at the meetings of Warwickshire Joint Commissioning Board on 2 April 2020, and the System Provider Support Group on 3 April 2020.[103] The decision to avoid face-to-face activity in order to reduce the risk of spreading disease is expressly included in the easement decision, thus highlighting once more the interface with social-distancing guidance. The rationale given was the lack of capacity to undertake standard Care Act assessments and reviews due to large staff absences (approximately 25 per cent were at that time absent through sickness or self-isolation, a figure that was expected to rise). The impact of

---

[98] Staffordshire County Council (2020) Recovery Plan – Health & Care, 17 June, ss 18–19.
[99] See Warwickshire County Council (2021) 'Population Report for Warwickshire from Census 2021', at https://data.warwickshire.gov.uk/population/#/view-report/63aed df1d7fc44b8b4dffcd868e84eac/___iaFirstFeature/G3, accessed 2 July 2024.
[100] Warwickshire County Council (2020) Officer Key Decision made under the Council's Urgency Procedure by the Strategic Director for People on 9 April 2020: 'Coronavirus COVID-19: Care Act Easements'.
[101] Warwickshire County Council (2020) Officer Key Decision 'Coronavirus COVID-19: Care Act Easements'.
[102] Response to FoI request made on 1 May 2020 by Liberty. Ref. MR/sh/MB47528.
[103] Response to FoI request on 2 September 2020. Ref. MR/sh/MB47528.

home working and the need to safeguard social care staff with underlying conditions was also highlighted. The need to support the hospital discharge pathway was also noted, as was the impact of reduced capacity in other areas, including the NHS and private providers".

This was set alongside the need to 'maintain the usual contact and triage arrangements for people in the community'. An adapted COVID-Assessment process was introduced with the aim of obtaining sufficient information 'based on the Care Act domains' to enable the making of care and support needs decisions which would reduce delays and be an efficient use of social work time. The intention was that this would largely be done remotely to reduce risk of infection, though they 'would consider the needs and wishes of customers and their families and carers wherever possible'.[104]

Existing planned reviews under the Care Act were to be suspended. In addition, where reviews arose otherwise on an unplanned basis they were to be assessed under the specific COVID-19 assessment pathway introduced and were treated as new assessments. Minimal detail was to be provided in support plans.[105] In those cases where new care and support needs were identified brief plans were to be prepared and it was intended that as the pandemic situation improved then plans in line with the Care Act 2014 would be developed.[106] Information was to be given to individuals to the effect that 'the care and support they receive at the current time may not be provided in the future or may be provided in a different way' along with information regarding changes to charging processes including the fact that these may be retrospective.[107]

There is a clear statement of prioritization to ensure that the most essential and pressing needs are met, meaning that certain practices usually implemented to promote social inclusion were paused:

> Assessments will be person specific to ensure their health and safety will but not person centred in terms of meeting wider social and life outcomes. For most people currently though, these outcomes are curtailed by the social isolation.
>
> Where we have to divert care to those most in need, some people will have some elements of their support withdrawn and their choices will be limited.[108]

---

[104] Warwickshire County Council (2020) Officer Key Decision made under the Council's Urgency Procedure by the Strategic Director for People, 9 April.
[105] Warwickshire County Council (2020) Officer Key Decision, 9 April.
[106] Warwickshire County Council (2020) Officer Key Decision, 9 April.
[107] Warwickshire County Council (2020) Officer Key Decision, 9 April.
[108] Warwickshire County Council (2020) Officer Key Decision, 9 April.

The document then considers 'Prioritising care and support for those with most pressing needs' – a key aspect of Stage 3 easements. It notes the pressures upon hospital discharge work, including on care providers 'most of whom also have contracts with the Council to provide social care and support'.[109] Similar pressures were noted on domiciliary care providers who were using 'business continuity processes'. Consequently, despite mitigation efforts, needs could not be met 'in line with normal practice under the Care Act'.[110]

If individuals were able to cope without 'regulated care for a short period' they would be referred to the voluntary and community sector, though at the 'conclusion of the coronavirus COVID-19 epidemic' they were to be contacted 'to determine whether they still wish to proceed to a Care Act compliant assessment'.[111] It remains uncertain when that cut-off date actually was given the continued prevalence of COVID-19, and it is also unclear from the records at the time of writing whether or when those people did ultimately come forward for assessments.

The statement also indicated what would happen were Stage 4 easements to be implemented; namely, that the actions would be reviewed every two weeks. It was noted that certain steps had been taken to mitigate the impact of easements before they were implemented. These included redeployment of social care staff to acute hospitals supporting patient discharge decision – making and annual leave was 'managed'. Due to technological changes staff were able to undertake work at home. Project work concerning change and performance had stopped. There was daily review of staffing measures and of demand by service managers and the Assistant Director Adult Social Care.[112] Staff absences are seen as a key factor, not only in the Council itself but also more generally across the NHS and commissioned services, for triggering easements.

The decision note is also accompanied by an Appendix explaining how the decision was assessed against the Ethical Framework, with a detailed table demonstrating analysis of the decisions against the criteria, as well as a 'Red, Amber, Green' (R-A-G rated) Equality Impact Initial Screening Template, which formed the basis of the Equality Impact Assessment.[113] External communications were considered and implemented, including a public statement with a simple explanation of the easement stages and

---

[109] Warwickshire County Council (2020) Officer Key Decision, 9 April.
[110] Warwickshire County Council (2020) Officer Key Decision, 9 April.
[111] Warwickshire County Council (2020) Officer Key Decision, 9 April.
[112] Warwickshire County Council (2020) Officer Key Decision, 9 April.
[113] Warwickshire County Council (2020) 'Appendix: analysis of recommendations against the COVID-19 Ethical Framework for Adult Social Care'.

which services might be impacted by the easements, posted on the Council website.[114]

By May 2020 it was clear that the position was improving. The Easement Review meeting involving key decision-makers, Nigel Minns (Strategic Director, People), Pete Sidgwick (Assistant Director), and Ian Redfern (PSW), dated 5 May 2020, recorded that staffing was at a good level and the market was able to meet demand, although there was some variance between providers and that choice remained 'restricted'.[115] Some aspects of work were still taking longer than hoped, such as telephone assessments; but operational managers were reporting that they were able to manage demand despite the pressures, and that they remained focused on 'making safe' rather than attending to the backlog of reviews and other deferred work:

> They no longer have wait lists which has enabled us to make sure current care needs are met. EDT has had significant increased adult demand – they continue to focus on making safe rather than doing more detailed Care Act work.
> Use of easements
> Residential review workers are still redeployed and supporting other teams so we are not undertaking these planned reviews. Other teams are doing planned reviews when they have capacity. Pressure at Team Leader level and Operations Manager level.

It was also commented that:

> There is stored demand with NHS hospital discharge cases that will need picking up – work has only just started on these cases. NHS locally is considering recommencing activity. We anticipate an upturn as people make contact again as restrictions are lifted. We need to go back to people where we/they have deferred non-urgent work due to risk of infection. We need to go back to people where the lack of group and community activity has meant we could not make these arrangements.[116]

---

[114] Warwickshire County Council (2020) 'Coronavirus – Care Act easements information', webpage. www.warwickshire.gov.uk/information-coronavirus/coronavirus-care-act-easements/1

[115] Warwickshire County Council (2020) Easement Review Meeting on 5 May, Minutes made available via FoI no. 6121208.

[116] Warwickshire County Council (2020) Easement Review Meeting on 5 May.

The easements were subsequently 'stood down'. A further Easement Review meeting was undertaken on 22 May 2020.[117] This indicated that staffing levels showed a good level of attendance, with the market meeting demand, and with no increased demand (though this was projected to rise in coming months). It was stressed that, while certain pressures and uncertainties remained, they were now able to move to Stage 2 (flexibilities), following the directives in the Guidance. Nonetheless, the possibility of revisiting the use of Care Act easements was left open. 'If some of the future demand and/or second wave occurs, we will need to consider moving back to stage 3.'[118]

In a response to an FoI request on 1 October 2020, it was confirmed that in the period 1 March 2020 to 29 May 2020 no one had been refused an assessment face-to-face or remotely due to lack of capacity because of the pandemic.[119] Warwickshire thus appeared to engage effectively with the easements Guidance.

(f) Reflections on approaches taken by West Midlands local authorities which formally notified the DHSC that they were implementing easements

The stated rationale for all the local authorities which formally activated Care Act easements was sustainability of adult social services in the context of increased demand and reduced workforce capacity. This was aligned with the DHSC Guidance. Pressure on NHS services and hospital beds were also a shared concern, particularly in Birmingham and Solihull with the construction of the Nightingale Hospital. As shown previously, communication and political buy-in with elected representatives was raised as an issue in Birmingham, whereas in Solihull, for example, there appeared to be political agreement with the decision-making process undertaken. The quality of communication with citizens regarding the introduction of easements was also criticized. For example, Clenton Farquharson, Chair of the organization Think Local Act Personal (TLAP),[120] tweeted on 21 April 2020 about the failure of Councils to communicate clearly and compassionately about the activation of easements: 'I'm not upset about the decision but in the way the decision was communicated, and the lack of clarity in the way the decision was made in the first place.'[121]

The public scrutiny and the impact of FoI requests were considerable. As we shall see in the excerpts from our stakeholder interviews that follow, some

---

[117] Warwickshire County Council (2020) Easement Review Meeting on 22 May. Minutes made available via FoI request. Ref. redacted.
[118] Warwickshire County Council (2020) Easement Review Meeting on 22 May.
[119] Response to FoI request dated 1 October 2020. Ref. redacted.
[120] TLAP and its work is discussed in more detail in Chapters 2 and 6.
[121] See, for example, https://twitter.com/clentonF/status/1252925838665961472?s=20

Councils were concerned about the adverse reputational impacts consequent upon the formal activation of Care Act easements during this period.

III. The approaches taken by West Midlands local authorities implementing Stage 2 'flexibilities' (which some describe as 'easements')

In the Guidance local authorities, the operation of Stage 2 'flexibilities' under the pre-amendment Care Act were not classed as being 'easements' per se, as this term applied to those Stages (3 and 4) which needed to be formally notified to the DHSC. However, several West Midlands local authorities operated such 'Stage 2 flexibilities' though they were described in council minutes as being 'easements'. This might be considered a simple 'misprint', but examination of the documents reveals that in relation to several of these local authorities the decision to implement such easements/flexibilities was accompanied by a considerable degree of formalization, in line with the decision-making approach taken by those West Midlands authorities which notified the DHSC that they were operating at Stages 3 and 4. Moreover, statements regarding 'moving to Stage 2' in some instances also suggest that these 'flexibilities' were viewed as outside of usual practice, and were perhaps pre-emptive measures with a view to the possibility of moving onto Stages 3 and 4 at some later time.

(a) Herefordshire Council

Herefordshire Council serves a predominantly rural population of some 188,700 citizens as of 2022.[122] The Council issued a decision on 4 May 2020 to state that 'under the Easement of the Care Act 2014 regulations, the council are at Stage 2 as set out in the guidance' and would 'move to Stage 3 and 4, when appropriate and necessary to do so'.[123] The decision document, applicable 'countywide', notes that there had been extensive consultation and communication with key stakeholders, including 'engagement to Adults and Communities workforce through three workforce Webex conferences. Verbal and written briefings to operational staff.'[124]

---

[122] Herefordshire Council (2022) 'Understanding Herefordshire: People and Places'.

[123] Herefordshire Council (2020) 'Record of Operational Decision: To make a formal decision to implement easements to the Care Act 2014, Introduced by the Coronavirus Act 2020 and associated Regulations', Stephen Vickers, Director of Adults and Communities, 4 April.

[124] S. Vickers (2020) 'Record of Operational Decision: To make a formal decision to implement easements to the Care Act 2014, Introduced by the Coronavirus Act 2020 and associated Regulations', Stephen Vickers, Director of Adults and Communities, 4 April.

What is striking here is (1) that this Council explicitly defines Stage 2 as 'Post Easement – but a continuation by the Council to continue to meet all of its duties under the Care Act 2014 but with some degree of flexibility used';[125] and (2) the date – 4 May 2020. This is relatively late to be deciding whether to implement easements or flexibilities, given the situation nationally. By this point the local authorities considered in the previous section were already operating at Stage 3 or Stage 4 and looking at options for cessation. The decision document states that the Council will:

(a) Introduce the new streamline COVID-19 assessment process.
(b) Suspend routine Care Act reviews.
(c) Triage new referrals, and broker home care for high and medium risk individuals, with home care for low risk individuals to be deferred.
(d) Work with home care providers to triage existing home care packages, continue care for high and medium risk individuals, and suspend care for low risk individuals.
(e) Put in place a system of welfare checks for low risk individuals for whom home care has been deferred or suspended.[126]

An Equality Impact Assessment was undertaken which identified several potentially negative impacts, though it also stated that these were not focused on a particular client group and that 'available resource is being prioritised across all client groups'.[127] The Council also produced a R-A-G rated prioritisation tool for home care, to aid social worker decision-making relating to levels of support needed by individuals.[128] The Council indicated that they had adapted to the pandemic challenges, including diversion of social work staff in relation to discharge to assess processes. Further, the fact that there had been 'increased capacity' through home working meant that they could 'adapt and effectively respond to the significant 33% additional assessment work through the COVID period'.[129]

The Report stated that: 'Social workers and social care assessors continued to operate a full service throughout the COVID period including emergency

---

[125] S. Vickers (2020).
[126] S. Vickers (2020).
[127] Herefordshire Council (2020) 'Equality Impact Assessment Form - Easement of Care Act duties', signed Mandy Appleby, Appendix 3, 4 May.
[128] Herefordshire Council (2020) 'Prioritisation tool for home care', Appendix 2, 4 May.
[129] Herefordshire Council (2021) Herefordshire Council's response to the COVID Pandemic. Meeting: General scrutiny committee. Meeting date: Friday 11 June. Report by: Solicitor to the council para 38.

social work response out of hours service.'[130] It noted that other functions such as safeguarding continued and that:

> Face to face work continued where it was judged as necessary for the immediate safeguarding and lawful assessment of an individual but with the full and early adoption of PPE and rigorous application of risk assessments for our staff regarding vulnerability to infection as set out by Human Resources department was successfully minimised.[131]

Although the Equality Impact Assessment had indicated that the operation of easements would be reviewed 'in line with the current emergency',[132] we were not able to identify the point at which Herefordshire Council decided to cease operating at Stage 2 from the publicly available council documentation.

(b) Sandwell Metropolitan Borough Council

Sandwell is a local authority serving a population of approximately 327,378 citizens.[133] Sandwell has ethnically diverse communities, several of which were hit particularly hard during the pandemic.[134] In 2021 it was ranked in the Office of National Statistics table as being the 12th most deprived local authority in England.[135] This council operated an 'Emergency Committee' and a 'COVID-19 Engagement Board' alongside Cabinet, which engaged with adult social care issues during the pandemic.[136] In documentation issued, express reference is made to 'Care Act Easements'. In his Report on 22 April 2020 to the Sandwell Council Emergency Committee, the Adult Social Care Lead Stuart Lackenby laid out his recommendations for 'approval for the implementation of Care Act easements' and 'approval for the implementation of a COVID-19 assessment process to support the

---

[130] Herefordshire Council (2021), point 39.
[131] Herefordshire Council (2021), point 39.
[132] Hereford Council (2020) 'Equality Impact Assessment Form – Easement of Care Act duties', signed Mandy Appleby, Appendix 3, 4 May.
[133] As of 2018, see www.sandwelltrends.info/sandwell-in-brief/
[134] 38.4 per cent were from BAME backgrounds in 2021; see further, Sandwell Metropolitan Borough Council (2021) *Sandwell COVID-19 Local Outbreak Management Plan*, April, p 29. The Report, p 29, also states that: 'In Sandwell, COVID-19 case rates have been consistently higher in BAME Groups. This includes a case rate among our Indian community that has been consistently at least twice as high as those found in the white British group.'
[135] See further discussion in Sandwell Metropolitan Borough Council (2021) *Sandwell COVID Local Management Plan*, April, p 27.
[136] Sandwell Metropolitan Borough Council (2020) 'COVID-19 Local Outbreak Plan', p 6.

hospital discharge pathway'.[137] However, it appears that this process had in fact begun. The document states that:

> The Care Act easements outlined above have been implemented with immediate effect as there is currently insufficient capacity to maintain normal Care Act assessments and reviews due to the following reasons:
>
> - Staff absence as result of self-isolating and sickness.
> - Social distancing – reducing the ability to undertake face to face intervention.
> - A requirement to support the Coronavirus COVID-19 hospital discharge pathway.
>
> The decision to implement easements is to be reviewed on a fortnightly basis, with a view to returning to normal practice as soon as is practically possible.[138]

Shortened needs assessments were integrated into the new COVID-19 assessment as part of the hospital discharge pathway:

> The COVID-19 assessment process would involve a short assessment, which would capture enough information to make a decision about whether an individual needs care and determine the most appropriate provision of care. Introduction of this process would avoid delays in the COVID-19 hospital discharge pathway and allow best use to be made of social work capacity.[139]

The approach and rationale given here seem to be very similar to those taken in local authorities which operated at Stage 3 and Stage 4. This document, in contrast to that of Herefordshire, did not mention any formal consultation process undertaken prior to implementation. However, it did indicate that following implementation there was to be a fortnightly report to the Cabinet Member for Healthy Lives and the Chair of the Health and Wellbeing Board as to 'the continued requirement of COVID-19 assessment process'.[140]

The minutes of that Emergency Committee meeting asked for approval to:

---

[137] S. Lackenby (2020) 'Adult Social Care' Sandwell Council, Appendix 1 Short Report, 22 April, 2.
[138] Lackenby (2020), para 2.2.
[139] Lackenby (2020), para 2.3.
[140] Lackenby (2020), para 2.3.

- implement Care Act easements, with immediate effect, including the suspension of charging for adult social care and the adoption of a revised care management pathway. These would be applied only when necessary;
- a COVID-19 assessment process to be implemented to support the hospital discharge pathway;
- develop an offer to providers of care and support to enable their ongoing sustainability through this difficult period, for consideration at a future meeting of the Committee.[141]

While there is reference to Care Act easements, and to the easements Guidance, it does not state whether this was actually intended to be a Stage 2 'easement' (a 'flexibility'). Moreover, the reasons given for implementation include 'social distancing' which, as previously discussed, was considered to be a public health directive. The language of easements continues to be used in later Council documentation. A report titled 'The Impact of COVID-19 on Operational Risks' for the subsequent meeting of the Emergency Committee on 6 May 2020 states that:

> As a result of the easements in respect of these areas, there will be a backlog in assessments and inspections which will need to be prioritised given the pressure on available resources when the easements are lifted.[142]

However in his Report to the Emergency Committee on 27 May 2020, Chief Executive David Stevens clearly states that the Council did not have to formally activate Care Act easements. He noted that they were assessing the impact of changes in service delivery going forward in the recovery plan with the intention that

> services that have continued but delivered differently (e.g. corporate contact centre staff working from home or adapting social work practices so that Level 3 Care Act easements (requiring notification to DHSC) have not had to be applied).[143]

This appears to be the last publicly available reference to easements or to flexibilities in the documentation produced by this Council. Thus, while

---

[141] Sandwell Metropolitan Borough Council (2020) Minutes of Emergency Committee, 22 April.

[142] Sandwell Metropolitan Borough Council (2020) 'Impact of COVID-19 on Operational Risks @ April 2020 (Appendix C)'.

[143] Sandwell Council (2020) Report to Emergency Committee on 27 May 2020, 'COVID-19 Reset and Recovery Planning – Roadmap of Activity' by Director: Chief Executive David Stevens para 3.4.2.1.

there was no formal notification of higher level easements, there had been changes in service delivery which were classed by the Council as 'easements'.

(c) Telford & Wrekin Council

Telford & Wrekin is a unitary authority with a fast-growing population of 185,500 people at the census of 2021.[144] This Council initially stated that it is operating 'stage 2 flexibilities' but a broader range of documentation refers to these as 'easements'. A report titled 'Care Act Easement: Implementation of the Coronavirus Act 2020' drafted by Jonathan Rowe, Executive Director Adult Social Care Health Integration & Wellbeing, in September 2020 outlined the approach taken in the Telford and Wrekin strategic plan to 'ensure sustainability of Adult Social Care during the coronavirus COVID-19 epidemic, and that planning and actions to sustain Adult Social Care link with planning and actions in the NHS' in an integrated manner, with many multi-agency meetings moved online.[145] Demand was to be managed with frontline staff being diverted to support the COVID-19 hospital discharge pathway. In addition, it stated that there would be a reduction in the risk of spreading COVID-19 via 'identifying key provisions to be delivered in a different way' and 'reducing staff-client contacts'.[146]

The report went on to state that Telford & Wrekin is 'operating flexibilities under the pre-amendment Care Act and, therefore, are at Stage 2 as set out within the guidance'.[147] However, it appears to conflate such flexibilities with easements and states that each of the three categories of changes identified are 'required due to the impact on service types and usual duties that have been changed, delayed or cancelled short term'.[148]

In relation to care and support needs it was noted that adjustments were made to the performance of needs and carer's assessments due to the suspension of non-essential visits. It was noted that this approach could

> impact on the details captured within an assessment and our ability to operate in a strength based way may also be affected. We will use a variety of ways to carry out assessments including video calling, the telephone, and/or email(s). This will ensure we are able to gather information

---

[144] Office for National Statistics (2021) 'How life has changed in Telford & Wrekin Census 2021'.
[145] Telford & Wrekin Council (2020) 'Telford & Wrekin Care Act Easements 2020', by Executive Director: Adults Social Care and Health & Wellbeing J. Rowe, presented to Meeting of the Health and Wellbeing Board, 10 September.
[146] Telford & Wrekin Council (2020) 'Telford & Wrekin Care Act Easements 2020'.
[147] Telford & Wrekin Council (2020) 'Telford & Wrekin Care Act Easements 2020'.
[148] Telford & Wrekin Council (2020) 'Telford & Wrekin Care Act Easements 2020'.

to carry out assessments. Pre-easement business processes should be followed, there have been no amendments to assessment paperwork.[149]

In relation to financial assessments, there was a three-month suspension of client contribution for all care and support delivered to any individuals in the community. Besides this, financial assessment activity, including requests for financial information from individuals or their representatives, continued. It was noted that there would be a delay in informing individuals of their required contribution, though this would be 'communicated at the earliest point'.[150] In relation to the review of care and support plans it was stated that:

> Scheduled reviews will continue to be completed, however these will be completed remotely where possible. Information should be gathered from the provider, all people important to the individual and consideration be given to an earlier review period if necessary to follow up any actions, particular that promote independence using a strength based approach, that are unable to be followed up at this time due to social distancing. Pre-easement business processes should be followed, there have been no amendments to review paperwork.[151]

The Report also indicated that they did not need to implement any changes to meeting care or support needs, nor did they use the easement enabling 'removal or reduction of support in order to allow the market to support those with the most pressing needs' because they had 'not experienced an impact on frontline staff or a surge in demand'.[152] It also noted the increased multi-agency working which had taken place.

Although Telford & Wrekin produced relevant documentation to explain decision-making internally at committee level, via correspondence to service providers, and through the website to the public, it is interesting to note the conflation of impacts of Stage 2 'easements' or 'flexibilities' with impacts resulting from social distancing. In many other local authorities, day centre closures and the shift from face-to-face contacts to virtual communications were not considered to be relating to easements since these were changes made in response to public health guidance.

There was some further confusion apparent when the Report was presented by Sarah Dillion, Director of Adult Social Care, to the Health &

---

[149] Telford & Wrekin Council (2020) 'Telford & Wrekin Care Act Easements 2020'.
[150] Telford & Wrekin Council (2020) 'Telford & Wrekin Care Act Easements 2020'.
[151] Telford & Wrekin Council (2020) 'Telford & Wrekin Care Act Easements 2020'.
[152] Telford & Wrekin Council (2020) 'Telford & Wrekin Care Act Easements 2020'.

Wellbeing Board on 10 June 2020.[153] The minutes of this meeting suggest a reiteration of the main 'flexibilities' in place. Having rated itself at 'level two', it was noted that the:

> biggest area of concern was the daytime support for individuals with disabilities while social distancing measures were in place. Work was being done to assess the types of support they can offer, but daytime support could not be resumed until social distancing measures were relaxed.[154]

In a further meeting on 3 December 2020, in a 'verbal update' Sarah Dillon 'advised that the Council had continued to complete its duties under Care Act throughout the pandemic, however, there had been some flexibility in how these duties were met'. There had not been a significant change to the care and support provided by the council but there had been some varation in the way in which it had been delivered.[155] Members had asked what services had been cancelled and the PSW stated that

> the services mostly impacted were the day centres due to the social distancing measures. Those impacted by these closures were identified and alternative support was established, such as the launch of MyOptions online weekly activity for individuals with learning difficulties, and smaller social bubbles for individuals with staff to access the community.[156]

This again demonstrates the impacts of public health measures on adult social care services which would ultimately impact on service provision, despite falling outside the provisions of the Coronavirus Act 2020. Overall, there were changes made to service provision and the language of 'easements' was utilized, though this was sometimes conflated with 'flexibilities' and no higher level easements were formally activated.

(d) Walsall Council

Walsall Council is a metropolitan borough council in the Black Country, serving a mix of urban, suburban, and semi-rural communities; it has

---

[153] Telford & Wrekin Council (2020) Minutes of meeting of the Health and Wellbeing Board, 10 June.
[154] Telford & Wrekin Council (2020) Minutes of meeting of the Health and Wellbeing Board, 10 June p.4.
[155] Telford & Wrekin Council (2020) Agenda of the Meeting of the Health and Wellbeing Board, 3 December, p 64.
[156] Telford & Wrekin Council (2020) Minutes of meeting, 3 December.

a population of some 285,500.[157] The local authority serves diverse communities, some with very high levels of socio-economic deprivation, which were consequently more vulnerable to COVID-19 than other parts of the country. The British Red Cross produced a COVID-19 vulnerability index which placed Walsall in the 20 per cent most vulnerable local authorities in England.[158] Walsall played an early role in the national Integrated Care Pilot scheme, and therefore had a relatively well-developed system of integrated working with regards to hospital discharge when the pandemic hit. In addition to following the standard Gold Command response, the local authority was also operating 'Walsall Proud' and 'Walsall Together' schemes, having established a 'Resilient Communities' model in 2019.[159] The wider local COVID-19 response was therefore mobilized using the pre-existing multi-agency community engagement forum of the Walsall Proud Programme.[160]

An undated Framework document, presumably from very early in the pandemic, outlines the emergency legislation and Government Guidance and asserts that 'the Council will do everything they can to continue meeting their existing duties prior to the Coronavirus Act provisions coming into force'.[161] There was a clear notification on the Council website from as early as March 2020 that there would be changes in approaches to service delivery from the 23rd of that month as a result of the pandemic. They announced that:

> Due to the additional pressures across the health and social care system, temporary changes have been made. These changes are to enable local authorities to prioritise the services they offer to ensure that the most urgent and serious care needs are met, even if this means not meeting everyone's assessed needs in full or delaying some assessments … service providers will be delivering care in a different way and [this] may mean changes to how your care is delivered.[162]

Although the term 'easements' was not explicitly used here, these changes resembled the kinds of changes that might be made under the emergency provisions. They included:

---

[157] According to Office for National Statistics figures in 2019.
[158] See Walsall Council (2020) 'COVID-19 Outbreak Management Plan', June, Draft V1.1, p 5.
[159] Walsall Council (2020) *A Review of the Resilient Communities Model*, presented to the Scrutiny Overview Committee, 28 July.
[160] J. Balmire, J. Rees & B. Sojka (2022) *Walsall Council Review of COVID-19 Response: Capturing the Learning*, Wolverhampton: University of Wolverhampton, p 7.
[161] Walsall Council (2020) 'Safeguarding Response to Cabinet – Appendix 1 Social Care Framework: Implementation of the Care Act Easements created as per the Coronavirus Act', 19 May, para 6(3).
[162] Walsall Council (2020) Service User Leaflet – COVID-19, 2 April.

1. Reducing frequency or duration of call times, if appropriate;
2. Replacing face to face calls with telephone contact;
3. Temporarily stopping home calls and services.[163]

In the minutes of a Cabinet meeting regarding safeguarding of 'vulnerable residents', replicated in information for service users, the Council spelled out its Care Act-compliant position more clearly:

> Adult Social Care have made the decision to move to stage 2 of the Care Act easements. This decision permits individual service types to prioritise short term allocation of care and support using current flexibilities within the Care Act.[164]

It notes that considerable operational changes have taken place in the light of social distancing measures. This includes home working of staff and a notice that 'day services have ceased' while staff prioritize working 'flexibly with health and social care colleagues in the provision of PPE and practical support to care homes'.[165]

In keeping with public health advice, there were restrictions in 'visits to care homes, hospitals and supported living' and local authority work was increasingly being undertaken via Teams, Skype, and WhatsApp video.[166] The department had established a R-A-G rating system and a schedule of direct checks to ensure that 'care and support needs continue to be met' among people receiving care at home. Nonetheless, the minutes state that: 'Home care providers are also facing considerable challenges and being supported to be flexible through Care Act easements.'[167] Throughout, there is an express intention to 'ensure oversight and accountability'.[168] There did not appear to be very much engagement with the matter of Care Act easements in the public record of the Health and Wellbeing Board, nor in the COVID-19 Local Outbreak Engagement sub-committee formed in part by its members. Instead, information regarding the easements can be discerned from segments of information posted on the Council website, in letters to service providers, and later in the year in the minutes of Scrutiny and Safeguarding meetings.

---

[163] Walsall Council (2020) Service User Leaflet.
[164] Walsall Council (2020) 'Safeguarding Response During COVID-19', Cabinet Agenda, Item 7(c), 19 May.
[165] Walsall Council (2020) 'Safeguarding Response During COVID-19', Cabinet Agenda, Item 7(c), paras 4.11 and 4.12.
[166] Walsall Council (2020) 'Safeguarding Response During COVID-19', Cabinet Agenda, Item 7(c), paras 4.11 and 4.12.
[167] Walsall Council (2020) 'Safeguarding Response During COVID-19', para 4.14.
[168] Walsall Council (2020) 'Safeguarding Response During COVID-19', Cabinet Agenda, Item 7(c), para 4.14.

By 9 April 2020, a co-signed letter was sent from Kerrie Allward, then Director of Commissioning at Walsall Council, and Andy Rust, Head of Commissioning at Walsall Clinical Commissioning Group, to local service providers, alerting them to the possibility of changes to provision under the Care Act, requesting participation in the R-A-G rating of their capacity, and explaining temporary changes to the usual payment system.[169] On 17 April 2020, a further co-signed letter was sent to local service providers, reiterating the message, reassuring providers that funding was still available, and explaining how a 'flexible' approach could mitigate against reduced staff capacity.[170] It also stated that: 'From Monday 23 March 2020, the Council has committed to paying Social Care providers against the Support Plan for services delivered to services users living in Walsall. The Care Act easements are formally implemented from 9th April 2020 and will be reviewed in 2 weeks' time.'[171] It continued that:

> This gives providers the mandate to deliver care flexibly based on their risk rating of individual needs and means that for some service users, some services will change, some will be reduced by frequency or call duration, some may be delivered by the offer of a virtual care calls and in some cases, calls will be temporarily stopped. We anticipate that by adopting this approach providers will create capacity to mitigate the risks of reduced staffing through sickness or self- isolation and can pick up anticipated additional packages.[172]

This letter suggests that Care Act easements have been implemented, but without an indication of the easement 'stage'. There is, however, a clear statement of prioritization 'to ensure the most urgent and serious care needs are met' as per the Guidance, and that delivery of care may be undertaken 'flexibly' with reference to the vulnerability and risk rating of the individual.

By 5 May 2020, a further update to providers of supported living and complex community-based support services confirmed that additional capacity was no longer required.[173] However, in terms of community-based provision, it appears that changes remained in place for much longer. In a letter dated 22 May 2020 from Kerrie Allward, then Interim Executive Director Adult Social Care, to community-based providers, it was confirmed post a Cabinet

---

[169] Walsall Council (2020) 'Safeguarding Response During COVID-19', para 4.14.
[170] Walsall Council (2020) Letter to providers, 17 April.
[171] Walsall Council (2020) Letter to providers, 17 April.
[172] Walsall Council (2020) Letter to providers, 17 April.
[173] Walsall Council (2020) Letter from K. Allward to care providers, dated 5 May.

meeting on 19 May 2020 that the arrangement to pay via individual support plan values can continue in the short term as follows: 'The service provider, shall continue to work flexibly, innovatively and prioritise their resources, ensuring that the service user's core assessed needs are met, as specified within the service user individual support plan, as agreed in collaboration with the service user and/or their relative/carer/representative.'[174]

In Walsall there was a clear statement that the 'easements' were activated early in April and remained in place well into the first pandemic winter. A letter dated 21 December regarding 'flexible delivery' from Kerrie Allward to providers of community-based support and NHS Continuing Healthcare (CHC) services, states that:

> *Therefore, the Care Act easements formally implemented from 09 April 2020 will also continue, this gives providers the mandate to deliver care flexibly based on their risk rating of individual needs.* For a number of service users this could mean a change to care and support for instance care could be reduced by frequency or call duration, care may be delivered by the offer of a virtual wellbeing care call and in some cases care could be temporarily stopped. We anticipate that by continuing this approach providers will create capacity to take on increased demand/additional packages specifically during the pandemic and to alleviate winter pressures.[175]

On a positive note on how local care homes had coped, Daren Fradgley, Walsall Together lead, presented a report to the Health and Wellbeing Board on 10 October 2020 that highlighted the area's healthy inter-agency working partnerships and that a review by the Care Quality Commission (CQC) 'had identified that only Walsall had arrangements in place under section 75 of the Care Act [re. integrated commissioning and provision] and that other authorities were looking to replicate this model'.[176]

The effectiveness of Walsall's multi-agency working practices, bolstered by its early uptake of integrated practices and principles through the pilot with Walsall Healthcare Trust in the Walsall Together approach, was also noted in a self-commissioned post hoc assessment of the local authority's overall COVID-19 response. The study, undertaken by researchers at the University of Wolverhampton, found that Walsall's response was characterized by agility,

---

[174] Walsall Council (2020) Letter from K. Allward, headed: 'COVID-19 Market Update: Community Based Provision', 22 May.

[175] Walsall Council (2020) Letter from K. Allward, dated 21 December regarding 'Flexible Delivery', emphasis added.

[176] Walsall Council (2020) Minutes of Meeting of the Health and Wellbeing Board, 10 October.

shared goals, and strong partnership working across services represented at the Command level, and especially between local authority and NHS staff. It was noted however that the Council had failed to make full use of a large and willing cohort of community volunteers and local voluntary sector organisations.[177] In its sole mention of the Care Act easements, the report also states that time-limited changes in legislation by Central Government – such as via the Care Act Easements created as per the Coronavirus Act 2020 – enabled local authorities to reduce certain services and relaxed other requirements (such as pertaining to GDPR) which eased the burden on Walsall Council. These factors were each reported to have facilitated the response.[178]

Overall it remains unclear precisely how these changes were operated in practice in Walsall as it appears that there were no specific records publicly available at the time of writing that detail impacts on service users resulting from them.

(e) Implementing and then not implementing Stage 2? Dudley Metropolitan Borough Council

Dudley Metropolitan Borough Council (MBC) serves a population of approximately 313,000 citizens. As of 22 June 2020, Dudley's COVID-19 infection rate was the lowest in the Black Country.[179] Dudley had undertaken its own Pandemic Flu planning work, titled Exercise Perinthus, in November 2019, just prior to the onset of COVID-19. Perinthus was a joint exercise between Dudley MBC, the Dudley Group NHS Foundation Trust, and Dudley Clinical Commissioning Group[180] Its usefulness was demonstrated in the prompt establishment of the local response in terms of the 'governance, command and control' approach, clear communication channels between strategic planners and staff delivering care, and effective utilization of local third-sector networks from early on in the pandemic. Retrospectively, the Director of Public Health noted that Perinthus had helped Dudley's pandemic response and that 'the steps we took to prepare for a pandemic and the "can do" attitude shared across all agencies made us ready to tackle what was ahead'.[181]

---

[177] J. Balmire et al (2022) *Walsall Council Review of COVID-19 Response: Capturing the Learning*, Wolverhampton: University of Wolverhampton.

[178] Balmire et al (2022), p 14.

[179] Dudley Metropolitan Borough Council (2020) 'COVID Situation in Dudley Borough', report presented to Health and Wellbeing Board, 1 July.

[180] Dudley Metropolitan Borough Council (2020) Health and Adult Social Care Scrutiny Committee, 'Report of the Acting Director of Public Health Update on COVID-19', 10 June.

[181] Dudley Metropolitan Borough Council (2022) 'Dudley for Everyone: COVID-19 Looking back and moving forward', Director of Health Annual Report 2022.

Dudley MBC is also notable as a local authority which stated that it had implemented Stage 2 easements, continuing well into October 2020; but then later stated that it had not done so. The Council had established an '8-Point Plan' to address challenges associated with the pandemic. This included objectives to 'Protect the most Vulnerable': (Point 4: 'Prioritising support to the most at risk groups in Dudley, such as the elderly and those with long term pre-existing medical conditions, and those shielding'); 'Support and Protect the Workforce' (Point 5: 'Continuing to review and updating HR policies and resources to support homeworking and redeployment of staff to business critical functions in line with national guidance'); and 'Support frontline services' (Point 6: 'Supporting NHS and Social Care partners to manage cases and outbreaks of COVID-19').[182]

There is little mention of Care Act easements in the minutes from the first half of 2020, though the DASS tweeted from an online Health and Adult Social Care Scrutiny Board meeting on 5 May 2020 — the minutes of which were not available online at the time of writing — that the Care Act easements were under review and that the Council had not triggered them. Yet at the Health and Adult Social Care Scrutiny Board on 15 October 2020, the Report of the Director of Adult Social Care stated that: 'Care Act Easements remained at level two and were reviewed on a weekly basis by the Director of Adult Social Care and the Principal Social Worker.'[183] Virtual consultations were being utilized in this period. Flexibilities and adaptations included redeployment of staff from working in closed day centres to instead operate the 'Pleased to Meet You' helpline for supporting those who felt socially isolated,[184] as well as a wider move towards online working for Council staff.

Confusingly, Dudley MBC stated in their Quarterly Management Report 2020–21 (Quarter 2 July to September 2020) that they 'did not enact any of the Care Act Easements during the pandemic and maintained a full statutory service'.[185] Of course, Stage 2 easements were defined as 'flexibilities' available within the Care Act, rather than 'easements' under the DHSC Guidance documents, but this statement is nonetheless striking given the pre-existing council documentation stating that 'stage 2 easements' were operational, as noted previously.

---

[182] Dudley Metropolitan Borough Council (2020) 'Report of the Acting Director of Public Health to Health and Adult Care Scrutiny Committee', 10 June.

[183] Dudley Metropolitan Borough Council (2020) Health and Adult Social Care Scrutiny Review. 'Report of the Director of Adult Social Care Council response to the COVID-19 Pandemic – Adult Safeguarding and Deprivation of Liberty Safeguards (DoLS)', 15 October.

[184] Dudley Metropolitan Borough Council (2020) Health and Adult Social Care Scrutiny Review Committee, 15 October.

[185] Dudley Metropolitan Borough Council (2020) 'Corporate Quarterly Management Report 2020-2021. Quarter 2 (1st July to 30th September 2020), Adult Social Care Performance Evaluation'.

Indeed, the management of Care Act easements were identified as 'the major point of comparison' for benchmarking in relation to neighbouring local authorities. This benchmark was presented in successive Quarterly Management Reports through until mid-2021.[186] Professor Paul Kingston, who was Head of Dudley's Safeguarding People Partnership Board, described the Council's governance and partnership working during the pandemic as 'exemplary' and that 'in referring to Care Act Easements, Dudley had kept these down at Level 2 whereas some Authorities, even across the West Midlands, had used easements at Level 4.'[187] Dudley MBC was nominated for a LaingBuisson Outstanding Response to COVID in Social Care Award in 2020, the only local authority shortlisted nationally in the category.[188]

IV. West Midlands local authorities which stated that they did not operate easements

(a) Shropshire Council

Shropshire has a population of approximately 320,300 residents, across a wide, mostly rural and semi-rural area, with a higher proportion of over 65-year-olds than the national average (this was reported in 2021 as being 24.3 per cent).[189] Overall this is a relatively affluent area, although 4.6 per cent of people live in areas which are included in the fifth most deprived Super Output areas in England.[190] Shropshire Council stated that it did not implement easements: 'Social Care Easements have not needed to be activated by Shropshire Council. A range of trigger points such as workforce capacity, staff absence, demand on teams, waiting lists will be continuously monitored against any need to enact easements.'[191]

---

[186] Dudley Metropolitan Borough Council (2020) 'Corporate Quarterly Management Report 2020-2021. Quarter 2 (1st July to 30th September 2020), Adult Social Care Performance Evaluation', p 28.

[187] Dudley Metropolitan Borough Council (2020) 'Meeting of the Scrutiny Committee: Adult safeguarding and deprivation of liberty safeguards (DOLS)', 15 October, p 20, para 83. See also Dudley Metropolitan Borough Council (2020) 'Dudley Metropolitan Borough Council and Partner Response to the COVID-19 Pandemic. Report of the Health and Adult Social Care Scrutiny Committee, November', p 21.

[188] D. Poole (2020) 'Dudley's adult social care team up for national award', *Dudley News*, 16 September.

[189] See further Shropshire Council (2021) 'Shropshire COVID-19 Outbreak Management Plan: Prevent, Contain and Live with COVID', March, p 5.

[190] Shropshire Council (2021) 'Shropshire COVID-19 Outbreak Management Plan', p 5. Super Output Area is a term used to describe units of geographic areas in England for statistical purposes.

[191] Shropshire Council (2020) Minutes of Meeting of the Health & Wellbeing Board, 12 November, p 29.

It did, however, adapt services to address issues such as social distancing through a shift to online working and communication for most Council staff, and a move from 'buildings based' day opportunities towards 'Good Things to do at Home' alternatives and online activities. The shift to digital and remote working went relatively smoothly as the Council was already moving in this direction pre-pandemic for unrelated workplace management reasons.[192]

Some of the challenges facing adult social care and how these were being addressed were set out in a report by Councillor Dean Carroll, then Portfolio Holder for Adult Social Care, Public Health and Climate Change at the Council meeting on 16 July 2020. This was nonetheless a markedly upbeat report and he described 'an amazing person-centred approach that reaches out to local people when they need support'.[193] In particular, he noted that there had been ongoing work in the Community Social Work teams to reduce waiting times and the use of 'digital transformation' and 'live data' had led to the 'lowest waiting list numbers that they have had for several years'.[194] The report noted the radical changes to daytime activities away from buildings and the lack of transport support, stating that:

> We are working with community partners on the Good Things to Do at Home project – inspired by the Happy Boxes that the teams immediately started to deliver to the people they would usually be supporting at the centres – and will learn from the project to create an exciting, creative, interactive and ambitious new stream of activity at the heart of our work.[195]

Additional financial and practical support was put in place for families and unpaid carers, including 'grant funding for both A4U, to support those caring for people living with autism, and for Taking Part, specifically to provide additional support for people caring for someone with a learning disability'.[196] The Council also provided 'carer's passes' to identify those who

---

[192] L. Todman (2018) 'Shropshire Council staff to work from home once a month to save money', *Shropshire Star*, 8 November.

[193] D. CarrollS (2020) 'Report of the Portfolio Holder for Adult Social Care/Public Health and Climate Change'. Portfolio Holder: Councillor Dean Carroll Shropshire Council, 16 July, p 1, para 4.1.

[194] Shropshire Council (2020) 'Report of the Portfolio Holder for Adult Social Care/Public Health and Climate Change', para 4.1.

[195] Shropshire Council (2020) 'Report of the Portfolio Holder for Adult Social Care/Public Health and Climate Change', p 1.

[196] Shropshire Council (2020) 'Report of the Portfolio Holder for Adult Social Care/Public Health and Climate Change', p 4.

would need more time outside for shopping and prescription collections during lockdowns. The shift to digital was noted among the informal carer population, as well as among Council workers: 'an increasing interest and take-up in the use of digital technology by carers to connect with support and with each other'.[197]

Going into winter 2020, a report for the Health and Social Care Overview and Scrutiny Committee on Adult Social Care Winter Planning on 9 November reiterated the team's successes in digital working and meeting needs and emphasized again that the Council had not needed to use easements. It was noted that there was a

> a strong domiciliary care market and good relationships with voluntary and community organisations. We have strengths and value based practice embedded across the teams. We have a loyal and dedicated workforce who are both flexible and open to change. New ways of working have been adopted, such as undertaking remote assessments through the use of a range of technology and IT has been provided to staff enabling them to work from home. Measures have been put in place to track both workforce availability and service demand. During lockdown 93% of the workforce were in work and whilst demand for adult social care initially dipped, when it did increase we were able to meet demand with many teams operating a 'business as usual' model.[198]

It commented on the experience of existing social work and therapy teams in application of the law and that:

> The paperwork processes direct practitioners to work in a legal and strengths based manner and there are quality assurance processes in place to measure this, e.g. assessments have to be approved by the worker's line manager. Thematic audits are carried out of practitioners' work and action is taken to address any areas for improvement.[199]

In Shropshire, as elsewhere in the UK, there were reports that day centres had been closed,[200] including those run by Age UK. Some remained closed or at

---

[197] Shropshire Council (2020) 'Report of the Portfolio Holder for Adult Social Care/Public Health and Climate Change', p 4.
[198] Shropshire Council (2020) 'Adult Social Care COVID-19 Winter Plan 2020/2021', p28.
[199] Shropshire Council (2020) 'Adult Social Care COVID-19 Winter Plan 2020/2021', p28.
[200] L. O'Brien (2021) 'Shropshire Day Services Centres to Remain closed until Mid-February', *Shropshire Star*, 27 January.

reduced capacity into March 2021 and beyond.[201] Healthwatch Shropshire, in its July 2020 report, indicated that there was some evidence from their surveys that a small number of individual service users had had their service provision adversely impacted.[202]

(b) City of Wolverhampton Council

In June 2020, the City of Wolverhampton area had a population of approximately 262,000; of these 50,000 were classified as 'at risk', with 28,500 classified as 'vulnerable' and a further 8000 people 'shielded'.[203] It is a diverse urban area stated to be of 'relative deprivation'.[204] Wolverhampton Council stands out as a local authority which did not ultimately enact Care Act easements, but which did undertake a considerable amount of reflective public preparatory work in relation to their potential implementation. Unlike other local authorities in the region, Wolverhampton Council produced and hosted a public consultation regarding the 'proposed Care Act easement procedure' between 15 and 25 May 2020.[205] Moreover, the consultation was facilitated through the production of 'An Easy Read Guide to Care Act easements in Wolverhampton: How local services may change because of Coronavirus and how it may impact you', following best practice in accessible communications.[206] The guide set out the four stages outlined in the Government easement Guidance and explained how different stages would have consequent impacts upon service users. As noted in Chapter 4, the consultation approach appears to have been well-received in the local community.[207] In addition, a very detailed proposed Operating Model for Care Act Easements was published in April 2020; this included a prioritization tool and analysis of easements against the Ethical Framework in its appendices.[208]

---

[201] Age UK Shropshire & Telford (2021) 'Age UK Day Centres Win an Award', Shropshire Telford & Wrekin Age UK, 31 March.
[202] Healthwatch Shropshire (2020) 'Health, care and well-being services during the COVID-19 pandemic', 7 July.
[203] City of Wolverhampton Council (2020) 'Wolverhampton COVID-19 Outbreak Control Plan', June, p 6.
[204] City of Wolverhampton (2020) 'Wolverhampton COVID-19 Outbreak Control Plan', p 6.
[205] City of Wolverhampton Council (2020) 'Consultation on Care Act easements', 17 June.
[206] City of Wolverhampton Council (2020) 'Care Act easements procedures'.
[207] City of Wolverhampton Council (2021) 'Principal Social Worker Annual Report 2020–2021', 28 July, para 3.7.
[208] City of Wolverhampton Council (2020) 'Operating Model for Care Act Easements', April. This was shared on the same webpage as the Consultation documentation.

After this initial activity in which the decision was effectively made, there appears to be relatively little mention or scrutiny of 'easements' or 'flexibilities' throughout the year. However, it does appear that some changes to working practices occurred, such as moving from face-to-face to online assessments, which had been defined by other local authorities as such. For example, the then DASS briefed the Adults and Safer City Scrutiny Panel on 15 September 2020 that

> the changes introduced by the Care Act Easements to allow Adult Social Care Directors to make decisions in consultation with other interested parties if changes were needed to be made about how the service would meet its statutory responsibilities. The Director of Adult Services gave examples of how new technology has been used to complete care assessments.[209]

Indeed, the 2019–2020 Adult Social Care Annual Report states that

> Adult Social Care in the City of Wolverhampton Council has continued to operate under the Care Act throughout the pandemic, with some flexibilities and minor changes to the way work has been carried out and support / services provided. As such there has not been any need to implement any Care Act easements and the Council has remained at Stage 2. Most services have continued to be delivered as business as usual, whilst observing all government guidelines.[210]

Ultimately, this Council – in contrast to some of those which we examined in the previous section of this chapter – interpreted the Guidance to mean that Stage 2 does not constitute the operation of easements: 'The Council's approach was that Care Act easements should only be implemented as a last resort and only when all other options and alternatives, including utilising any other available resource, had been explored.'[211]

(c) Worcestershire County Council

Worcestershire is a county which had a population of some 609,665 citizens in 2021.[212] The Council, with the guidance of its legal and democratic

---

[209] City of Wolverhampton Council (2020) Adults and Safer City Scrutiny Committee. Minutes from meeting on 15 September 2020, p 4.
[210] City of Wolverhampton Council (2021) 'Adult Social Care: Annual Report. Local account 2019/20', para 12.3, presented to Cabinet on 17 February.
[211] City of Wolverhampton Council (2020) Operating Model for Care Act easements, para 3.6.
[212] Worcestershire County Council (2022) Population Projections Dashboard.

services team, provisionally put in place procedures for the enactment of Care Act easements if required, but they were not in the end deemed necessary.[213] The PSW was reporting weekly to the designated DASS on whether the Council was experiencing either a 'significant impact on its workforce or a significant increase in demand' and 'as neither of these scenarios has applied to Worcestershire County Council, no easements have been sought or applied and, based on current predictions, it is highly unlikely that any will be'.[214] The Council established a Gold-Silver-Bronze Command structure as per national guidelines, and 'put in place a robust review of demand for social care and capacity to respond,' and this was to be reported weekly to the Directorate Leadership Team.[215] In June 2010 it stated that.having noted that five West Midlands local authorities had enacted and then ceased the operation of Care Act easements, 'the Council does not anticipate enacting any easements in the future.'[216]

Collaboration with local partners, including West Midlands Association of Directors of Adult Social Services (WMADASS), was emphasized along with statements that the Council was involved in sharing data and developing a robust communications strategy.[217] The Commissioning team established a 'Worcestershire Care Home Hub' to coordinate infection control and other support for providers across the local authority area.[218] As with other councils, day services were closed in the early stages of the pandemic, and it was also clear that service delivery had been impacted in other ways during this period. The teams had undertaken a review 'within the first 3 weeks' of those receiving care and support to ascertain where they might be:

> 12. ... at higher risk of carer breakdown or other pressures due to the withdrawal of services by providers, the loss of community support, the restrictions imposed by 'lockdown' or by virtue of being in the 'shielded' cohort. Any person who was considered at high risk has been offered weekly 'welfare check' calls.

---

[213] Worcestershire County Council (2021) 'Adult Care and Well Being Overview and Scrutiny Panel, "Care Act Easements as a Result of COVID-19"', 15 March Agenda item 17.

[214] Worcestershire County Council (2020) 'Adult Care and Well Being Overview and Scrutiny Panel, Agenda Item 5: COVID-19 People Directorate Response for Adult Services', 11 June paras 10 and 11.

[215] Worcestershire County Council (2020) 'Cabinet: COVID-19 Response', 4 June, Agenda Item 4.

[216] Worcestershire County Council (2020) 'Cabinet: COVID-19 Response', 4 June, point 14.

[217] Worcestershire County Council (2020) 'Cabinet: COVID-19 Response', point 40.

[218] Worcestershire County Council (2020) 'Cabinet: COVID-19 Response', point 39.

13. Where a person requires additional support or a change in the way it is delivered, this has been provided. In some cases, people and their families have declined to use services due to understandable concerns about the risk of COVID-19 infection. Again, support has been provided to enable this to happen in the best way possible under the circumstances, including providing alternative care arrangements. All arrangements will be reviewed at the declared end of the pandemic.[219]

The 'Update on the County Council's COVID-19 response' contained in the papers for Cabinet on the 22 October 2020, as with the documentation produced by other councils, noted how the cessation of the majority of specific financial support for suppliers provided during COVID-19 and ongoing impact of social-distancing requirements were impacting the way in which services were provided, and that 'Services are therefore engaging with our customers to bring forward different opportunities for supporting them'.[220]

Later in this document, it is commented that there had been a rise in individuals seeking support following lockdown.[221] It appears that 'flexibilities' had been utilized here as elsewhere.

(d) Stoke-on-Trent City Council

Stoke-on-Trent is both a city and a unitary authority within Staffordshire. It has a population of approximately 258,400 according to the 2021 census.[222] There are high levels of socio-economic deprivation. It is one of the 20 per cent most deprived districts/unitary authorities in England, where life expectancy is lower than the English average.[223] As of April 2020, there were 'approximately 1,500 residents across the city receiving home care organised by the city council.'[224]

---

[219] Worcestershire County Council (2020) Agenda Item 4, Cabinet – 25 June 2020, 'COVID-19 Response and Restart Update Relevant Cabinet Member Mr S E Geraghty Relevant Chief Officer Chief Executive' para 12.

[220] Worcestershire County Council (2020) 'Cabinet: Update on the County Council's COVID-19 Response and Recovery', 22 October para 33.

[221] Worcestershire County Council (2020) 'Cabinet: Update on the County Council's COVID-19 Response and Recovery', 22 October para 46.

[222] Office for National Statistics (2023) 'How life has changed in Stoke-on-Trent: Census 2021', 19 January.

[223] Public Health England (2020) 'Stoke-on-Trent Local Authority Health Profile 2019', 3 March.

[224] Stoke-on-Trent City Council (2020) 'Care for your city', 1 April, web news.

The Council did not formally adopt Care Act easements, and the publicly available minutes of Council meetings and related reports during this period[225] do not appear to make explicit reference to Care Act easements until December 2020, when the DASS had indicated that there had been meetings on a fortnightly basis since the onset of the pandemic between the DASS, Assistant DASS, PSW, and legal officer to assess whether easements were needed.

> Adult Social Care in-house provider services continue to operate as close to normal as possible whilst ensuring they services remain safe for our vulnerable citizens. The Director of Adult Social Services (DASS) meets fortnightly with the Assistant Director for Adult Social Care (Provider Services), the Principal Social Worker and a legal officer to consider whether the City Council needs to look for Care Act Easement. We have done this since the Pandemic started earlier in the year and we continue to be absolutely confident that we are operating at all times safely and within the Care Act and so do not need to seek any easement.[226]

In a Cabinet meeting on 21 April 2020, John Rouse, City Director, presented a COVID-19 update stating that by this stage, Stoke-on-Trent had 'suffered less from this terrible virus than the majority of the country' and that the emergency was being managed under the Gold and Silver Command system.[227] Changed working practices for both Council staff and community providers are noted in the document and the 'exceptionally brave work of our front-line social care teams, including redeployed staff who have retrained to join the front-line' were commended.[228] With regard to supporting vulnerable adults, extended working hours were introduced and there was a renewed focus on hospital discharge.[229]

Rouse also noted that many staff were still working in the community, sometimes redeployed in new face-to-face roles as carers and it was noted

---

[225] See, for example, Stoke-on-Trent (2020) 'COVID-19 Local Outbreak Control Plan', V23, 14 December, which doesn't mention easements, but provides detail on PPE, social distancing, additional funding, and 'support for vulnerable residents' and so on.

[226] Stoke-on-Trent Council (2020) Public Document Pack City Council Supplementary Papers COVID-19 Update, 10 December, supplementary papers, para 3.2.1.

[227] Stoke-on-Trent Council (2020) COVID-19 statement and update from the city Director, Agenda item 4, supplementary papers, 21 April.

[228] Stoke-on-Trent Council (2020) Public Document Pack City Council Supplementary Papers COVID-19 Update, 21 April 2020, para 1.9.

[229] Stoke-on-Trent Council (2020) Public Document Pack City Council Supplementary Papers COVID-19 Update, 21 April 2020, para 2.1.

that 'the domiciliary care companies we commission in the City are fragile but managing'.[230] Such changes might well have been considered to be 'flexibilities' or 'Stage 2 easements' in other local authority areas. By February 2021, explicit reference was made to the decision not to formally activate easements:

> We continue to meet on a fortnightly basis to review provision, and are absolutely confident that we are operating at all times safely and within the Care Act so we do not need to seek any easement. We continue to operate in-house provider services as close to normal as possible whilst maintaining social distancing and ensuring the safety of service users and staff, which does mean reduced numbers in some services and a consolidation of some services to enable this to happen.[231]

Although not specific to social care provision, it was noted that Council managers were monitoring capacity, that some services were closed or paused, and that staff were working from home and there had been training and redeployment of staff to 'front line services' notably to maintain capacity in the 'care team'.[232] In addition, Government COVID-19 funding was added to the budgets of local third-sector groups to provide increased community support.

Concluding thoughts on the approaches taken by local authorities

The declared approaches taken by local authorities fell into three specific categories. While only the first category formally notified the DHSC that they had decided to operate higher level (Stage 3 or 4) easements, there were notable changes in approach to service provision made by local authorities across the West Midlands. The disparate utilisation of the word 'easement' demonstrated at times a lack of understanding regarding the application of the Guidance documents or indeed a lack of clarity within the Guidance documents themselves. But in some instances, there were indications that a degree of prioritisation of services had been undertaken without use of the statutory easements provision. Thus although formal approaches were different between "easement" and other councils the

---

[230] Stoke-on-Trent City Council (2020) COVID-19 Update, 10 December, supplementary papers, para 2.2.
[231] Stoke-on-Trent City Council (2021) 'COVID-19 Update and statement to Cabinet, Agenda item 3', 23 February, para 3.1.
[232] Stoke-on-Trent City Council (2020) COVID-19 Update, 10 December, supplementary papers, para 12.2; see also 'Care for your City' web news.

review of the documentary evidence indicates that in fact responses were very similar. This section of the chapter has examined those documents available in the public domain regarding the approaches local authorities took in the period under examination. In the next section we look to the reflections of people working in local authorities and adult social care in the West Midlands as they recount the impact of COVID-19 and the legislative mitigations on the delivery services during this period.

V. Reflections from stakeholders in the West Midlands on the experience of the delivery of adult social care in 2020

In this section we turn to examine the insights and perspectives of a number of key stakeholders in the West Midlands interviewed during the research for our ESRC project. It explores the views of stakeholders regarding the activation or non-activation of Care Act easements, and the meaning ascribed to these decisions by professionals with responsibility for sustaining adult social care provision in 2020–21.

The first theme that stood out was that of values. Could it be seen that the utilization of such easements was fundamentally at odds with how individuals viewed their role as social care professionals? This certainly was the approach of one PSW we spoke with:

> I think that from a social work perspective, a value base, how would you prioritize people's needs? And how could you say, "You deserve to get care and support but then you don't"? And it just felt like a hugely difficult position that I just didn't want to be in. So, I think from my perspective I wanted to work as hard as I could in order to put everything in place where people continued to have the care and support, they needed, and we put all our commitments, our energies, and our finance in place ... And the Council were very behind us with that. From our point of view, we didn't want to do it unless we had no choice. Unless it was a last resort. (Principal Social Worker in a West Midlands local authority that did not formally activate easements)

Some stakeholders we spoke to appeared relieved not to have to activate easements, and had gone to some lengths to demonstrate that they were managing without reaching that tipping point. Indeed, some local authority professionals in councils which had activated them expressed scepticism and some regret.

Second, there were suggestions from interviewees in local authorities in the West Midlands which had formally implemented easements that they considered the operational changes and practices which they had used to be very similar to or the same as those utilized in local authorities which stated that they were *not* operating easements. Three statements from stakeholders illustrate this point clearly. One Director of Adult Social Services stated that:

> We know from conversations around the region and nationally that most local authorities made some sort of adjustment or another that you could quite easily interpret as, strictly speaking, a derangement from the Care Act, and therefore they should have declared an easement. But they didn't, they just sort of kind of got on with it. (Director of Adult Social Services in a West Midlands local authority)

This was also reflected in the comment of a Principal Social Worker, who stated that

> I talked to a colleague, somebody I used to work with at another local authority, who phoned me to see how I was because he'd heard we'd used the easements and [assumed] things must be really bad. And I said, 'No, we're doing really well.' And I know for a fact that they were doing the same things as us, in terms of not doing reviews, etc. Those kinds of things. (Principal Social Worker in a local authority that formally activated easements)

Another Principal Social Worker in a West Midlands local authority that formally activated easements echoed these comments and went further, indicating that the disparate interpretation of the easements Guidance was reflected more broadly nationwide:

> Random scattergun right across the country ... I could find no pattern or rationale; it was literally, I think, word of mouth. So there were some people who just said 'This is due to easements' and sort of quoted that when actually there were no easements. And when you went further up the ranks, they would say 'No', and the senior managers would confirm there weren't. So it was almost as if there were some frontline workers who ... used it as an excuse. But that's the way it was. It was almost as if they used it as an excuse instead of saying 'Things are really difficult in COVID at the moment and I am going to be delayed'. The easements were used as a reason. (Principal Social Worker in a West Midlands local authority that formally activated easements)

This view also reflected in findings at the national level in relation to 'easement and non-easement local authorities' by ADASS and TLAP,[233] and by Baginsky et al.[234]

Notably, across the grey literature and in council announcements and minutes which we examined there was a degree of inconsistency in the terminology used to describe both easements and flexibilities within the pre-amendment Care Act; the terms were often used interchangeably. This was particularly the case where councils were ostensibly operating at Stage 2 and were not clear whether or not this constituted a formal 'easement' or a 'flexibility'.

There is also some suggestion that those who formally notified the DHSC of their intention to activate easements later regretted having done so so:

> And then after the event, the event being publication on the CQC website, I think the relevant directors were surprised, not only for the national attention they were getting, but actually more importantly from the local attention. And it created a lot of fuss and admin and so forth … From what they told me, some probably regretted declaring stage three or four. I couldn't find much difference between what those three and four declared authorities were actually doing and all other DASSs were doing around the country. So, the second point linked to that was … I think they'd probably say, 'Look, we think we did the right thing at the time and didn't realise how much attention we attracted which was unhelpful and distracting when we were trying to do other important things. I'm pretty sure that what we were facing and what we were doing was not a lot different from the average other.' You know what I mean? And I think they're right on that. (Regional ADASS associate)

One important reflection related to whether formal legislative changes and the Care Act easement framework issued in the Guidance was in fact, the most appropriate avenue to follow or whether a broader, more fluid discretion could have been given to local authorities:

> I guess even Care Act easements, what the Government could have said that would have made it quite easy was words to the effect of

---

[233] Think Local Act Personal Insight Group (2020) *A Telling Experience: Understanding the Impact of COVID-19 on People Who Access Care and Support – A Rapid Evidence Review with Recommendations.* TLAP Insight Group, October.

[234] See M. Baginsky, E. Thomas, and J. Manthorpe (2023) 'Reasons for not adopting COVID-19 permitted changes to legal duties: accounts from English local authorities', *Health & Social Care in the Community.*

nationally: 'Don't worry about the precise details of the Care Act right now; if you have to deviate from them a bit, it's okay.' ... it could've made a sort of general derogation, couldn't it? 'As long as you are acting reasonably and proportionality in all of that, etc.' Rather than having the level 1, level 2, rather than that nit-picky bureaucratic way of doing it, if you see what I mean. (Director of Adult Services in a West Midlands local authority that formally activated easements)

Even where considerable time was put into meetings to discuss the legal and operational detail, there was ambivalence about the Guidance and about the decision-making taking place across the national context of local government:

> We wanted to make sure we were getting it right to the legislation and we thought: 'We're going on to [level] 3 and others aren't.' But what we realized after the event was that others should have, and I think when they've seen us getting a battering for it, for going onto easement 3, I think they thought, 'We don't want to go there, we don't want to go there.' But, actually, that's what they [the easements] were there for, and at no point did we stop people having a service. [Others] were on easements 3, but they couldn't actually offer services to people in their own homes. We never got to that stage; we were not withdrawing services or asking for alternatives. We didn't even need to enact the change that direct payments could be used to pay for families. We didn't have to enact that, because we were thinking of suggestions and what we might deem as easement 4. We didn't think we were at easement level 4, but we did think that we were not doing our responsibilities under the Care Act. (Principal Social Worker in a West Midlands local authority that formally activated easements)

This lack of clarity and consequent uncertainty in relation to interpretation was reflected by other interviewees. This was particularly the case where a substantial number of councils were ostensibly operating at Stage 2 and were not clear whether or not this constituted an 'easement' or a 'flexibility' within the pre-amendment Care Act.

> I think Stage 2 is a grey area. We never really came to the conclusion that we're in Stage 2 ... I mean, we did do things differently. So day centres, for example, shut down. Therefore, we had to think differently about how we provided somebody with support during the daytime. So does that mean we're in Stage 2? But we never officially went to Stage 2. (Principal Social Worker in a West Midlands local authority that did not formally activate easements)

Another notable finding was that some of the changes in adult social care provision were not driven by policy changes but rather by a change in demand from those who would usually request or require services. Some individuals and families were understandably concerned that social care workers visiting their homes could risk clinically vulnerable individuals being infected by the virus;[235] they therefore contacted the council and cancelled their care visits.

> Interestingly, the demand on the service in the first wave in March, the amount of requests coming into adult social care dipped. So there was a very clear drop of demand on the service. We weren't quite sure what that was about. By the time we finished the financial year and we look back over that year, from the April through to the April, the demand coming in for service was back up to the same levels that it had been ... So we think that people just sort of huddled inside and decided they didn't want to ask for help or have other people coming. There was a lot of fear. (Principal Social Worker in a West Midlands local authority that did not formally activate easements)

This in turn meant that family or third-sector volunteers got involved to provide day-to-day support on an informal, unpaid basis; others increased the level of support they were already providing.[236] For example, one interviewee told us that:

> We had some people who cancelled their support. Especially early on. They just rang up and said 'No, I don't want carers in my home. I'll manage.' Or some family members provided the support instead, especially if they've been furloughed. So family members stepped in. Communities stepped in as well. So, we had someone from the Polish community who was struggling; she couldn't go out, she was shielding and there was a local Polish café and shop, and they delivered food to her and some meals and things. (Principal Social Worker in a West Midlands local authority that did not activate easements)

A further theme from interviewees was that of potential long term impacts flowing from local authorities decisions to utilize easements or general "flexibilities" Some interviewees from third sector organisations

---

[235] This fear was exacerbated because supplies of PPE were particularly difficult to secure for social care providers in the community.
[236] Unpaid carers, family, and friends reported that they were more able to provide this additional support during the early months of the pandemic, particularly when the furlough scheme was operating and some people were working from home or not at all. Their availability and capacity of course changed as time passed.

expressed concerns that because people were seen to have 'coped' during the pandemic, it might not consequently be seen as necessary for certain services to be reinstated.

> Obviously, the local authority was in significant financial dire straits before COVID. I think there was a suspicion that ... for those local authority areas where easements were put in place, I think there was that concern that this would be a shield for effecting change to people's care and support, without there really being a lot of social work intervention, assessment. That was the thing that worried people most, that the potential of assessment of individual care packages would be taken at quite a superficial level and not in the way that people would normally be reassessed or have their care needs reviewed. So, there was a lot of anxiety. We were very anxious as an organization because for a lot of people there's been a background narrative of potential service cuts in the local authority and over the whole period of austerity there has been a massive reduction in support services for people with disabilities, learning disabilities. So, I think there was that angst. No communication from the council as to what their intentions were. (CEO of a major learning disabilities charity in the West Midlands)

Further concerns were also expressed by another interviewee.

> We've had local authorities who have used the last lockdown period as a piece of evidence as to why someone may now not need to return to their day service, if they haven't had it ... and they've coped during that time. (Member of a social care advocacy organization)

The consequences of lingering impacts were expressed by someone with direct experience of navigating the system:

> It created a huge amount of fear ... I mean 'why social care?' Like why this thing that is actually really important to people's lives? It seemed disproportionate to us ... And I guess because perhaps historically there's been great relationships with people: between people and their local authority, and not a huge amount of trust always ... And so I think there was this sense that social care wasn't great anyway and suddenly like this almost opened the floodgates to massive changes. 'We don't have to do anything anymore, we can really cut back what we're doing.' ... There was just a real sense of, what could this mean? And would we ever get back to even what we had before? (Social care rights spokesperson, with lived experience)

The broader issue as to whether the impact of COVID-19 and consequent reduction of services during the pandemic may have had a lasting 'chilling effect' is something which we return to in Chapter 6.

VI. Conclusions

The provision of adult social care across the West Midlands local authorities – whether or not they regarded themselves as having operated Care Act easements – was clearly impacted during the first phase of the pandemic. While each local authority was undertaking their own internal, officer-level decision-making, it is nonetheless notable from the interviews that there were extensive ongoing discussions and meetings – both formal and informal – taking place between members of the professional groups of Directors of Adult Social Care in the West Midlands and of PSWs during this time. This reflects what we saw earlier, in relation to ADASS' role during the pandemic planning process where it was suggested that regional ADASS groupings could provide 'mutual aid' in such a situation. In addition, despite new Regional Assurance Leads being established by the DHSC to perform a kind of bridging role between central and local government; it was clear that communication channels had not been working well. These were recruited from senior ranks of the social care sector including, ex-CQC, leaders Care Providers, ex-directors of Adult Social Care, and senior nurses to 'act as a conduit between DHSC and local areas ... provide opportunities for the sector to influence and inform DHSC as to the way in which current policies are working at local level'.[237]

Yet while there was discussion, across professional groups ultimately each authority reached their own decision. That small group of local authorities went ahead with higher-level easements rapidly, but then withdrew from them equally rapidly. The adverse impacts in terms of press publicity, the approach taken by campaigning groups, and legal action itself were clearly noted by the other local authorities. This may have proved a cautionary lesson to all the local authorities when in later waves none made use of higher-level easements.

> I was genuinely very surprised by how few authorities ended up doing it in the end. And I'm fascinated whether we were like a little West Midlands bubble where – because we – it could just be a coincidence that there's a few of us in the West Midlands ... my conversations with PSWs were in the West Midlands about other's thinking of doing it, etc. It was those email exchanges about what you're doing, and how you're doing it, etc. And then it was almost like, once we'd done it and we looked round and nobody else in the country was doing it,

---

[237] S. Eldridge (2021) 'Giving assurances', *GOV.UK*, 25 June.

virtually, it felt like – it was, like, oh, okay that's interesting. Yeah, very interesting experience. (Principal Social Worker in a West Midlands local authority that formally activated easements)

Yet it is striking that the approaches taken in West Midlands 'easement', 'Stage 2', and 'non-easement' councils were in fact decidedly similar in many respects. In both groups the pressures on NHS provision, the consequent redeployment of staff to assist in hospital discharge, the proliferation of home working practices, the advent of increased 'technological solutions', and the movement away from in-person assessments and reviews all featured. There is less evidence of overt reduction of services and prioritization attributable to the Care Act easement provisions. It is notable that while the language of fundamental rights formed part of the national level discussion as to the legitimacy of easements, this was far less apparent in the documentation of local authorities. It was unclear as to the extent to which there was a full appreciation of the differences between Equality Act 2010 impact assessments and the Human Rights Act 1998 requirements. Where measures differed between local authorities, we must also consider that there were likely different local pressures in their care provider markets and differing levels of staff absence due to illness.

While certain activities and aspects of service delivery may have been stopped ostensibly under the auspices of Care Act easements, in other instances, such as the decision to close day centres and respite care, for example, was made expressly in order to comply with social-distancing requirements under the Health Protection (Coronavirus, Restrictions) (England) Regulations 2020.[238] As we shall see in the next chapter, the legacy of such closures has lingered for a very long time.

During the second wave of the pandemic no local authority in England decided to operate Stage 3 or 4 easements despite the provision being available to them. Did this mean that they were simply sufficiently well able to cope as they had adapted to remote working and the additional burdens created by pandemic conditions? Was staff illness and absence now less of a problem, despite the intensity of the second wave? It is certainly the case that the NHS in Birmingham was under extreme pressure in the winter of 2020.[239] There is one interesting reference, however, in the minutes of a meeting in a non-Stage 3/4 council, which perhaps sheds a different light on this. The minutes of a Worcestershire County Council

---

[238] SI 2020/350.

[239] J. Hayes (2021) 'Birmingham hospitals have more COVID patients than anywhere else in country', *Birmingham Mail*, 20 November.

Adult Care and Well Being Overview and Scrutiny Panel meeting on 15 March 2021 stated that:

> At a meeting of West Midlands Association of Directors of Adult Social Services on 14 January 2021 it was acknowledged that the process of enacting the easements during the first lockdown caused significant anxiety and distress to the public and would not be considered unless as a last resort.[240]

This statement that 'the process of enacting easements caused significant anxiety and distress to the public' is notable. While concerns were expressed at the outset about the operation of easements nationally, accounts of anxiety and distress resulting specifically from the use of Care Act easements were not apparent in the public documentation issued or recorded by the other West Midlands councils. So, for example, in a report on 27 June 2020, Coventry's DASS Pete Fahy noted that:

> For Local Authorities that activated the easements, Coventry included, there was a significant amount of scrutiny and challenge from national organisations and law firms. It is worth noting that none were able to identify any individual who has suffered detriment as a result of the easements and no complaints or challenges were made locally in this respect.[241]

Ultimately the legislative easements gave legitimacy to hard resource allocation choices during the COVID-19 pandemic. They were put in place to provide structure and formality for departures from the Care Act 2014 and transparency for the public as to how those decisions had been taken. Understandably, as we saw in Chapter 4, the very existence of these provisions, in addition to their implementation, gave rise to grave concerns. Yet those local authorities who formally implemented these statutory processes as we saw in the previous chapter were subject to heavy public criticism at national level. In the West Midlands as elsewhere in the country the formal operation of easements was only operational for a very fleeting period. However the detailed examination of the West Midlands local authorities, both through the formal documentation of local authorities

---

[240] Worcestershire County Council (2021) 'Care Act Easements as a result of COVID-19', Adult Care and Well Being Overview and Scrutiny Panel, 15 March.

[241] Coventry City Council (2020) Report to Coventry Health and Wellbeing Board Date: 27 July 2020; From: Pete Fahy, Director of Adult Services; Title: 'Adult Social Care – Key programmes of work to support COVID-19 to date', para 6.4.

available in the public domain and the reflection of our interviewees, demonstrated that the position across differences between local authorities was far less clear cut than might have been anticipated. In the next chapter, we explore first how local authorities responses and adaptations we have examined West Midland case study compare with the broader national picture. Then we go on to examine how adult social care fared after the formal withdrawal of Care Act easements provision and as the country was urged to start 'living with COVID-19'.

6

Pandemic Legacies: 'Living with COVID-19' in Adult Social Care

I. Introduction

As the COVID-19 restrictions began to be lifted towards the end of 2021,[1] some people celebrated the return to a more 'normal' existence. Others – including those deemed clinically vulnerable, many people who draw on care and support services, and those working in health and social care – wondered what this would mean for them.[2] Winter 2020–21 had been an extremely difficult time health and social care. Despite a cautious re-opening in summer 2020 parts of the country- including the West Midlands remained subject to additional restrictions as part of what was known as the "Tier System".[3] The UK was then subject to a national lockdown in November 2020, though less restrictive than spring 2020, followed by parts of the country, including the West Midlands, again re-emerging into Tiers. Further restrictions at a higher level were imposed on certain areas of the country later in December 2020.[4]

---

[1] Institute for Government (2022) 'Timeline of UK Government coronavirus lockdowns and measures March 2020 to December 2021'.
[2] J. Lee and F. Gillett (2021) 'COVID-19 "For us it's not freedom day, is it?"' *BBC News*, 6 July.
[3] Health Protection (Coronavirus, Local COVID-19 Alert Level) (Very High) (England) Regulations 2020, SI No 1105; Health Protection (Coronavirus, Local COVID-19 Alert Level) (High) (England) Regulations 2020 SI 1104; Health Protection (Coronavirus, Local COVID-19 Alert Level) (Medium) (England) Regulations 2020 SI No 1103; and see also House of Lords Library 'Covid-19 Alert Levels: Three Tiers for England', at https://lordslibrary.parliament.uk/covid-19-local-alert-levels-three-tier-system-for-england/, accessed 10 July 2024; and see A. Wagner (2022) *Emergency State: How We Lost Our Freedoms in the Pandemic and Why it Matters*, London: Bodley Head, chapter 7.
[4] UK Government (2020) 'Press Release: Prime Minister announces Tier 4: "Stay At Home" Alert Level in response to new COVID variant', 19 December, at https://www.gov.uk/government/news/prime-minister-announces-tier-4-stay-at-home-alert-level-in-response-to-new-covid-variant, accessed 10 July 2024.

However, far from recovering from these measures, the UK went into a further lockdown on 6 January 2021, with consequent impacts on quality of life and delivery of services.

The new 'stay at home' order ended on 29 March 2021, but it was not until 19 July 2021, the so-called 'Freedom Day',[5] that most of the restrictions on contact were removed. However, by autumn and winter 2021–22 the virus was again spreading fast, fuelled this time by the new 'Omicron' variant. On 8 December 2021, Prime Minister Boris Johnson announced a move to 'Plan B' which required an increase in lateral flow testing and compulsory mask wearing in most indoor venues.[6] There were of course more stringent infection control rules applied in health and social care settings.[7]

This chapter explores the pandemic legacies for adult social care as the country began 'living with COVID-19' in the expectation that the virus would soon become endemic and more manageable following the vaccination programme.[8] Section II begins by reflecting on the pandemic's legacies and the lessons that can be drawn from the specific provisions of the Coronavirus Act 2020 relating to Care Act easements at national level in England. We compare and contrast the national-level findings with those of the West Midlands case study we considered in Chapter 5, and we examine their perceived legacy for future pandemic planning through the lens of those organizations given the task of monitoring and evaluating their impact. Section III then explores the lingering impacts of the pandemic for adult social care from 'Freedom Day' onwards as England adjusted to the 'new normal' of 'living with COVID-19'. We consider the ongoing and ever-increasing pressures on the delivery of adult social care in both community and residential care settings and, by extension, the profound pressures on unpaid carers and the social care workforce. In Section IV we focus in on the legacy of COVID-19 for two important aspects of delivery of care and support which, while they were already apparent pre-pandemic, intensified and accelerated in the pandemic years and are becoming fully embedded post-2023. The first of these is the movement towards digitization in data management, working practices, and in the direct provision of services. Here we explore the potential benefits and challenges of maintaining pandemic-era working practices – for social care professionals, for people who draw on care and support, and for carers. Second, we revisit the impact of COVID-19

---

[5] See W. James (2021) 'England's "freedom day" marred by soaring cases and isolation chaos', *Reuters News*, 19 July.

[6] Prime Minister's Office 10 Downing Street (2021) 'Prime Minister confirms move to Plan B in England', press release, 8 December.

[7] Department of Health and Social Care (2021) 'Adult social care: COVID-19 winter plan 2021 to 2022', Policy paper, 3 November.

[8] Cabinet Office (2022) *COVID-19 Response: Living with COVID* (updated 6 May).

closures on the provision and availability of day centres and day opportunities, a vital resource for many people living in the community which has yet to be fully restored. This analysis shows that the legacy of the COVID-19 pandemic runs deep. We also see how the foundational paradigms of care, vulnerability, and fundamental rights, which we explored in Chapter 2, were drawn into sharp relief during times of both 'unprecedented' crisis and indeed in the face of the well-precedented and chronic funding crisis in adult social care.

II. Reflections on the implementation of Care Act easements across England and their aftermath

After the initial, brief period of Care Act easement operation there was a degree of review at national level to gauge their impact and consider whether they should remain available to local authorities. As we saw in Chapter 4, the Coronavirus Act was enacted in some haste, so meaningful parliamentary- and committee-level scrutiny was only engaged later in 2020.[9] The House of Commons Women and Equalities Committee (then chaired by Caroline Noakes MP), for example, undertook an extensive piece of work to gather evidence regarding the 'unequal impact' of the Coronavirus Act on disabled people and other groups needing access to services.[10] Following on from the the first interim report of that Committee which found that the pandemic had "highlighted and exacerbated pre-existing systematic problems in the social care system,[11] December's final Report concluded that 'the Coronavirus Act, which was fast-tracked into statute in March, had clear and adverse effects on disabled people's rights', and in relation to easements the Committee called for their 'swift repeal should the pandemic become more clearly under control'.[12] The Report of the House of Commons Women's and Equalities Committee called for a discrete independent inquiry specifically examining issues pertaining to the disproportionate impact of COVID-19 on disabled people; the underlying causes of the disproportionate death rates; and the

---

[9] See Chapter 4; and also P. Grez Hidalgo, F. de Londras and D. Lock (2022) 'Parliament, the pandemic, and constitutional principle in the United Kingdom: a study of the Coronavirus Act 2020', *Modern Law Review*, 85(6): 1463–1503.

[10] House of Commons Women and Equalities Select Committee (2020) *Unequal Impact? Coronavirus, Disability, and Access to Services: Full Report*. Fourth report of session 2019–21, 22 December, HC 1050.

[11] House of Commons Women and Equalities Select Committee (2020a) *Unequal Impact? Coronavirus, Disability, and Access to Services: Interim Report on Temporary Provisions in the Coronavirus Act*. First report of session 2019–21, 22 September, HC 386 paras 27-29.

[12] House of Commons Women and Equalities Select Committee (2020 para 37), at pp 7 and 16 respectively.

need for 'consideration of the role of Government's and local authorities' policies and decisions in adverse outcomes for disabled people'.[13] The Report also called for extensive reform of the social care sector, including greater accountability and transparency; a more equitable funding model; and the integration of co-production and improved communication in future policy decisions – indeed, these are some of the themes that emerged during our own contemporaneous research.

Although concerns were raised about the extent and quality of consultation and co-production in policymaking, we saw in Chapter 4 that a selection of key organizations did have a seat at the table. 'Think Local Act Personal' (TLAP) – a partnership organization working to promote personalization, co-production, and community-based approaches to adult social care, hosted in the Social Care Institute for Excellence – was involved in discussions with the Department of Health and Social Care (DHSC) and major social care stakeholders both before[14] and throughout the immediate and ongoing sector-wide response to the pandemic. The TLAP Insight Group (TIG) was launched early in the pandemic to gather intelligence and views from across the sector and the wider community. The TIG's membership was comprised of 'partners and friends' drawn from key organizations and professional bodies involved with social care provision, from the Association of Directors of Adult Social Services (ADASS) and the British Association of Social Workers (BASW), Healthwatch, and the Care Quality Commission (CQC), along with charities and service providers, and others.[15]

The TIG published *A Telling Experience: Understanding the Impact of COVID-19 on People Who Access Care and Support - A Rapid Evidence Review with Recommendations*[16] in October 2020. This report drew on insights from all the group's members and focused on the experiences of those who directly access services, as well as carers and providers. It therefore used a mixture of methodologies. It noted the challenge of making a full assessment given that the 'data varied tremendously in scope and depth, and it is important to note this variation and the impact this had on the subsequent analysis'.[17] As our own research,[18] and that of Baginsky

---

[13] House of Commons Women and Equalities Select Committee (2020), pp 39–46.
[14] See Chapter 4 for more detail about the role of TLAP, ADASS, and other associated organizations in pandemic-preparedness exercises.
[15] The full list can be seen here: www.thinklocalactpersonal.org.uk/covid-19/tlap-insight-group/, accessed 10 July 2024.
[16] See Think Local Act Personal (2020) *A Telling Experience: Understanding the Impact of COVID-19 on People Who Access Care and Support – A Rapid Evidence Review with Recommendations*.
[17] Think Local Act Personal (2020).
[18] J.V. McHale and L. Noszlopy (2021) *Adult Social Care Provision under Pressure: Lessons from the Pandemic*, Birmingham: University of Birmingham.

et al,[19] and Price et al,[20] has shown, there were many similarities in the approaches taken by those local authorities that formally introduced easements and those that explicitly stated that they had not. As noted in the previous chapters, those few councils that did operate the formal easements were promptly subject to considerable scrutiny and public criticism. The TIG report stated that the lack of real-time monitoring and data gathering had made it difficult to identify whether issues experienced by service users during this period were directly caused by the implementation of Care Act easements.[21] It also reported a paucity of data about how the easements did or did not affect the quality of care and support received during the early months of the pandemic.[22]

Subsequently, the DHSC Guidance on easements, updated on 29 June 2021, noted that:

> Work has been undertaken by TLAP, ADASS, CQC and partners to understand the impacts of the Care Act easements on individuals. Chief Social Workers have had conversations with Principal Social Workers to provide assurance that the guidance has been applied as intended, and to offer support if needed. TLAP and ADASS have had discussions with the local authorities who have operated under easements to consider the reasons for this and the impact on adults with care and support needs.[23]

Having noted the TLAP-TIG report, it states that 'there is insufficient evidence to conclude that the easements have impacted on care and support'.[24] It then goes on to state that the 'CQC are working with providers to understand the impact of Care Act easements on them, to complement their Emergency Support Framework activities', though 'this information will not be published'.[25] This partial approach to information

---

[19] M. Baginsky, E. Thomas and J. Manthorpe (2023) 'Changing English local authority duties by the adoption of easements in the COVID-19 pandemic: findings from an interview-based study', *British Journal of Social Work*, 52(2): 939–55; and M. Baginsky, E. Thomas and J. Manthorpe (2023) 'Reasons for not adopting COVID-19 permitted changes to legal duties: accounts from English local authorities', *Health & Social Care in the Community*, 1–7.

[20] D. Price, P. Drake, N. Allen and J. Astbury (2022) *The Impact of Care Act Easements under the Coronavirus Act 2020 on Older Carers Supporting Family Members Living with Dementia at Home*, NIHR Older People and Frailty Policy Research Unit, Final Report, November.

[21] Think Local Act Personal (2020).

[22] Think Local Act Personal (2020).

[23] Department of Health and Social Care (2020) *Care Act Easements: Supporting Guidance*, updated 29 June 2021; withdrawn 22 July 2021.

[24] Department of Health and Social Care (2020) *Care Act Easements: Supporting Guidance*.

[25] Department of Health and Social Care (2020) *Care Act Easements: Supporting Guidance*.

gathering, and particularly information sharing, is puzzling given the well-established oversight role of the CQC, and its emphasis on the importance of transparency and accountability.[26] Given the task of learning from the events of the pandemic and feeding into subsequent resilience planning, it would be reasonable to consider this information as a matter of public interest.

In October 2020, the ADASS published a further report, titled *Themes and Learning from ADASS Members on the Local Response to COVID-19 in Spring and Early Summer 2020*.[27] This was co-authored by then ADASS President James Bullion and TLAP Chair Clenton Farquharson CBE. It drew on the intelligence shared within the TLAP-TIG group, along with a number of interviews with Directors of Adult Social Services (DASSs) in the eight local authorities which had operated Care Act easements and a small selection (five) which had not. Unsurprisingly, in the light of the findings of the other reports and the contemporaneous academic research, one of the key findings reiterated that 'many of the approaches used by councils that did not operate the easements were similar to those used by councils that did'.[28]

As discussed in Chapter 4, the ADASS had substantial input into the development of the Care Act easements model as part of the pandemic influenza preparedness planning of 2018. Their report identifies 44 points of learning for sharing with Government at central, regional, and local levels. The focus on decision-making re-emphasizes the 'last resort' nature of Care Act easements, to be triggered only once every other remedy has been explored. The 'Learning for Sharing' section recommends that councils should prepare in every possible way and hold off as long as possible before activating easements, which should only be used 'at the last possible moment ... when the house is on fire'.[29] It recommends that part of this preparation should involve extensive consultation with local stakeholders, such as council members, NHS boards, and Healthwatch teams, and the report reiterates the importance of consistency in the channels and content of cross-agency messaging.[30] Yet there are conflicting messages on the need for greater levels of consultation and communication, perhaps due

---

[26] See Chapter 4 in reference to the COVID-19 Local Outbreak Management Plans (known as LOMPs) which the DHSC required of every local authority from June 2020, and which ultimately provided basic, roughly systematic data on local impacts, and a range of public health and mitigation efforts. See UK Health Security Agency (2020) *COVID-19 Contain Framework: A Guide for Local Decision Makers*, 17 July 2020, updated 7 October 2021; withdrawn 7 April 2022.

[27] Association of Directors of Adult Social Services (2020) *Themes and Learning from ADASS Members on the Local Response to COVID-19 in Spring and Early Summer 2020*.

[28] Association of Directors of Adult Social Services (2020), p 28.

[29] Association of Directors of Adult Social Services (2020), para 30.

[30] Association of Directors of Adult Social Services (2020), para 31.

to the strain between ideal best practice and what is considered possible or reasonable when operating in fast-paced 'fire-fighting' mode. As the ADASS report notes:

> In times of real crisis, when local leaders are already fire-fighting, there should be a clear principle of 'No surprises' and minimal requests for unnecessary additional reporting. In relation to the Care Act Easements the expectation on local authorities to widely consult with stakeholders was not realistic given the unprecedented nature of the Pandemic and the need to act swiftly and decisively.[31]

Yet while such consultation and communication activities are burdensome and 'not realistic', the report also considers them to be 'crucial':

> Consultation and communications at a local level is crucial. Some national work was undertaken which would have been much better done at a local level. Some local systems were over-ridden by requirements to use national communications and then reverted to local management. Some regions had sophisticated data and intelligence systems that were over-ridden by national requirements. The sector needs national frameworks and permissions, which support local implementation and prioritisation. National messaging is required for the public and stakeholders to support the sector at a local and regional level.[32]

The need for clearer and more standardized national frameworks and permissions that support local systems, implementation, and priorities was itself clearly echoed in our own stakeholder interviews. Lack of clear and timely communication and messaging from central Government was a recurrent complaint, but there was also a sense that there was too much distance and a lack of understanding in Westminster of what is required locally and of how social care works in practice One of our interviewees highlighted this:

> It was an inefficient way to prioritize resources, and a more efficient way would be some sort of general derogation of not just the care act but a whole range of acts, because there are aspects of all sorts of things which we do by necessity during peace time that you could suspend for a period of a few weeks or months, without any detriment to citizens.

---

[31] Association of Directors of Adult Social Services (2020), para 66.
[32] Association of Directors of Adult Social Services (2020), para 69.

> It's like a minister from Whitehall trying to micromanage everything, the analogy I've used before is it's like someone with a really, really long screwdriver trying to change a plug in the next room; they can't see what they're doing, you know the instrument is far too far away to be effective, and there's no feedback if they're doing it wrong and getting the screwdriver in the live wire. You know it does frustrate us quite a lot, and I think the whole care act easement is a microcosm of that wider problem really. (Director of Adult Social Services in a West Midlands local authority that formally activated easements)

This frustration was exacerbated by the negative attention received by those local authorities who had made use of the emergency provisions and followed 'the letter of the law' as they saw it which we discussed in the previous chapter.

> The letter of the law is: if we can't follow an element of the Care Act, we have to enact easement level 3. And I think we got penalized a little bit in the press and penalized quite a lot across the country. And I believe we were penalized very unfairly because we did it correctly … some other regions have been telling me that they were doing the same things that we were doing, but they hadn't enacted easements. (Principal Social Worker [PSW] in a West Midlands local authority that formally activated easements)

Similar frustration was expressed by a DASS in a local authority that formally activated easements, who told us:

> Because things at that time were moving very, very quickly and what you don't want to have to do when things are moving very, very quickly is go through a full democratic process, because it's slow. So, we wanted to make sure that we had [covered] all eventualities – 'in the event that things are really bad we will do this …'. And other local authorities didn't do that. That doesn't mean they didn't do the planning and it doesn't mean that they didn't make modifications to the processes – pretty much everybody did. But there were varying interpretations of whether or not it formally constituted a Care Act easement, and I think most local authorities just did it under the radar. So, we were very transparent about it, as a consequence of which we then found ourselves [facing accusations, such as] 'Isn't it disgraceful what these local authorities are doing, and it will affect the care of the most vulnerable', and all of that sort of stuff. So, we then spent the next six to nine months answering all sorts of freedom Freedom of

Information requests, letters from all sorts of advocacy groups, from 'Outraged' – and none of these were our residents ... It left us feeling just a bit bruised really, and it was all a bit unnecessary. (Director of Adult Social Services in a West Midlands local authority that formally activated easements)

Other concerns regarding the relationship between local government departments and the DHSC, and the consequences of following the Guidance and implementing easements, were demonstrated in the following comments from one of our interviewees:

So, I think the easements process was pushed through Parliament, etc., with all good intent to get that balance right between, having to respond practically and effectively to an emergency, whilst ensuring service user and carer needs, human rights, needs, expectations, safety etc. were respected. Making sure that the Care Act 2014, the main bits, the principles of it, were still sound and followed and all that sort of thing. But on the other hand, the balance of the emergencies and the contingencies and the need to shift capacity and scarce resources around due to the pandemic. But I think it was a bit of a rough stick to control it with if you see what I mean. And, because of the urgency of it, not really thought through well enough, i.e. some of the unintended consequences of doing it.

I think nationally, some of it was perhaps a bit harsh. It was almost like DHSC [were saying] yes, we'd done this, we've got this legislation through, these emergency regulations through. But they were then asking: Do you really mean that? Do you really want to do it? Tell us again why you've done it?

You could see this pattern of experience repeating over the years in different ways. Do we want to stick our head above the parapet on this? Or wait for somebody else to do it? (Regional ADASS associate)

While the messaging from central government in relation to Care Act easements and other changes was highlighted by some interviewees, concerns were also expressed regarding lack of consultation and clear communication by local authorities to other local stakeholders.[33] It was suggested that this resulted in local providers, voluntary sector organizations, and communities

---

[33] The central–local government disconnect seen during the pandemic was also highlighted in A. Giovannini (2021) 'In the eye of the storm: English local government and the COVID-19 crisis', in J.R. Bryson et al (eds) *Living with Pandemics: Places, People and Policy*, Cheltenham: Edward Elgar Publishing.

being left out, or unaware, of certain significant decisions. For example, the following interviewee commented that

> There wasn't any consultation or any discussion that the Council were enacting easements. I heard it from a third party who told me where I could go to find the information to confirm that. And with no disrespect to the local authority, it was deeply hidden on their website. You have to be able to navigate through what is a very complicated website anyway to actually find the fact that the local authority had gone down the route of easement.
>
> There was no announcement, and I think that was one of the bits that took us by surprise, that the decision had obviously been taken at director level, I suspect, and then out to the Cabinet, that the city might need to suspend some services or whatever. But I think it's genuinely fair to say that that was not communicated to the people likely to be affected by it, the users of services. It certainly wasn't advised to us, and I think it came as quite a shock. (CEO of a major learning disabilities charity in the West Midlands)

Similar concerns were raised by a local Healthwatch lead:

> That decision [to activate easements] was taken very quickly ... And that was done behind closed doors without any engagement, not even involvement. Actually, there was no communication around it either. The result of that meant that health and local authority moved into the different pathways, with no sign of having supported organizations within the same system, who were completely unaware that the pathways had changed. And therefore there was a lack of understanding, not only from the community perspective, but also from partners within the voluntary sector as well around 'What do Care Act easements mean for us? What does that mean our own roles in terms of organizations? Or what does that mean for our community members that have been discharged from hospital?' So, though it happened quickly, we had no comms or engagement around it, which caused quite a bit of confusion, especially with partners who actually support older people or people with learning disabilities. (Healthwatch Lead in a West Midlands local authority that formally activated easements)

In areas where more systematic consultation took place early on, local third-sector partners tended to report a more positive collaborative experience. One Healthwatch Lead in a local authority that did not formally activate easements said that the pandemic experience had 'made their relationship stronger; they've all come together'.

Interestingly, the ADASS report indicates that from a national-level perspective certain local authorities may have avoided engaging with the Care Act easement provision and Guidance, either due to a perception that it would create additional work, or due to fear of negative repercussions whether legal or political; it then states that this 'leaves a risk that some could have been operating easements informally'.[34] Some of our own interviewees echoed these concerns about increased administrative load and certainly some of those that did formally activate easements felt strongly the effects of 'political difficulty', both internally and from outside. One interviewee stated that

> as it turned out, once we'd made the decision to do the easements, I'm sure hindsight has shown us that we could have got away with not doing them. I suspect that there are local authorities around the country that reduced things, and stopped doing some things like we did, probably, more than we did, who didn't use the easements.
>
> So I talked to a colleague, somebody I used to work with at another local authority, who phoned me to see how I was, because he'd heard we'd used the easements and things must be really bad. And I said, 'No, we're doing really well.' And I know for a fact that they were doing the same things as us, in terms of, you know, clearly, not doing reviews, etc. Those kinds of things. (Principal Social Worker in a West Midlands local authority that formally activated easements)

Some others also felt the decision to formally activate easements was a 'sensible' part of 'contingency planning':

> We saw the easements come through. We looked at what they were. When we were really worried that the market was, probably, going to have a serious problem delivering care to people – mainly the sickness absence rates looked to be going up in the private sector, as well as our own Reablement Service – we thought we were going to, potentially, look to use Stage 4, the Level 4 of the easements, that we might have to think about moving care from some people to cover safety issues.
>
> So I think our initial conversation around that – certainly, my thinking as the PSW – was that this is contingency planning. This is us being ahead of what we think may happen. I saw the easements as something that we could have in place and use as necessary. Later, when there seemed to be a growing questioning of the use of easements, and when it surprised me that most local authorities weren't using

---

[34] Association of Directors of Adult Social Services (2020), para 70.

easements, it was clear that other people viewed them very much as a reactive thing. In the press, in the community care articles, etc., they were described as, if you're using easements, God, your local authority must be in a right state, not able to do stuff. And I'd certainly seen them as a proactive thing.

And when you look at what hospitals were doing ahead of their Intensive Care Unit's being full, they were moving everybody out of hospital that could possibly be moved out. It seemed a very, very sensible thing to do facing a pandemic. I actually have very strong personal feelings about how different people reacted to the use of the easements in social care, when the impact of doing it – the decision to do it – I still think, seemed quite reasonable and logical to me. (Principal Social Worker in a West Midlands local authority that formally activated easements)

Nonetheless, concerns remained about the potential adverse reputational consequences that implementation of the easements had caused, and some raised valid questions as to whether a lesson for the future might be that rather than going through the formal legislative easement process, changes could be implemented in other ways instead.

I think we would argue that at the time we followed the letter of the law, so the letter of the law said that if you change things that are not strictly Care Act-compliant you have to declare it as an easement. Again, you know, most local authorities did something similar but without declaring it, so we possibly made life more difficult for ourselves than we needed to, frankly. And yes, if we were facing a similar situation again, we might well see what we could do under the radar, rather than making it sort of legally overt. (Director of Adult Social Services in a West Midlands local authority that formally activated easements)

The October 2020 ADASS report had picked up on this discontent and commented that:

There is a residual sense of injustice. DASSs who implemented the easements felt obliged to keep explaining themselves and justify their actions, even after they had done all that was asked of them in the guidance, with a genuine intent to be transparent. Some questioned why the reaction was so different from the reaction to NHS acute hospital service cancellations?

and noted that the DHSC 'was perceived as overly focused on the NHS, and within that, "hospital-centric", to the exclusion of the wider health and care system, and that this contributed to a lack of public understanding of the wider system, and adult social care, in particular'.[35]

Many, though not all, of the findings, suggestions and learning from the ADASS report were echoed in the data gathered during our own interviews. While local authorities and their social services teams tried to adjust to this changing policy landscape, amid increased demand, an exhausted and depleted workforce, and ever-stretched resources, these decisions were felt by people in communities who relied on the availability and consistency of services to maintain their well-being and quality of life.[36] The core findings reiterate that existing socio-economic and health inequalities, already acutely felt among people who draw on care and support services, resulted in disproportionately adverse impacts from COVID-19.

The 2020 motto that suggested we were 'all in it together' rang hollow under any closer scrutiny.[37] The unequal impacts of COVID-19 were felt across the intersections of different demographic groups, but it is widely accepted that those drawing on adult social care services, and those providing care and support, were particularly affected. Adverse impacts and outcomes flowing from the pandemic were disproportionately experienced by those classified as clinically vulnerable, older people, disabled people, people living in socio-economic deprivation, and people of Black, Asian, and minority ethnic backgrounds.[38] In a damning report in 2020 Michael Marmot and the UCL Institute of Heath research team found that social, economic, and resultant health inequalities had contributed to the high and unequal death toll from COVID-19 in the UK; moreover, they found that existing health inequalities had been further exacerbated by the pandemic.[39] Marmot et al showed how the pandemic had dragged these failings into the light, opening up our

---

[35] Association of Directors of Adult Social Services (2020), para 70.
[36] See J. MacLochlainn, J. Manthorpe, J. Mallett et al (2023) 'The COVID-19 pandemic's impact on UK older people's social workers: a mixed-methods study', *British Journal of Social Work*, 53(8): 3838–59; and further A. Ratzon, M. Farhi, N. Ratzon and B. Adini (2022) 'Resilience at work, burnout, secondary trauma, and compassion satisfaction of social workers amidst the COVID-19 pandemic', *International Journal of Environmental Research and Public Health*, 19(9): 5500.
[37] See, for example, discussion in M. Whitehead, B. Barr and D. Taylor-Robinson (2020) 'COVID-19: we are not "all in it together"—less privileged in society are suffering the brunt of the damage', *The BMJ Opinion* (22 May).
[38] NHS Confederation (2022) *The Unequal Impact of COVID-19: Investigating the Effect on People with Certain Protected Characteristics. How Health and Care Systems Are Devising Innovative Approaches to Mitigate the Direct Effects of COVID-19*, 15 June.
[39] M. Marmot et al (2020) *Build Back Fairer: The COVID-19 Marmot Review. The Pandemic, Socioeconomic and Health Inequalities in England*, London: Institute of Health Equity, The Health Foundation.

systems and policies of social care and support to the prospect of greater visibility and increased scrutiny:

> Albert Camus in *The Plague* wrote that the "pestilence is at once blight and revelation. It brings the hidden truth of a corrupt world to the surface." Echoing Camus, we argue that this pandemic exposes the underlying inequalities in society and amplifies them.[40]

Hospital discharge decisions have long been a pressure point in the health and social care system, but problems in this area also intensified during the pandemic. As we saw in Chapter 3, rapid hospital discharge under COVID-19 was facilitated with the acceleration of the Discharge to Assess model and the redeployment of some social workers from community-based roles to ward-based work. While this approach was effective in relation to removing people from hospital beds in the first half of 2020, the rapidity of discharge coupled with the lack of COVID-19 testing led to sometimes-lethal consequences for the residents of care homes and the workers who cared for them.[41] These discharge decisions raised ethical issues for practitioners. In an empirical study by Banks and Rutter that examined responses from 41 social workers to ethical challenges raised by the pandemic, one respondee described the dilemmas and distress as follows:

> A senior manager in adult social care (R24, F) recounted 'bullying' in an acute hospital, where the primary drive was to meet the patient discharge target of three hours from being assessed as medically safe. If patients were unsafe to return home without support, they were placed in care homes, without assessment of patients' or homes' COVID-19 status. This resulted in patients transferring COVID-19 to care homes and developing COVID-19 once placed in an infected home. The manager commented: 'I escalated my thoughts on how this was implemented, but it has gone unheard ... I have *lost sleep* over the decision-making I am seeing around me and the *distress* this is causing frontline workers, my managers, families and carers.'[42]

Even where the main issue was not fear of infection, the removal of choice became a matter of concern. A 2020 Healthwatch England report

---

[40] M. Marmot et al (2020) *Build Back Fairer*, p 5.
[41] M. Daly (2020) 'COVID-19 and care homes in England: what happened and why?', *Social Policy and Administration*, p 985.
[42] S. Banks and N. Rutter (2022) 'Pandemic ethics: rethinking rights, responsibilities and roles in social work', *British Journal of Social Work*, 52(6): 3460.

commented that: 'Care home staff often encountered families refusing to accept their relative's discharge placement as they found it difficult to explain that people no longer had a choice about where they went to after leaving hospital.'[43]

By October 2020, as pressures on hospitals began to mount once more, COVID-19-positive patients were again being discharged to 'designated care settings'.[44] Beyond residential health and care settings, the situation was at least as precarious in domiciliary care, in people's own homes in the community.[45] Assessment of impacts experienced by this group of adults with care needs has been particularly difficult, though it is clear that reductions in community-based services during the pandemic caused stress and affected the well-being of all people in such situations.[46] What if individuals and their families who had 'survived' the worst of times were now simply viewed as able to 'cope'? There were uncertainties about whether the requisite state support would be returned once those on furlough who had stepped in to care for relatives returned to work. Given the backdrop of austerity, there were concerns that what might have been a quiet and stoic acceptance of lack and less during the peak pandemic years might in fact become a 'new normal'. Would these latest cuts and restrictions be subsumed under the broader malaise of the post-COVID 'cost of living crisis' and the ever-tightening squeeze on local government budgets? These concerns were voiced by many of our research interviewees:

> There's a massive worry from people on the ground now is that because they didn't have five days' service, or because they didn't have such a support and the family did it instead, that the social workers come round and say 'Well, your family can carry on doing it can't they? Or you know you don't need that, you managed, you survived.' So there's a level of 'what's going to be the view of social workers and others going forward?' Is the view that social care support is purely to survive

---

[43] Healthwatch England, working with the British Red Cross (2020) *590 People's Stories of Leaving Hospital during COVID-19 – A Joint Report*, October, p 25; see also discussion in J.V. McHale (2023) 'Choosing Home'.

[44] P. Dunn et al (2021) *Adult Social Care and COVID-19 after the First Wave*, Health Foundation Briefing, May, p 7.

[45] K. Hodgson et al (2020) *Briefing: Adult Social Care and COVID-19: Assessing the impact on social care users and staff in England so far*, London: The Health Foundation, July.

[46] R. Tuijt (2021) 'Life under lockdown and social restrictions: the experiences of people living with dementia and their carers during the COVID-19 pandemic in England', *BMC Geriatrics*, 21(301); see also D. Price et al (2022) *The Impact of Care Act Easements under the Coronavirus Act 2020 on Older Carers Supporting Family Members Living with Dementia at Home*, Final Report, November, NIHR Older People and Frailty Policy Research Unit.

rather than live? And, if so, then the pandemic is given really the bad legacy that people can survive without five days service, can survive with the parents doing it. (Principal Social Worker in a West Midlands local authority that did not formally activate easements)

Similar concerns were expressed by another of our interviewees:

Having now done it for this length of time, are we going to see people, not necessarily brought back into the fold of services, but actually told to carry on as they are, and so are we going to have people that are reluctant carers, going forward? And then you've got all the issues around when people do things reluctantly, they can become quite agitated, quite easily, because they resent the fact that they've been pushed into doing something that they don't want to do. And therefore, you end up with safeguarding issues and all sorts of other issues that come out of it, because people are forced into a situation. (CEO of a West Midlands branch of a national mental health charity)

While there was no formal use of the statutory Care Act easements after Summer 2020, this should not suggest that the experience of those receiving social care or support, or those who were working in the care sector, immediately returned to a pre-pandemic position.

There was widespread unease that impacts were not being properly tracked as formal provisions were reduced or stopped, with long-term consequences for those with care needs and their unpaid carers and relatives at home:

It's all of the other bits, the impact of social isolation, the loss of contact with family and friends, and services. And of course, a lot of people caught COVID and coped. But how? We don't know. And of course, we're now seeing long-COVID. It's a real phenomenon, and it's a race for the bottom when it comes to health inequalities for people with disabilities, learning disabilities particularly. So, it's that bit for me: we took our eye off the ball a little bit. Because I think there is this sense that people got through it, but what's the impact on carers who for 15, 16, 17 months have had to care for somebody full time with no support from anywhere? (CEO of a major learning disabilities charity in the West Midlands)

Price et al's study with an 'especially hidden group' of unpaid or family carers, specifically older people caring for a spouse living with dementia at home, found that 'carers seem unprotected with few options. They are dealing with an unclear legal situation and widespread stress and burden'; this was found to be the case in both easement and 'non-easement' local authority areas.[47]

Pressures were also felt by personal assistants. The role of personal assistants directly employed by the person needing care and support is something which has grown over time facilitated by the use of directments and personal budgets.[48] Norrie et al, in their survey of the experiences of some 104 personal assistants during the pandemic, found that many expressed feeling 'overlooked and undervalued' during this period, compounded by a lack of understanding of the role.[49] There was also concern about the shortage of personal assistants in general, with lack of availability exacerbated by the pandemic. This led to adverse consequences for the personal assistant employers left without or with limited support, and the safeguarding concerns that would automatically arise in such circumstances.[50] Research involving healthcare workers, domiciliary care agencies, and nursing homes in the Midlands region by Nyashanu, Pfende, and Ekpenyong reported of impacts on respondents, such as adverse mental health outcomes due to pressures in the early pandemic period of 2020 arising from stressors including the lack of available personal protective equipment (PPE) and unsafe discharge to care homes with inadequate testing, as well as distress about the COVID deaths of residents, colleagues, and relatives.[51] They also noted that staff shortages in the social care sector meant that those who did go into work were subject to considerable pressures, leading to staff feeling 'physically and mentally drained'.[52]

These issues, and changes in service delivery, had an impact upon unpaid family carers, the ranks of whom grew rapidly at the outset of the pandemic as fear of infection set in. In June 2020, research by Carers UK estimated

---

[47] Price et al (2022), p 11.
[48] See M. Leverton et al (2023) '"I have enough pressure as it is, without the worry of doing something wrong because of ignorance": the impact of COVID-19 on people who employ social care personal assistants', *British Journal of Social Work*, 53(2): 1243; see also Chapter 3.
[49] See further C. Norrie et al (2023) '"You're out on a limb, on your own": social care personal assistants' (PAs') reflections on working in the COVID-19 pandemic – implications for wider health and care services', *PLOS ONE*, December p 5.
[50] N.C. Norrie et al (2023).
[51] M. Nyashanu, F. Pfende and M.S. Ekpenyong (2022) 'Triggers of mental health problems among frontline healthcare workers during the COVID-19 pandemic in private care homes and domiciliary care agencies: lived experiences of care workers in the Midlands region, UK', *Health and Social Care in the Community*, 30: e370–e376.
[52] M. Nyashanu, F. Pfende and M.S. Ekpenyong (2022).

that some 4.5 million additional people had become carers since March 2020.[53] As one of our own interviewees commented:

> Many care homes were seeing their occupancy down to 60 per cent, which is just not viable. I think many care providers now are looking at pre-pandemic occupancy levels. There was a lot of commentary that occupancy levels would be, would never go back because people actually realized they could look after loved ones at home, and furlough enabled that. And then, you know so could the Government look at furlough type payments for carers, for family carers. I think an awful lot of people realized that looking after somebody with quite challenging dementia is a really difficult job, and it's 24/7. You can't do that on your own. And that's been a sad, a really sad part of it as well. And some people have made themselves very ill through exhaustion from trying to deal with those type of situations. Been an incredibly tough 18 months. And it continues, because COVID hasn't gone away. (Representative of the care sector in the Midlands)

The pressures they faced grew considerably as their regular day care and respite services, and other crucial forms and forums of social support, were closed due to social-distancing rules or staffing issues. As Gleibel et al noted in relation to the impact on people living with dementia and their unpaid carers:

> For carers, being unable to access previously utilized activities significantly predicted their well-being. Unpaid carers provide a large proportion of dementia care, worth over £13 billion each year in the UK. ... While carers might not always acknowledge themselves how much care they provide, ranging from preparing a hot meal to dressing the PLWD or supporting them to use the toilet, carers can become increasingly burdened as the dementia progresses and symptoms advance with PLWD requiring more support. ... Accessing respite care and having some time to themselves whilst the PLWD is attending a day care centre is therefore crucial to support the carer.[54]

Conversely, some family or unpaid carers – despite high levels of stress during the pandemic – became wary of accessing those residential respite

---

[53] Carers UK (2020) *Carers Week 2020 Research Report: The Rise in the Number of Unpaid Carers during the Coronavirus (COVID-19) Outbreak*, 8 June p 4.
[54] In C. Giebel et al (2021) 'A UK survey of COVID-19 related social support closures and their effects on older people, people with dementia, and carers', *International Journal of Geriatric Psychiatry*, 36(3): 393; see also C. Giebel et al (2021) 'Impact of COVID-19 related social support service closures on people with dementia and unpaid carers: a qualitative study', *Aging & Mental Health*, 25(7): 1281.

opportunities that did remain available, weighing up the risks to benefits for people who were clinically vulnerable to the virus.[55]

Research also indicates that disabled people from Black, Asian, and minority ethnic backgrounds were particularly severely adverse impacted by the pandemic. A 2023 report by the Voluntary Organisations Disability Group (VODG) Commission on COVID-19, Ableism and Racism reported that:

> Disabled Black, Asian and minority ethnic people were severely affected by changes to their social care and support during the pandemic. For example, two thirds of those who responded to our easy read survey said that their care and support had changed during the pandemic.[56]

The Commission set out to explore how the 'intersections of race and disability impacted people's outcomes' and found that 'the Government failed Disabled people of Black, Asian and minority ethnic communities because it did not recognise them as citizens'.[57] It went on to state that:

> There were delays and difficulties accessing new or changed support, as well as reductions in the care and support people received pre-pandemic. Mostly this was the result of social services reducing hours of funded support or staffing shortages impacting the quality and consistency of care. This included carers cancelling at short notice or stopping work entirely due to safety concerns for either themselves or their families.
>
> These delays and difficulties resulted in long-term impacts on physical and mental health and a greater reliance on families taking on additional caring responsibilities.[58]

This echoes findings elsewhere about the increased pressures experienced by unpaid or family carers, and relatives, friends, or neighbours who took on a caring role at the start of the pandemic. The impact of day centre closures was also acutely felt by these service users and carers, given that such services are so crucial for providing respite and avoiding carer burnout.[59]

---

[55] K. Samsi, L. Cole, K. Orellana and J. Manthorpe (2022) '"Is it worth it?" Carers' views and expectations of residential respite for people living with dementia during and beyond the COVID-19 pandemic', *International Journal of Geriatric Psychiatry*, 1.

[56] Voluntary Organizations Disability Group (2023) *Commission on COVID-19, Ableism and Racism 'A spotlight on Injustice'*, 21 July, London: VODG para 2.5.

[57] Voluntary Organizations Disability Group (2023) *Commission on COVID-19*, pp 1–2.

[58] Voluntary Organizations Disability Group (2023) *Commission on COVID-19*, para 2.5.1.

[59] J. Onwumere et al (2021) 'COVID-19 and UK family carers: policy implications', *Lancet Psychiatry*, 8(10): 929; see also C. Giebel et al (2022) 'Navigating the new normal: accessing community and institutionalised care for dementia during COVID-19', *Aging & Mental Health*, 26(5): 905.

(We return to the issue of day centre closures later.) The report found that all these problems disproportionately affected disabled people living in the community, as the Government focus was on institutional settings:

> Challenges were exacerbated by a narrow policy approach to social care throughout the pandemic. This focused on large institutional settings, especially care homes for older people, and overlooked community based support. For example, disabled people who employed their own personal assistants (PA) had little to no support throughout the pandemic and faced difficulties accessing PPE and a lack of guidance about what to do if they or their PA became infected ... This contrasted with significant amount of guidance made available to care homes.[60]

The survey showed that these people also experienced difficulties in obtaining support and had reductions in the level of support they received, due to local authorities reducing funded hours of provision, along with staffing shortages, and the cancellation of care at short notice due to safety concerns. Here, family members again stepped in to provide informal care,[61] as did voluntary sector organizations and ad hoc groups of community volunteers, though these were not in a position to provide higher-level or complex care and support. There was also great pressure on social care workers, themselves impacted by COVID-19 with the rise of sickness absences,[62] and many exhausted residential or agency care workers quit the sector, due to burn-out or to seek better pay and conditions outside social care.

The impact was also heavy on providers.[63] An Association of Directors of Adult Social Services survey in June 2020 noted that 43 per cent of local authority leaders reported that there were closures of care homes and care home providers, either through ceasing to trade or handing back contracts; by October and November 2020 this figure had grown to 60 per cent.[64] The rapid financial decline that followed in 2022 and 2023 resulted in untenable running costs and combined with workforce shortages, care homes continued to struggle. The impact of such closures on service users remains to be fully measured, but it is clear that when care homes close, for

---

[60] Voluntary Organizations Disability Group (2023), p 25.
[61] Voluntary Organizations Disability Group (2023), para 2.5.1–2.5.2.
[62] See also the discussion in N. Curry, C. Oung, N. Hemmings, A. Comas-Herrera and W. Byrd (2023) *Building a Resilient Social Care System in England: What Can Be Learnt from the First Wave of COVID-19?*, Research Report, May, Care Policy and Evaluation Centre and Nuffield Trust, p 19.
[63] M. Fotaki et al (2023) *Bailed Out and Burned Out? The Financial Impact of COVID-19 on UK Care Homes for Older People and their Workforce*, Coventry: Warwick Business School.
[64] Directors of ADASS (2020) *ADASS Autumn Survey 2020*.

example, and older people need to be 're-assessed and resettled' there is a substantial risk of consequent physical and mental harm.[65]

With or without Care Act easements, workforce pressures seemed only to be increasing with time. As one of our own interviewees commented:

> It's very difficult to summarize all the twists and turns of how it felt and the emotions and how different parties felt and reacted over the course of ... a short period of time. But a lot happened. A lot happened. And a lot of it was necessarily reactive and I think, as we speak, I suppose we don't want to set too many nerves a-jangle, but I mean, I know we're in the heat of winter [2020–21] but we're starting to worry about next winter and hospitals and the knock-on effect on adult social care and the state of adult social care, particularly its workforce. Not just tired ... but actually we're losing particularly home care staff a lot back, ironically, to the NHS, which is almost like robbing Peter to pay Paul. (Regional ADASS associate)

Under such multifarious pressures, this shows the difficulty during this period in ensuring that the baseline Care Act principles of supporting and promoting well-being, dignity, and choice were fulfilled.

A further shift in the profile of social care and support is the way in which third-sector organizations and more impromptu networks of local volunteers and 'mutual aid' groups stepped up to respond to unmet needs in their communities.[66] Beyond the self-directed activity of these volunteers, local authority resilience teams soon harnessed this rise in neighbourly goodwill and community support to fulfil roles usually undertaken by staff who were being redeployed elsewhere.[67] A local government survey in 2020 found that

---

[65] In relation to impacts of care home closures, see further research J. Glasby, S. Robinson and K. Allen (2024) *Achieving Closure: good practice in supporting older people during residential care home closures,* University of Birmingham-ADASS report, in association with SCIE, July, pp 4 and 5; and A. Iqbal et al (2023) 'A scoping review of the costs, consequences, and wider impacts of residential care home closures in a UK context', *Health and Social Care in the Community,* 2023; see also K. Sams et al (2023) 'Understanding factors influencing residential respite service use by carers of people living with dementia using Andersen's behavioural model of health services use: a qualitative study', *Aging & Mental Health,* 1–10. DOI: 10.1080/13607863.2023.2196254

[66] See Centre for People, Work, Organisational Practice (2021) *Respond, Recover, Reset: The Voluntary Sector and COVID-19,* CWOP Report, May; see also D. King et al (2022) *Respond, Recover, Reset: Two Years On,* Nottingham: Nottingham Trent University, Centre for People, Work, Organisational Practice.

[67] See Centre for People, Work, Organisational Practice (2021). For an examination of the relationship between mutual aid groups and council bodies in Scotland, see J. Rendall, M. Curtin, M.J. Roy and S. Teasdale (2022) 'Relationships between community-led

95 per cent of Council Chief Executive Officers believed the contribution of voluntary and community groups was 'very significant' or 'significant'.[68] The response of individuals and communities operating at local level, often filling gaps where immediate needs such as access to food and medicines, and social contact, were not being met by statutory providers during the first peak of the pandemic, was organised with remarkable speed, agility and good will.[69]

While this intensified the usual level of interaction between the public sector and third-sector employees and community volunteers, and very many positive benefits were evident, it was not always a straightforward process to negotiate roles, as we found in some of our research interviews.[70]

III. Experiences of adult social care delivery from winter 2021

In the previous section we have explored a range of insights and experiences of adult social care delivery from the peak pandemic period from March 2020, when the the Coronavirus Act came into force, through to so-called 'Freedom Day' in July 2021. The Westminster Government and large portions of the public were wearying of COVID-19 news and mitigations, yet the huge stress on health and social care continued unabated. COVID-19, despite the very successful vaccination campaign, continued to exert a heavy toll on lives, health, and well-being. In this section of the chapter, we explore experiences from winter 2021 onwards into 2022, a period when legislative 'solutions' in the form of Care Act easements under the Coronavirus Act 2020 were no longer available to local authority adult services teams.

In the retrospective view of one of our interviewees, as the dust began to settle:

> There is a legacy of increased demand, there is a legacy of work force shortages, because I think the fact that so many people worked so hard for so long has been material in influencing their decision about future careers.

---

mutual aid groups and the state during the COVID-19 pandemic: complementary, supplementary, or adversarial?', *Public Management Review*.

[68] New Local (2020) 'Council's response to COVID-19 - Leadership Index Edition 9', May, cited in Locality (2020) *We Were Built for This: How community groups helped us through the coronavirus crisis - and how we can build a better future*. London, June, p 12.

[69] Locality (2020) *We were Built for This*.

[70] See further the discussion in Chapter 5.

I think we are much more familiar now with the challenges, the direct challenges that the virus presents and have quite mature systems and processes, so we're not sort of making things up as we go along in quite the same way as we were initially. And I think, again, we're back to what feels like a more normal way of operating, albeit given that we're dealing with quite a lot of demand pressure. My point about the early stages is – don't forget then that no-one knew how this was going to pan out, right? There was an awful lot of uncertainty and a very wide range of plausible outcomes ranging from a best-case scenario to a quasi-apocalyptic worst-case scenario. And, again, in the context of that I think it is still surprising that we maintained all of the usual legal checks and balances that exist in peace time. (Director of Adult Social Services in a West Midlands local authority that formally activated easements)

In December 2021 ADASS issued an urgent plea from social services teams and from the wider adult social care sector:

Despite phenomenal increases in the amount care delivered in recent months, more is needed than there are care givers to deliver it. This means that excruciatingly painful choices are being made about who gets support and how much. It means deciding between helping someone to get out of bed and ensuring they are able to eat and drink during the day. This situation is getting worse by the hour as more and more staff go off sick or isolate because of the Omicron variant of COVID-19. Given that the Government has not announced any further restrictions over recent days, we are appealing to people to do the right thing.[71]

In the same press release, then ADASS Director Stephen Chandler made the stark admission that 'rationing' of care and support had become widespread across the sector:

Even before COVID-19 and Omicron, adult social care was struggling with severe funding and workforce challenges. Staff absences due to the rapid spread of Omicron and the need to self-isolate now mean that there are not enough pairs of hands to provide care for everyone who needs it. *Every day we are rationing care in ways that we never have before. We are making incredibly difficult decisions about who gets care, how*

---

[71] Association of the Directors of Adult Social Services (2021) *Press Release: A National Emergency for Social Care*, 22 December.

much care they get and who misses out – with obvious concerns that this will lead to people becoming isolated and, ultimately, to the loss of lives ... This is now a national emergency for social care.[72]

Around a week later, on 29 December 2021, a letter was sent by Michelle Dyson, Director General of Adult Social Care, and Lyn Romeo, then Chief Social Worker, to all local authorities, in response to communications that despite 'doing all they can to meet their statutory Care Act duties to provide care and support to individuals and to meet their duties to the health and well-being of their wider population', they now needed 'greater flexibility to prioritise resource in these very challenging times'. The letter was headlined 'Supporting the COVID response in adult social care'.[73] It noted the additional challenges facing the adult social care sector as a result of the Omicron variant, with staff shortages where workers had to take time off to isolate due to sickness and mentioned that there would be an additional £69 million in funding to support infection control measures and direct payments 'if required to meet care needs'.[74]

The letter then went on to say that:

In recent days, we have heard that local authorities need greater flexibility to prioritise resource in these very challenging times. Government recognises that the Care Act does allow for flexibility in how local authorities prioritise resources to meet the most urgent needs and / or significant risks, whilst still fulfilling their statutory duties.

The Care and Support Statutory guidance (particularly chapter 10) provides more detail on the flexibilities that can be used to assess, review and prioritise services, which may be particularly helpful during times of increased pressure, while still fulfilling statutory duties. Where these flexibilities are used, local authorities should be satisfied that it is an appropriate, proportionate, and effective way of meeting needs and care must be taken to ensure that the process is person-centred. *Recognising increasing pressures and demand, it might become necessary to make challenging decisions on how to redirect resources where they are most needed and to prioritise individual care needs.* The Ethical Framework that was published in response to the pandemic

---

[72] Association of Directors of Adult Social Services – ADASS (2021) *Press Release: A National Emergency for Social Care*, emphasis added.
[73] Shared by Care England, at www.careengland.org.uk/sites/careengland/files/20211229%20Supporting%20the%20covid%20response%20in%20adult%20social%20care.pdf, accessed 10 July 2021, cited below under Care England (2021).
[74] Care England (2021).

also provides a checklist when considering decision-making and policy responses to COVID-19.[75]

This is, strikingly, the language of the Care Act easements guidance, albeit used at a time when the statutory frameworks facilitating their operation were no longer in place. The letter is also suggestive of some concern as to the scope and legitimacy of actions which might be taken in this situation by local authorities, as it goes on to recommend that they seek legal guidance about the validity of any operational changes:

> Whilst we are confident about the general advice regarding flexibility within the Care Act, we would advise you to take your own legal advice regarding any specific measures you are considering to ensure you continue to comply with your legal obligations, including those in Part 1 of the Care Act 2014.[76]

This latter statement itself raises questions as to the use of the statutory easements in the first place. The Care Act easements were introduced precisely to provide explicit legislative protection yet local authorities, arguably bruised or wary following the public reaction to their brief implementation in spring 2020, chose not to utilize them after the summer of 2020. Ultimately the statutory powers were expired on 16 July 2021. As such, this letter goes far beyond expressing thanks for the continuing service and resilience of local authority staff; it also shows that the Government recognized that delivery of services remained under strain, while making clear to local authorities that it would be a matter of local governance to ensure that any actions undertaken to mitigate the strain remained lawful.

These harsh realities played out against a backdrop of Government announcements pledging moral, and some further financial, support for the social care sector; the pandemic had certainly brought care into the public awareness. On 2 January 2022, the Government announced that they were already planning to invest £462 million to support adult social care sector recruitment and retention, along with a range of other measures to mitigate the impact of the Omicron variant.[77] But the strains on the system continued, and in some cases worsened. Staffing challenges had been

---

[75] Care England (2021), emphasis added where the wording is repeated verbatim from the Ethical Framework prose.
[76] Care England (2021).
[77] Cabinet Office and the Rt Hon Steve Barclay Press release (2022) *Government Takes Action to Mitigate Workforce Disruption*, 2 January.

exacerbated not only by COVID-19, but also by the restrictions imposed on workers after Brexit, and ongoing poor pay and working conditions.[78] There were some attempts made by Government to address staffing issues in social care. On 7 September 2020 the Johnson Government had announced plans for a new Health and Social Care Levy via a 1.25 per cent increase in National Insurance contributions.[79] It was intended that of this levy some £500 million would be used to support social care workforce well-being and development. However, this pledge was subsequently abandoned during the brief Truss Government,[80] and was replaced in April 2023 by a reduced figure of £250 million. Focused funding was made available in the form of grants to support workforce capacity in January 2021 of some £120 million, a Workforce Recruitment and Retention Fund in October 2021 of £162.5 million, and £300 million in December 2021 to address winter pressures: but these amounts were not adequate for the scale of the problem.[81]

To further compound the strain on the social care workforce, a 2021 policy requiring that social care and NHS workers should be fully vaccinated against COVID-19 led to further disruption, having proved controversial among some staff.[82] By winter 2021 only some 83% of care home staff had any vaccination as compared with 91 per cent of 'frontline' NHS Trust healthcare staff.[83] A statutory instrument was enacted requiring social care workers to be vaccinated in order to be able to work in the sector. This was subject to an unsuccessful judicial review challenge.[84] Provisions also introduced which would have required those working in the NHS to be similarly vaccinated were ultimately never implemented.[85] The social care mandatory vaccination

---

[78] R. Booth (2022) 'England's social care workforce shrinks for first time in 10 years', *The Guardian*, 11 October.

[79] Cabinet Office HMG (2021) *Build Back Better Our Plan for Health and Social Care*, 7 September.

[80] H.M. Treasury (2022) 'National Insurance increase reversed', *GOV.UK*, 22 September.

[81] Department of Health Policy Paper (2023) *Next Steps to Put People at the Heart of Care*, *GOV.UK*, 4 April.

[82] See Department of Health and Social Care (2023) *Guidance. Coronavirus (COVID-19) vaccination as a condition of deployment for the delivery of CQC-regulated activities in wider adult social care settings*. Updated 1 March 2022, J. Otte (2021) '"No jab, no job": care home workers in England on the COVID vaccine mandate', *The Guardian*, 11 November.

[83] See further P. Dunn et al (2021) *Adult Social Care and COVID-19 after the First Wave*, Health Foundation Briefing, May, p 19.

[84] E. Waitzman (2021) *Mandatory vaccines for health and care workers: latest regulations*, House of Lords Library, 13 December, and *R (Peters and Findlay) v Secretary of State for Health and Social Care* [2021] EWHC 3182 (Admin).

[85] M. McKee and M.C.I. van Schalkwyk (2022) (eds) 'England's U turn on COVID-19 vaccine mandate for NHS staff'. *BMJ*, 376: o353 h.

policy was reversed in February 2022.[86] However, a substantial number of care workers had already left the sector in that period due to the policy. Girma and Paton have argued that 'the mandate substantially decreased the proportion of care home workers who remained unvaccinated (equivalent to between 28,000 and 41,000 fewer unvaccinated staff), but this came at the cost of a reduction in staffing levels of between 3% and 4% (equivalent to 14,000 to 18,000 staff)'.[87]

Further concerns regarding the employment conditions and demands of care workers, and indeed on the resultant quality of care that could be provided were raised. The House of Commons Levelling Up, Housing and Communities Report 'Long Term Funding of Adult Social Care', commented that:

> For those working in domiciliary care, who are often electronically tagged so that their progress through their visits can be tracked, Jane Townson described 'the number of 15-minute visits, short visits, makes it really stressful because they feel that they cannot meet the needs of the people who they are supporting, then they go around in this permanent sense of guilt and worry'.[88]

Efforts to counter the negative impacts of post-Brexit restrictions on freedom of movement included the introduction of a five-year Health and Care Worker visa in 2022, though this appears to have resulted, according to the CQC, in exploitation and modern slavery becoming 'a feature' of the adult social care sector.[89]

At the day-to-day operational level, the legal requirement to self-isolate following a positive test remained in place until 18 March 2022. In the period between mid-December 2021 and mid-March 2022 some 15,000 people died in England who had tested positive for COVID-19. During this period local authorities still continued to struggle with the provision of services – the situation remained grave. The ADASS also published a highly critical report on the state of adult social care, titled *Waiting for Care and Support*, in May

---

[86] S. Learner (2022) 'Government U-turn on mandatory COVID vaccine branded "a joke" and "too late" by care homes', *Carehome.co.uk*, 1 February, at www.carehome.co.uk/news/article.cfm/id/1664289/u-turn-covid-vaccine-care-homes

[87] S. Girma and D. Paton (2024) 'COVID-19 vaccines as a condition of employment: impact on uptake, staffing, and mortality in elderly care homes', *Management Science*, 70(5).

[88] House of Commons Levelling Up, Housing and Communities Committee (2022) *Long-term Funding of Adult Social Care*, Second Report of Session 2022–23, HC 19, para 106.

[89] R. Booth (2023) 'Modern slavery "a feature" of care sector in England since Brexit', *The Guardian*, 19 December.

2022.⁹⁰ It stated that in the period between November 2021 and February 2022 there had been a 28 per cent increase in the number of people who were waiting for assessments, care and support, direct payments, or reviews. In the same period there had been a 71 per cent increase in the number of people waiting for care and support or a direct payment to begin. Also in that period 26 per cent of the people who were waiting for an assessment had been waiting for six months or more. The report concluded that such statistics translated into a very dire situation indeed for those in need of care and support:

> We saw in the last two surveys (January and March 2022) that 61% of DASSs are having to prioritise their assessment capacity to only people with life and limb safeguarding or at the point of hospital or reablement discharge. This means that people will be waiting without support and relying on unpaid/family carers (33% of respondents in the last two surveys reported that they were having to ask unpaid carers to take paid or unpaid leave from work as care wasn't available). Others will not be living a decent life and are likely to be deteriorating (becoming dehydrated or malnourished or falling for example). A proportion will need admission to hospital or will see their health and wellbeing deteriorate significantly.⁹¹

This level of strain again suggests that some social services teams were no longer able to be Care Act-compliant with regard to their obligation to assess people's needs, much less ensure the promotion of their well-being, choices, and dignity. In our interview with the Social Care Lead of the Local Government and Social Care Ombudsman (LGSCO) in August 2021, she stated that

> the general picture we're seeing is that overall COVID has exacerbated or aggravated what was already poor in some councils and care provision. COVID has not had a huge impact on those councils who had good systems – for example, joined-up systems with health – because a lot of the cracks in terms of the interface between health and social care, for example, hospital discharge complaints, were coming to the fore before. For some councils who were already poor, it just made things worse, because obviously there has been a lack of resource and a

---

⁹⁰ Association of Directors of Adult Social Services (2022) *Waiting for Care and Support Report*, May.
⁹¹ Association of Directors of Adult Social Services (2022), May 2022, p 4.

lack of funding, which have been an issue for many years. (Social Care Lead of Local Government and Social Care Ombudsman)

Specific findings relevant to the provision of services under the Care Act 2014 were highlighted in the LGSCO's report, *Unprecedented Pressure,* published in February 2022.[92] The Ombudsman in this period decided 1,123 complaints and enquiries with COVID-19 identified 'as a primary or secondary factor' and of these some 505 cases were subject to an in-depth investigation.[93] Of these, 20 per cent concerned adult social care.[94] The Ombudsman found maladministration in relation to 'care plans not being properly developed and/or reviewed as circumstances changed during the pandemic', inadequate record-keeping, and 'pre-existing delays and backlogs in service provision exacerbated and compounded by the impact of COVID-19 meaning important actions further delayed'.[95] Specific findings relevant to the provision of services under the Care Act 2014 requirements included:

> Significant delays carrying out Care Act assessments, sometimes preventing or delaying moves out of hospital or moves between providers.
>
> The needs of people receiving care not being put at the centre for decisions about what happened …
>
> Difficulties prioritising key decisions about longer-term care during the pandemic.
>
> Inflexibility about the creative use of direct payments to secure appropriate care when normal provision was affected by lockdown.[96]

The report also noted that the Ombudsman had found fault in relation to: '[c]onfusing changes and fluctuations in care, sometimes without consultation required by the Care Act' and '[v]arious problems with transfers between hospital and care and between different care providers particularly involving hospitals'.[97]

As the pandemic continued the intense strain on hospitals prompted further directions to increase the rapid discharge of patients into community settings when they were deemed medically fit for discharge. In a letter sent on 13 December 2021 by Amanda Pritchard, the NHS Chief Executive, and Professor Stephen Powis, the Chief Executive of NHS Improvement

---

[92] Local Government and Social Care Ombudsman (2022) *Unprecedented Pressure Learning from Complaints about Council and Care Provider Actions during the COVID-19 Pandemic,* February.
[93] Local Government and Social Care Ombudsman (2022), p 8.
[94] Local Government and Social Care Ombudsman (2022), p 10.
[95] Local Government and Social Care Ombudsman (2022), p 15.
[96] Local Government and Social Care Ombudsman (2022), p 21.
[97] Local Government and Social Care Ombudsman (2022), p 28.

to NHS bodies, hospital managers were urged to 'maximise capacity' by discharging the 'maximum number of people' both 'safely and quickly'.[98] This was to be achieved via integrated working practices, with medics expected to 'work together with local authorities and partners across your local system including hospices and care homes to release the maximum number of beds (and a minimum of at least half of current delayed discharges)' through working with local authorities to facilitate rapid discharge of patients.[99]

By winter 2022, the situation had again worsened. NHS England reported that in December 2022 there were on average around 13,440 patients in hospital who were waiting for discharge – some 30 per cent more than during the same period in December 2021.[100] The early signs following a new statutory framework for moving Care Act and CHC assessment outside of the hospital context were not, however, propitious. Hospitals in winter 2022–23 were again overwhelmed by the numbers of patients with consequent shortages of available beds which led to the Government announcing that it was providing 'up to £200 million of additional funding to immediately buy short-term care placements to allow people to be discharged safely from hospitals into the community where they will receive the care they need to recover before returning to their homes'.[101]

Nonetheless the level of pressure in winter 2022–23 was also emphasized in press reports that described how in Bristol, Cornwall, and Devon problems with space in hospitals had led to individuals being discharged into 'care hotels' in the period until end of March 2023 being cared for by a provider of homecare services and NHS rehabilitation and primary care staff.[102]

As we saw in Chapter 3, concerns in relation to the operation of hospital discharge processes continue to be reported, following the discharge to assess processes introduced under the Health and Care Act 2022 and reforms to the Care Act 2014 discussed earlier.[103] The NHS guidance highlights the importance of ensuring that such discharge is safe and includes active risk management.[104] Safety is obviously critical, as is avoiding a repeat of the

---

[98] NHS England and NHS Improvement (2021) C1487-letter-preparing-the-nhs-potential-impact-of-omicron-variant-and-other-winter-pressures-v4.pdf, p 4.

[99] NHS England and NHS Improvement (2021), p 5.

[100] See further D. Foster (2023) 'Insight: Delayed Hospital Discharges and Adult Social Care', House of Commons Library, 9 February.

[101] Up to £250 million to speed up hospital discharge – GOV.UK (www.gov.uk).

[102] D. Campbell (2023) 'Hospitals in England discharging patients into "care hotels"', *The Guardian*, 5 January.

[103] J.V. McHale (2023) 'Choosing home: discharge to assess and the Health and Care Act 2022' *Northern Ireland Legal Quarterly*, 74(4): 713–38.

[104] Department of Health and Social Care (2020) *Hospital Discharge Requirements*, p 22.

unsafe discharge decisions of 2020. The matter of what constitutes a 'safe discharge' is not clearly defined, however. It remains to be seen how effective these new measures will prove to be in the longer term.[105]

Although delays and backlogs were gradually being reduced, there was little optimism heading into 2023 and these concerns have been continued to be expressed subsequently.[106] The Autumn 2022 ADASS survey of DASSs in 76 per cent of 152 local authorities found that some 9 out of 10 of their members were of the opinion that workforce and funding were not sufficient to meet the needs of persons who were older and those with disability in their area.[107] The broader pressures on the sector, shortages of care workers and resultant pressures on delivery of care, reduced care packages, waiting lists for assessments, and concerns that employment of care workers being linked to modern slavery were all continuing themes highlighted by the CQC in its *The State of Health Care and Adult Social Care in England 2022/23*.[108]

Jackie Mahoney, a social worker and co-chair of the BASW Adult Group, noted that:

> rebound demand and pressure, following the initial COVID restrictions and possible reluctance to have support from some of the community, has been relentless over the past 18 months ... Social care is at the forefront of responding to the most challenging needs and circumstances within communities and is fundamentally key to 'levelling up'. In this respect, I would say the government is failing and is not focused enough on social care.[109]

Returning to some pre-pandemic level of 'business as usual' would have anyway been suboptimal for local authorities and service providers, but the reality was even worse. By early 2023, the ADASS stated that local authorities are 'caught in a vicious cycle, struggling to prioritize support to keep people healthy, independent and working, so they can continue to contribute to the economy and their communities'[110] and to reduce the number of people

---

[105] J.S. MacInnes, L. Bertini and S. Walker (2023) 'Does a discharge to assess programme introduced in England meet the quadruple aim of service improvement?', *Journal of Integrated Care*, 33(1): 16.

[106] Association of Directors of Adult Social Services – ADASS (2023) *Spring Survey 2023*.

[107] Association of Directors of Adult Social Services – ADASS (2022) *Autumn Report 2022*, November, cited in the Care Quality Commission (2023) *The State of Health Care and Adult Social Care in England 2022/23*, HC1871, p 35.

[108] CQC (2023) *The State of Health Care and Adult Social Care in England 2022/23*, HC1871.

[109] Quoted in M. Samuel (2022) 'Drop in adult social workers employed by councils as vacancies and turnover mount', in *Community Care*, 3 March.

[110] Association of Directors of Adult Social Services – ADASS (2023) Spring Survey Press Release 'Care waiting lists down but needs increasing'.

with higher and complex needs longer-term. Where provision is not available or insufficient, they acknowledge, 'family and unpaid carers are bearing the brunt of an under-resourced and over-stretched system'.[111]

IV. Digitisation of adult social care and changes to day centre services

In this section of the chapter we now move to focus in particular upon two elements of adult social care provision which were undergoing changes before 2020, but which faced dramatic transformations from March 2020 onwards. We look at how these changes to service delivery are embedding as a tangible legacy of the pandemic and the potential and challenges of such a legacy.

(a) Digitisation of adult social care

The drive towards enhanced online working practices and digital delivery in adult social care, also known as the 'digital agenda', had started well before the pandemic.[112] 'Digital transformation' is a key component of the Partners in Care and Health programme led by the Local Government Association and the ADASS, and it is also core to the Conservative Government's 2023 *Next Steps to Put People at the Heart of Care* policy, which notes that 'the adult social care sector lags behind the NHS in its digital working'.[113] The agenda includes increased use of virtual communications within teams to enable remote-working practices, expansion of reporting software with a view to greater integration between health and social care systems, and a sharp increase in the use of technology-enabled care (TEC) in the form of devices, responsive online systems, or apps. There was, however, an unprecedented acceleration in this use of digital technology from March 2020, as local authorities, the NHS, care providers, and service users pivoted to what became an increasingly online interface.[114]

Many local authorities had already begun to provide laptops, communications apps, and some relevant IT training to their staff before remote or hybrid working became obligatory in the early months of the

---

[111] Association of Directors of Adult Social Services – ADASS (2023).

[112] D. Maguire, H. Evans, M. Honeyman and D. Omojomolo (2018) *Digital Change in Health and Social Care*, King's Fund, June.

[113] Department of Health and Social Care (2023) *Policy paper: Next steps to put People at the Heart of Care*; Local Government Association (2023) *Digital Transformation in Adult Social Care*.

[114] M. Harvey, D.P. Hastings and G. Chowdhury (2023) 'Understanding the costs and challenges of the digital divide through UK council services', *Journal of Information Science*, 49(5): 1153–67.

pandemic. As discussed in previous chapters, due to the requirements to stay at home and, where outside the home, to maintain social distancing, many local authority employees, including some social workers, moved quite abruptly from face-to-face meetings to undertaking routine meetings and so on via Zoom, Teams, or Webex.[115] As one of our interviewees noted:

> [It was] just a massive change at the end of March, April [2020] where a lot of the way that services previously had been delivered changed almost overnight ... on a practical level, the face-to-face delivery, the mainstay that a lot of local authorities had done, what a lot of the community sector had also done, certainly wasn't possible. We were in lockdown, and even though there were certain easings for charities and essential services there was a sort of reluctance to put staff and volunteers in harm's way. [It] is difficult to imagine now in some ways, but we just didn't know enough about this virus, did we? We didn't know about its transmissibility and the effects of it really. There was a lot of reluctance to do face-to-face work, even if it was legally permissible.
>
> With Teams, Zoom, we had to do a lot of stuff over the phone where we previously did them face-to-face. The stuff that actually needed a face-to-face interaction, a lot of that got paused, didn't it, for a period of time. Pretty much everything got paused for certainly a couple of months. It was really only the absolutely crucial stuff that didn't. Even when in June, July we started to get back out there and there was a semblance of a normal service, there was a huge backlog. (Community resources manager in a West Midlands local authority that formally activated easements)

Remote working had obvious benefits in terms of protecting the workforce and public from potential COVID-19 infections, and it proved to work well for staff-to-staff committee, team, and interprofessional meetings. In addition many social workers and, of course, most care home staff continued to deliver face-to-face services and support throughout the pandemic. In fact, some social workers were redeployed from community teams into hospital-based teams to support the increased activity around discharge. There were different challenges and some serious shortcomings when digital communication approaches were applied to direct contact between frontline workers and service users. This issue was noted by the care-sector stakeholder respondents in our own study, in contrast to other local authority responses. For example, one of our interviewees noted the limitations of moving to

---

[115] F. Mishna, E. Milne, M. Bogo et al (2021) 'Responding to COVID-19: new trends in social workers' use of information and communication technology', *Clinical Social Work*, 49: 484–94.

Zoom and Teams for work, including such things as multi-disciplinary teams in relation to hospital discharge.

> To get a holistic assessment completed you cannot do that for a vulnerable older person through a screen, you need to be with them, you need to be understanding their needs. So I think we, I mean certainly this local authority always continued to meet the needs of their community and they have continued to place all the way through the pandemic, and they have done a sterling job. But the practicalities ... and the impact of social workers in particular moving to virtual ways of working, it has had a significant impact on care home and ancillary managers and supervisors because they're trying to work out the gaps. Lots more paperwork, lots more risk assessments, lots more in fact finding which one would normally expect to be within a holistic social work assessment. And less available to families. I'm not being overtly critical because actually I have been absolutely overwhelmed by the support that the council has given to providers. But it's the unforeseen circumstances of moving frontline workers, social workers, to virtual working. (Senior care provider in the West Midlands)

The same respondent identified the importance of providing face-to-face meetings for certain groups:

> The issue now is with social workers not being as available because I think there's some preference to online working. It's great that you can all work from home ... However, actually meeting people face-to-face makes a fundamental difference. And you cannot assess and appropriately support vulnerable adults through a screen. And hybrid works, but fundamentally in adult social care you need to be communicating with families, you need to be communicating with people who need care and support. And when you are dealing with often quite elderly people who are not necessarily tech-savvy, and certainly if you're dealing with people who have cognitive impairment, talking to a flat screen just doesn't work. So thought needs to be given not just to about what is in the worker's best interests, but what's in the client group's best interest. And I think what's happened is a lot of that burden of explaining, supporting, and guiding through the process that would be done by a social worker has ended up at the door of care home managers and domiciliary care managers ... it's one of those unintended consequences. (Senior care provider in the West Midlands)

This concern around lack of access to in-person care was also noted by Thomas et al in their interviews with social workers and occupational therapists drawn from five English local authorities which had not implemented Care Act easements, which stated that:

> Apart from those working in hospitals and in mental health teams, all had undertaken 'remote' telephone or online assessments and reviews with what was described as 'variable effectiveness.' There were instances where home care workers had asked for their clients to be assessed or visited by social workers in-person, but social workers had not been able to make face to face visits other than in emergencies.[116]

In contrast, the view from one of our local authority interviewees was more positive:

> We were actually in a really good place with the homeworking. We'd all got the right kit anyway. All our frontline staff [had] Surface Pros, Teams was set up, so that worked really well. We've always encouraged staff to work flexibly. And they work from various bases ... I mean, mostly every council I'm sure is the same. Most organizations you can log on any computer anywhere and your laptop syncs to the Wi-Fi in any office. Some people would have worked at home. But I think mainly the frontline staff, so the social workers and social care practitioners, more often than not would have been office based. So yeah, so quite a significant change for them. (Principal Social Worker in a West Midlands local authority that formally activated easements)

Nonetheless, as Machin comments, social care practitioners' roles, as with medics, teachers, and care workers, differ from those of usually office-based staff:

> The adjustment to home working and relying on digital communication posed similar issues as for other staff, but the responsibility to protect and engage with citizens presented unique issues. An important element of face-to-face working with the public (through home visits or office appointments) is the assessment of need, weighing up visual cues, assessing environmental factors, developing ongoing relationships where important information or vulnerability can be shared.[117]

---

[116] E. Thomas, M. Baginksy and J. Manthorpe (2024) 'The views of practitioners on Care Act easements during the COVID-19 pandemic', *Practice: Social Work in Action*, 36(1): 61.

[117] R. Machin (2023) 'UK local government experience of COVID-19 lockdown: local responses to global challenges', *Local Economy*, 0.

Research on the impact for service users and carers identifies mixed outcomes from the movement online or to hybrid working.[118] For example, Caton et al suggested that while the move to an offering of online activities (as opposed to day centre attendance and other community-based activities) for service users with profound and multiple learning disabilities was seen as positive by some, others indicated how challenging this was due to difficulties getting online, as well as sensory and other communication issues.[119] In the first period of lockdown, studies involving individuals with dementia and their carers highlighted how digital communication tools such as Zoom were not ideal for service provision. Tuijt et al's[120] research found that:

> Carers reported that alternative activities were being arranged, using online technology such as Zoom or WhatsApp. However, this was not always a satisfactory replacement for regular social activity. Some people living with dementia struggled with the necessary technology, and even telephone calls did not always replace the social engagement that benefitted people living with dementia.[121]

This finding was also reflected in the LGA COVID-19 Adult Safeguarding Project Insight Report of December 2021, which stated that:

> Over the duration of the pandemic there was increased use of videoconferencing with people with learning disabilities, which had a mixed response. For some people with a learning disability the use of virtual formats had a negative impact on them, others preferred the use of remote meetings. Some teams continued with face-to-face meetings where there were urgent visits (as required).[122]

---

[118] Also it should be noted that a review of literature concerning effects on older persons' access to health and social care services undertaken in 2021 indicated that the impacts of those technologies on equitable access was unclear; see T.P. Kunonga et al (2021) 'Effects of digital technologies on older people's access to health and social care umbrella review', *Journal of Medical Internet Research*, 23(11), published online 24 November.

[119] S. Caton et al (2022) 'Digital participation of people with profound and multiple learning disabilities during the COVID-19 pandemic in the UK', *British Journal of Learning Disability*, 163.

[120] R. Tuijt et al (2021) 'Life under lockdown and social restrictions: the experiences of people living with dementia and their carers during the COVID-19 pandemic in England', *BMC Geriatrics*, 21: 301.

[121] Tuijt et al (2021).

[122] Local Government Association (2021) *COVID-19 Adult Safeguarding Insight Project*, Third Report, December.

Other research also highlighted how the move towards digital delivery might be seen as detrimental to individual well-being. As noted in Chadwick et al's review of the literature concerning digital inclusion and participation of those with learning disabilities during the pandemic, this impact may not have been adequately considered: 'where an activity was lost or reduced in quality due to the lack of a digital alternative the negative impact on the general well-being of the person with ID [intellectual disability] was inferred but not evaluated in the studies reviewed, few of which directly addressed well-being as their primary aim'.[123] They went on to highlight the impacts of digital exclusion and dependency on others to access digital technologies, demonstrated in a lack of support and initial training for people with learning disabilities and for carers and support staff.[124] This lack of training and implementation, despite directives, had direct impacts on service users in some cases, particularly in the roll-out of TEC devices or apps:

> service providers, educational, health and social care professionals and caregivers, despite feeling pressure to move online, often failed to rise to the challenge of implementing digital solutions during Government sanctioned lockdowns and social distancing imperatives. Although awareness of digital exclusion was raised these stakeholder groups: underestimated people's ability to use ICT; were unwilling to provide the effort to train and support ICT use; and were often not adequately trained (digitally competent/literate) themselves. Despite awareness being raised, the extent to which this has led to action and actual change in the lives of people with ID [intellectual disabilities] remains unclear.[125]

The need for further, specific support needed for adults with intellectual disabilities, along with their carers or support staff, in relation to obtaining or enhancing digital access and skills, has also been noted in a study by Flynn et al.[126]

New challenges are emerging from the confluence of fast-paced technological innovation. Wright et al have suggested that:

---

[123] D. Chadwick et al (2022) 'Digital inclusion and participation of people with intellectual disabilities during COVID-19: a rapid review and international bricolage', *Journal of Policy and Practice in Intellectual Disabilities*, 19: 247.
[124] Chadwick et al (2022), p 247.
[125] Chadwick et al (2022), p 252.
[126] S. Flynn, S. Caton, A. Gillooly et al (2021) 'The experiences of adults with learning disabilities in the UK during the COVID-19 pandemic; qualitative results from wave 1 of the coronavirus and people with learning disabilities study', *Tizard Learning Disability Review*, 26(4): 224–9.

In the prolonged absence of national political leadership in the U.K. in proposing solutions to the myriad challenges of adult social care, relatively cheap, ubiquitous, and approachable consumer technologies such as Alexa seem [...] to be fast becoming one of the most important elements of a de facto strategy among LAs for a technologized future of care less centred on in-person human interaction. However, as new, more complex care assemblages come to include a fragmented patchwork of generic consumer electronic devices, yoking together a fast-moving and global consumer technologies marketplace characterised by the epithet 'move fast and break things', with the slow commissioning practices and long telecare contracts of local government, they introduce both new opportunities and new areas of risk, uncertainty, and fragility that could redefine the future role of LAs ... The increasing digitisation of care services in broad terms is likely to exacerbate an already significant digital divide, jeopardising equality of access.[127]

Pascoe also highlights concerns in relation to the use of digital technology in social work practice raised during a study of 14 frontline social workers in Northern Ireland during the pandemic.[128] These social workers were concerned that where such practices were exclusively used, it could inhibit the building of relationships and obstruct the ability to provide some 'small acts of kindness', such as making cups of tea; it also made it difficult to utilize silence during contact.[129] Pascoe's respondents also raised concerns regarding the digital divide and suggested that the use of new technology was 'leaving the service user behind'. There were also concerns about reduced collaboration:

> Reflecting on processes of remote assessments, social workers feared decisions were being made without the active involvement of service users, increasing the risk of inappropriate interventions or service users being misunderstood, unheard and undervalued.[130]

---

[127] J. Wright (2021) 'The Alexafication of adult social care: virtual assistants and the changing role of local government in England', *International Journal of Environmental Research and Public Health*, 18(2): 812, at p 9.

[128] K.M. Pascoe (2022) 'Remote service delivery during the COVID-19 pandemic: questioning the impact of technology on relationship-based social work practice', *British Journal of Social Work*, 52(6): 3268–87.

[129] Pascoe (2022), pp 3275–8.

[130] Pascoe (2022), p 3278.

Digital exclusion was also an issue for some older people during the pandemic,[131] though many in this age group were anyway defying stereotypes with their technical abilities or learnt new skills during the lockdowns in response to limits on face-to-face contact. Researchers from the Centre for Ageing Better found that 'the pandemic has further exposed and deepened the divide between the digital haves and have nots'.[132]

They comment that the lack or limited availability of online alternatives put those without online access at an even further disadvantage. This finding was echoed by Seifert, who noted that:

> A focus only on digital events as a means of social participation during the COVID-19 pandemic has the potential to perpetuate ageism – that is, older non-users of technology are viewed as outsiders, additional to the already prevailing view of older adults as rendered frail and physically isolated by the COVID-19 pandemic.[133]

This concern about digital exclusion was echoed by some of our interviewees, particularly where they perceived a lack of choice over digital engagement:

> If you had access to the internet, you could use it, and you were comfortable using it, you had a much easier passage through the whole pandemic than if you didn't. And it's highlighted the fact that actually there are a large number of people in our communities that do not have those digital advantages.
>
> Of course, everything suddenly then went even more digital. So progressively local authorities have had that move to digital provision over the last 10–15 years, but suddenly everything has gone, 'Right, we'll do this digitally. We'll do it solely digitally'. And even if you've got the connectivity, even if you're reasonably comfortable, most people have a level of which: 'I'm comfortable doing my shopping', or, 'I'm comfortable renewing my car tax online'. Suddenly as local authorities we were asking them to do much, much more. (Community resources manager in a West Midlands local authority that formally activated easements)

---

[131] A. Seifert (2020) 'Letter the Digital Exclusion of Older Adults during the COVID-19 Pandemic', *Journal of Gerontological Social Work*, 63(6–7): 674.
[132] Centre for Ageing Better (2020) 'How has COVID-19 changed the landscape of digital inclusion?', Briefing.
[133] Seifert (2020), p 675.

As we have seen, the digitization of service delivery was extensive across local authorities. Many local authority offices, including public-facing forums, were closed and the majority of local authority staff worked from home from early 2020, with hybrid working becoming the norm in many cases long after lockdowns had ended. Some face-to-face provision did continue, of course, particularly in relation to social work assessments and other crucial frontline support work with safeguarding considerations.

Certain aspects of using digital technology to deliver services have been viewed as advantageous. Meetings between professionals were often better attended when they could be dialled into from anywhere with Wi-Fi. Online video conferencing facilitated new and faster ways of information sharing, though many noted that something in the quality of team relationships was lost in this disembodied working environment. For example, one PSW who we interviewed commented that:

> Some of our multi-agency meetings have been a lot better attended, because you can be very efficient on that. And so, what we're probably going to do is try and have a hybrid model where we've got enough time in our office together, and particularly get together when we need to do something creative. We've tried to replace the ad-hoc informal conversations by having regular catch-ups, and things like that. It's not as good as making somebody a cup of tea in the office … it's a stressful phone call. (Principal Social Worker in a West Midlands local authority that formally activated easements)

At the same time there were concerns that digital delivery and home working could inhibit continuing professional development and training, with consequent impacts on service delivery. Another interviewee commented on how difficult it can be to support staff morale and mutual learning when people are not in a shared office:

> But we're talking at the minute about well-being, especially staff well-being, and the importance of student social workers and new workers, and you learn as social workers sometimes by osmosis. By being in the office, hearing conversations and listening to things and saying: 'Can I come with you on that visit so I can see what you do?' Or observing practice or observing phone calls. And what we were seeing is students that are coming through now who have done their final year during COVID and perhaps are a bit, not confident about going out there, because they haven't done it as much. So, it's thinking about the skills deficit that we might find, and the competence building that we need to do. Especially in social work, and as a Principal Social Worker.

(Principal Social Worker in a West Midlands local authority that did not formally activate easements)

Clearly, the future of online and hybrid delivery of social care provision needs to address broader issues of digital inequality. This was clearly highlighted by the House of Lords COVID-19 Committee report *Beyond Digital Planning for a Hybrid World*, which held that 'while those from marginalised and less advantaged groups are more likely to lack digital access, digital inequality also compounds marginalisation and disadvantage'.[134] This includes lack of home broadband 'for all' and the Committee was of the view that there should be a statutory right to internet access and digital infrastructure coupled with appropriate redress rights where needed.[135] While the report contains an interesting analysis in a specific chapter directed at health there is unfortunately no separate chapter addressing the challenges of digital access in the social care context.

The shift to more digital and hybrid social work practices received mixed reviews from social workers during the pandemic. Many expressed concerns about the risk of missing non-verbal cues and contextual or environmental information that would inform an assessment outcome or raise a safeguarding concern, while others highlighted that any form of remote communication could be problematic for those with severe mental health problems, learning difficulties or disabilities, or other communication issues.[136] Further issues that have been raised in relation to the use of digital platforms are the potential impacts on privacy and confidentiality. So, for example, someone with intellectual disabilities may require carer support to understand the risks of a platform or the nature of a discussion.[137] As with the rapid development and roll-out of new technologies or IT systems, there is also ample scope for bugs, and for problems relating to system glitches or systemic issues relating to data processing.[138]

---

[134] House of Lords COVID-19 Committee (2021) *Beyond Digital: Planning for a Hybrid World*, First Session of 2019–21, para 26.
[135] House of Lords (2021) COVID-19 Committee, para 39.
[136] See S.T. Tong et al (2021) *Social Work during COVID-19: Learning for the Future. Challenges, Best Practice and Professional Transformation*, BASW Research Report.
[137] See, for example, G.H. Rawlings, C. Gaskell, K. Rolling and N. Beail (2021) 'Exploring how to deliver videoconference-mediated psychological therapy to adults with an intellectual disability during the coronavirus pandemic', *Intellectual Disabilities Research*, 15(1): 1–10; and see also P.M. Keenan and O. Doody (2023) 'An update of the reported effects of the COVID-19 pandemic on persons with intellectual disability and their carers: a scoping review', *Annals of Medicine*, 55(1).
[138] See, for example, the events regarding the COVID-19 app, T. Polzer and G. Goncharenko (2022) 'The UK COVID-19 app: the failed co-production of a digital public service', *Financial Accountability & Management*, 38(2): 281–97.

Certainly local authorities faced with financial constraints may find that reducing the amount of office space and increasing hybrid working may be an appropriate response. The ADASS argues that the pandemic has already 'radically reshaped the role of technology in adults social care', and that digital transformation is the most effective way to improve integrated practice; the changes made during COVID 'are here to stay'.[139] The DHSC is promoting the uptake of digital practices and digitisation schemes across local authorities, with an 'aspirational framework' for good practice in adult social care.[140] How this will play out in terms of service delivery and the experiences of service users remains to be seen.[141]

(b) Changes to day centre provision

Due to public health measures to slow the spread of COVID-19, day centres across the country closed at the start of the pandemic. These closures had a considerable impact on service users and carers. The development and use of day centres to support older people and those with disabilities goes back many years and was facilitated by the National Assistance Act 1948 (Amendment) Act 1962.[142] Further, as Thane comments:

> A succession of measures in the 1970s were designed to assist older and disabled people to remain in the community, partly impelled by activism by disabled people. The Chronically Sick and Disabled Act 1971 required all local authorities to register disabled people and publicize services. It encouraged, but did not require or adequately fund, expanded community based services such as home helps and day centres.[143]

This, as we saw in Chapter 1, was followed by increasing emphasis on community care and this provided the backdrop for the Care Act 2014. Day centres providing care, company, community, activities, and sustenance

---

[139] ADASS (2022) *Digital Transformation in Social Care: How to Get It Right*, November.
[140] Department for Health and Social Care (2023) *Digital Working in Adult Social Care: What Good Looks Like*, 17 May.
[141] S. Pink, H. Ferguson and L. Kelly (2022) 'Digital social work: conceptualising a hybrid anticipatory practice', *Qualitative Social Work*, 21(2): 413; see also S.-T. Kong, C. Noone, and J. Shears (2022) 'Social workers' sensual bodies during COVID-19: the suspended, displaced and reconstituted body in social work practice', *British Journal of Social Work*, 52(5): 2834 for a more ambivalent appraisal of digital practices.
[142] P. Thane (2009) 'Memorandum submitted to the House of Commons' Health Committee Inquiry: Social Care', October.
[143] P. Thane (2009).

became a key part of local authorities' offering to their citizens. However, their purpose and use, and the running of other 'buildings-based services', have been under challenge for well over two decades.[144] It was suggested that day centres – for people with learning disabilities, or older people, for example – could be seen as providing spaces for them separated and set apart from the rest of the community. As cuts to public funding took hold, more centres came under private or third-sector ownership, so people could either access them directly or be provided with a local authority-funded placement by their social work team. As Orellana et al commented: 'The policy of personalisation, marketisation of social care, a shift to competitive tendering and budget cuts are impacting on day centres for older people. Tensions arise when implementing policy in a context of cuts with differing interpretations of a key driver, and when assumptions predominate over evidence.'[145]

There are differing views of the value of day centres and other non-residential care and support settings. Some regard them as outdated and part of the architecture of 'institutionalisation'.[146] Needham argues that the widespread closure of day centres was fed by various narratives that are used to underpin the personalization (and marketization) of the social care agenda. These narratives, she claims, were used to delegitimize the status and use of day centres: 'Existing day centres are part of the "one size fits all" provision of the pre-personalization era (delegitimizing place).'[147]

The second narrative is: 'People who seek to protect day centre resources are special interests or illegitimate voices (delegitimizing people).'[148] The third narrative she terms 'delegitimizing financing', which argues that types of 'hidden cross-subsidy that were apparent in earlier forms of social care funding, and particularly in building-based services, were unfair or inefficient'.[149] The final narrative is that: 'The closure of day centres is not an individualisation of care, but the unlocking of capacity so that people

---

[144] See, for example, P. Seed (1988) *Day Care at the Crossroads*, Costello: Tunbridge Wells; C. Clark (ed) (2001) *Adult Day Services and Social Inclusion. Better Days. Research Highlights in Social Work*, London & NY: Jessica Kingsley, p 39; Department of Health (2001) *Valuing People: A New Strategy for Learning Disability for the 21st Century*, CM 5086, paras 4.7 and 7.21.

[145] K. Orellana, J. Manthorpe and A. Tinker (2020) 'Day centres for older people: a systematically conducted scoping review of literature about their benefits, purposes and how they are perceived', *Ageing and Society*, 40(1): 73.

[146] For further discussion in relation to the historical backdrop concerning disability use of day centres by young people, see C.G. Barnes (1990) *Cabbage Syndrome: The Social Construction of Dependence*, London: Taylor & Francis.

[147] C. Needham (2013) 'Personalization: from day centres to community hubs?', *Critical Social Policy*, 90: 94; see also C. Needham (2011) *Personalising Public Services: Understanding the Personalisation Narrative*, Bristol: Policy Press.

[148] C. Needham (2013), p 95.

[149] C. Needham (2013), p 96.

can develop alternative ways of getting together.'¹⁵⁰ Needham finds that these 'intersecting story-lines delegitimize the day centre model' yet failed to bolster the development and embedding of alternative community spaces or 'hubs'.¹⁵¹

Many people who draw on social care services, especially those facing social isolation, continue to see them as a valuable asset, though there is little clear evidence to measure exactly how many remain in operation as there is no requirement for day centres to be centrally registered.¹⁵² In their review of the literature, Orellana et al identified four main categories of day centre activity: (1) provision of day centres as 'social and preventive alternatives;' (2) provision of support for individuals continued independence; (3) the support of 'health and daily living needs' of centre attendees; and (4) enabling 'family carers to have a break and/or continue with employment.'¹⁵³ Although the offering will vary from place to place, most centres provide company, social or creative activities, food and/or refreshments, and in some cases access to health and care resources. They also provide crucial respite to carers. Overall the research indicated that these centres were an invaluable source of community and well-being for the people who use them.¹⁵⁴

Orellana et al found that the profile of most people who were attending the day centres fell within the National Institute for Health and Care Excellence category of 'vulnerable older people' who are 'most at risk of a decline in their independence and mental wellbeing'.¹⁵⁵ They found that: 'Attendance enhanced quality of life, sometimes significantly, and made a unique contribution to their "vulnerable" attenders' lives ... thus demonstrating their policy-relevance.'¹⁵⁶ Further:

> People growing up after World War II are said to recognise welfare as a reassuring 'safety-net' ... Day centres were identified as providing attenders with two such 'safety-net' outcomes: monitoring attenders'

---

[150] C. Needham (2013), p 97.

[151] C. Needham (2013), p 90.

[152] Orellana et al (2020), p 76; see also K. Orellana, J. Manthorpe and A. Tinker (2020b) 'Day centres for older people: attender characteristics, access routes and outcomes of regular attendance: findings of exploratory mixed methods case study research', *BMC Geriatrics*, 20(1): 158.

[153] Orellana et al (2020), p 85.

[154] See, for example, C. Bilotta et al (2020) 'Day care centre attendance and quality of life in depressed older adults living in the community', *European Journal of Ageing*, 7: 29; see also K. Orellana, J. Manthorpe and A. Tinker (2021) 'Making my day. Volunteering or working at a day centre for older people: findings of exploratory research in English day centres', *Journal of Long Term Care*, 177.

[155] Orellana et al (2020) Day Centres for Older People attendee characteristics, p 14.

[156] Orellana et al (2020) Day Centres for Older People attendee characteristics, p 14.

health and wellbeing, and providing practical support, information and facilitating access to other services. Thus, centres offered added value beyond the purposes for which they were commissioned or funded, beyond what may be assumed to be covered by a service aim of improving quality of life or supporting people to remain at home, and beyond what attenders may have wanted or expected, given their reasons for attending.[157]

Thus the mass closure of day centres during the pandemic had a significant impact on this cohort of service users. Price et al, in their study of the impact of Care Act easements on carers of people with dementia living at home, found that:

Carers' experience of diminished day centre services was almost universally negative and the lack of respite that the day centres had previously provided was and remained a very serious problem ... support groups for both carers and their partners, including dementia cafes, memory groups, singing groups, carers groups, and lunch clubs, were reported to have closed at the start of the pandemic for varying time periods, with many having not reopened or been re-established at the time of the interviews, some of which took place two years after the start of the pandemic.[158]

Our own research interviews confirmed this stark view, with advocates concerned about the very serious long-term impacts on people in need of respite services:

There have been several families where they ... have survived but they are absolutely at breaking point. We had one call, a couple of weeks ago, which was around a family which had no respite service throughout the whole of the pandemic. It was supposed to open and then the last lockdown happened, and so from their perspective, yes, you know, they're all alive and they're still standing but ... it's not, it's not coping at all. So yes, you know, I guess if you're talking about coping from the perspective of, we haven't yet heard about any major safeguarding issues or God forbid, someone dying who didn't get the support. But I mean, I think that's the bar that we're working towards,

---

[157] Orellana et al (2020) 'Day centres for older people, attendee characteristics', p 14.
[158] D. Price et al (2022) *The Impact of Care Act Easements under the Coronavirus Act 2020 on Older Carers Supporting Family Members Living with Dementia at Home*, NIHR Older People and Frailty Policy Research Unit, Final Report, November, p 16.

in terms of coping. I don't think it's any more than ... we don't know of a serious incident, and I'm not convinced there hasn't necessarily been one. (Advisor at a legal advocacy organization)

Impacts were also raised by another stakeholder we interviewed:

[We saw ...] changes to day services and the increased pressure on individuals that care for people in our own home. So, family carers – there was a delay locally to get some form of offer of support to individuals who have suddenly gone to 24/7 care and responsibility. It did get better, but actually we heard from a number of individuals at breaking point more or less – because they were left to their own devices to care for their relative or child, when usually they relied on respite from day services. (Healthwatch Lead in a West Midlands local authority that formally activated easements)

This was also reflected by one of our national-level respondents:

A huge, significant impact – closure of day centres, lack of access to respite, shortage of time being available to spend in homes or inconsistency and people just reporting that they're falling away and falling out of the system. (Director of Services of a major national charity)

The repercussions were also felt by those third-sector organizations which attempted to 'fill the gap':

The process that happened was the usual statutory services, in terms of social care and those services, were very quickly and immediately withdrawn. And thankfully the voluntary sector across [the city], did step up and identify quickly where the gaps were, where need was, and like other areas in the country, the kind of social response and mutual aid response that the city was amazing. They just stepped up and filled the gap. And I think it was that voluntary sector action that suddenly made the local authority go: 'We need to get this feeding in from it.' At that time, there didn't seem to be any consideration of whether their decisions to withdraw services would then have a knock-on effect to other partners within the system, who would then have to pick it all up because the need still remained for individuals. (Healthwatch Lead in a local authority that formally activated easements)

Another research project – 'Rights in Peril: Exploring the Impact of Care Act Easements under the Coronavirus Act 2020 on Access to Adult Social Care' – was undertaken by the Central England Law Centre in

2020–22[159] to examine the impact of Care Act easements on service users in the area of Birmingham, Coventry, Solihull, and Warwickshire. They conducted surveys in conjunction with the University of Warwick (Law in the Community) in relation to domiciliary care, day centres, residential respite, and direct payment brokers, and found that the Care Act easements 'significantly diluted legal rights'.[160] Their findings reported a reduction in day centre services and inconsistency in provision of alternative services, contrary to section 5 of the Care Act 2014. They also reported that once a number of day centres eventually reopened, their clients had not been able to return at previous service levels due to continuing public health restrictions or other ongoing reductions in capacity:

> some social care services, such as day centres and residential respite services, closed permanently during the pandemic. This left adults with care and support needs with no service to return to once the COVID-19 restrictions were lifted. For some, this meant needs remained unmet for long periods and in other cases alternative support was offered that may not have been sufficient to meet needs or may not have been appropriate as it was not safe due to the specific nature of needs.[161]

A growing body of research on the health and psychosocial impacts of loneliness, particularly among marginalized people and those 'who may have lost physical and cognitive function during lockdowns' and throughout the pandemic, show that day care centres and the kinds of communal and interactive activities and services they provide, remain more important than ever.[162]

IV. Conclusions

While the emergency provisions of the Coronavirus Act 2020 were expired by July 2021, and the fleeting formal use of Care Act easements ended long before that in July 2020, the Pandemic and may of its mitigations revealed the fault lines in adult social care structures and the vulnerabilities of those

---

[159] Full details of this Baring Foundation-funded project are available at www.centralenglandlc.org.uk/rights-in-peril-project, accessed 10 July 2023. The CELC was an original project partner to the authors' ESRC-funded COVID-19 rapid response project.

[160] CELC (2022).

[161] CELC (2022).

[162] C. Lunt, C. Shiels, C. Dowrick and M. Lloyd-Williams (2021) 'Outcomes for older people with long-term conditions attending day care services delivered by paid staff or volunteers: a comparative study', *Palliative Care and Social Practice*, 15.

accessing care and support. In this chapter, we reflected on the operation of easements at national level and saw how studies have highlighted how similar issues arose and approaches were taken across local authorities across the country as a whole, as reflected, in our West Midlands case study discussed in Chapter 5. In relation to the organisational aspects of easements, as we saw in Chapter 4, while these had been long in the planning with local authorities, the manner of their implementation left questions as to how effective this planning had been. Moreover it appeared that the relationship between central and local government in relation to the easement process was by no means optimal.

While from 'Freedom Day' onwards the easements themselves were not available, adult social care provision remained under notable pressures and this was repeatedly highlighted by ADASS at national level. There were further tensions between the language of business as usual in an era where Coronavirus Act provisions were not applicable and the realities of service delivery from the perception of local authority representatives and their concerns as to the position of those using services. During this period local authorities were again reminded of the 'flexibilities' which can be used under the Care Act 2014. This again demonstrates one of the challenging aspects of the Care Act, as we discussed in Chapter 3 – levels of interpretation and discretion with regards to addressing the well-being principle.

As the Local Government Association has pointed out, the pandemic revealed a 'perfect storm' of socio-economic factors underpinning overall health inequalities, the same social determinants that resulted in such starkly disproportionate COVID outcomes experienced across society.[163] As the literature discussed in this chapter illustrates, there were notable additional pressures facing those needing care and support during that period. Here again the nested realities and complexities of the relationships of care were evident through the pressures felt by those needing care and by carers themselves – both family and professionals. Questions of equality and fundamental rights and concerns regarding delivery of services were raised at national level. However, although with the exception of the early stage in the pandemic, as we saw in Chapter 4, there was no attempt to challenge actions through litigation.

The chapter also illustrated some of the concerns regarding the consequences of changes to service delivery in the pandemic period, such as those raised by the Local Government Ombudsman. We saw this also with reference to the impact of digital delivery of services in the broadest sense and in relation to the availability of day centres and opportunities. In

---

[163] Local Government Association (2021) *A Perfect Storm: Health Inequalities and the Impact of COVID-19*, April.

both instances aspects of these changes were had been initiated prior to the pandemic but the pandemic accelerated developments. The digital delivery of services, while having perceptible advantages in terms of cost and also flexibility of delivery, leaves concerns regarding digital exclusion and the effectiveness of this as a mode of operation. Whether day centres are in fact appropriate for 21st century care remains a matter of debate by policy makers. What is evident, though, from our work and other studies, is that their closure both as an immediate response to the pandemic and often in the longer-term, has in many cases curtailed vital respite support.

In general, our interviews and the review of literature demonstrated growing concern about the pandemic's impact in the context of adult social car reads "legacy of the pandemic", both in terms of the measurable impacts on people's lives and well-being and whether there may have been a wider 'cultural shift' wherein people have become accustomed to less, and lack of support and provision.

What then are the broader lessons that can be learned from the COVID years to help inform future pandemic planning and adult social care law and policy? We explore some of the lessons and possibilities in the next chapter.

7

Adult Social Care Law and Policy: Learning Lessons from the Pandemic

I. Introduction

The COVID-19 pandemic still casts a long shadow of trauma and loss, of chronic illness, and of physical, mental, and emotional exhaustion. The lingering impacts of post-COVID syndrome alone are likely to compromise adult social care, for both those seeking support and for those providing it, in the years ahead.[1] People working in the sector were on the 'frontline', part of the largest grouping of essential 'key workers'[2] alongside those employed in the NHS. The adult social care funding shortfall remains entrenched in the aftermath of short-term COVID-19 emergency boosts, and local government finance remains gravely weakened. As we have seen in the preceding chapters, the condition of the social care workforce needs to be viewed in the context of deep-set systemic problems which pre-dated COVID-19, but which were dramatically exacerbated by the pandemic experience.

To some extent, the years 2020–2022 shone a light on the importance of the role played by both formal and informal carers. Nonetheless, as we saw in earlier chapters, caring during the pandemic took its toll. For informal or family carers the day-to-day challenges of providing care and support were accentuated by the strains of the pandemic lockdowns.[3] Reduction

---

[1] See Industrial Injuries Advisory Council (2022) *COVID-19 and Occupational Impacts*, Independent Report, 16 November, paras 194–209. See also M. McKee (ed) (2021) *Drawing Light from the Pandemic: A New Strategy for Health and Sustainable Development. A Review of the Evidence or the Pan-European Commission on Health and Sustainable Development*, WHO Europe Publications, European Observatory on Health Systems and Policies.
[2] Office of National Statistics Census (2020) *Coronavirus and Key Workers in the UK*, 15 May.
[3] Carers UK (2020) *Caring Behind Closed Doors*, April 2020; and Carers UK (2020) *Caring Behind Closed Doors; Six Months On*, October 2020.

of respite care impacted on well-being as did the inability of carers to visit loved ones if they were admitted to hospital or residential care.[4] Concerns have also been highlighted regarding the pressure on professional carers in this period, for example Humphries comments that

> it has brought out the best in our care services, the way staff went beyond the call of duty in, for example, covering the work of colleagues who were sick or self-isolating, prioritising the protection of people they were caring from over their own needs and those of their own families.[5]

This level of compassion and the commitment to keep going under terrible pressure is admirable, but functioning in this way is not sustainable.[6] Humphries also identified the pressure on terms and conditions and reliance on agency staff and similarly the Health Foundation described the situation as 'dire' and noted that some but definitely not all of the entrenched problems around recruitment and retention could be attributed to the 'long tail of the pandemic'.[7] As we saw through the discussion of Needham and Hall's typology of the 'care crisis' in Chapter 1, the pandemic pushed this complex, interconnected sector from a state of 'slow decay into a rapid and deadly crisis'.[8]

As we suggested in Chapter 2, in order to understand the nature of adult social care law and policy in England today it is necessary to interrogate the theoretical paradigms which underpinned its development over time. Drawing on Nedelsky's model of 'nested relationality' as developed by Harding, we posited that 'care' is a complex, nuanced, multi-dimensional, and inherently relational concept, rather than simply a category of activity, work, or emotional connection.[9] The primacy of fundamental rights, and the need to understand, recognize, and respect these, is also crucial to the development and upholding of adult social care law and policy. We suggested that Nussbaum's capabilities approach provides a flexible framework in which to understand the potential for

---

[4] J. Onwumere et al (2021) 'COVID-19 and UK family carers: policy implications', *The Lancet Psychiatry*, 8: 329.

[5] R. Humphries (2022) *Ending the Social Care Crisis: A New Road to Reform*, Bristol: Policy Press, p 158.

[6] M. Brown (2020) 'The social care workforce: Overworked, undervalued and poorly paid', *Integrated Care Journal*, News, 26 May.

[7] L. Allen and N. Shembavnekar (2023) 'Social care workforce crisis: How did we get here and where do we go next?', *The Health Foundation Blog*, 13 October.

[8] C. Needham and P. Hall (2023) *Social Care in the UK's Four Nations: Between the Two Paradigms*, Bristol: Policy Press, p 1.

[9] J. Nedelsky (2011) *Law's Relations: A Relational Theory of Self, Autonomy and Law*, Oxford: Oxford University Press; and R. Harding (2017) *Duties to Care: Dementia, Relationality and the Law*, Cambridge: Cambridge University Press; and see further discussion in Chapter 2.

achieving individual human well-being and the utilization of such fundamental rights. We saw how the Care Act's well-being principle can be viewed through the prism of a capabilities approach, although its application in practice, as we saw in subsequent chapters, may not be straightforward.

Adult social care law, policy and practice is also underpinned by recognition of individual vulnerabilities, as evident for example in relation to safeguarding. Examining theories of vulnerability – both universal and individual – demonstrated the importance of the concept when devising and implementing law and policy in this area, despite the complexity of integrating appropriate and flexible options to respond to the specifics of a person's situation, desires and needs.[10] At the same time, as the discussion demonstrated, the use of 'vulnerability' as a term has been popularized in the public consciousness in recent years, and especially when attributed from a position of power to other people or groups, remains contentious in policy terms. Given these tensions there remain notable challenges in translating our theoretical understandings of the importance of the universality of vulnerability to day-to-day law and policy solutions.

Chapter 3 demonstrated both how the Care Act 2014 and related legislation function as a means of providing people (including carers) with services that support their individual (and relational) well-being. The legislation is framed in the language of 'care' as opposed to the terminology of 'assistance' as in the National Assistance Act 1948, or illness and disability as in the case of the Chronically Sick and Disabled Persons Act 1970. Yet as we saw the legislative scope of 'care' has its limits. To fall within the remit of the legislation, an individual will first need to demonstrate eligibility in terms of needs, and this in turn will include a consequent assessment of financial means. While the core principle of promoting 'well-being' can be viewed in terms of supporting individual rights, in reality its interpretation is loose and somewhat fluid. The Care Act also provides for notable degrees of discretion in relation to decisions concerning the provision of certain services. While there is scrutiny of local authority actions in relation to providing care and support through fundamental rights principles, as we saw in the chapter application of such rights in the context of resource allocation decisions is inevitably subject to the discretionary nature of the statutory provisions concerning delivery of adult social care and is subject to the margin of appreciation which is afforded to member states.[11] Local authority powers and duties also need to be viewed alongside certain provisions which are not subject to charge because they fall under the auspices of NHS continuing healthcare (CHC) or specific aftercare under section 117 of the Mental Health Act 1983.

---

[10] See, for example, Office for Health Improvement and Disparities (2022) *Vulnerabilities: Applying All Our Health,* Guidance, (formerly Public Health England), 29 March.

[11] See further Chapter 3.

This analysis of the theoretical paradigms and legislative framework underpinning of adult social care services provided a basis for us to then critically examine the impacts of the COVID-19 pandemic on delivery. We began this examination in Chapter 4 by evaluating how policy and legislative responses to address pandemic challenges in general and with specific reference to adult social care had been developed in England. The nature and focus of pandemic preparedness planning work under successive national governments in the two decades before COVID-19 was interrogated. We saw that a significant impact on the social care sector in the event of a pandemic had indeed been envisaged and that proposals and blueprints had been developed at national level to try to maintain continuity and protect health services. Moreover, as we showed in Chapter 5 in relation to our West Midlands case study, pandemic planning exercises had also been undertaken at regional and local level, including in the early months of 2020. In Chapter 4, we also explored the evolution of the Coronavirus Act 2020 and how section 15 and Schedule 12 of that Act enabled local authorities to depart from certain provisions of the Care Act 2014 in certain circumstances. The implementation of care Act easements and the resultant controversy highlighted the challenges with this approach. Why was it that such a response planned over such a long period of time was met with so many problems at the outset? It raises broader issues of the need for greater transparency in pandemic planning as it was only through campaigning, Freedom of Information requests, and the publication of documentation by the COVID-19 Inquiry itself that various aspects of the recommendations and proposals for draft legislation emerged into the public domain. One of the lessons of this period is that surely greater transparency is needed for effective public health policy evolution and policy development regarding emergency planning. We also analysed the related Guidance documents and the updated Ethical Framework for adult social care, before exploring in Chapter 5 how these were interpreted at pace and under pressure by local authority employees from March 2020 onwards.

Chapter 5 presented a West Midlands regional case study of local authority responses to COVID-19 and to the variable operation of 'Care Act easements' and other changes in working practices and service delivery. This region contained a notable 'cluster' of local authorities that formally activated these provisions, alongside several others that did not. Using documentation in the public domain, such as local reports and minutes from local authority meetings, we analysed the responses taken by those local authorities which formally notified the Department of Health and Social Care (DHSC) that they had activated Care Act easements, as well as those authorities that did not. We explored the declared rationales for notification (or not) in the formal documentation, the recorded contemporaneous impacts and discussions at local level, and the decisions to withdraw from notified statutory easements. We sought to compare and contrast these approaches. A more complex picture emerged, one that highlighted the similarity of approach between those authorities which formally activated easements and those which stated that they had not. The documentation was also striking for the diverse utilization of 'easements' terminology by those local authorities which did not formally activate the provisions, as well as a generalized sense of unease around both the introduction of this legislative device and the points of comparison with other authorities. The final section of this chapter drew upon our semi-structured interviews with stakeholders in the West Midlands. We shared the voices of some of the people involved in making these local-level decisions at the start of the pandemic, alongside others who found themselves navigating some of the consequences of such decisions in relation to service provision for communities and individuals. All were tasked with maintaining care and support services in their respective communities. Inside local authorities, employees reflected on their engagement and communications with national-level actors during this period, within professional networks, and with the wider public. Some who had formally activated easements also commented on the pushback and criticism they received from campaign organizations and the media.

One of the recurrent questions raised with regard to the Care Act easements period was what legacy might remain after their formal withdrawal. There were concerns that changes made during the emergency period might simply remain in situ, marking a silent shift in both provision and expectation. We explored some of these legacy questions in Chapter 6. We reflected on the reported experiences of implementation and its impacts on service provision contained in a series of national-level stakeholder reports and related academic research findings; we found that that these findings aligned overall with those in our own case study. One issue that inevitably arose was the question of whether the Care Act easements and the related statutory provisions (or something equivalent) should have remained in place to confer legitimacy upon subsequent adult social care decision-making. We looked, for example, at the acceleration of the digitization agenda and changes to day centre services, both of which serve as examples of service delivery for which the pandemic and its mitigations were a catalyst for temporary or permanent change. Acute challenges remained for the safe and appropriate delivery of care across the sector, and there were concerns about how to maintain full Care Act compliance in such depleted circumstances.[12]

Now, as most people accept the day-to-day reality of 'living with COVID' and as memories of those challenging months of 2020–2021 start to fade, what useful lessons can we learn from the pandemic experience for the future

---

[12] See, for example, Association of Directors of Adult Social Services (2023) *Spring Survey 2023*.

of adult social care law and policy? We suggest that there are two major areas for which learning can be drawn: first, to inform future pandemic preparedness planning; and second, to identify some more general lessons for adult social care law and policy. We explore each of these respectively in sections II and III of this concluding chapter.

II. What are the lessons for future pandemic preparedness planning in relation to adult social care?

In Chapter 4, we saw that pandemic planning had been underway in England (and involving all four nations) over a period of two decades. However, a considerable amount of this planning was focused on the specific modelling for pandemic influenza, and blueprints for mitigating the potential impacts of such a pandemic for adult social care only emerged in the later planning exercises. Eventually, and critically, such blueprints did emerge. There was a realization that measures needed to be taken to address the challenges which would face the sector at the time of a pandemic. This planning was the subject of consultation with organizations such as the Association of Directors of Adult Social Services (ADASS), Think Local Act Personal (TLAP), and a range of third sector organizations. As we saw in the discussion in Chapter 4, considerable amounts of that resultant planning were repurposed during the consideration of what may have been required for social care in the event of a 'no deal' Brexit.[13]

As noted previously, emergency legislation was enacted in the form of the Coronavirus Act 2020, and a series of sector-specific Guidance documents, along with an Ethical Framework, was produced for adult social care. As we saw in Chapter 4, further guidance was also made available in the form of Government webinars, including one led by Rhia Roy from the DHSC and James Bullion, then Chair of the ADASS. Local authorities also had the benefit of access to legal advice and support from their in-house legal teams.[14] In addition, as we saw in Chapter 5, the West Midlands has strong local and regional professional networks of principal social workers and directors of adult social services respectively, which liaised regularly during 2020–21. Despite all this background information, our West Midlands case study literature review and the data drawn from the interviews both suggest that there was considerable uncertainty and some confusion as to the purpose and operational thresholds of the Care Act easements, and as to precisely what fell within the bounds of the emergency legislation and the statutory guidance. This finding is echoed in the findings of the other

---

[13] See further discussion in Chapter 4.
[14] See discussion in Chapter 4.

research projects we have cited in previous chapters. Thus, although the DHSC had worked together with professional bodies from social care, social work, care provision, and the third sector to devise the form of the Care Act easements in contingency planning exercises, it appeared that relatively little was known about them among adult social care practitioners or even senior management teams in some local authorities. As some of our interviewees from West Midlands local authorities suggested, the introduction of the easements option almost blindsided them.[15]

We suggest that there are both lessons to be learnt and issues to be explored further at central government level which relate to the form and nature of the emergency legislation and some of the terms given to statutory measures in the legislation and Guidance. We need to learn to utilize and adapt existing facilities that harness the collective knowledge and capacity of professional and government bodies.

Some of these lessons have been highlighted in the UK COVID-19 Inquiry Module 1 Report published in July 2024 while this book was in production and we reflect on those here.[16] Other lessons go beyond the scope of that Report and are drawn from our own findings in our own project. We begin by reflecting upon the recommendations of the UK COVID-19 Inquiry Module 1 Report. The Inquiry Report concluded that while there had been the belief that the UK was well-prepared to address a major pandemic, in fact this was not the case. It found that the UK lacked sufficient resilience. Moreover, it cast this in terms of the need for effective resources to be spent on pandemic preparedness. While it recognized that politicians have to make resource allocation decisions, the Report went on to state as follows:

> Proper preparation for a pandemic costs money. It involves preparing for an event which may never happen. However, the massive financial, economic and human cost of the COVID-19 Pandemic is proof that, in the area of preparedness and resilience, money spent on systems for our protection is vital and will be vastly outweighed by the cost of not doing so.[17]

The Inquiry Report found that pandemic preparedness planning in the UK had been in relation to what was ultimately the 'wrong pandemic' – that of influenza – and was 'outdated and lacked adaptability, strategy had

---

[15] See further discussion in Chapter 5.
[16] UK COVID-19 Inquiry (2024) *Module 1: The resilience and preparedness of the United Kingdom: A Report by the Rt Hon Baroness Hallett, DBE Chair of the UK Covid-19 Inquiry*, 18 July 2024, HC 18.
[17] UK COVID-19 Inquiry (2024), p 2.

not learnt from the various planning exercises and disease outbreaks'.[18] The Report highlighted the failure to address proportionality. The various emergency planning structures which were discussed earlier in Chapter 4 of this book were seen by the Inquiry Report as being 'labyrinthine in their complexity'.[19] The assessment of risks was seen as subject to 'fatal strategic flaws'. Expert advice given could be improved – concerns around 'group think' were identified. Critically, the Inquiry found that pandemic planning processes failed the UK public.[20]

The fragmentation of decision-making between departments is highlighted by UK COVID-19 Inquiry Module 1 Report. The intention is to provide greater oversight and ensure that lessons from, for example, pandemic planning exercises are learnt. It recommends the establishment at national level of a new statutory body 'with expertise in whole-system civil emergencies'.[21]

The Report states that

> The new body should be given responsibility for:
>
> - providing independent, strategic advice to the UK government and devolved administrations on their planning for, preparedness for and building resilience to whole-system civil emergencies;
> - consulting with the voluntary, community and social enterprise sector at a national and local level and directors of public health on the protection of vulnerable people in whole-system civil emergencies;
> - assessing the state of planning for, preparedness for and resilience to whole system civil emergencies across the UK; and
> - making recommendations on the capacity and capabilities that will be required to prepare for and build resilience to whole-system civil emergencies.[22]

The Report also makes recommendations for oversight at governmental level. It is recommended that there should be a committee responsible for 'whole system civil emergency preparedness and resilience'.[23] This should operate at 'Cabinet level or equivalent ministerial committee'.[24] The Report also

---

[18] UK COVID-19 Inquiry (2024), p 2.
[19] UK COVID-19 Inquiry (2024), p 2.
[20] UK COVID-19 Inquiry (2024), p 3.
[21] UK COVID-19 Inquiry (2024), para 6.93.
[22] UK COVID-19 Inquiry (2024), p 161.
[23] UK COVID-19 Inquiry (2024), p 4.
[24] UK COVID-19 Inquiry (2024), p 4.

suggests that risk assessment should be 'collaborative', 'applying to central government but also at the devolved, regional and local levels'.[25]

One of the issues found by the Inquiry was the failure to learn effectively from the various exercises and that action plans and follow-up reports needed to be published by the government in response to the various exercises. Such transparency in the future is to be welcomed – it is vitally important to enable effective learning and policy development. It remains a matter of concern that, for example, public access to Exercise Cygnus was only eventually the result of freedom of information requests by campaigners and an application to the Information Commissioners Office.[26]

The Inquiry Report recommends that there should be a UK-wide pandemic preparedness exercise, as well as reports to national legislatures on pandemic planning, every three years.[27] Finally, to avoid 'group think', the Report proposes the establishment of what are known as 'Red Teams', which are defined as being 'groups of people external to the advisory and decision-making structures involved in developing policies, strategies and plans'.[28] This follows an approach previously utilized in military and defence activities.[29] The intention would be that such Teams would be more detached and thus better able to challenge received thinking.[30]

These are important recommendations. One notable aspect will be the relationship between statutory oversight and pandemic planning at legislative level along with related parliamentary scrutiny in the mechanisms which are proposed here. The Inquiry recommendations, if implemented, would result in new actors in the form of oversight through such a national statutory body along with a more centralized overview at executive level, rather than disparate policy development across government departments.

Nonetheless, in relation to adult social care law and policy in a future pandemic, challenges will remain in translating between national level planning and the operation of law and policy at local government level. As we saw in Chapter 4, some local authorities in the West Midlands had undertaken local-level contingency exercises in the lead up to and including early 2020. As the discussion in Chapters 4 and 5 illustrated, there was

---

[25] UK COVID-19 Inquiry (2024), para 3.6.3.
[26] Leigh Day (2024) 'Exercise Cygnus documents finally disclosed following ICO Complaint', at https://www.leighday.co.uk/news/news/2021-news/exercise-cygnus-documents-finally-disclosed-following-ico-complaint/#:~:text=The%20Information%20Commissioner%27s%20Office%20has,and%20Community%20Care%20briefing%20paper, accessed 25 July 2024.
[27] UK COVID-19 Inquiry (2024), para 5.93.
[28] UK COVID-19 Inquiry (2024), para 6.60.
[29] UK COVID-19 Inquiry (2024), para 6.64.
[30] UK COVID-19 Inquiry (2024), paras 6.61 and 6.62.

nonetheless some disconnect between the fact that some exercises had taken place and the variable levels of comprehension and readiness within local authorities as to how specific measures taken nationally in response to COVID-19 were to become operational locally.

This is a classic example again of the need for 'joined up' thinking, as highlighted in the UK COVID-19 Inquiry Module 1 Report, not only to avoid creating more work and duplication but also to avoid confusion. It is clearly important that Local Resilience Forums' work should continue and that there should be an interface with relevant professional organizations and central and local government departments. That planning in turn should be undertaken against a backdrop of the details of pandemic legislation 'in waiting' which would be utilized. For example, at the time pandemic-planning exercises were being utilized in the West Midlands, the Draft Pandemic Influenza Bill, which formed the basis of the Coronavirus Act, was not available in the public domain. The proposed new statutory oversight body may help to ensure that such draft measures should be transparent in order that they can be usefully factored into ongoing pandemic-planning exercises. We know now the importance of planning for different epidemiological situations, but this does not detract from the need for transparency and access to information and contingency frameworks. Moreover, going further than the initial Inquiry recommendations in Module 1, we suggest that there should be a full re-evaluation at national level as to the utility of current Civil Contingencies Act provisions, the work of Local Resilience Forums and their relationship with Public Health Act measures, and indeed the consequent need for any separate bespoke pandemic legislation in the future. The Red Teams concept proposed by the UK COVID-19 Inquiry is particularly interesting. One challenge in the future will be that of effective selection of team members to ensure that a diverse range of views are included and sufficient agency is given to challenge orthodoxy in practice – in particular if these concern areas, whether (for example) drawn from scientists or social scientists, where there may in fact be only a limited number of experts in existence in a particular field.

The UK COVID-19 Inquiry Module 1 Report provides a sobering series of findings and very important recommendations. While we see challenges with parts of these, we very much hope that they are subject to serious consideration by the new Labour Government. The Inquiry also recognizes that there is need for further reflection and development in this area and has highlighted the need for an 'ambitious, widespread and better-funded programme of hibernated research studies' linked to a new pandemic preparedness strategy.[31] The Report defines hibernated or 'sleeping' studies as being 'flexible draft protocols that are designed in advance, then maintained

---

[31] UK COVID-19 Inquiry (2024), para 4.85.

in a state of readiness so they can be initiated as soon as a new infectious disease outbreak strikes'.[32]

We are very conscious that the Inquiry's work concerning adult social care is still ongoing and that further issues regarding specific pandemic preparedness and social care may emerge in the subsequent Module 6 (hearings for this Module are not due to begin until later in 2025). Here we highlight some further lessons which we suggest should be considered in developing future law and policy concerning pandemic planning, with specific reference to adult social care in the future. First, language is important. We can learn from the choice of terms used to describe the statutory measures introduced to temporarily amend the Care Act 2014. The terminology of 'easements' remains baffling and is an anomaly of the pandemic planning work. As we noted in Chapter 4, the term 'easement' has a very specific legal meaning. A legal easement, in accepted usage, is a legal right which one piece of land has over another piece of land, such as a right of way.[33] In the vernacular, we can understand the verb 'to ease' can mean 'to loosen' or 'relax' and this might conceivably have been applied to a loosening or 'easing' of statutory obligations – but this seems unlikely in the context of legislative drafting. We have been unable to find a clear explanation of why a term which has a clear legal meaning in Land Law was utilized in this way to describe situations in which local authorities could depart from specific statutory provisions in the Care Act 2014.

It is likely that those drafting the legislation recognized this anomaly as, while it appears in the Coronavirus Act Guidance, it is notably absent from the legislation itself – unsurprisingly, given that it is a distinct legal interest wholly different from the issues under consideration. It may be that those drafting the Guidance wanted by utilizing such terminology to distinguish the process of 'easing' the Care Act 2014 from utilizing 'flexibilities' under the Act, which is standard practice in exercising statutory discretions, as shown in Stages 1 and 2 of the easements framework. We would argue, however, that this phrasing is inappropriate and, should similar provisions be included in future legislation, such unfamiliar and out-of-place terminology should be avoided.

Secondly, exceptional situations such as a global pandemic may of course require exceptional measures. One enduring question from the legacy of the Care Act easements is whether such legally sanctioned departures

---

[32] UK COVID-19 Inquiry (2024), para 4.84.
[33] *Re Ellenborough Park* [1955] EWCA Civ 4 and in relation to the fact that an easement is capable of existing as a legal interest, see Law of Property Act 1925, s 1(2)(a); see further M. George and A. Layard (2022) *Thompson's Modern Land Law* (8th edn), Oxford: Oxford University Press, ch 11 'Easements'.

from statutory obligations ought to have been viewed as something to be avoided – or whether they can be viewed as effective legal device to enable transparency and accountability in relation to very difficult policy and operational choices. Systems of delivery inevitably underwent changes at operational level, not least due to the contemporaneous Public Health regulations and guidance on social distancing. However, as we saw in Chapter 4, the concern about the potential impact of Care Act easements on those drawing on care and support services was notable. There was clear alarm about the potential risk they might pose to services and consequently to the people who relied on them, thus putting them in an increasingly perilous and vulnerable position during a time when they were already at extreme risk. This led to strong national-level campaigning to withdraw the Coronavirus Act and specifically the easements provisions in the associated Guidance. However, this national-level attention, as we saw in Chapter 4, was focused on the specific legislative provisions and their withdrawal rather than on what would be happening at ground level after formal easements were withdrawn. Moreover, while in those early months very similar steps were in practice taken by both easement and non-easement local authorities in our West Midlands case study discussed in Chapter 5, and more generally at national level as we saw in Chapter 6, it was only those local authorities which activated Care Act easements which were subject to a higher level of public scrutiny and accountability.

The paradox of the campaigning was that while the focus was on dissuading local authorities from using the easements, and persuading the Government to reduce or remove the powers – neither eventuality protected all services or modes of delivery from undergoing changes. In addition, as we saw in the discussion of local authority decision-making in Chapter 5, there was some suggestion that one of the motivations for not revisiting the option of easements was to avoid the consequences of the probable backlash.[34]

The further issue with the application of the Care Act easements goes to the heart of the Care Act 2014 itself. The Act, as we saw in Chapter 3, provides considerable flexibility for interpretation in relation to the provision of services, something which was reflected in the Care Act easement guidance under Stages 1 and 2 which we examined in Chapter 4. By identifying the departures from usual practice, the Care Act easement process also highlighted the innate discretion built into certain provisions of the Care Act 2014 itself. As we saw in Chapter 3, the legislation involves, on a day-to-day basis, flexibilities and what may ultimately be very uncomfortable choices in service provision linked to issues regarding 'efficiencies' rather

---

[34] See Chapter 5.

than being seen through the frame of safeguarding fundamental rights for a specific service to be satisfied.

Would it have made a difference if the Coronavirus Act 2020 and the provisions for the Care Act easements were seen as a means of holding local authorities effectively to account? Would this have provided reassurance and legitimacy for the structured mitigation of pandemic challenges, thus rendering local authorities accountable for any service changes? Instead, easements were understandably regarded as posing a risk to services and service users, thus putting them in an increasingly perilous and vulnerable position at a time when they were already at extreme risk. Yet the existence of the statutory easements did provide legitimacy and at least some limited degree of transparency. A better approach would have been greater overall transparency and detailed provision of information. The operation of greater 'flexibilities' should have been subject to clearly recorded public documentation and resultant direct oversight rather than focusing simply the 'higher level' easements. This would promote accountability by making transparent the manner in which local authority service provision under the Care Act 2014 is operated. It remains questionable as to whether there would be support at local authority level for such statutory easements in the future. But this is an issue which, if the new UK statutory body proposed by the UK COVID-19 Inquiry Module 1 is implemented, should be considered by them as part of discussions as to the structure and content of any future pandemic emergency legislation.

Thirdly, it is also important to reflect further on the precise drafting of the provisions of the Coronavirus Act 2020 concerning adult social care. As we saw in Chapter 4, one key and interesting aspect of the 2020 Act provisions was that infringement of the ECHR rights was the threshold set below which services should not be reduced under section 18 of the Act. However, this drafting assumes that the people undertaking Care Act assessments, and in pandemic conditions possibly even simplified assessments, have a working knowledge not only of the Coronavirus Act and its impacts on assessments, but also of the nature and applicability of the relevant ECHR human rights provisions and their relationship in turn with the Human Rights Act 1998 and related jurisprudence. This is arguably presuming or demanding a level of knowledge of legal principles which is likely greater than that held by many of those tasked with undertaking the relevant social care assessments on a day-to-day basis. This also raises further questions as to the effectiveness of attempting to make such judgments in making service decisions regarding care and support in the context of exceptional pandemic conditions of pace and pressure such as those we encountered in early 2020. While most needs and carers assessments would be undertaken by qualified social workers, others would be conducted by 'trusted assessors' who undergo some training but are not professionally registered. Pritchard-Jones, in her comparative work on the Mental Capacity Act 2005 and the Care Act 2014, highlighted the problems which can arise consequent to the (mis)interpretation of the Mental Capacity Act which may arise if people have insufficient legal knowledge. She then rightly states in relation to the Care Act 2014 that:

> The same problems of interpretation perhaps arise in the Care Act because that Act, too, requires complex legal provisions on how and when assessments are to be conducted and when eligibility criteria for services are met to be understood, applied and delivered by non-legally trained professionals. If, as noted above, evidence suggests that the Mental Capacity Act depends on the strength of training, it would seem to be common sense that the same is true of the provisions of the Care Act.[35]

It is therefore suggested that regular training in relevant legislation and related international human rights provisions and how these relate to operational and discretionary decision-making should be a mandatory addition to the ongoing training offering for social work professionals, assessors, and care providers. But even so, training can only go so far and making such decisions as to where the threshold sits in terms of service provision in a pandemic will inevitably remain very challenging.

Fourthly there is a lesson to be learned regarding the clarity and standardization of communication and explanation from policy makers and those drafting legislation and guidance. There were notable variations in the ways local authorities interpreted how and when the Care Act easements ought to be used. This may in part reflect the differing interpretations, and levels, of 'flexibility' routinely applied within Care Act compliant practice in social work teams under 'normal' conditions. Given the diversity of systems, structures, and operational processes found across England's local authorities in general, it is easy to see how interpretations of swiftly drafted guidance could vary and were subject to localized discretion. Alternatively, such disparate and uneven approaches may simply be reflective of the more immediate and urgent responses in the tumultuous spring of 2020. Perhaps understandably, updates to the guidance were shared by the DHSC incrementally rather than in a cohesive announcement. Ultimately, as noted throughout, it appears that the actions undertaken by some local authorities which self-declared

---

[35] L. Pritchard-Jones (2020) 'The Care Act 2014 and the Mental Capacity Act 2005: learning lessons for the future', in S. Braye and M. Preston-Shoot (eds) *The Care Act 2014: Wellbeing in Practice*, London: Sage.

under the 'non-easement' category were in fact little different to those where easements had been formally notified.

There was also some divergence between the interpretation by some local authorities as to whether measures such as day centre closures should be categorized as Stage 2 'flexibilities' within the Care Act easement guidance or whether the local authority was taking such measures in response to social-distancing requirements.[36] For future pandemic planning it is important that the relationship between public health measures and the precise scope of measures concerning the provision of adult social care services is clarified so that local authorities can better communicate their decisions to the communities they serve. This is something which again the new statutory body proposed by the UK COVID-19 Inquiry Module 1 Report may be well placed to address.

The next major lesson is the need to fully understand and address the compound challenges facing local government and local authority-level service provision at national level. As we noted in Chapter 5, there appeared to be a serious disconnect between central and local government regarding legislative and operational changes to adult social care; this was evident in many of the interviews we undertook in the West Midlands.[37] The CEPEC and Nuffield Trust's 2023 report *Building a Resilient Social Care System in England* found that the DHSC social care team had been dwindling for some time, leaving 'too few staff to cope with the scale of the crisis'; moreover, there had not been a director general for social care since 2016, nor was one instated until June 2020.[38] Their interviewees, like our own, often expressed the view that social care was treated as 'an afterthought', and that there was a lack of clarity in relation to responsibility for social care,[39] and a lack of clear processes for implementing crucial guidance at local level.[40] Also echoing our own findings in the West Midlands, they identified a problem with those on the ground having to respond to rapidly changing guidance.[41] They suggest that the Government Guidance itself needed to recognize the diverse types of providers of social care, the diversity of the sector's workforce,[42] the role of unpaid carers,[43] and of the individuals who draw on care and support

---

[36] See Chapter 3.
[37] See further Chapter 5.
[38] See N. Curry et al (2023) *Building a Resilient Social Care System in England: What Can Be Learnt from the First Wave of COVID-19?*, Care Policy and Federation Centre and Nuffield Trust Research Report, May, pp 24–5.
[39] Curry et al (2023), pp 26–9.
[40] Curry et al (2023), p 29.
[41] Curry et al (2023), pp 48–50.
[42] Curry et al (2023), pp 50–6.
[43] Curry et al (2023), pp 55–61.

services.[44] They also commented that in the DHSC social care team 'lacked the capacity and the deep operational knowledge needed to navigate a crisis on this scale'.[45] At local authority level, it would be useful to have a dedicated contact point at DHSC available to respond to immediate queries and crises. The newly formed DHSC Regional Assurance team has gone some way to bridging the communication gap between central and local government.[46] It is suggested that ensuring that there are experienced staff in place to address any emergency challenge is crucial to maintaining an effective and consistent approach.

While the UK COVID-19 Inquiry Module 1 Report recommendations are as we saw above likely to be important in raising awareness and greater transparency regarding pandemic planning processes this needs also to be consistently translated at local government level for future pandemics. As we saw in Chapter 4 the Care Act Easements Guidance required that where easements were formally implemented local authorities were required to inform citizens and the DHSC, and the information was then to be listed on the website of the Care Quality Commission (CQC).[47] Decisions to depart from statutory powers and duties thus became very visible. This could be seen as particularly important for the purposes of accountability not least because during this period the CQC had paused its formal inspections. Nonetheless, as we saw in Chapters 4 and 5, in practice the effectiveness of communication was variable at best. There were examples of situations where Stage 3 Care Act easements were introduced without clear communication of the information to citizens in the locality, or indeed to voluntary sector partners, or some elected representatives.[48] Subsequent decisions made at local level need to be subject to appropriate consultation, with the involvement of elected representatives to ensure clarity as to what form they take, how they are implemented, and how services are to be subsequently recovered.

Finally, we would argue that if difficult resource allocation decisions have to be made then these should be rooted in legislation which itself has undergone clear and proper legislative scrutiny, something which was limited in the case of the Coronavirus Act.[49] We hope that this is the result of the new statutory

---

[44] Curry et al (2023), p 47.

[45] Curry et al (2023), p 46.

[46] See S. Elwick (2021) 'Giving assurances', *DHSC Social Care Blog*, 25 June.

[47] See Care Quality Commission (2020) *The Care Act and the 'Easements' to It*.

[48] As we saw, for example, in Birmingham City Council minutes revealed disquiet among certain elected representatives as to the manner in which this was undertaken. In other parts of the country concerns were also raised in relation to this process. See further discussion in Chapter 5.

[49] P.G. Hidalgo, F. de Londras and D. Lock (2022) 'Parliament, the pandemic and the constitutional principle in the United Kingdom: a study of the Coronavirus Act 2020', *Modern Law Review*, 85(6): 1463–503.

body proposed in the UK COVID-19 Inquiry Module 1 Report. As we saw in Chapter 4, there was, of course, draft legislation already in existence concerning pandemic influenza. However, while the table of contents of that draft Bill is now in the public domain as part of the release of documentation consequent upon the UK COVID-19 Inquiry, at the time of writing in summer 2024 the full Bill had not been released, even in redacted form, into the public domain. We would argue that as part of future pandemic planning, draft emergency legislation should be published in advance and then be subjected to pre-legislative scrutiny, a process which has been adopted in relation to the adoption of other legislation.[50] This can be valuable in providing governments with effective engagement with a large piece of legislation which raises a myriad of important public policy issues at an early stage.

III. Lessons from the pandemic for the future of social care law and policy

The international organization Inclusion International in their 2021 report, *A Global Agenda for Inclusive Recovery: Ensuring People with Intellectual Disability and Families Are Included in a Post-COVID World*, stated that international governments should 'build back better … to ensure no one is left behind'.[51]

> 'Building back better' will require recognition of the barriers in place prior to the pandemic, as well as the exclusion that was amplified due to the global crisis. 'Building back better' does not only mean restoring the pre-pandemic status quo but aims to create a recovery that addresses the systemic issues which predated and were amplified by COVID-19, to ensure that our 'new normal' is inclusive.[52]

This statement is applicable more broadly than those with intellectual disability. Emerging from COVID does potentially provide an opportunity to reflect on and reconsider adult social care law and related policy. As Marmot and his team have suggested, there is an imperative to learn from the consequences of entrenched health inequalities and instead aim to 'build back fairer'.[53] We saw

---

[50] See, for example, R. Kelly (2015) 'Pre-legislative scrutiny under the Coalition Government: 2010–2015', House of Commons Library Briefing Paper, Number 05859, 13 August.

[51] Inclusion International (2021) *A Global Agenda for Inclusive Recovery: Ensuring People with Intellectual Disabilities and their Families are Included in a Post-COVID World*, London: Inclusion International.

[52] Inclusion International (2021), p 8.

[53] M. Marmot et al (2020) *Build Back Fairer: The COVID-19 Marmot Review. The Pandemic, Socioeconomic and Health Inequalities in England*, London: Institute of Health Equity, The Health Foundation.

in Chapter 1 that social care has long been regarded as a 'Cinderella service' operating very much in the shadow of the NHS.[54] Unless substantive reform is undertaken, this position is unlikely to change.[55]

At the time of the pandemic, the Care Act 2014 had not been in operation for very long. The 2014 Act came into force from 1 April 2015 in relation to its provisions concerning matters such as eligibility for care and support, and market provision. However, as we saw in Chapter 3, other aspects of the legislation, such as proposals to include a cap on care costs, were not taken forward.[56] There were initially positive statements from the vast majority of local authorities as to their ability to implement the legislation, as shown in a survey undertaken by the Local Government Association, the ADASS and, the then Department of Health.[57] However, there were also concerns contemporaneously expressed as to the availability of the requisite funding for adult social care.[58] The legislation was being introduced in the middle of a decade of austerity. A survey undertaken by the ADASS in 2015 found that local authorities were under an expectation of having to make some 8 per cent of net budget in savings from adult social care (at that time this was around £1.1 billion). This was reported as being due to reductions in available finance along with demographic pressures and inflation.[59] In 2018 the Communities and Local Government Committee stated that: 'Fewer than one in twelve Directors of Adult Social Care are fully confident that their local authority will be able to meet its statutory duties in 2017–18.'[60] This view was also reflected in the Local Government Association's 2018 report, which stated that:

> People's needs are not being met, services are being withdrawn, quality is deteriorating, improvement is stalling and in some cases is in reverse, the ability to prevent the need for social care in the first place is rapidly being rapidly being lost, providers are unable to stay

---

[54] See further Chapter 1.
[55] See N. Curry et al (2023), pp 24–5.
[56] Care Act 2014, s 15.
[57] M. Samuel (2016) 'One year on, what has the Care Act achieved?', *Community Care*, 1 April.
[58] See, for example, D. Kelly (2013) 'Editorial: Reflecting on the implications of the Care Act 2014 for care providers', *Journal of Care Services Management*, (7): 74–5; and S. Braye and M. Preston-Shoot (2020) 'The Care Act 2014: outcomes in context', in S. Braye and M. Preston-Shoot (eds) *The Care Act 2014: Wellbeing in Practice*, London: Sage.
[59] A. McNicoll (2015) 'Social workers forced to cut care packages as £1bn wiped off social care budgets', *Community Care*, 4 June.
[60] House of Commons Communities and Local Government Committee (2017) *Adult Social Care*, Ninth Report of Session 2016–17, HC 1103, p 3.

afloat and unpaid carers and the care workforce are being put under impossible and unbearable pressure.[61]

By 2023, relatively little appeared to have changed and ADASS reported that 'family and unpaid carers are bearing the brunt of an under-resourced and over-stretched system.'[62] Nearly a decade since the Care Act 2014 was introduced, and after a considerable amount of political discussion and Government proposals, the problems regarding the dividing lines in health and care funding from 1948, and the complexities of adult social care funding and commissioning structures, remain a matter of concern.[63] Some of our West Midlands interviewees expressed concerns regarding the short notice provided in relation to emergency funding packages from central Government to address specific pressures; even where additional funding was received, there wasn't always time to plan and to spend it effectively.[64] Nonetheless it is important to note that the goal of respecting people's rights, needs, and expressed choices, and providing appropriate support and proportionate safeguarding measures, cannot be viewed in the abstract, separated from the socio-political and economic context.

Responses during the pandemic period also raised questions in relation to the extent to which the Care Act 2014 in its current form provides an effective means with which to address both individual well-being and social care needs. The range of interpretation during the pandemic and indeed in the recognition of flexibilities in the Care Act easement Guidance, show that the 2014 Act incorporates considerable degrees of discretion and allows for flexibility of interpretation. Concerns were expressed by our interviewees about the 'chilling effect' of changes to the provision of services during the pandemic, and many of these changes were not attributed to the Care Act easement process, but to the built-in flexibilities of statutory interpretation.

What is clear, however, is that effective engagement and actualization of individual well-being under the provisions of the Care Act itself or indeed our expectations of what constitutes respect for fundamental human rights, whether under the ECHR or the UN Convention on the Rights of Persons with Disabilities, may be seen as being in tension with

---

[61] Local Government Association (2018) *The Lives We Want to Lead: The LGA Green Paper for Adult Social Care and Wellbeing LGA Consultation Response*, London: Local Government Association.

[62] Association of Directors of Adult Social Services – ADASS (2023) *Spring Survey 2023*.

[63] See Chapter 3.

[64] See further Chapter 5; also see, for example, the discussion in C. Needham and R. Humphries (2022) *Ending the Social Care Crisis: A New Road to Reform*, Bristol: Policy Press.

the resources which are available to underpin social care.[65] This also leads to the prospect of a 'postcode lottery' for social care with differences in interpretation regarding care provision across local authority areas. While some differences may be due to different demographics, it has been argued that aspects of disparity cannot otherwise be justified.[66] A 'postcode lottery' has also been found to have been operational pre-pandemic in relation to the standards of social care provided for older people.[67] But this lottery and its inequities pre-date the implementation of the Care Act and were already being discussed by Dilnot in the 2011 *Fairer Social Care Funding* report.[68]

Needham and Hall, as we saw in Chapter 1, included a 'crisis in community' in their typology of the 'care crisis', and they suggested that this was an area where positive changes could be identified.[69] One of the heartening findings from our research in the West Midlands was the way in which community groups, both formal and informal, stepped up in the early months of the pandemic to work alongside third-sector organizations.[70] In many cases, these smaller organizations were proven to be responsive and agile in a way that larger public sector bodies were not. There was at times also an ability to cut through bureaucracy and 'to make things happen'.[71] Although many third-sector organizations, and especially charities, struggled enormously during the pandemic through loss of income and volunteers, this partnership working should be a positive legacy which it would be hoped could be maintained in the future.

The move to more digital delivery as we saw in Chapter 6 has been accelerated by the pandemic developments. Digitization and remote working provided the potential for efficiencies in service delivery, while at the same time raising concerns about the effectiveness and safety of undertaking some assessments in this form for some people.[72] The broader

---

[65] See, for example, concerns raised in R. Siemans (2023) 'UKIM's joint submission to the UN committee on the rights of persons with disabilities', Equality and Human Rights Commission blog, 27 September.

[66] See, for example, C. Thomas (2022) *Community First Social Care*, London: Institute for Public Policy Research.

[67] See, for example, M. Savage (2018) 'New data confirms postcode lottery of care for the old', *The Observer*, 3 June.

[68] Commission on Funding of Care and Support (2011) *Fairer Care Funding: The Report of the Commission on Funding of Care and Support*, July (the Dilnot Report).

[69] See C. Needham and P. Hall (2023) *Social Care in the UK's Four Nations: Between Two Paradigms*.

[70] See Birmingham Voluntary Service Council, Walsall Together, and the examples from the individual local authorities in Chapter 5.

[71] See Chapter 5.

[72] See further the discussion in Chapter 6.

digitization agenda can be also seen as facilitating the integration between health and social care. There have been attempts over decades to facilitate this integration as through Primary Care Trusts,[73] and today much of this work is taking place in Integrated Care Boards.[74] The Government's plan for digital health and social care was published in 2022. Its plan includes the digitization of health and social care records, enabling these to be fully linked and accessible to both NHS and social care staff.[75] Increased digitalization can facilitate delivery at local level, for example by providing up-to-date data to support effective hospital discharge decisions. The intention was that by March 2024 80 per cent of social care providers would have digitized their records, and that some 20 per cent of providers would be utilizing sensor technology to detect falls, for example.[76] The general movement away from in-person service provision remains controversial but shows no signs of slowing.

As we also saw in Chapter 6 one fundamental issue which came to the fore throughout the pandemic was that of social justice, and how health inequalities, underpinned by glaring socio-economic inequalities,[77] resulted in unequal impacts for different communities and individuals, as demonstrated by Marmot et al.[78] The UK COVID-19 Inquiry Module I Report in July 2024 also stressed the importance of this issue.[79] Moreover the Inquiry highlighted that while vulnerability had been identified as something which needed to be built into COVID-19 planning, definitions of vulnerability provided by the Cabinet Office in related guidance 'were too vague to have any utility'.[80] The National Security Risk Assessment introduced in 2022 included a section on guidance for vulnerable groups which noted the need to take into consideration 'the disproportionate impact the risk may have on vulnerable groups'; this, the Inquiry Report stated, did not go far enough.[81] The Report stated that: 'There needs to be a move away from

---

[73] See Chapter 1.
[74] Department of Health and Social Care (2022) *A plan for digital health and social care*, Policy paper, 22 June.
[75] Department of Health and Social Care (2022) *A plan for digital health and social care*, Policy paper, 22 June.
[76] M. Marmot et al (2020) *Build Back Fairer*, UCL Institute of Health Equity, commissioned by the Health Foundation, December.
[77] See C. Bambra, J. Lynch and K.E. Smith (2021) *The Unequal Pandemic: COVID-19 and Health Inequalities*, Bristol: Policy Press; and EHRC (2020) *How Coronavirus Has Affected Equality and Human Rights*, Is Britain Fairer? Series, October.
[78] Marmot et al (2020) *Build back fairer*; see also C. Bambra, J. Lynch and K.E. Smith (2021) *The Unequal Pandemic: COVID-19 and Health Inequalities*, Bristol: Policy Press.
[79] M. Marmot et al (2020).
[80] UK COVID-19 Inquiry (2024), para 3.6.1.
[81] UK COVID-19 Inquiry (2024), para 3.6.2.

the causes of risks towards minimising their impact, particularly for people who are the most vulnerable'.[82]

The Report recommended that in relation to pandemic planning

> there should be a single definition of vulnerability for the UK government and devolved administrations. This should take into account the protected characteristics under the Equality Act 2010 but also be sufficiently broad and capable of adaptation to the circumstances of a major emergency as information about its potential wider impact is gathered. There should be consideration of the effect that both action and inaction may have on those most at risk of harm and suffering. If this approach were taken to all aspects of preparedness and resilience, the risk of suffering and harm – not only from a pandemic but from the response – would be reduced.[83]

The recognition of the importance of vulnerability as a concept is to be welcomed in principle, however the scope and nature of this concept in terms of policy development, as we have seen in Chapter 2 of this volume, remains very much a matter of discussion and indeed debate. We suggest that before there is any attempt for a general definition of this type, there needs to be much further engagement at national government level with these broader debates. Moreover we suggest that this should go far wider than the context of pandemic and emergency planning as it raises far-reaching questions of the positions of all citizens in society.

Highlighting the nature of embedded inequalities in future law and policy in this area is important but is not in itself sufficient. As we saw in Chapter 2, we need to recognize the importance of the nested relationality of personal decision-making and its interface with the principle of solidarity.[84] Unless these fundamental tensions are addressed in the aftermath of the COVID-19 pandemic, promptly and in earnest, they will be compounded and further entrenched, and our society will be left vulnerable in the face of future public health emergencies.

IV. Conclusions

It is difficult to overstate quite how challenging the pandemic and its aftermath have been for adult social care, both for those who work in the sector and especially for those who draw on services and support. Already

---

[82] UK COVID-19 Inquiry (2024), para 3.6.2.
[83] UK COVID-19 Inquiry (2024), para 3.6.4.
[84] See Chapter 2.

straining under acute pressure prior to 2020, adult social care was, as far back as the Griffiths Report, characterized as a 'poor relation' to the NHS.[85] The term more recently used is that of a 'Cinderella service',[86] but while the fairy-tale Cinderella went on to enjoy a life radically transformed, the trajectory of the last two decades does not inspire confidence that the necessary radical transformation will easily happen for adult social care.[87] While we are now in an era of 'living with COVID-19', major pressures still remain for adult social care, and the typology of forms of 'crises' for social care identified by Needham and Hall are very much in evidence.[88] There has been retrenchment in relation to governmental pledges regarding funding reform and sustained budgetary boosts. In September 2023, Birmingham City Council issued what is known as a section 114 notice, which is a formal notification to the UK Government that a local authority is unable to balance its accounts. The ramifications of this are major for the citizens of Birmingham. It was decided that new expenditure, other than for maintaining statutory services, would cease – and this is now being followed with swingeing budget cuts.[89] As this book was being finalized in spring 2024, there were fears that many other local authorities were likely to imminently follow suit unless funding is radically reformed.[90] In March 2024, the Public Accounts Committee stated that 'Government is falling short on its promise to "fix the crisis in social care" as chronic underfunding, rising waiting lists and patchwork funding place sustained pressure on local authorities'.[91]

The specifics of the nature and scope of the details of reform of adult social care law and policy in general and its delivery go beyond our present remit as

---

[85] R. Griffiths (1988) *Community Care: Agenda for Action. A Report to the Secretary of State for Social Services*, London: HMSO; and see also C. Needham and J. Glasby (2023) 'Forgotten, neglected and a poor relation? Reflecting on the 75th anniversary of adult social care', in M. Exworthy, R. Mannion and M. Powell (eds) *The NHS at 75: The State of UK Health Policy*, Bristol: Policy Press.

[86] See A. Charlesworth (2018) 'Even on its 70th birthday, social care remains a Cinderella service', *Health Foundation*, 12 July.

[87] S. Scown (2018) 'Is the Care Sector really a "Cinderella?"', *Huffington Post*, 23 February.

[88] Needham and Hall (2023); see also Chapter 6.

[89] J. Sandiford and S. Gilbert (2024) 'Birmingham City Council signs off "devastating" cuts', *BBC News*, 6 March.

[90] See E. Ames (2024) '14 councils likely to issue s114s in the next year', *LocalGov*, 28 February; and Local Government Association (2023) 'Section 114 fear for almost 1 in 5 council leaders and chief executives after cashless Autumn Statement', 6 December.

[91] House of Commons Committee of Public Accounts (2024) 'Adult social care: PAC raises alarm as Government fall short of promise to fix crisis', News article, 20 March; see also House of Commons Committee of Public Accounts (2024) *Reforming Adult Social Care in England, Twenty-second report of session 2023-24*, HC 427, 20 March.

we highlighted in Chapter 1.[92] At the time this book was in production, there have been reports that the new Labour Government may be establishing a Royal Commission on Social Care and, if so, that broader question will soon begin to be unpacked.[93] As we have seen, an understanding of the nested realities of relationships of care and questions of fundamental rights should inform the task of structuring effective pandemic responses to better serve adult social care in the future. We need to ensure that there is engagement with and understanding of the requisite legal principles and the Care Act itself by those accessing care and support in adult social care services and their advocates and those working in adult social care. The broad definition of 'well-being' needs to be revisited, to explore how a piece of legislation can be expected to work effectively and specifically from such a generic principle.

As we have noted, of vital importance is transparency in the way in which decisions are reached; we are of course not the first to recommend proper public consultation, and ideally co-production, at all stages.[94] During our empirical research, we found some examples of good supportive practice, based on open communication and collaboration, designed to meet individual needs. But there was also a widespread sense of frustration from the interviewees in our empirical study, that the same themes of what needs fixing in adult social care policy are brought up decade after decade. Issues of funding, of course, remain key, as does the need for better integration and partnership working across health and social care systems and teams; clearer and more responsive communications from central to local government; and greater understanding of the challenges of putting policy into practice when the quality of people's lives is at stake. Real concerns were raised among some of our interviewees as to whether the different approaches to and reductions in service provision rolled out during the peaks of the pandemic years would ultimately lead to an acceptance of less and lack, and that ever-lower expectations would become the norm.

The COVID-19 pandemic left an impact on all of us who lived through those early years from 2020 – a more devastating and deeper impact on some, though, than others. As we have seen, this has been particularly the case for those who draw on adult social care and support in England and also for their carers, whether in a formal or informal capacity. It is critical that the lessons of those turbulent years are addressed in earnest and used to inform pandemic planning and adult social care law and policy for England in the future.

---

[92] For further analysis, see Humphries (2022); Needham and Hall (2023); and Needham and Glasby (2023).

[93] C. Smyth (2024) 'Labour plans cross-party Royal Commission to fix social care', *The Times*, 12 July 2024.

[94] T. Brandsen, B. Verschuere and T. Steen (eds) (2018) *Co-Production and Co-Creation: Engaging Citizens in Public Services*, London: Routledge.

Bibliography

Abbott, S. (2019) 'Navigating practice at the interface between mental health and social care law', in S. Braye and M. Preston-Shoot (eds) *The Care Act 2014: Wellbeing in Practice*, London: Sage.

Age UK (2021) 'Age UK day centres win award', Shropshire Telford & Wrekin Age UK, 31 March.

Allen, L. and Shembavnekar, N. (2023) 'Social care workforce crisis: How did we get here and where do we go next?', *The Health Foundation Blog*, 13 October.

Allmark, P. (1995) 'Can there be an ethic of care?', *Journal of Medical Ethics*, 21(1): 19–24.

Ames, E. (2024) '14 councils likely to issue s114s in the next year', *LocalGov*, 28 February.

Amnesty International (2020) *As if Expendable: The UK Government's Failure to Protect Older People in Care Homes during the COVID-19 Pandemic*, 4 October, Index Number: EUR 45/3152/2020.

Anderson, B. and Adley, P. (2012) 'Governing events and life: 'emergency in UK civil contingencies', *Political Geography*, 31: 24.

Andoh, B. (2005) 'An analysis of aftercare under section 117 of the Mental Health Act 1983', *Medicine Science and the Law*, 45(1): 7–16.

Anka, A., Thacker, H. and Penhale, B. (2020) 'Safeguarding adults practice and remote working in the COVID-19 era: challenges and opportunities', *Journal of Adult Protection*, 22(6): 415–27.

Antova, I. (2020) 'Disability rights during COVID-19: emergency law and guidelines in England', *Medical Law Review*, 28(4): 804.

Arden, A. and Dymond, A. (2022) *Manual of Housing Law*, London: Legal Action Group.

Association of Directors of Adult Social Services – ADASS (2015) *Care Act and Whole Family Approaches*.

Association of Directors of Adult Social Services – ADASS (2018) *A Report Identifying the Regulatory and Process Easements that DASSs Require to Manage the Reprioritisation of Needs and Delivery of Services in a Future Pandemic Flu Response*.

Association of Directors of Adult Social Services – ADASS (2018) *Guide to Pandemic Flu Planning*.

Association of Directors of Adult Social Services – ADASS (2018) *The Communications and Support Infrastructure Required by DASSs to Support Them Communicating Service Reprioritisation in a Future Pandemic Flu Response*.

Association of Directors of Adult Social Services – ADASS (2018) *Proposals to Support Directors of Adult Social Care and Local Areas to Prepare Now for a Future Flu Pandemic*.

Association of Directors of Adult Social Services – ADASS (2020) *Autumn Survey 2020*.

Association of Directors of Adult Social Services – ADASS (2020) *Themes and Learning from ADASS Members on the Local Response to COVID-19 in Spring and Early Summer 2020*.

Association of Directors of Adult Social Services – ADASS (2021) ADASS *Press Release: A National Emergency for Social Care*, 22 December.

Association of Directors of Adult Social Services – ADASS (2022) *Autumn Report*.

Association of Directors of Adult Social Services – ADASS (2022) *Digital Transformation in Social Care: How to Get it Right*.

Association of Directors of Adult Social Services – ADASS (2022) *Waiting for Care and Support Report*, May.

Association of Directors of Adult Social Services – ADASS (2023) *Spring Survey 2023*.

Asthana, A. and Elgot, J. (2017) 'Theresa May ditches manifesto plan with "'dementia tax'" U-turn', *The Guardian*, 22 May.

Astin, D. (2022) *Housing Law Handbook* (5th edn), London: Legal Action Group.

Atlee, C. (1920) *The Social Worker* (1st edn), London: G. Bell, reprinted Sharpe Books, 2019.

Baginsky, M., Thomas, E. and Manthorpe, J. (2023) 'Reasons for not adopting COVID-19 permitted changes to legal duties: accounts from English local authorities', *Health and Social Care in the Community*, 1–7.

Baginsky, M., Thomas, E. and Manthorpe, J. (2023) 'Changing English local authority duties by the adoption of easements in the COVID-19 pandemic; findings from an interview-based study', *British Journal of Social Work*, 53(2): 939–55.

Baldwin, R. and Black, J. (2016) 'Driving priorities in risk-based regulation: what's the problem?', *Journal of Law and Society*, 43(4): 565–95.

Balmire, J., Rees, J. and Sojka, B. (2022) *Walsall Council Review of COVID-19 Response: Capturing the Learning*, Wolverhampton: University of Wolverhampton.

Bambra, C., Lynch, J. and Smith, K.E. (2021) *The Unequal Pandemic: COVID-19 and Health Inequalities*, Bristol: Policy Press.

Banks, S. and Rutter, N. (2022) 'Pandemic ethics: Rethinking rights, responsibilities and roles in social work', *British Journal of Social Work*, 52(6): 3460–79.

Barclay, P. (1978) *Social Workers Their Role and Tasks*, London: National Institute for Social Work.

Barnes, C. (2019) 'Understanding the social model of disability: past, present and future', in N. Watson, A. Roulstone and C. Thomas (eds) *Routledge Handbook of Disability Studies*, London: Taylor and Francis.

Barnes, C.G. (1990) *Cabbage Syndrome: The Social Construction of Dependence*, London: Taylor & Francis.

Barnes, M. (2011) 'Abandoning care? A critical perspective on personalisation from an ethic of care', *Ethics and Social Welfare*, 5(2): 153.

Barnes, M. (2012) *Care in Everyday Life: An Ethic of Care in Practice*, Bristol: Policy Press.

Bartlett, P. (2012) 'The United Nations Convention on the Rights of Persons with Disabilities and the future of Mental Health Law', *Modern Law Review*, 75(5): 752–78.

Baxter, K, Heavey, E. and Birks, Y. (2020) 'Choice and control in social care: experiences of older self-funders in England', *Social Policy and Administration*, 54(3): 460–74.

BBC News (2019) 'Whorlton Hall abuse: Watchdog defends inspection', 12 June.

BBC News (2020) 'Coronavirus: Care workers "shocked" by virus treatment guidance', 3 April.

Bell, D., Comas-Herrera, A., Henderson, D., Jones, S., Moro, M., Murphy, S., O'Reilly, D. and Patrignani, P. (2020) 'COVID-19 mortality and long-term care: a UK comparison', International Long Term Care Policy Network, CPEC-LSE, 29 August.

Beresford, P. and Slasberg, C. (2020) 'The Care Act: the service user's experience', in S. Braye and M. Preston-Shoot (eds) *The Care Act 2014: Wellbeing in Practice*, London: Sage.

Beveridge, W. (1942) *Social Insurance and Allied Services* (Beveridge Report), Cmd 6404.

Beyleveld, D. and Brownsword, R. (2001) *Human Dignity in Bioethics and Biolaw*, Oxford: Oxford University Press.

Bilotta, C. et al (2010) 'Day care centre attendance and quality of life in depressed older adults living in the community', *European Journal of Ageing*, 7: 29–35.

Birmingham City Council (2024) *Social Care for Adults in Birmingham: A Fair Deal in Times of Austerity*.

Birmingham City Council (2020) *Birmingham City Council's Response to COVID-19 Report of: Cabinet Report author: Professor Graeme Betts, Gold Commander March to May 2020 and Director, Adult Social Care*.

Birmingham City Council (2020) 'Local guidance during COVID-19', webpage.
Birmingham City Council (2020) Minutes of meeting of the City Council, 9 June.
Birmingham City Council (2020) 'Health and Social Care Overview and Scrutiny Committee – COVID-19 Update', 16 June.
Birmingham City Council (2020) *COVID-19 Decision Log*, June.
Birmingham City Council (2020) 'Minutes of meeting of the City Council', 15 September.
Birmingham City Council (2020) 'Minutes of Cabinet Meeting regarding Impact on Day Centres', 13 October.
Birmingham City Council (2020) 'Minutes of the meeting of the City Council', 3 November.
Birmingham City Council (2021) 'Local Outbreak Management Plan.'
Birmingham City Council (2021) *Annual Governance Statement 2020/2021*.
Birmingham City Council (2022) 'Mid-year Population Information Estimate'.
Birmingham City Council (2024) 'Your day, your say – adult social care day centre consultation', webpage, 7 May.
Birmingham City University and Birmingham Voluntary Service Council (2021) *Community-based Responses to COVID-19 in Birmingham: Insights and Experiences*, research report, 28 June.
Birmingham Mail (2021) 'Birmingham Nightingale Hospital closes without treating a single patient', *Birmingham Mail*, 1 April 2021.
Birmingham Voluntary Service Council (2020) 'COVID-19 support brum partnership weekly briefing bulletins'.
Booth, R. (2020) 'Stop using coronavirus powers to neglect care duties, UK councils told', *The Guardian*, 7 May.
Booth, R. (2022) 'England's social care workforce shrinks for first time in 10 years', *The Guardian*, 11 October.
Booth, R. (2023) '"A bowl of spaghetti": COVID Inquiry opens with flowchart on UK's pandemic planning', *The Guardian*, 3 June.
Booth, R. (2024) 'Modern slavery in social care surging since visa rules eased', *The Guardian*, 21 January.
Borowski, A. (2022) 'On human dignity and social work', *British Journal of Social Work*, 52(2): 609–23.
Bows, H. and Herring, J. (2022) 'DNACPR decisions during COVID-19: an empirical and analytical study', *Medical Law Review*, 30(1): 60–80.
Brammer, A. (2020) *Social Work Law*, Harlow: Pearson.
Brammer, A. and Pritchard-Jones, L. (2019) *Safeguarding Adults: Focus on Social Work Law* (2nd edn), London: Red Globe Press.
Brandsen, T. and Honingh, M. (2018) 'Definitions of co-production and co-creation', in T. Brandsen, B. Verschuere and T. Steen (eds) *Co-Production and Co-Creation: Engaging Citizens in Public Services*, London: Routledge.

Brandsen, T., Verschuere, B. and Steen, T. (2018) 'The dark side of co-creation and co-production: seven evils', in T. Brandsen, B. Verschuere and T. Steen (eds) *Co-Production and Co-Creation: Engaging Citizens in Public Services*, London: Routledge.

Braun, V. and Clarke, V. (2021) 'One size fits all? What counts as quality practice in (reflexive) thematic analysis?', *Qualitative Research in Psychology*, 18(3): 328–52.

Braun, V., Clarke, V. et al (2022) 'Doing reflexive thematic analysis', in S. Bager-Charleson and A. McBeath (eds) *Supporting Research in Counselling and Psychotherapy*, Cham: Palgrave Macmillan.

Braye, S. and Preston-Shoot, M. (2019) 'Adult safeguarding', in S. Braye and M. Preston-Shoot (eds) *The Care Act 2014: Wellbeing in Practice*, London: Sage.

Braye, S and Preston-Shoor, M. 'The Care Act 2014- outcomes in context', in S. Braye and M. Preston-Shoot (eds) *The Care Act 2014: Wellbeing in Practice*, London: Sage.

Brisenden, S. (1986) 'Independent living and the medical model of disability', *Disability and Society*, 1(2): 173–8.

British Association of Social Workers – BASW (2021) *The Code of Ethics for Social Work*, statement of principles.

British Association of Social Workers – BASW (2024) 'Professional Capabilities Framework'.

British Institute for Human Rights (2020) 'Human rights implications of the coronavirus bill: the risk of making vulnerable adults and children even more vulnerable', 24th March 2020.

British Institute for Human Rights (2020) 'Explainer: JCHR Report on the Government's response to COVID-19: human rights implications', September.

British Medical Association (2023) *The Public Health Response by UK Governments to COVID-19*, report, 7 July.

Broach, S. (2020) 'COVID-10: banana bread, blankets, beans and the law', blog post by K. Runswick-Cole, available at https://rightsinreality.wordpress.com/2020/06/03/covid-19-banana-bread-blankets-beans-and-the-law/

Broderick, A. (2019) *International and European Disability Law and Policy*, Cambridge: Cambridge University Press.

Brown, J. and Kirk-Wade, E. (2022) *Coronavirus: A History of 'Lockdown Laws' in England*, House of Commons Library Research Briefing, No 9068.

Brown, M. (2020) 'The social care workforce: Overworked, undervalued and poorly paid', *Integrated Care Journal*, News, 26 May.

Burn, E(eta.) (2023) 'Implementing England's Care Act 2014: was the Act a success and when will we know?', *International Journal of Care and Caring*, 8(1): 47–63.

Bushby, H. (2022) 'Permacrisis declared Collins Dictionary word of the year', *BBC News*, 1 November.

Bynam, W.F. (1993) 'Policing hearts of darkness: aspects of the international sanitary conferences', *History and Philosophy of the Life Sciences*, 15(3): 421–34.

Cabinet Office (2002) *Risk, Improving Government's Capability to Handle Risk and Uncertainty*, November 2002.

Cabinet Office (2013) *Guidance: Preparation and Planning for Emergencies*, last updated May 2018.

Cabinet Office (2013) *Preparing for Pandemic Influenza: Guidance for Local Planners*, July.

Cabinet Office (2013) *The Role of Local Resilience Forums: A reference document.*

Cabinet Office HMG (2021) *Build Back Better. Our Plan for Health and Social Care.* 7 September. CP 506.

Cabinet Office (2022) *COVID-19 Response: Living with COVID.* Guidance, 21 February, updated 6 May 2022.

Cabinet Office (2022) *UK Government Resilience Framework*, Policy paper, updated 4 December 2023.

Cabinet Office and Rt Hon Steve Barclay (2022) 'Government takes action to mitigate workforce disruption', Press release, 2 January.

Cabinet Office, Prime Ministers Office, 10 Downing Street and the Rt Hon Lord Cameron (2010) 'PM's speech on wellbeing', 25 November 2010.

Caiels, J. Silarova, B., Milne, A. and Beadle-Brown, J. (2022) *Perspectives on Strengths-based Approaches: Social Workers, Commissioners and Managers.* NIHR Policy research unit in adult social care discussion paper 2021–22.

Campbell, A. (2007) *The Blair Years: Extracts from the Alastair Campbell Diaries*, London: Hutchinson.

Campbell, D. (2023) 'Hospitals in England discharging patients into "care hotels"', *The Guardian*, 5 January.

Cardwell, M. (2020) 'Day centre closures in Birmingham having "terrible" impact on families due to COVID-19 pandemic', *Express and Star*, 7 December.

Care Provider Alliance (2017) 'Developing Trusted Assessments Schemes: essential elements', *Improvement.nhs.uk*, July.

Care Quality Commission (2017) *Guidance: Trusted Assessors. Requirements when People Are Discharged from Hospital into Adult Social Care Services under 'Trusted Assessor' Schemes.*

Care Quality Commission (2018) *Guidance on Trusted Assessors Agreements V2.*

Care Quality Commission (2018) *Our Updated Approach to Regulating Independent Healthcare Services*, June, updated 12 May 2022.

Care Quality Commission (2020) *Guidance: COVID-19 Trusted Assessor Guidance.*

Care Quality Commission (2020) 'Routine Inspections Suspended in Response to Coronavirus Outbreak', Web news, 16 March, updated 12 May 2022.

Care Quality Commission (2021) *Protect, Respect, Connect – Decisions about Living and Dying Well during COVID-19,* April.

Care Quality Commission (2022) *The Care Act and the 'Easements' to it. Local Authorities that Have Exercised the Easements,* last updated 12 May 2022.

Care Quality Commission (2023) 'Our Approach to Assessing Local Authorities', Web news, 28 February, updated 4 July.

Care Quality Commission (2023) *The State of Health Care and Adult Social Care in England 2022/23,* HC1871.

Carers UK (2020) *Carers Week 2020 Research Report. The Rise in the Number of unpaid Carers during the Coronavirus (COVID-19) Outbreak,* June.

Carers UK (2020) *Caring Behind Closed Doors.*

Carers UK (2020) *Caring Behind Closed Doors: Six Months On,* October 2020.

Carers UK (2024) *Unpaid Carers in Employment: Occupation and Industry,* Research report, April.

Carers UK (2024) 'Financial support: Carer's Allowance', webpage.

Carr H. (2011) 'Rational men and difficult women – *R (on the application of McDonald) v. Royal Borough of Kensington and Chelsea* [2011] UKSC 33', *Journal of Social Welfare and Family Law,* 34: 219.

Carroll, D. (2020) *Report of the Portfolio Holder for Adult Social Care/Public Health and Climate Change Portfolio Holder,* 16 July, Shropshire Council.

Carter, C. (2020) 'Government to drop coronavirus provisions weakening mental health protections' *Community Care,* 2 October.

Carter, P. and Martin, G. (2016) 'Challenges facing Healthwatch, a new consumer champion in England', *International Journal of Health Policy Management,* 5(4): 259–63.

Caton, S. et al (2022) 'Digital participation of people with profound and multiple learning disabilities during the COVID-19 pandemic in the UK', *British Journal of Learning Disability,* 51: 163–74.

Central England Law Centre (2022) *Rights in Peril Project Report,* available at www.centralenglandlc.org.uk/Handlers/Download.ashx?IDMF=78650142-2ab3-45d0-8fe1-02d9cc6d314d

Centre for Ageing Better (2020) *Briefing: How Has COVID-19 Changed the Landscape of Digital Inclusion?*

Centre for People, Work, Organisational Practice (2021) *Respond, Recover, Reset: The Relationship with Local Authorities,* CWOP report, April.

Chadwick, D. et al (2022) 'Digital inclusion and participation of people with intellectual disabilities during COVID-19: a rapid review and international bricolage', *Journal of Policy and Practice in Intellectual Disabilities,* 19: 242–56.

Charlesworth, A. (2018) 'Even on its 70th birthday, social care remains a Cinderella service', *Health Foundation,* 12 July.

Chua, L.J. and Engel, D.M. (2021) 'Legal consciousness reconsidered', *Annual Review of Law and Science*, 15: 335–53.

City of Wolverhampton Council (2020) 'Adults and Safer City Scrutiny Panel Minutes', 15 September.

City of Wolverhampton Council (2020) 'Care Act easements procedures'.

City of Wolverhampton Council (2020) 'Consultation on Care Act easements', available at https://consultation.wolverhampton.gov.uk/cwc/care-act-easement-procedure/

City of Wolverhampton Council (2020) 'Operating Model for Care Act Easements', April.

City of Wolverhampton Council (2020) 'An Easy Read Guide to Care Act easements in Wolverhampton: How local services may change because of Coronavirus and how it may impact you', webpage.

City of Wolverhampton Council (2021) 'Adult and Safer City Scrutiny Panel, Adults Social Work Health Check 2020,' 16 March.

City of Wolverhampton Council (2021) 'Adult Social Care: Annual Report. The Local Account 2019–2020', presented to Cabinet on 17 February.

City of Wolverhampton Council (2021) 'Principal Social Worker Annual Report 2020–2021', 28 July.

Civil Contingencies Secretariat (2007) *Preparing for Pandemic Influenza: Guidance to Local Planners*, 3 December.

Civil Contingencies Secretariat (2008) *Preparing for Pandemic Influenza. Supplementary Guidance for Local Resilience Forum Planners*, May.

Clark, C. (ed) (2001) *Adult Day Services and Social Inclusion. Better Days. Research Highlights in Social Work,* London and NY: Jessica Kingsley.

Clements, L. (2022) 'Holidays and Poor Law Commissioners', Blog (21 January), available at https://www.lukeclements.co.uk/holidays-and-poor-law-commissioners/

Clements, L., Ashton, K., Garlick, S., Goodhall, C., Mitchell, C. and Pickup, A. (2019) *Community Care and the Law. 7th edition*, London: Legal Action Group.

Clifford, D. (2014) 'Limitations of virtue ethics in the social professions', *Ethics and Social Welfare*, 8(1): 2–19.

Coggon, J. (2012) *What Makes Health Public?: A Critical Evaluation of Moral, Legal, and Political Claims in Public Health*, Cambridge: Cambridge University Press.

Coggon, J., Syrett, K. and Viens, A. (2017) *Public Health Law Ethics, Governance, and Regulation*, London: Routledge.

Coker, R. (2001) 'Civil liberties and the public good: detention of tuberculous patients and the Public Health Act 1984', *Medical History*, 45(3): 341–58.

Cole, A. (2016) 'All of us are vulnerable, but some are more vulnerable than others: the political ambiguity of vulnerability studies, an ambivalent critique', *Critical Horizons: A Journal of Philosophy and Social Theory*, 17(2): 260–77.

Commission on Funding of Care and Support (2011) *Fairer Care Funding: The Report of the Commission on Funding of Care and Support* (Dilnot Report), July.

Comas-Herrera, A. et al (2020) 'The COVID-19 Long Term Care Situation in England', International Long Term Care Policy Network, CPEC-LSE, 19 November.

Cooper, B. and Harrop, A. (2023) *Support Guaranteed: The Roadmap to a National Care Service*, London: Fabian Society.

Coventry City Council (2020) 'Independent Travel Training', webpage.

Coventry City Council (2020) 'Exercise of emergency functions – Use of the Care Act Easements, created under the Coronavirus Act 2020', 2 June.

Coventry City Council (2020) 'One Minute Guide. The Care Act Easements,' Coventry Safeguarding Adults Board, April.

Coventry City Council (2020) Document signed by Chief Executive Coventry City Council on 2 June 2020, 'Exercise of emergency functions – Use of the Care Act Easements, created under the Coronavirus Act 2020'.

Coventry City Council (2020) Report to Coventry Health and Wellbeing Board Date: 27 July 2020 From: Pete Fahy, Director of Adult Services; Title: 'Adult Social Care – Key programmes of work to support COVID-19 to date.'

Coventry City Council (2020) *Coventry Adult Social Care Annual Report and Key Areas of Improvement 2019/20 (Local Account)*.

Coventry City Council (2020) 'Adult Social Care – Care Act Decision Report – Care Act Easements, 27 May 2020 from: Andrew Errington, Adults Principal Social Worker, Sally Caren, Head of Social Work, Mental Health and Sustainability to: Pete Fahy – Director of Adult Services.'

Coventry City Council (2020) Response to FoI Request REQ07090, 21 May.

Coventry City Council (2020) Response to FoI Request REQ07114, 28 May.

Coventry City Council (2020) Response to FoI from Liberty, 1 June.

Coventry City Council (2020) 'Exercise of emergency functions - use of the Care Act Easements, created under the Coronavirus Act,' 2 June.

Coventry City Council (2020) Minutes of meeting of Coventry Health and Well-Being Board 27 July.

Coventry City Council (2021) 'Report to Coventry Health and Wellbeing Board Date: 25 January 2021. From: Pete Fahy, Director Adult Services COVID-19 – The Impact on Adult Social Care.'

Coventry City Council (2021) *Our Key Achievements Adult Social Care: Annual Report and Key Areas of Improvement 2020/21 (Local Account)*.

Crossland, J. (2020) 'Implementing the Care Act: assessing need and providing care and support', in S. Braye and M. Preston-Shoot (eds) *The Care Act 2014: Wellbeing in Practice*, London: Sage.

Crowther, M.A. (2016) *The Workhouse System 1834–1929: The History of an English Social Institution*, London: Routledge.

Curry, N. et al (2023) *Building a Resilient Social Care System in England: What Can Be Learnt from the First Wave of COVID-19?*, research report, Care Policy and Evaluation Centre and Nuffield Trust, May.

D'Astous, V. et al (2016) 'Retracing the historical social care context of autism: a narrative overview', *British Journal of Social Work*, 46: 789–807.

Dalley, G. (2022) *Caring in Crisis: The Search for Reasons and Post-Pandemic Remedies*, Cham: Palgrave Macmillan.

Daly, M. (2020) 'COVID-19 and care homes in England: what happened and why?', *Social Policy and Administration*, 54(7): 985–98.

Dare, T. (2020) 'Concern for vulnerable as Birmingham no longer obliged to assess people over care needs', *Birmingham Mail*, 28 April.

Davis, F. and Cowie, G. (2020) *Coronavirus Bill: What Is the Sunset Clause Provision?*, House of Commons Library Insight, 20 March.

Day, M. (2020) 'COVID-19 Nightingale hospitals set to shut down after seeing few patients', *BMJ*, 369: m1860.

de Beco, G. (2021) *Disability in International Human Rights Law*, Oxford: Oxford Academic.

Deeny, S. et al (2017) *Reducing Hospital Admissions by Improving Continuity of Care in General Practice*, Health Foundation Briefing, February.

Denger, T. (2016) 'A human rights model of disability', in P. Blanck and E. Flynn (eds) *Routledge Handbook of Disability Law and Human Rights*, London: Routledge.

Department of Health (2001) *Valuing people: a new strategy for learning disability for C21st, CM 5080*.

Department of Health (2002) *Getting Ahead of the Curve: A strategy for combating infectious disease*.

Department of Health (2007) *Exercise Winter Willow: Lessons Identified*.

Department of Health (2011) *UK Influenza Pandemic Preparedness Strategy*, 10 November.

Department of Health, Association of Directors of Adult Social Services, NHS England (2015) *Quick Guide – Discharge to Assess. Transforming Urgent and Emergency Care Services in England*, NHS England Publications Gateway, Reference 05871.

Department of Health/Cabinet Office (2007) *Pandemic Flu: UK National Framework for Responding to an Influenza Pandemic*, Cabinet Office, November.

Department of Health and Social Care (2022) *Guidance: National Framework for NHS Continuing Healthcare and NHS-funded Nursing Care*, 28 November, updated 31 October 2022.

Department of Health (2015) *Code of Practice Mental Health Act 1983* (2015), last updated 2017.

Department of Health, Local Government Association, Association of Directors of Adult Social Services, the Children's Society and the Carers Trust (2015)

Department of Health and Social Care (2016) 'Three Conversations, Multiple Benefits', *Social Work with Adults* blog post, 26 September, Lyn Romeo and Sam Newman (Partners4Change),

Department of Health and Social Care (2019) *'Right to Be Heard': The Government's Response to the Consultation on Learning Disability and Autism Training for Health and Care Staff.*

Department of Health and Social Care (2019) *Strengths-based Approach: Practice Framework and Practice Handbook*, February.

Department of Health and Social Care (2020) 'Care Act Easements', Adult Social Care COVID-19 Forum – weekly teleconferences, 8 April 2020, 13:00–14:00.

Department of Health and Social Care (2020) *Care Act Easements: Guidance for Local Authorities*, 1 April 2020, updated 29 June 2021; withdrawn 22 July 2021.

Department of Health and Social Care (2020) *Care Act Easements: Supporting Guidance*, updated 29 June 2021; withdrawn 22 July 2021.

Department of Health and Social Care (2020) *Coronavirus Action Plan: A Guide to What You Can Expect Across the UK*, 3 March.

Department of Health and Social Care (2020) *COVID-19 Hospital Discharge Service Requirements*, 19 March; withdrawn 25 August 2020.

Department of Health and Social Care (2020) *Guidance: What the Coronavirus Bill Will Do*, updated 26 March 2020; withdrawn 1 April 2022.

Department of Health and Social Care (2020) *Responding to COVID-19: The Ethical Framework for Adult Social Care*, 19 March 2020, updated 21 April 2021; withdrawn 1 April 2022.

Department of Health and Social Care (2020) *Impact Assessment. Coronavirus Bill: Summary of Impacts*, 19 March, updated 23 March 2020.

Department of Health and Social Care (2020) 'UK Pandemic Preparedness Policy Paper', Policy paper, updated 5 November 2020.

Department of Health and Social Care (2021) *People at the Heart of Care. Adult Social Care Reform White Paper*, CP 560, 1 December, updated 18 March 2022.

Department of Health and Social Care (2021) 'Adult social care: COVID-19 winter plan 2021 to 2022', Policy paper, 3 November.

Department of Health and Social Care (2022) 'Vulnerabilities; applying All Our Health', March.

Department of Health and Social Care (2022) 'A plan for digital health and social care', Policy paper, 22 June.

Department of Health and Social Care (2022) *A plan for digital health and social care*, Policy paper, 22 June.

Department of Health and Social Care (2022) *Chief Social Workers' Annual Report (2021–22)* (applies to England), 11 May.

Department of Health and Social Care (2023) *Closed Consultation Oliver McGowan Draft Code of Practice on Statutory Learning Disability and Autism Training*.

Department of Health and Social Care (2023) *Digital Working in Adult Social Care: What Good Looks Like*, 17 May.

Department of Health and Social Care (2023) *Next Steps to Put People at the Heart of Care*, Policy paper, 4 April.

Department of Health and Social Care (2024) *Written Statement Update on Implementation of the Down Syndrome Act 2022*, 21 March.

Department of Health and Social Care and Cabinet Office (2021) *Build Back Better: Our Plan for Health and Social Care*, CP 500.

Department of Health and Social Care and Helen Whately MP (2022) *Our Support for Adult Social Care this Winter*, Policy paper, updated 11 January 2023.

Department of Health and Social Care (2023) *Guidance Coronavirus (COVID-19) vaccination as a condition of deployment for the delivery of CQC-regulated activities in wider adult social care settings*, updated 1 March 2022.

Department of Health and Social Care (2022) 'Social Care; Charging for Care and Support: local authority circular', LAC(DHSC)(2022), 28 February.

Department of Health and Social Care (2024) *Care and Support Statutory Guidance*, updated 24 March 2024.

Devanney, J. and Harris, J. (2014) *The National Security Council: National security at the centre of government*, London: Institute of Government.

Diver, A. and Schwehr, B. (2022) 'The significance of *R (BG and Anor) v Suffolk CC* (2021): meeting 'eligible need[s]' in social care?', *Liverpool Law Review*, 43: 539.

Dodds, S. (2013) 'Dependence, care and vulnerability', in C. Mackenzie, W. Rogers and S. Dodds (eds) *Vulnerability: New Essays in Ethics and Feminist Philosophy*, Oxford: Oxford University Press.

Dudley Metropolitan Borough Council (2020) 'Report of the Acting Director of Public Health Update on COVID-19 to Health and Adult Social Care Scrutiny Committee', 10 June.

Dudley Metropolitan Borough Council (2020) 'COVID Situation in Dudley Borough', report presented to Health and Wellbeing Board, 1 July.

Dudley Metropolitan Borough Council (2020) 'Corporate Quarterly Management Report 2020-2021. Quarter 2 (1st July to 30th September 2020), Adult Social Care Performance Evaluation'.

Dudley Metropolitan Borough Council (2020) 'Meeting of the Scrutiny Committee: Adult safeguarding and deprivation of liberty safeguards (DOLS)', 15 October.

Dudley Metropolitan Borough Council (2020) Health and Adult Social Care Scrutiny Review, 'Report of the Director of Adult Social Care Council response to the COVID-19 Pandemic – Adult Safeguarding and Deprivation of Liberty Safeguards (DOLS)', 15 October.

Dudley Metropolitan Borough Council (2020) 'Dudley Metropolitan Borough Council and Partner Response to the COVID-19 Pandemic: Report of the Health and Adult Social Care Scrutiny Committee', November.

Dudley Metropolitan Borough Council (2022) 'Dudley for Everyone: COVID-19 Looking back and moving forward', Director of Health Annual Report 2022.

Dunn, P. et al (2021) *Adult Social Care and COVID-19 after the First Wave. Assessing the Policy Response in England*, London: Health Foundation.

Eldridge, S. (2021) 'Giving assurances', *Department of Health and Social Care* blog, 25 June.

Elves, C. and Herring, J. (2020) 'Ethical framework for adult social care in COVID-19', *Journal of Medical Ethics*, 662.

Elwick, S. (2021) 'Giving assurances', *DHSC Social Care blog*, 25 June.

Engster, D. (2007) *The Heart of Justice: Care Ethics and Political Theory*, Oxford: Oxford University Press.

Equality and Human Rights Commission (2020) *How Coronavirus Has Affected Equality and Human Rights*, Is Britain Fairer? Report Series, 20 October.

Errington, A. (2020) 'Adult Social Care – Care Act Decision Report – Care Act Easements, 27 May 2020 From: Andrew Errington Adults Principal Social Worker, Sally Caren Head of Social Work, Mental Health and Sustainability To: Pete Fahy – Director of Adult Services: response to FOI request 07144', Coventry City Council.

European Observatory on Health Systems and Policies (2021) *Drawing Light from the Pandemic: A New Strategy for Health and Sustainable Development. A Review of the Evidence*, M. McKee (ed), WHO.

Ewing, K (2020) 'COVID-19: government by decree', *King's Law Journal*, 31(1).

Farrar, J. with Ahuja, A. (2021) *Spike: The Virus v the People: The Inside Story*, London: Profile Books.

Feldon, P. (for BASW) (2020) *Adults Social Work Group Response to Coronavirus Crisis*.

Feldon, P. (2023) *The Social Worker's Guide to the Care Act 2014* (2nd edn), St Albans: Critical Publishing.

Fell, G. (2008) 'Preparedness of residential and nursing homes for pandemic flu', *Journal of Public Health*, 30(1): 99–102.

Ferguson, I. and Lavalette, M. (2013) 'The crisis in adult social care', in I. Ferguson and M. Lavalette with responses from B. Jordan, M. Lymbery, D. Whitfield, I. Hood, B. Smith and C. Cairns *Adult Social Care*, Bristol: Policy Press.

Fernandez, J.-L. et al (2020) *Supporting Carers Following the Implementation of the Care Act 2014: Eligibility, Support, and Prevention*, The Carers in Adult Social Care Study, end of project report, LSE and NIHR.

Fine, M.D. (2007) *A Caring Society? Care and the Dilemmas of Human Service in the 21st Century*, New York: Palgrave Macmillan.

Fineman, M.A. (2000) 'Myths: independence, autonomy and self sufficiency', *American University Journal of Gender, Social Policy and the Law*, 8(1): 13–29.

Fineman, M. (2000) 'Cracking the foundational myths; independence, autonomy and self-sufficiency', *American University Journal of Gender, Social Policy and the Law*, 8(13): 13–29.

Fineman, M.A. (2020) 'The vulnerable subject: anchoring equality in the human condition', in M.A. Fineman (ed) *Transcending the Boundaries of Law: Generations of Feminism and Legal Theory*, New York: Routledge Cavendish.

Fisher, B. and Tronto, J. (1993) 'Towards a feminist theory of care', in E.K. Abel and M.K. Nelson (eds) *Circles of Care: Work and Identity in Women's Lives*, New York: State University of New York Press.

Flynn, S. Caton, S., Gillooly, A., Bradshaw, J., Hastings, R., Hatton, C., Jahoda, A., Mulhall, P., Todd, S., Beyer, S. and Taggart, L. et al (2021) 'The experiences of adults with learning disabilities in the UK during the COVID-19 pandemic: qualitative results from wave 1 of the coronavirus and people with learning disabilities study', *Tizard Learning Disability Review*, 26(4): 224–9.

Folbre, N. (2006) 'Measuring care: gender, empowerment and the care economy', *Journal of Human Development*, 7(2): 183–99.

Foley, N. and Foster, D. (2022) *Impact of COVID-19 Pandemic on Social Work*, research briefing, 21 March.

Forrester-Jones, R. et al (2021) 'The impact of austerity measures on people with intellectual disabilities in England', *Journal of Long-Term Care*, 241–55.

Foster, D. (2022) *Coronavirus: Adult Social Care Key Issues and Sources*, Commons Library Research Briefing, No. 9019, 14 February.

Foster, D. (2023) *Adult Social Care Workforce in England*, House of Commons Research Briefing No. 9615, 22 January 2024.

Foster, D. (2023) *Insight Delayed Hospital DIscharge and Adult Social Care*, House of Commons Library, 9 February.

Fotaki, M. et al (2023) *Bailed Out and Burned Out? The Financial Impact of COVID-19 on UK Care Homes for Older People and Their Workforce*, Coventry: Warwick Business School.

Friede, D. (2013) 'The historical decline of virtue ethics', in D.C. Russell (ed) *The Cambridge Companion to Virtue Ethics*, Cambridge: Cambridge University Press.

George, M. and Layard, A. (2022) *Thompson's Modern Land Law* (8th edn), Oxford: Oxford University Press.

Giebel, C. et al (2020) 'A UK survey of COVID-19 related social support closures and their effects on older people, people with dementia, and carers', *International Journal of Geriatric Psychiatry*, 36(3): 393–402.

Giebel, C. et al (2021) 'Impact of COVID-19 related social support service closures on people with dementia and unpaid carers: a qualitative study', *Aging and Mental Health*, 25(7): 1281–8.

Giebel, C. (2022) 'Navigating the new normal: accessing community and institutionalised care for dementia during COVID-19', *Aging and Mental Health*, 26(5): 905–10.

Gilligan, C. (1993) *In a Different Voice: Psychological Theory and Women's Development*, Cambridge, MA: Harvard University Press.

Gingrich, J.R. (2011) *Making Markets in the Welfare State: The Politics of Varying Market Reforms*, Cambridge: Cambridge University Press.

Giovannini, A. (2021) 'In the eye of the storm: English local government and the COVID-19 crisis', in J.R. Bryson et al (eds) *Living with Pandemics: Places, People and Policy*, Cheltenham: Edward Elgar Publishing.

Girma, S. and Paten, P. (2023) 'COVID-19 vaccines as a condition of employment: impact on uptake, staffing, and mortality in elderly care homes', in *Management Science*, 17(5).

Glasby, J., Robinson, S. and Allen, K. (2024) *Achieving Closure: Good Practice in Supporting Older People During Residential Care Home Closures*, University of Birmingham-ADASS report, in association with SCIE, July.

Goodin, R.E. (1985) *Protecting the Vulnerable: A Re-analysis of our Social Responsibilities*, Chicago, IL: University of Chicago Press.

Gorsky, M. (2013) '"Searching for the People in Charge": appraising the 1983 Griffiths NHS Management Inquiry', *Medical History*, 57(1): 87–107.

Gostin, L.O. (2004) 'International infectious disease law: revision of the World Health Organisation's international health regulations', *Journal of the American Medical Association*, 29(2): 2623–7.

Gostin, L.O. (2006) 'The international health regulations: a new paradigm for global health governance', in S.A.M. McLean (ed) *First Do No Harm: Law, Ethics and Healthcare*, London: Routledge.

Gostin, L.O. (2014) *Global Health Law*, Cambridge, MA: Harvard University Press.

Gostin, L.O. and Katz, R. (2016) 'The international health regulations: the governing framework for global health security', *Milbank Quarterly*, 96(2): 264–313.

Gostin, L.O., Wiley, L.F. and Frieden, T.R.F. (2016) *Public Health Law: Power, Duty and Restraint* (3rd edn), Beley, CA: University of California Press.

Gouws, A. and van Zyl, M. (2015) 'Towards a feminist ethics of *ubuntu*: bridging rights and *ubuntu*', in D. Engster and M. Harrington (eds) *Care Ethics and Political Theory*, Oxford: Oxford University Press.

Grech, S. (2009) 'Disability, poverty and development: critical reflections on the majority world debate', *Disability and Society*, 24(6): 771–84.

Greene, A. (2020) *Emergency Powers in a Time of Pandemic*, Bristol: Bristol University Press.

Greene, A. (2021) 'Falling at the first hurdle? *Terhes v Romania*: lockdowns and normalising the exception', *Strasbourg Observers*, 18 June.

Grez Hidalgo, P., de Londras, F. and Lock, D. (2022) 'Parliament, the pandemic, and constitutional principle in the United Kingdom: a study of the Coronavirus Act 2020', *Modern Law Review*, 85(6): 1463–1503.

Griffiths, R. (1983) *NHS Management Inquiry*, London: Department of Health and Social Security.

Griffiths, R. (1988) *Community Care: Agenda for Action. A Report to the Secretary of State for Social Services*, London: HMSO

Grove, H. (2021) 'Ageing as well as you can in place: applying a geographical lens to the capability approach', *Social Science and Medicine*, 288: 113525.

Ham, C. (2017) 'Theresa May is right to drop the "'dementia tax'" – the social care system needs considered reform', *The Telegraph*, 22 May.

H.M. Government (2008) *Shaping the Future of Care Together*, Cm 7673, London: HMSO.

H.M. Government (2013) *Guidance: Preparation and Planning for Emergencies*, 20 February.

H.M. Government (2021) *The National Strategy for Autistic Children, Young People and Adults: 2021 to 2026*.

H.M. Government (2020) Pandemic Influenza (Emergency) Bill, INQ000023118_1–3. Draft issued to UK COVID-19 Inquiry, dated 21 January 2020.

H.M. Treasury (2022) 'National Insurance increase reversed', News story, 22 September.

Hallett, C. (1983) 'Social workers: their role and tasks', *British Journal of Social Work*, 13(4): 395–404.

Halwani, R. (2003) 'Care ethics and virtue ethics', *Hypatia*, 18(3): 161–92.

Hamlin, C. and Sidley, P. (1998) 'Revolutions in public health: 1848, and 1998?', *BMJ*, 317(7158): 587–91.

Hampton, J. (2016) *Disability and the Welfare State in Britain: Changes in Perception and Policy 1948–79*, Bristol: Policy Press.

Hancock, M. (2020) HC Coronavirus Bill Debate, Hansard Volume 674, Column 59, March 2020.

Hardhill, I, Grotz, J. and Crawford, L. (eds) (2022) *Mobilising Voluntary Action in the UK: Learning from the Pandemic*, Bristol: Policy Press.

Harding, R. (2017) *Duties to Care: Dementia, Relationality and the Law*, Cambridge: Cambridge University Press.

Harding, R. (2021) 'COVID-19 in adult social care: futures, funding and fairness', in D. Cowan and A. Mumford (eds) *Pandemic Legalities: Legal Responses to COVID-19 Justice and Social Responsibility*, Bristol: Bristol University Press.

Harding, R. and Taşcıoğlu, E. (2017) 'Everyday Decisions Project: Supporting Legal Capacity Through Care, Support and Encouragement', November, Birmingham Law School, available at www.legalcapacity.org.uk/research-findings

Harris, J. (2024) 'Birmingham's cuts reveal the ugly truth about Britain in 2024: the state is abandoning its people', *The Guardian*, 17 March.

Harvey, M., Hastings, D.P. and Chowdhury, G. (2023) 'Understanding the costs and challenges of the digital divide through UK council services', *Journal of Information Science*, 49(5): 1153–67.

Harwood, A. (2019) 'Whorlton Hall: advisers quit government review in protest at CQC's handling of abuse scandal', *BMJ*, 365.

Hayes, J. (2021) 'Birmingham hospitals "have more COVID patients than anywhere else in country"', *Birmingham Mail*, 20 November.

Healthwatch Network (2020) *A Guide to Running Healthwatch*, guidance, 12 February.

Healthwatch Shropshire (2020) 'Health Care, Social Care and Well-being Services during the COVID-19 Pandemic', 7 July.

Healthwatch England, working with the British Red Cross (2020) *590 People's Stories of Leaving Hospital during COVID-19: A Joint Report*, October.

Held, V. (2006) *The Ethics of Care: Personal, Political and Global*, Oxford: Oxford University Press.

Hemmings, N., Oung, C. and Schlepper, L. (2022) *New Horizons: What Can England Learn from the Professionalisation of Care Workers in Other Countries?*, Research report, London: Nuffield Trust.

Henderson, G. and Bryan, W.V. (2011) *Psychosocial Aspects of Disability* (4th edn), Springfield, IL: Charles C. Thomas.

Henwood, M. et al (2022) 'Self-funders: still by-standers in the English social care market?', *Social Policy and Society*, 21(2): 227–41.

Herefordshire Council (2022) 'Understanding Herefordshire: People and Places', webpage.

Herefordshire Council (2020) 'Record of Operational Decision: To make a formal decision to implement easements to the Care Act 2014, Introduced by the Coronavirus Act 2020 and associated Regulations', Stephen Vickers, Director of Adults and Communities, 4 May.

Herefordshire Council (2020) 'Equality Impact Assessment Form – Easement of Care Act duties', signed Mandy Appleby, Appendix 3, 4 May.

Herefordshire Council (2021) 'Herefordshire Council's response to the COVID Pandemic Meeting: General scrutiny committee Meeting date: Friday 11 June 2021. Report by: Solicitor to the council'.

Herring, J. (1999) 'The Human Rights Act and the welfare principle in family law: conflicting or complementary?', *Child and Family Law Quarterly*, 11(3): 223–35.

Herring, J. (2013) *Caring and the Law*, Oxford: Bloomsbury.

Herring, J. (2019) *Family Law* (9th edn), Harlow: Pearson.

Herring, J. and Foster, C. (2012) 'Welfare means relationality, virtue and altruism', *Legal Studies*, 32(3): 480–98.

Hidalgo, P.G., de Londras, F. and Lock, D. (2022) 'Parliament, the pandemic, and constitutional principle in the United Kingdom: a study of the Coronavirus Act 2020', *Modern Law Review*, 85(6): 1463–1503.

Hill, J. (2020) 'Exclusive: five councils start by-passing Care Act duties amid Covid pressure', *Local Government Chronicle*, 24 April.

Hill, A. (2012) 'Winterbourne View care home staff jailed for abusing residents', *The Guardian*, 26 October.

Hill, J. (2020) 'Military planners tasked with assisting local virus response', *Local Government Chronicle*, 16 March.

Hill, J. (2021) 'ADASS president: social care system is "past breaking point – it's broken"', *Local Government Chronicle*, 24 September.

Hine, D. (2010) *The 2009 Influenza Pandemic. An Independent Review into the Response to the 2009 Swine Flu Pandemic*, Cabinet Office, July.

Hodgson, K., Grimm, F., Vestesson, E., Brine, R. and Deeny, S. (2020) *Briefing: Adult Social Care and COVID-19: Assessing the impact on social care users and staff in England so far*, London: The Health Foundation, July.

Horovitz, J. and Bucciarelli, F. (2020) 'The lost days that made Bergamo a coronavirus tragedy: behind the curve', *The New York Times*, 29 November.

House of Commons Communities and Local Government Committee (2017) *Adult Social Care*, Ninth Report of Session 2016-7 HC 1103.

House of Commons Levelling Up, Housing and Communities Committee and Health and Social Care Select Committee (2018) *Long-term Funding of Adult Social Care*, First Joint Report of the Health and Social Care and Housing, Communities and Local Government Committees of Session 2017–19.

House of Commons Levelling Up, Housing and Communities Committee and Health and Social Care Select Committee (2022) *Long-term Funding of Adult Social Care*, Second Report of Session 2022–23, HC 19.

House of Commons Women and Equalities Select Committee (2020a) *Unequal Impact? Coronavirus, Disability, and Access to Services: Interim Report on Temporary Provisions in the Coronavirus Act*, First Report of Session 2019–21, HC 386, 22 September.

House of Commons Women and Equalities Select Committee (2020b) *Unequal Impact? Coronavirus, Disability, and Access to Services: Full Report*, Fourth Report of Session 2019–21, HC 1050, 22 December.

House of Commons Health and Social Care, and Science and Technology Committees (2021) *Coronavirus: Lessons Learned to Date*, Sixth Report of the Health and Social Care Committee and Third Report of the Science and Technology Committee of Session 2021–22, HC 92, 12 October.

House of Commons Committee of Public Accounts (2024) *Reforming Adult Social Care in England*, Twenty-Second Report of Session 2023–24, HC 437.

House of Commons Committee of Public Accounts (2024) 'Adult social care: PAC raises alarm as Government fall short of promise to fix crisis', News article, 20 March.

House of Commons and House of Lords, Joint Committee on the National Security Strategy (2020) *Biosecurity and National Security*, First Report of Session 2019–21, HC 611; HL 195, 18 December.

House of Commons and House of Lords (2022) Joint Committee on Human Rights Protecting Human Rights in Care Settings Fourth Report of Session 2022-23, HC 216, HL Paper 51, 22 July.

House of Commons House of Lords Joint Committee on Human Rights (2020) *The Government's Response to COVID-19: Human Rights Implications.* Seventh Report of Session 2019–21, HC 265; HL Paper 125, 21 September.

House of Lords Adult Social Care Committee (2022) *A 'Gloriously Ordinary Life': Spotlight on Adult Social Care*, Adult Social Care Committee Report of Session 2022–23, HL Paper 99.

House of Lords COVID-19 Committee (2021) *Beyond Digital: Planning for a Hybrid World*, First Report of Session 2019–21, HL Paper 263.

House of Lords COVID-19 Committee Report (2022) *Living in a COVID World: A Long-term Approach to Resilience and Wellbeing*, 3rd Report of Session 2021–22, 16 March, HL Paper 117.

Hudson, B. (2021) *Clients, Consumers or Citizens: The Privatisation of Adult Social Care in England*, Bristol: Policy Press.

Humphries, R. (2022) *Ending the Social Care Crisis: A New Road to Reform*, Bristol: Policy Press.

Hunter, D.J. (2020) 'Strictly come partnering: are health and wellbeing boards the answer?', in A. Bonner (ed) *Local Authorities and the Social Determinants of Health*, Bristol: Policy Press.

Hunter, D.J. and Judge, K. (1988) *Griffiths and Community Care: Meeting the Challenge*, London: King's Fund Institute.

Hunter, D.J., Perkins, N., Visram, S. et al (2018) *Evaluating the Leadership Role of Health and Wellbeing Boards as Drivers of Health Improvement and Integrated Care across England*, report.

Hursthouse, R. (2001) *On Virtue Ethics*, Oxford: Oxford University Press.

Iacobucci, G. (2018) 'New CQC-style inspections don't raise standards or improve patient safety, say RCGP members', *BMJ*, 363.

IMPACT (2024) 'IMPACT's co-production approach', webpage.

Inclusion International (2021) *A Global Agenda for Inclusive Recovery: Ensuring People with Intellectual Disabilities and their Families are Included in a Post-COVID World*, report, London: Inclusion International.

Industrial Injuries Advisory Council (2022) *COVID-19 and Occupational Impacts*, independent report, 16 November.

Institute for Government (2022) 'Timeline of UK Government coronavirus lockdowns and measures March 2020 to December 2021', webpage.

Iqbal, A. et al (2023) 'A scoping review of the costs, consequences, and wider impacts of residential care home closures in a UK context', *Health and Social Care in the Community*, vol. 2023.

Industrial Injuries Advisory Council (2022) *COVID-19 and Occupational Impacts*, independent report, 16 November.

Irwin, D. (2021) '"Viruses are much cleverer than we are" – Solihull public health chief on why COVID battle has changed but isn't over', *Birmingham Mail*, 17 August.

Jagger, S. and Harris, P. (2024) 'Whorlton Hall; four carers sentenced for abusing hospital patients', *BBC News*, 19 January.

James, W. (2021) 'England's "freedom day" marred by soaring cases and isolation chaos', *Reuters News*, 19 July.

Jaspers, S. and Steen, T. (2019) 'Realizing public values: enhancement or obstruction? Exploring value tensions and coping strategies in the co-production of social care', *Public Management Review*, 21: 606–27.

Jenkinson, A.J. and Chamberlain, J. (2019) 'Social workers' knowledge and skills and the Care Act: Practice Advice Note', November, NIHR Policy Research Unit in Health and Social Care Workforce, The Policy Institute, King's College London.

Kayess, R. and French, P. (2008) 'Out of darkness into light: introducing the United Nations Convention on the Rights of Persons with Disabilities', *Human Rights Law Review*, 8(1): 1–34.

Keenan, P.M. and Doody, O. (2023) 'An update of the reported effects of the COVID-19 pandemic on persons with intellectual disability and their carers: a scoping review', *Annals of Medicine*, 55(1).

Kelly, D. (2013) 'Editorial: Reflecting on the implications of the Care Act 2014 for care providers,' *Journal of Care Services Management*, (7): 74–5.

Kelly, R. (2015) 'Pre-legislative scrutiny under the Coalition Government 2010-2015', House of Commons Library Briefing Paper no 05859, 13 August.

King, D. et al (2022) *Respond, Recover, Reset: Two Years On*, Nottingham: Trent University, Centre for People, Work, Organisational Practice.

Kingstone, T. et al (2022) 'Exploring the Impact of the First Wave of COVID-19 on Social Work Practice: A Qualitative Study in England, UK', *British Journal of Social Work*, 52(4): 2043–62

Kong, S.-T. Noone, C. and Shears, J. (2022) 'Social workers' sensual bodies during COVID-19: the suspended, displaced and reconstituted body in social work practice', *British Journal of Social Work*, 52(5): 2834–53.

Kunonga T.P. et al (2021) 'Effects of digital technologies on older people's access to health and social care umbrella review', *Journal of Medical Internet Research*, 23(11) (online 24 November).

Lackenby, S. (2020) 'Adult Social Care', Appendix 1, short report, 22 April, Sandwell Council.

Lancet (2020) 'Editorial: Redefining vulnerability in the era of COVID-19', *The Lancet*, 395(10230): P1098.

Law Commission (2008) *Adult Social Care Scoping Review*, 26 November.

Law Commission (2010) *Adult Social Care Consultation Paper*, 24 February, Law Com No 192.

Law Commission (2011) *Adult Social Care Law*, Law Com No 326, HC 941, 10 May.

Lawson, A. and Beckett, A.E. (2021) 'The social and human rights model of disability: towards a complementarity thesis', *International Journal of Human Rights*, 25(2): 348.

Lawson, J. on behalf of the ADASS and the LGA (2017) *Making Safeguarding Personal. For Safeguarding Adults Boards.*

Learner, S. (2022) 'Government U-turn on mandatory COVID vaccine branded "a joke" and "too late" by care homes', *Carehome.co.uk*, 1 Feb. https://wwwwww.carehome.co.uk/news/article.cfm/id/1664289/u-turn-covid-vaccine-care-homes

Learning Disability England (2020) 'Disabled peoples' rights, DNR, and COVID-19', webpage.

Learning Disability England (2020) 'Do not resuscitate notices and people with learning disabilities. January–April 2020 in COVID-19: Findings from our survey', May.

Leckey, R. (2008) *Contextual Subjects: Family, State and Relational Theory*, Toronto: University of Toronto Press.

Lee, J. and Gillett, F. (2021) 'COVID-19: "For us it's not freedom day, is it?"', *BBC News*, 6 July.

Leigh Day (2021) 'Eleven pandemic simulation exercises were staged between 2015–2019', 10 June, available at www.leighday.co.uk/news/news/2021-news/eleven-pandemic-simulation-exercises-were-staged-between-2015-19/

Lewis, S. (2023) 'Care homes closing at twice rate of openings, study finds', *Care Home Professional*, 27 February.

Leverton, M. Samsi, K. Woolham, J. and Manthorpe, J. (2023) '"I have enough pressure as it is, without the worry of doing something wrong because of ignorance": the impact of COVID-19 on people who employ social care personal assistants', *British Journal of Social Work*, 53(2): 1243–62.

Liberty (2020) 'Liberty and Disability Charities Warn Councils not to Weaken Social Care During Coronavirus Pandemic', 7 May, available at www.libertyhumanrights.org.uk/issue/liberty-and-disability-charities-warn-councils-not-to-weaken-social-care-during-coronavirus-pandemic/

Livrani, M. and Coker, R. (2012) 'Protecting Europe from diseases: from the international sanitary conferences to the ECDC', *Journal of Health Politics, Policy and Law*, 37(6): 915–34.

Local Government and Social Care Ombudsman (2021) 'Decision: Staffordshire County Council (20 004 894)', dated 3 February.

Local Government and Social Care Ombudsman (2022) *Unprecedented Pressure: Learning from Complaints about Council and Care Provider Actions during the COVID-19 Pandemic*, February.

Local Government Association (2018) *The Lives We Want to Lead: The LGA Green Paper for Adult Social Care and Wellbeing LGA Consultation Response*, London: Local Government Association.

Local Government Association (2019) *What a Difference a Place Makes: The Growing Impact of Health and Wellbeing Boards*, report, June.

Local Government Association (2020) 'Emergency response structures during the COVID-19 pandemic. Councillor guidance', May.

Local Government Association (2020) *Digital Innovation in Adult Social Care: How We've Been Supporting Communities during COVID-19. What We Have Done, What We Have Learned and What Next for Digital Innovation in Adult Social Care*, August. REF 25.172.

Local Government Association (2021) *A Perfect Storm – Health Inequalities and the Impact of COVID-19*, April.

Local Government Association (2021) *COVID-19 Adult Safeguarding Insight Project – Third Report*, December.

Local Government Association (2023) 'Section 114 fear for almost 1 in 5 council leaders and chief executives after cashless Autumn Statement', 6 December.

Local Government Association (2024) 'Digital transformation in adult social care', available at www.local.gov.uk/our-support/partners-care-and-health/informatics/digital-transformation-adult-social-care

Lord Phillips (2000) *The BSE Inquiry Volume 1 Findings and Conclusions*.

Locality (2020) *We Were Built for This: How community groups helped us through the coronavirus crisis - and how we can build a better future*, London, June.

Lotinga, A. (2015) 'Context matters: general practice and social work: the Birmingham story', *Journal of Integrated Care*, 23(2): 88–95.

Lunt, C. et al (2021) 'Outcomes for older people with long-term conditions attending day care services delivered by paid staff or volunteers: a comparative study', *Palliative Care and Social Practice*, 15.

McKee, M. and van Schalkwyk, M.C.I. (2022) 'Editorial: England's U-turn on COVID-19 vaccine mandate for NHS staff', *BMJ*, 376: o353 h.

Macdonald, K. and Morgan, H.M. (2021) 'The impact of austerity on disabled, elderly and immigrants in the United Kingdom: a literature review', *Disability and Society*, 36(7):1125–47.

Macfarlane, F., Exworthy, M. and Willmott, M. (2011) 'The 1983 Griffiths Inquiry', in M. Exworthy et al (eds) *Shaping Health Policy: Case Study Methods and Analysis*, Bristol: Policy Press, pp 135–50.

MacInnes, J.S., Bertini L. and Walker, S. (2023) 'Does a discharge to assess programme introduced in England meet the quadruple aim of service improvement?', *Journal of Integrated Care*, 33(1): 16.

Machin, R. (2023) 'UK local government experience of COVID-19 lockdown: local responses to global challenges', *Local Economy*, 38(1): 80–91.

Mackenzie, C. (2013) 'The importance of relational autonomy and capabilities for an ethics of vulnerability', in C. Mackenzie, W. Rogers and S. Dodds (eds) *Vulnerability: New Essays in Ethics and Feminist Philosophy*, New York: Oxford University Press.

Mackenzie, C. (2021) 'Relational autonomy', in K.Q. Hall and Ásta (eds) *The Oxford Handbook of Feminist Philosophy*, Oxford: Oxford University Press.

Mackenzie, C. and Stoljar, N. (2000) 'Introduction: autonomy refigured', in C. Mackenzie and N. Stoljar (eds) *Relational Autonomy: Feminist Perspectives on Autonomy, Agency and the Social Self*, Oxford: Oxford University Press, pp 3–31.

MacLochlainn, J., Manthorpe, J., Mallett, J. et al (2023) 'The COVID-19 pandemic's impact on UK older people's social workers: a mixed-methods study', *British Journal of Social Work*, 53(8): 3838–59.

Madianou, M. (2020) 'A second-order disaster? Digital technologies during the COVID-19 pandemic', *Social Media + Society*, 6(3).

Maguire, D. et al (2018) *Digital Change in Health and Social Care*, King's Fund report, June.

Mao, G., Fernandes-Jesus, M., Ntontis, E. and Drury, J. (2021) 'What have we learned about COVID-19 volunteering in the UK? A rapid review of the literature', *BMC Public Health* 21: 140.

Marczak, J. et al (2022) 'How have the Care Act 2014 ambitions to support carers translated into local practice? Findings from a process evaluation study of local stakeholders' perceptions of Care Act implementation', *Health and Social Care in the Community*, 30(5): e1711–e1720.

Marmot, M. et al (2020) *Build Back Fairer: The COVID-19 Marmot Review. The Pandemic, Socioeconomic and Health Inequalities in England*, London: Institute of Health Equity, The Health Foundation.

Marshall, F., Gordon, A., Gladman, J. and Bishop, S. (2021) 'Care homes, their communities, and resilience in the face of the COVID-19 pandemic: interim findings from a qualitative study', *BMC Geriatrics*, 21: 102.

May, J.R. and Daly, E. (2020) *Advanced Introduction to Human Dignity and Law*, Cheltenham: Edward Elgar.

McBride, S. (2020) 'Government stays silent on draft coronavirus pandemic emergency bill after Belfast meeting cancelled', *The Independent*, 27 February.

McCarey, M. et al (2022) *Health and Brexit: Six Years On*, Nuffield Trust report.

McClelland, A.G. and Shaw, D. (2023) 'Resilience to disruptions: the role of regional soft spaces', *Regional Studies*, 1–13.

McGowan, V.J. and Bambra, C. (2022) 'COVID-19 mortality and deprivation: pandemic, syndemic, and endemic health inequalities', *Lancet Public Health*, e-966–e-975.

McHale, J.V. (2023) 'Choosing home: discharge to assess and the Health and Care Act 2022', *Northern Ireland Legal Quarterly*, 74(4): 713–38.

McHale, J.V. and Noszlopy, L. (2021) *Adult Social Care Provision under Pressure: Lessons from the Pandemic*, initial report, Birmingham: University of Birmingham, available at www.birmingham.ac.uk/documents/coll ege-artslaw/law/research/adult-social-care-provision-under-pressure-less ons-from-the-pandemic-november-2021.pdf

McKee, M. and Van Shalwyk, M.C.I. (2023) 'England's U turn on COVID-19 vaccine mandate for NHS staff', *The BMJ*, 376: 0353H.

McNicholl, A. (2025) 'Social workers forced to cut care package', *Community Care*, 4 June.

McClelland, A.G. and Shaw, D. (2023) 'Resilience to disruption; the role of the regional safe space', *Regional Studies*, October.

MENCAP (2020) *Easy Read Guide about the Care Act Easements*, 3 April.

Migration Advisory Committee (2022) *Adult Social Care and Immigration: A Report from the Migration Advisory Committee*, April, CP665.

Minns, N. (2020) 'Officer Key Decision made under the Council's Urgency Procedure by the Strategic Director for People on 9th April 2020: Coronavirus COVID-19: Care Act Easements', Warwickshire County Council.

Mishna, F., Milne, E., Bogo, M. et al (2021) 'Responding to COVID-19: new trends in social workers' use of information and communication technology', *Clinical Social Work*, 49: 484–94.

Mitra, S. (2006) 'The capability approach and disability', *Journal of Disability Policy Studies*, 16(4): 236–47.

Moore, V.L. and Graham, L.D. (2022) 'R *(Gardner and Harris) v Secretary of State for Health and Social care and Others* [2022] EWHC 967: scant regard for COVID-19 risk to care homes', *Medical Law Review*, 30(4): 734–43.

Moosavian, R., Walker, C. and Blick, A. (2021) 'Coronavirus legislative responses in the UK: regression to panic and disdain of constitutionalism', *Northern Ireland Legal Quarterly*, 72(1): 1–36.

Morciano, M., Stokes, J., Kontopantelis, K., Hall, I. and Turner, A.J. (2021) 'Excess mortality for care home residents during the first 23 weeks of the COVID-19 pandemic in England: a national cohort study 2021', *BMC Medicine*, 19(71).

Moral and Ethical Advisory Group (2020) 'Meeting note', 1–10 March.

Moritz, J. (2020) 'COVID-19 volunteers 'not being called upon' to help NHS', *BBC News*, 24 April.

Munro, V. and Scoular, J. (2012) 'Abusing vulnerability? Contemporary law and policy responses to sex work in the UK', *Feminist Legal Studies*, 20(3): 189–206.

Murray, L. and Barnes, M. (2010) 'Have families been rethought? Ethic of care, family and "whole family" approaches', *Social Policy & Society* 9(4): 533–44.

Murray, J. (2023) 'Birmingham City Council declares itself in financial distress', *The Guardian*, 5 September.

National Audit Office (2017) *Investigation into NHS Continuing Healthcare Funding*, Report by the Comptroller and Auditor General, Session 2017–19, HC 239, 5 July.

Nayashanu, M., Pfende, F. and Ekpenyung, H. (2020) 'Exploring the challenges faced by frontline workers in health and social care amid the COVID-19 pandemic: experiences of frontline workers in the English Midlands region, UK', *Journal of Interprofessional Care*, 34(5): 655–61.

Nedelsky, J. (2011) *Law's Relations: A Relational Theory of Self, Autonomy, and Law*, Oxford: Oxford University Press.

Needham, C. (2007) *Reform of Public Services under New Labour: Narratives of Consumerism*, Basingstoke: Palgrave Macmillan.

Needham, C. (2011) *Personalising Public Services: Understanding the Personalisation Narrative*, Bristol: Policy Press.

Needham, C. (2013) 'Personalization: from day centres to community hubs?', *Critical Social Policy*, 34(1): 90–108.

Needham, C. and Glasby, J. (eds) (2014) *Debates in Personalisation*, Bristol: Policy Press.

Needham, C. and Glasby, J. (2023) 'Forgotten, neglected and a poor relation? Reflecting on the 75th anniversary of adult social care', in M. Exworthy, R. Mannion and M. Powell (eds) *The NHS at 75: The State of UK Health Policy*, Bristol: Policy Press.

Needham, C. and Hall, P. (2023) *Social Care in the UK's Four Nations: Between Two Paradigms*, Bristol: Policy Press.

Needham, C. and Humphries, R. (2022) *Ending the Social Care Crisis: A New Road to Reform*, Bristol: Bristol Policy Press.

New Local (2020) 'Council's response to COVID-19 – Leadership Index Edition 9', May.

NHS Confederation (2022) *The Unequal Impact of COVID-19: Investigating the Effect on People with Certain Protected Characteristics. How Health and Care Systems Are Devising Innovative Approaches to Mitigate the Direct Effects of COVID-19*, 15 June.

NHS South West of England (2012) *Report of the NHS Review of the Commissioning of Care and Treatment at Winterbourne View*.

Norrie, C., Luitnenburg, O., Moriarty, J., Samsi, K. and Manthorpe, J. (2023) ' "You're out on a limb, on your own": social care personal assistants' (PAs') reflections on working in the COVID-19 pandemic – implications for wider health and care services', *PLOS One*, 18(12).

Nuffield Council on Bioethics (2007) *Public Health: Ethical Issues*, London: Nuffield Council on Bioethics.

Nussbaum, M.C. (2011) *Creating Capabilities: The Human Development Approach*, Cambridge, MA: Harvard University Press.

Nyashanu, M., Pfende, F. and Ekpenyong, M.S. (2023) 'Triggers of mental health problems among frontline healthcare workers during the COVID-19 pandemic in private care homes and domiciliary care agencies: lived experiences of care workers in the Midlands region, UK', *Health and Social Care in the Community*, 30: e370–e376.

O'Brien, L. (2021) 'Shropshire day services centres to remain closed until mid-February', *Shropshire Star*, 27 January 2021.

Ó Néill, C. (2022) 'This is no country for old (wo)men'? An examination of the approach taken to care home residents during the COVID-19 pandemic', *Medical Law Review*, 31(1): 25–46

O'Neill, O. (1983) 'I. Kant after virtue', *Inquiry*, 26(4): 387–405.

Office for Health Improvement and Disparities (2022) *Vulnerabilities: Applying All Our Health*, guidance (formerly Public Health England), 29 March.

Office for National Statistics (2020) *Deaths involving COVID-19 in the Care Sector, England and Wales: Deaths Registered between Week Ending 20 March 2020 and Week Ending 21 January 2022*.

Office for National Statistics (2020) *Deaths involving COVID-19 by Local Area and Socioeconomic Deprivation: Deaths Occurring between 1 March and 17 April 2020*, statistical bulletin, 1 May.

Office for National Statistics (2021) 'How life has changed in Telford & Wrekin: Census 2021'. 19 January.

Office for National Statistics (2023) 'How life has changed in Stoke-on-Trent: Census 2021', 19 January.

Oliver, D. (2016) 'NHS continuing care is a mess', *BMJ*, 354.

Oliver, D. (2019) 'NHS continuing care confusion', *BMJ*, 366.

Oliver, M. (1990) The individual and social models of disability', paper presented at the Joint Workshop of the Living Options Group and the Research Unit of the Royal College of Physicians on People with established Locomotor Disabilities in Hospitals, 23 July.

Onwumere, J., Creswell, C., Livingston, J. et al (2021) 'COVID-19 and UK family carers: policy implications', *The Lancet Psychiatry*, 8(10): 929–36.

Orellana, K., Manthorpe, J. and Tinker, A. (2020a) 'Day centres for older people: a systematically conducted scoping review of literature about their benefits, purposes and how they are perceived', *Ageing and Society*, 40(1): 73–104.

Orellana, K., Manthorpe, J. and Tinker, A. (2020) 'Day centres for older people – attender characteristics, access routes and outcomes of regular attendance: findings of exploratory mixed methods case study research', *BMC Geriatrics*, 20(1): 158.

Orellana, K., Manthorpe, J. and Tinker, A. (2021) 'Making my day. Volunteering or working at a day centre for older people: findings of exploratory research in English day centres', *Journal of Long Term Care*, 177–91.

Ostrom, E. (1996) 'Crossing the great divide: coproduction, synergy, and development', *World Development*, 24(6): 1073–87.

Otte, J. (2021) '"No jab, no job": care home workers in England on the COVID vaccine mandate', *The Guardian*, 11 November.

Ottway, S. (2013) 'The elderly in the eighteenth century workhouse', in J. Reinarz and L. Schwartz (eds) *Medicine and the Workhouse*, Rochester, NY: University of Rochester Press/Boydell & Brewer.

Our Legal Correspondent (1985) 'Detaining patients with AIDS', 19 October, *BMJ*, 291, 1102.

Parliamentary and Health Service Ombudsman (2020) 'NHS continuing healthcare failing to provide care for most vulnerable, says Ombudsman', blog, 4 November.

Pascoe, K.M. (2022) 'Remote service delivery during the COVID-19 pandemic: questioning the impact of technology on relationship-based social work practice', *British Journal of Social Work*, 52(6): 3268–87.

Pink, S., Ferguson, H. and Kell, L. (2022) 'Digital social work: conceptualising a hybrid anticipatory practice', *Qualitative Social Work*, 21(2): 413–30.

Plomin, J. (2019) 'Whorlton Hall hospital abuse and how it was uncovered', *BBC News*, 22 May.

Polzer, T. and Goncharenko, G. (2022) 'The UK COVID-19 app: the failed co-production of a digital public service', *Financial Accountability and Management*, 38(2): 281–97.

Poole, D. (2020) 'Dudley's adult social care team up for national award', *Dudley News*, 16 September.

Priaulx, N. (2002) 'Charging for after-care services under section 117 of the Mental Health Act 1983 – the final word?', *Journal of Mental Health Law*, 313–22.

Priaulx, N. (2007) *The Harm Paradox: Tort Law and the Unwanted Child in an Era of Choice*, Abingdon: Routledge.

Price, D., Drake, P., Allen, N. and Astbury, J. (2022) *The Impact of Care Act Easements under the Coronavirus Act 2020 on Older Carers Supporting Family Members Living with Dementia at Home*, NIHR Older People and Frailty Policy Research Unit, final report, November.

Prime Minister's Office 10 Downing Street (2020) 'Prime Minister's Statement on Coronavirus (COVID-19),' 23March.

Prime Minister's Office 10 Downing Street (2021) 'Prime Minister confirms move to Plan B in England', press release, 8 December.

Pritchard-Jones, L. (2015) 'Night-time care, Article 8 and the European Court of Human Rights: a missed opportunity?', *Journal of Social Welfare and Family Law*, 37(1): 108–10.

Pritchard-Jones, L. (2020) 'The Care Act 2014 and the Mental Capacity Act 2005: learning lessons for the future', in Braye, S. and Preston-Shoot, M. (eds) *The Care Act 2014: Wellbeing in Practice*, London: Sage.

Pritchard-Jones, L., Mehmi, M., Eccleston-Turner, M. and Brammer, A. (2022) 'Exploring the changes and challenges of COVID-19 in adult safeguarding practice: qualitative findings from a mixed-methods project', *Journal of Adult Protection*, 24(3–4): 132–48.

Public Administration Committee (2020) *Parliamentary Scrutiny of the Government's Handling of COVID-19*, 10 September.

Public Health England (2016) *Report: Exercise Alice Middle East Respiratory Syndrome Coronavirus (MERS-Cov)*, 5 February.

Public Health England (2017) *Exercise Cygnus Report. Tier One Command Post Exercise. Pandemic Influenza – 18 to 20 October 2016*, 13 July.

Public Health England (2020) *Summary Note on Exercise Nimbus Novel Coronavirus Preparation*, 12 February, COVID-19 Inquiry paper INQ000273915_001.

Public Health England (2020) *Disparities in the Risks and Outcomes of COVID-19*, 11 August.

Public Health England (2020) 'Stoke-on-Trent Local Authority Health Profile 2019', 3 March.

Qizilbash, M. (2020) 'Historical antecedents and philosophical debates', in S. Osmani, E. Chiappero-Martinetti and Qizilbash (eds) *The Cambridge Handbook of the Capability Approach*, Cambridge: Cambridge University Press.

Quigley, W.P. (1996) 'Five hundred years of the English Poor Laws, 1349–1834: regulating the working and nonworking poor', *Akron Law Review*, 30(1/4).

Quinn, G. and Degener, T. (2002) 'The moral authority for change: human rights values and the worldwide process of disability reform', in G. Quinn and T. Degener (eds) *Human Rights and Disability: The Current Use and Future Potential of UN Human Rights Instruments in the Context of Disability*, Geneva: United Nations.

Rajan, S., Comas-Herrera, A. and McKee, M. (2020) 'Did the UK Government really throw a protective ring around care homes in the COVID-19 pandemic?', *Journal of Long-Term Care*, (0): 185–95.

Raleigh, V. (2022) *What Is Happening to Life Expectancy in England?*, King's Fund Long Read, 9 August.

Ratzon, A., Farhi, M., Ratzon, N. and Adini, B. (2022) 'Resilience at work, burnout, secondary trauma, and compassion satisfaction of social workers amidst the COVID-19 pandemic', *International Journal of Environmental Research and Public Health*, 19(9): 5500.

Rawlings, G.H., Gaskell, C., Rolling, K. and Beail, N. (2021) 'Exploring how to deliver videoconference-mediated psychological therapy to adults with an intellectual disability during the coronavirus pandemic', *Intellectual Disabilities Research*, 15(1): 1–10.

Razavi, S. (2007) *The Political and Social Economy of Care in a Development Context Conceptual Issues, Research Questions and Policy Options*, United Nations Research Institute for Social Development, Gender and Development Programme Paper, Number 3, June.

Redhead, C.A.B. et al (2022) 'Relationships, rights and responsibilities: (re) viewing the NHS constitution for the post-pandemic "new normal"', *Medical Law Review*, 31 (1): 83–108.

Renda, A. and Castro, R. (2020) 'Toward stronger EU governance of health threats after the COVID-19 pandemic', *European Journal of Risk Regulation*, 1–10.

Rendall, J. et al (2022) 'Relationships between community-led mutual aid groups and the state during the COVID-19 pandemic: complementary, supplementary, or adversarial?', *Public Management Review*.

Rothstein, M. (2002) 'Rethinking the meaning of public health', *Journal of Law, Medicine and Ethics*, 30(2): 144–9.

Royal Commission on Long Term Care (1999) *With Respect to Old Age: Long Term Care – Rights and Responsibilities*, Cm 4192, London: HMSO.

Ruck-Keene, A. (2020) 'Capacity at the time of coronavirus', *International Journal of Law and Psychiatry*, 70: 101560.

Rummery, K. and Fine, M. (2012) 'Care: a critical review of theory, policy and practice', *Social Policy and Administration*, 46(3): 321–43.

Ryan, S. (2017) *Justice for Laughing Boy: Connor Sparrowhawk – A Death by Indifference*, London: Jessica Kingsley.

Samsi, K. et al (2022) 'Is it worth it? Carers' views and expectations of residential respite for people living with dementia during and beyond the COVID-19 pandemic', *International Journal of Geriatric Psychiatry*, 37(2): 10.1002.

Samsi, K. et al (2023) 'Understanding factors influencing residential respite service use by carers of people living with dementia using Andersen's behavioural model of health services use: a qualitative study', *Aging and Mental Health*, 27(10): 1946–55.

Samuel, M. (2016) 'One year on what has the Care Act achieved?', *Community Care*, 1 April.

Samuel, M. (2020) 'Council faces legal challenge for suspending Care Act duties', *Community Care*, 7 May.

Samuel, M. (2020) 'Council says it has "learned lessons" after Care Act legal challenge dropped', *Community Care*, 5 June.

Samuel, M. (2022) 'Council adopted "restrictive and wrong interpretation" of Care Act in cutting brothers' care, finds court', *Community Care*, 5 August.

Samuel, M. (2022) 'Drop in adult social workers employed by councils as vacancies and turnover mount', *Community Care*, 3 March.

Sandiford, J. and Gilbert, S. (2024) 'Birmingham City Council signs off "devastating" cuts', *BBC News*, 6 March.

Sandwell Metropolitan Borough Council (2020) 'Sandwell COVID-19 Local Outbreak Plan'.

Sandwell Metropolitan Borough Council (2020) 'Impact of COVID-19 on Operational Risks @ April 2020 (Appendix C).'

Sandwell Metropolitan Borough Council (2020) Minutes of Emergency Committee 22 April.

Sandwell Metropolitan Borough Council (2020) 'Report to Emergency Committee on 27 May 2020. COVID-19 Reset and Recovery Planning – Roadmap of Activity by Director: Chief Executive David Stevens'.

Sandwell Metropolitan Borough Council (2021) 'Sandwell COVID Local Management Plan', April.

Sargeant, J. (2020) *Co-ordination and Divergence. Devolution and Coronavirus*, Institute for Government, IfG Insight, October.

Scottish Government (2023) *Exercise Nimbus: FOI reference FOI/ 202300362536, Information Request and Response under the Freedom of Information (Scotland) Act 2002*, 25 July.

Scown, S. (2018) 'Is the care sector really a "Cinderella?"', *Huffington Post*, 23 February.

Seebohm, F. (1968) *Report of the Committee on Local Authority and Allied Personal Social Services*, Cmnd 3703, London: HMSO.

Seed, P. (1988) *Day Care at the Crossroads*, Tunbridge Wells: Costello.

Seifert, A. (2020) 'Letter: the digital exclusion of older adults during the COVID-19 pandemic', *Journal of Gerontological Social Work*, 63(6–7): 674–6.

Sen, A. (1979) *Equality of What?*, Tanner Lecture on Human Values, Stanford University, 22 May.

Series, L. (2019) 'Disability and human rights', in N. Watson, A. Roulstone and C. Thomas (eds) *Routledge Handbook of Disability Studies*, London: Taylor & Francis.

Series, L. and Clements, L. (2013) 'Putting the cart before the horse: resource allocation systems and community care', *Journal of Social Welfare and Family Law*, 32(2): 207–26.

Shakespeare, T. (2013) *Disability Rights and Wrongs Revisited*, London: Taylor & Francis.

Shannon, B. (2019) 'Words that make me go hmmm: service user', Rewriting Social Care Blog, 30 November.

Sharland, A. (2017) '*R (Davey) v Oxfordshire CC* in the Court of Appeal', *11KBW* Community Care blog, 7 September.

Shropshire Council (2020) 'Adult Social Care COVID-19 Winter Plan 2020/2021'.

Shropshire Council (2020) 'Report of the Portfolio Holder for Adult Social Care/Public Health and Climate Change'. Portfolio Holder: Councillor Dean Carroll Council, 16 July.

Shropshire Council (2020) 'COVID-19 Outbreak Control Plan: Prevent, Contain and Recover'. V2.1, 22 June.

Shropshire Council (2020) Minutes of Meeting of the Health & Wellbeing Board, 12 November.

Shropshire Council (2021) 'Shropshire COVID-19 Outbreak Management Plan: Prevent, Contain and Live with COVID', March.

Siemens, R. (2023) 'UKIM's joint submission to the UN committee on the rights of persons with disabilities', *Equality and Human Rights Commission blog*, 27 September.

Simpson, P. (1992) 'Contemporary virtue ethics and Aristotle', *Review of Metaphysics*, 45(3): 503–24.

Skills for Care, in partnership with TLAP (2018) *Using Conversations to Assess and Plan People's Care and Support: The Principles of Conversational Assessment.*

Slack, P. (1995) *The English Poor Law, 1531–1782* (2nd edn), Cambridge: Cambridge University Press.

Slasberg, C. and Beresford, P. (2014) 'Government guidance for the Care Act: undermining ambitions for change?', *Disability and Society*, 29(10): 1677–82.

Slasberg, C. and Beresford, P. (2020) 'The Care Act: the service user's experience', in S. Braye and M. Preston-Shoot (eds) *The Care Act 2014: Wellbeing in Practice*, London: Sage.

Slasberg, C., Beresford, P. and Schofield, P. (2015) 'Further lessons from the continuing failure of personal budgets', *Research Policy and Planning*, 31(1): 43–53.

Sloan, B. (2021) '"Easing" duties and making dignity difficult: COVID-19 and the Care Act 2014', *Public Law*, 37.

Slote, M. (2007) *The Ethics of Care and Empathy*, London: Routledge.

socialcarefuture (2021) *Whose Social Care is it anyway? From permanent lockdown to an equal life*, report.

socialcarefuture (2023) *Towards an Equal Life; from here to there: What next for social care future?* strategy briefing.

socialcarefuture (2024) *Living Good Lives in the Place We Call Home: An Outline Programme for the Next Government to Ignite the Transformation of Care and Support.*

Social Work England (2019) *Professional Standards*, available at www.socialworkengland.org.uk/standards/professional-standards/

Solihull Observatory on behalf of Solihull Metropolitan Borough Council (2019) *People and Place*, August.

Solihull Metropolitan Borough Council (2020) 'CPH Adult Social Care and Health Decision Session, Care Act Easements', 6 April.

Solihull Metropolitan Borough Council (2020) 'Report to: Health and Adult Social Care Scrutiny Board. Care Act Easements', 15 June.

Solihull Metropolitan Borough Council (2020) 'Minutes: Meeting of the Health and Adult Social Care Scrutiny Board. Care Act Easements', 15 June.

Solihull Metropolitan Borough Council (2020) 'News item: How COVID-19 is affecting care and support for adults', website news item.

Solihull Metropolitan Borough Council (2021) 'Local Outbreak Management Plan, Revised 2021', March.

Smyth, C. (2024) 'Labour plans cross-party Royal Commission to fix social care', *The Times*, 12 July 2024.

Spencer-Lane, T. (2020) 'Overview of the Care Act 2014', in S. Braye and M. Preston-Shoot (eds) *The Care Act 2014: Wellbeing in Practice*, London: Sage

Spencer-Lane, T. (2020) *The Care Act Manual* (3rd edn), London: Sweet & Maxwell.

Staffordshire County (2020) 'Staffordshire County Council's Response to Coronavirus COVID-19', Council Cabinet Meeting on 17 June 2020.

Staffordshire County Council (2020) 'Report Staffordshire CC Coronavirus/COVID-19 Update'.

Staffordshire County Council (2020) 'Staffordshire County Council's Response to COVID-19', Cabinet meeting on 15 April 2020.

Staffordshire County Council (2020) 'Statement on Care Act easements', Newsroom item, 23 April.

Staffordshire County Council (2020) 'Executive Officer Delegated Decision Form Decision Title: Coronavirus COVID-19: implementation of Care Act easements', 9 April.

Staffordshire County Council (2020) 'Staffordshire County Council's Response to COVID-19', Cabinet meeting on Wednesday 15 April 2020.

Staffordshire County Council (2020) 'Staffordshire County Council's Response to Coronavirus COVID-19', Cabinet meeting on Wednesday 20 May 2020.

Staffordshire County Council (2020) Coronavirus/COVID-19 Update, 27 May.

Staffordshire County Council (2020) iCare Campaign report, Cabinet meeting, Agenda item 7, 15 April.

Staffordshire County Council (2020) Recovery Plan – Health & Care, 17 June.

Starns, B. (2019) *Safeguarding Adults Together under the Care Act 2014: A Multi-Agency Practice Guide*, St Albans: Critical Publishing.

Stewart, E., Desia, A. and Zoccatelli, G. (2023) 'Our NHS? The changing involvement of patients and the public in England's health and care system', in M. Exworthy, R. Mannion and M. Powell (eds) *The NHS at 75: The State of UK Health Policy*, Bristol: Policy Press.

Stoke-on-Trent City Council (2020) 'Care for your city', 1 April, web news.

Stoke-on-Trent City Council (2020) 'COVID-19 statement and update by the City Director', Supplementary Cabinet papers, 21 April.

Stoke-on-Trent City Council (2020) 'COVID-19 update', Public document pack, City Council supplementary papers, 10 December.

Stoke-on-Trent City Council (2020) 'Local Outbreak Control Plan', V23, 14 December.

Stoke-on-Trent City Council (2021) 'COVID-19 update and statement to Cabinet', Agenda item 3, Supplementary papers, 23 February.

Symonds, J., Williams, V., Miles, C. and Steel, M. (2018) 'The social care practitioner as assessor: people, relationships and professional judgement', *British Journal of Social Work*, 48(7): 1910–28.

Szmulker, G. (2017) 'The UN Convention on the Rights of Persons with Disabilities: "rights, will and preferences" in relation to mental disabilities', *International Journal of Law and Psychiatry*, 54: 90–7.

Tanner, D., Beedell, P., Willis, P., Nosowska, G., Noszlopy, L., Powell, J., Ubhi, M. and Wakeham, M. (2024) *Social Work with Older People. SWOP Project Final Report*, University of Birmingham; University of Bristol, Effective Practice.

Tarrant, A. (2020) 'Personal budgets in adult social care: the fact and the fiction of the Care Act 2014', *Journal of Social Welfare and Family Law*, 42(3): 381.

Telford & Wrekin Council (2020) Minutes of meeting of the Health and Wellbeing Board, 10 June.

Telford & Wrekin Council (2020) Minutes of meeting of the Health and Wellbeing Board, 3 December.

Telford & Wrekin Council J. Rowe (2020) 'Telford & Wrekin Care Act Easements 2020', by Executive Director: Adults Social Care and Health & Wellbeing J. Rowe, presented to Meeting of the Health and Wellbeing Board, 10 September.

Telford & Wrekin Council (2020) Agenda of the Meeting of the Health and Wellbeing Board, 3 December.

Tew, J., Duggal, S., Carr, S., Ercolani, M., Glasby, J., Kinghorn, P., Miller, R., Newbigging, K., Tanner, D. and Afentou, N. (2019) *Implementing the Care Act 2014: Building Social Resources to Prevent, Reduce or Delay Needs for Care and Support in Adult Social Care in England. Final Report for the Department of Health and Social Care*, University of Birmingham Department of Social Work and Social Care.

Thane, P. (1983) 'The history of provision for the elderly to 1929', in D. Jerrome (ed) *Ageing in Modern Society: Contemporary Approaches*, New York: Croom Helm/St Martin's Press.

Thane, P. (2000) *Old Age in English History: Past Experiences, Present Issues*, Oxford: Oxford University Press.

Think Local Act Personal Insight Group (2020) *A Telling Experience: Understanding the Impact of COVID-19 on People Who Access Care and Support – A Rapid Evidence Review with Recommendations*, TLAP Insight Group, October.

Thomas, C. (2022) *Community First Social Care*, London: Institute for Public Policy Research.

Thomas, E., Baginksy, M. and Manthorpe, J. (2024) 'The views of practitioners on Care Act easements during the *COVID-19* pandemic', *Practice: Social Work in Action*, 36(1): 55–67.

Thomas, E., Baginsky, M. and Manthorpe, J. (2024) 'The Views of Practitioners on Care Act Easements during the COVID-19 Pandemic', *Practice: Social Work in Action*. 36(1), 55–67.

Thomas, R. (2023) 'The English Local Government and Social Care Ombudsman: systemic administrative justice and bureaucratisation. Part 1', *Public Law*, 240–64.

Thomas, R. (2023) 'The English Local Government and Social Care Ombudsman: systemic administrative justice and bureaucratisation. Part 2', *Public Law*, 2: 424–47.

Todman, L. (2018) 'Shropshire Council staff to work from home once a month to save money', *Shropshire Star*, 8 November.

Toebes, B. et al (2022) *Health and Human Rights: Global and European Perspectives* (2nd edn), Cambridge: Intersentia.

Tong, S.T. et al (2021) *Social Work during COVID-19: Learning for the Future. Challenges, Best Practice and Professional Transformation*, BASW research report.

Trani, J.F., Bakhshi, N., Bellanca, M., Biggeri and Marchetta, F. (2011) 'Disabilities through the Capability Approach lens: implications for public policies', *European Journal for Disability Research*, 5(3): 143–57.

Tronto, J. (1993) *Moral Boundaries: A Political Argument for an Ethics of Care*, London and New York: Routledge.

Tuijt, R., Frost, R., Wilcock, J., Robinson, L., Manthorpe, J., Rait, G. and Walters, K. (2021) 'Life under lockdown and social restrictions: the experiences of people living with dementia and their carers during the COVID-19 pandemic in England', *BMC Geriatrics*, 21(1): 301.

UK COVID-19 Inquiry (2023) Statement of Professor Alexander. Module 1, Day 3, 15 June.

UK COVID-19 Inquiry (2023) Witness statement of Dr Ben Warner, former special advisor. Evidence, Module 2 INQ000269182, 8 September.

UK COVID-19 Inquiry (2024) *Module 1: The Resilience and Preparedness of the United Kingdom: A Report by the Rt Hon Baroness Hallett, DBE Chair of the UK COVID-19 Inquiry*, 18 July HC 18.

UK Government (2020) *Press Release: Prime Minister announces Tier 4 'Stay At Home Alert Level' in Response to New COVID Variant*.

UK Health Security Agency (2020) *COVID-19 Contain Framework: A Guide for Local Decision Makers*, 17 July; updated 7 October 2021; withdrawn 7 April 2022.

UK Health Security Agency (2020) *Research and Analysis NHS Test and Trace Statistics (England): Methodology*, 18 June; updated 18 May 2022.

UK Health Security Agency (2023) *Guidance Ebola: Overview, History, Origins and Transmission*, January.

UN Committee on the Rights of Persons with Disabilities (2016) *Inquiry Concerning the United Kingdom of Great Britain and Northern Ireland Carried Out by the Committee under Article 6 of the Optional Protocol to the Convention Report of the Committee*, 6 October.

Unia, E. and Rhodes, D. (2014) 'Thousands died while waiting for NHS funding decisions', *BBC News*, 24 August.

University of Birmingham Policy Commission (2014) *Report: Healthy Ageing in the C21st: The Best Is Yet to Come,* Birmingham.

University of Strathclyde (2022) 'Care homes reliant on agency staff more than twice as likely to spread COVID-19, study confirms', web news, 25 January.

Valeska, H. (2006) 'The unification of the globe by disease? The international sanitary conferences on cholera, 1851–1894', *Historical Journal*, 49(2): 453–76.

Vickary, S., Stone, K., McClusker, P., Davidson, G. and Spencer-Lane, T. et al (2020) '"It's about how much we can do, and not how little we can get away with": coronavirus-related legislative changes for social care in the United Kingdom', *International Journal of Law and Psychiatry*, 72: 1101601.

Vickers, S. (2020) 'Decision title: To make a formal decision to implement Easements to the Care Act 2014 introduced by the Coronavirus Act 2020 and associated Regulations', 4 May. Decision maker: Stephen Vickers, Directors of Adults and Communities, Herefordshire Council.

Voluntary Organisations Disability Group (2023) *Commission on COVID-19, Ableism and Racism: 'A Spotlight on Injustice'*, 21 July, London: VODG.

Waitzman, E. (2021) *Mandatory vaccines for health and care workers: latest regulations*, House of Lords Library, 13 December.

Waghid, Y. and Smeyers, P. (2012) 'Reconsidering *Ubuntu*: on the educational potential of a particular ethic of care', *Educational Philosophy and Theory*, 44(2): 6–20.

Wagner, A. (2022) *Emergency State: How We Lost Our Freedoms in the Pandemic and Why it Matters*, London: Bodley Head.

Walsall Council (2020) Service user leaflet – COVID-19, 2 April.

Walsall Council (2020) Letter from K. Allward to care providers, 17 April 2020.

Walsall Council (2020) Letter from K. Allward to care providers, 5 May.

Walsall Council (2020) Letter from K. Allward, headed: 'COVID-19 Market Update: Community Based Provision', 22 May.

Walsall Council (2020) Letter from K. Allward dated 21 December 2020 regarding ''Flexible Delivery'.

Walsall Council (2020) 'Report to Cabinet agenda item 18 on 9 December 2020 – To approve extension to flexible arrangements for Adult Social Care providers during COVID-19 pandemic'.

Walsall Council (2020) 'COVID-19 Outbreak Management Plan', June.

Walsall Council (2020) 'A Review of the Resilient Communities Model.' Presented to the Scrutiny Overview Committee, 28 July.

Walsall Council (2020) 'Safeguarding response during COVID-19', Cabinet Agenda Item 7(c), 19 May.

Walsall Council (2020) 'Safeguarding Response to Cabinet Appendix 1 Social Care Framework: Implementation of the Care Act Easements created as per the Coronavirus Act', 19 May.

Walsall Council (2020) Minutes of Meeting of the Health and Wellbeing Board, 10 October.

Ward, W. (2011) *Beatrice Webb and Her Quest for a Fairer Society: A Hundred Years of the Minority Report*, October, The Smith Institute.

Warren, S. (2022) 'Austerity 2.0: why it's critical for our health that the government learns the lessons of Austerity 1.0', *King's Fund blog*, 1 November.

Warwickshire County Council (2020) 'Appendix: analysis of recommendations against the COVID-19 Ethical Framework for Adult Social Care'.

Warwickshire County Council (2020) 'Coronavirus - Care Act easements information', webpage.

Warwickshire County Council (2020) Officer Key Decision made under the Council's Urgency Procedure by the Strategic Director for People on 9 April 2020: 'Coronavirus COVID-19: Care Act Easements'.

Warwickshire County Council (2020) Easement Review Meeting on 5 May 2020, Minutes made available via FoI REQ 6121208.

Warwickshire County Council (2020) Easement Review Meeting on 22 May 2020, Minutes made available via FoI request. Ref. Redacted.

Warwickshire County Council (2021) 'Population Report for Warwickshire from Census 2021'.

Watson, S. (2020) *On Hospitals: Welfare, Law, and Christianity in Western Europe, 400–1320*, Oxford: Oxford University Press.

Weinstein, D. (2020) 'Intellectual history and defending the capabilities approach', in E. Chiappero-Martinetti, S. Osmani and M. Qizilbash (eds) *The Cambridge Handbook of the Capability Approach*, Cambridge: Cambridge University Press.

Williams, C. (2022) 'First Witness Statement of Cathie Williams Chief Executive of the Director of Adult Social Services Local Government Association, In The Matter of Module 1 of The UK COVID-19 Public Inquiry 14 December 2022'.

Whitehead, M., Barr, B. and Taylor-Robinson, D. (2020) 'COVID-19: we are not "all in it together"—less privileged in society are suffering the brunt of the damage', *BMJ Opinion* (22 May).

Whittington, C. (2016) 'The promised liberation of adult social work under England's 2014 Care Act: genuine prospector false prospectus?', *British Journal of Social Work*, 46(7): 1942–61.

Wilson, G. (1994) 'Co-production and self-care: new approaches to managing community care services for older people', *Social Policy and Administration*, 28(3): 236–50.

Winslow, C.E. (1920) 'The untilled fields of public health', *Science*, 51(1306): 23–33.

Women's Budget Group (2020) 'COVID-19 Report: The Impact on Women in Coventry'.

Woodroofe, K. (1977) 'The Royal Commission on the Poor Law and the unemployed (1905–09)', *International Review of Social History*, 22(2): 137–64.

Woolham, J.G., Norrie, C.M., Samsi, K. and Manthorpe, J. (2019) *Roles, Responsibilities, and Relationships: Hearing the Voices of Personal Assistants and Directly Employed Care Workers*, NIHR Policy Research Unit in Health and Social Care Workforce, The Policy Institute, King's College London.

Worcestershire County Council (2020) 'Cabinet: COVID-19 Response and Restart Update, Relevant Cabinet Member', Mr S.E. Geraghty Relevant Chief Officer Chief Executive', 25 June.

Worcestershire County Council (2020) 'Cabinet: COVID-19 Response', 4 June.

Worcestershire County Council (2020) 'Adult Care and Well Being Overview and Scrutiny Panel', Agenda Item 5: COVID-19 People Directorate Response for Adult Services, 11 June.

Worcestershire County Council (2020) 'Cabinet: Update on the County Council's COVID-19 Response and Recovery', 22 October.

Worcestershire County Council (2020) 'COVID-19 Response and Restart Update Relevant Cabinet Member Mr S E Geraghty Relevant Chief Officer Chief Executive', Cabinet – Agenda Item 4, 25 June.

Worcestershire County Council (2021) 'Care Act Easements as a result of COVID-19', Adult Care and Well Being Overview and Scrutiny Panel, 15 March.

Worcestershire County Council (2022) 'Population Projections Dashboard'.

World Health Organization (2001) *International Classification of Functioning, Disability and Health*. Geneva: WHO.

World Health Organization (2005) *International Health Regulations* (3rd edn), Geneva: WHO Press.

World Health Organization (2023) *Coronavirus Disease (COVID-19) Pandemic: Overview*, available at www.who.int/europe/emergencies/situations/covid-19

World Health Organization (2022) *Ageing and Health* (1 October), available at www.who.int/news-room/fact-sheets/detail/ageing-and-health#:~:text=At%20this%20time%20the%20share,2050%20to%20reach%20426%20million

Wright, J. (2021) 'The Alexafication of adult social care: virtual assistants and the changing role of local government in England', *International Journal of Environmental Research and Public Health*, 18(2): 812.

Zoccatelli, G. et al (2021) 'Finding the voice of the people in the pandemic: an ethnographic account of the work of local Healthwatch in the first weeks of England's COVID-19 crisis', in P. Beresford et al (eds) *COVID-19 and Co-production in Health and Social Care Research, Policy, and Practice. Volume 1: The Challenges and Necessity of Co-production*, Bristol: Bristol University Press.

Index

A

abuse 66, 78, 95–8, 109
  abuse in care homes 5, 18, 88
accommodation 57, 66, 67, 73
  homelessness 100
accountability 52, 62, 112, 161, 162, 177, 234
acute respiratory syndrome coronavirus *see* COVID-19 pandemic
adaptations/equipment 7, 82
adult social care 115, 132
  crisis in 1, 6, 15–18
  definitions/terminology 6–7
  delivery of 8–16, 252–63
  in draft Pandemic Flu Bill 142–3
  future of 245–6, 297, 303
  history of 9–13
  impacts of pandemic 1–6, 23, 116–17, 280
  legal regulation 2, 6–7, 10, 12, 62–3
  lessons from pandemic 285–96
  multi-faceted complexity of 15
  National Adult Social Care (COVID-19) Group (NACG) 60
  oversight bodies 99–101, 107–14, 288–9
  paradigms in 2, 26
  pressures in 232, 261
  reports on 14–17, 26, 53, 97, 116, 233, 257–9, 276, 299
  see also Care Act 2014; care market; COVID-19 pandemic; funding for adult social care; paying for care
advocacy scheme 98–9, 104
affluent areas 186, 212
African philosophy and care 29
aftercare services (mental health) 106–7
ageing in place 49–50
ageing population 15, 17, 50
Age UK 214
Alice, Exercise 140
Amnesty International 5
Aristotelian philosophy 29, 46
Asian people 174, 176, 243, 249
assessments of need 7, 10, 49, 73–81
  delays in 187, 190, 206, 258, 259
  digitisation of 58, 183, 216, 264, 265
  fluctuating needs 83
  by phone 196, 203, 214
  streamlined 179, 192, 194, 199, 201
Association of Directors of Adult Social Services (ADASS) 19, 20, 170
  Coventry City Council 182
  implementing easements 159
  pandemic planning 140–4
  report on digitisation 272
  role of 7, 10, 13, 63, 108
  and safeguarding 97
  Waiting for Care report 257–8
  see also West Midlands easements
austerity 16, 17, 95, 176, 226, 245, 297
  budget cuts 16, 115, 177, 178, 226, 245, 302
Australian de-institutionalization 59
autism 18, 88, 213
  Autism Act 2009 71–2
autonomy 26, 37, 53, 88
  over day-to-day life 66, 74, 78
  and relationality 31–2
  and vulnerability 53, 56

B

BBC *Panorama* 18
Bergamo, Italy 147
Beyond Digital Planning for Hybrid World 271
biological security 144
Birmingham City Council 176–81, 302
Black Swan, Exercise 181
Blair, Tony 121
Brexit 144, 285
  and workers' restrictions 256
British Association of Social Workers (BASW) 44–5, 67, 160, 163
British Institute of Human Rights 155
British Red Cross 16

C

campaign organizations 284, 291
capabilities approach 45–50, 282
  central capabilities 46–7
cap on care costs 13, 297

342

INDEX

care 64
　care diamond 8, 13, 15
　concept of 24, 27–37, 60
　crisis of 15–18
　ethic of care 26, 27, 30, 31
　principles of care 28–9
Care Act 2014 1, 10, 12–13, 282, 298
　advocacy scheme 98–9
　assessment of needs 73–81
　and capabilities approach 48
　cap on costs 13, 297
　and family care 16
　local authorities' duties 63–5
　and relationality 35
　reviews 194, 204, 228
　and vulnerable adults 60
　see also financial assessment
Care Act easements 19, 20, 24, 140–1, 172, 290
　ambiguity/uncertainty 156–7, 174, 224, 285–6
　and disability groups 169–70
　Central England Law Centre research 276–7
　flexibilities in 156
　impacts of 233–4, 275
　implementation of 156–66, 233–52
　legacy of 283
　and local authorities 1–2, 150–2
　and non-easement 174, 223, 228, 235–42
　stakeholders views 221–7
　statutory Guidance 159, 160–2
　see also West Midlands easements
Care and Support (Eligibility Criteria) Regulations 2015 81–3
care diamond 8, 13, 15
care homes 105, 133, 167
　abuse in 5, 18, 88
　closure of homes 250
　and discharge patients 3–4, 166–9, 244, 260
　inspections of 5, 109, 140
　personal protective equipment (PPE) 247
　planning for flu pandemic 134
　staff shortages 188, 250
　staff staying on site 3
　visiting restrictions 5, 14, 207
care market
　care providers 65, 199, 220
　crisis of the 17
　effective markets 65
　fragility of 6
　Griffiths Report 11, 302
　oversight 99–101
　privatisation of care 9, 11–12, 14
　provider failure 100, 185
　service range 100, 113–14, 179
　support for providers 202, 207–8
　trifurcated market 17

care packages 133, 191, 199, 226, 261
care plans 11, 93, 183, 259
Care Providers Alliance 143
Care Quality Commission (CQC) 100, 109–13, 143, 164
　inspections of care homes 5, 140
　report on adult social care 261
carers/care workers 3, 4, 7, 18
　affected by pandemic 133
　cancellation of visits 225
　and closures of day centres 275
　employment conditions 57
　leaving career 250
　needs of 31, 68, 83
　PPE 3, 4, 185, 188, 247
　role of 280–1
　support for 13, 35, 75, 77, 91–2, 152, 185, 214
　unpaid carers 14, 30, 185, 247–8, 258
　see also staffing/workforce
Carers UK 247–8
care services 14, 73, 195
　complaints 113–14
　delivery of 2
　home care services 191, 199, 213, 220, 257
　during pandemic 3
　pressures on 132–6, 252
　quality of care 65
　users as 'customers' 12
case study of West Midlands 2, 20–4, 173–230
　see also West Midlands easements
challenges to care decisions 85–90, 101–2, 115, 229
changes in social care *see* easements
charging, suspension of 202, 204
China 119, 146
cholera epidemics 118
Chronically Sick and Disabled Persons Act 1970 10
City of Wolverhampton Council 215–16
Civil Contingencies Act 2004 121–9, 171, 176
Civil Defence Act 1948 121
civil partnerships 9
Clements, L. 62, 66, 67
　language of care 27
Clinical Commissioning Groups (CCGs) 166, 190, 193
COBR/COBRA 125, 136, 146
communication 4, 144, 164–5, 217, 236–40, 303
　from government 227, 293
　information/communication flows 135, 144
　to service users 178, 182, 197
　in Wolverhampton 215
community 161, 162, 299
　access to services 82
　community-based support 250

community care 10–12
Community Care (Direct Payments) Act 1996 12
Community Care Act 1990 11, 63, 102
Community Risk Register 123
community spirit 180
crisis in the community 18–19, 299
see also day centres
co-morbidities 15–16
complex care 162, 188, 250, 268
complex organizational structures 285
Confucian philosophy 30
Conservative Government 262
　care in the community 10–12
　and social care funding 255–6
Conservative-Liberal Coalition Government 126
co-operation with partners 65, 97
co-production 49, 50–2, 234, 303
Coronavirus Act 2020 1, 19, 129, 146–56, 283
　concern about 169–71, 290–1
　and human rights 292
　impacts on disabled people 169–71, 233
　implementing easements 156–66
　Rights in Peril report 276–7
　and the West Midlands 20, 22
cost of care *see* paying for care
Coventry City Council 165, 181–6
COVID-19 pandemic 146
　and autonomy 53, 59
　CHC assessments paused 105
　communication issues 144
　CQC inspections paused 109
　Delta/Omicrom variants 173, 232, 253, 254
　experiences from Winter 2021 252–63
　and health inequalities 57
　illness/absences caused by 6
　impacts of 1–6, 61, 233, 243, 252–61, 283
　legacies of 25, 232
　lessons from 20, 285–96, 296–301
　'living with COVID-19' 1, 25, 231, 232, 284, 301
　media focus during 14
　as a national security risk 116
　restrictions 59, 87, 120, 204, 207, 218, 220, 228, 232
　social work ethics 45
　see also day centres; digitisation; hospital discharge
COVID-19 pandemic Inquiry 2–3, 117, 285–90
　and 2011 Strategy 138–9, 147–8, 171
　complex care structures 145
　and Local Resilience Forums 124
　reorganisation and resilience 126
　and vulnerability 144
crisis in adult social care 15–18, 302

cuts, budget 16, 115, 177, 178, 226, 245, 302
　austerity 16, 17, 95, 176, 226, 245, 297
Cygnus, Exercise 140–1, 144

D

data management *see* digitisation
Davies, Lord Justice 89
day centres 7, 59, 205, 214, 228
　in Birmingham 180–1
　in Coventry 184–5
　impact of closures 249
　provision of 272–7
　in Solihull 188
　in Worcestershire 217
deaths 130, 146, 247, 257
　death rates 132, 178, 233
　excess deaths 4, 5, 59, 142
　and inequalities 243
　modelling predictions 147
decision-making 224
　capacity 34, 67, 68
　by government 287
　by individuals 36
　process 90, 161–3
　in Solihull 189
deferred payment agreement 93
Delta variant 173
demand, crisis of 15–16, 253, 254
dementia 34, 248
　and day centres 275
　and online services 266
Department of Health and Social Care (DHSC) 182
　Care Act Guidance 156–9
　Coronavirus action plan 147
　criticism of 294–5
　recording decision-making 164
　strategic planning 141–3
　strengths-based approach 78–9
deprivation 9, 57, 174, 181, 189, 206, 243
　in Sandwell 200
　in Stoke-on-Trent 218
　in Wolverhampton 215
Derbyshire County Council 171
digitisation 232, 262–72, 284, 299–300
　online assessments 183
　and service users 58
　see also online/phone services
dignity 46, 66, 67, 88
Dilnot Report 299
Directors of Public Health 124, 287
direct payments 7, 12, 90, 94
　in Birmingham 176
　challenge to decision 171
　delays in 258–9
disabilities, people with 1, 5, 6, 10, 133, 249
　capabilities approach 45–50
　and day centres 272

human rights model 41–4
impact of easements 169–70, 233–4
and legal capacity 43–4
medical/social model 38–40
rights and easements 36, 156
UN Convention on the Rights of 38, 41–4, 51, 67, 70, 95
Women and Equalities Report 233–4
Disability Alliance 39
Disability Rights UK 170
discrimination 40, 50, 64
diverse populations 174, 181, 206
Donaldson, Lord 114
Down Syndrome Act 2022 72–3
drug and alcohol abuse 6
Dudley Metropolitan Borough Council 174, 210–12

E

easements *see* Care Act 2014 easements
Ebola 119, 139
Economic and Social Research Council (ESRC) 19, 157
eligibility criteria 81–3, 152
emergencies, managing
  emergency legislation 149
  emergency powers 118–29, 124, 153, 297
  Emergency Powers Act 1920 121
  Gold Command structure 176, 179, 206, 217, 219
  proposed new body 287
  SAGE 117, 136
  see also Coronavirus Act 2020
empathy 28, 29
English Land Law 141
epilepsy 88
Equality Act 2010 189, 195, 228
  discrimination 64
  Equality Impact Assessment 199
  and vulnerability 301
ethic of care 26, 27, 30, 31
ethics 137
  ethical dilemmas 134
  Ethical Framework for Adult Social Care 161–3, 195, 283, 285
European Convention of Human Rights (ECHR) 44, 85, 86, 152, 163, 292
  and Care Act easements 1, 158
  incompatibility with 37
  violation of 64
European Court of Human Rights (ECtHR) 87, 153

F

face-to-face activity 193, 200, 207, 215, 219, 265
Fair Deal in Times of Austerity 176
Fairer Social Care Funding 299
falls, detecting 300

family 8–9, 73, 77, 88
  family care 14, 16, 245–8, 258, 297
  family visits 5, 14
  financial assessments 93
  impacts of pandemic on carers 275–6
feminist thought 30, 55
financial assessment 92, 151, 183
flexibilities 156, 161, 174–5, 254–5, 290
  in Staffordshire 190
  in Stoke-on-Trent 220
  in Telford & Wrekin 203
  in Walsall 207–8
  in Worcestershire 218
  see also Care Act easements; West Midlands easements
foot and mouth crisis 121
Freedom Day 232, 252
Freedom of Information (FOI) requests 170, 175, 197, 239, 283, 288
funding for adult social care 253, 280, 297–9
  additional funding for beds 260
  aftercare funding 106–7
  cap on costs 13
  Dilnot Report 299
  future of 302–3
  grant funding 12
  Griffiths Report 11
  Health and Social Care Levy 256
  House of Commons report 16–17, 116, 257
  tensions with NHS 115
furlough scheme 14

G

gender and care 28, 30
Gold-Silver-Bronze Command structure 176, 179, 206, 217, 219
grant funding 12
Griffiths Report 11, 302
Guidance, statutory 64
  interpretations of the 174
gym membership 7

H

H1N1 Swine Flu pandemic 134–5
Hale, Lady 87
Hallett, Heather 2
Hancock, Matt 2, 146, 148, 168, 237
health, right to 85
Health and Care worker visas 257
Health and Social Care Act 2008 109, 111
Health and Social Care Act 2012 108
Health and Social Care Levy 256
Health and Well-being Boards 108–9
health inequalities 57, 243, 296, 300
Healthwatch 108, 111–12
  and communication 239–40
Herefordshire Council 198–200
Hine, Dame 134–5
HIV-positive patients 120

holiday funding 82, 88–9
homelessness 100
home working 186, 228, 263–5, 269, 299
  in Coventry 184
  in Dudley 211
  in Herefordshire 199
  in Sandwell 202
  in Walsall 207
  in Warwickshire 194
hospices 260
hospital discharge 3–4, 105, 228, 244–5, 259–61
  and adult social care 166–9
  in Coventry 183–5
  risk assessments 140
  in Sandwell 201
  in Solihull 187–8
  in Staffordshire 191, 192
  in Stoke-on-Trent 219
  in Telford & Wrekin 203
  in Warwickshire 195
House of Commons reports
  on disabilities 233–4
  on funding 16–17, 116, 257
House of Lords
  Adult Social Care Committee 14–15
  Beyond Digital Planning for Hybrid World 271
human rights 31, 37, 53, 60, 303
  and the Coronavirus Act 2020 152–5
  ECHR 44, 64, 85, 86, 152, 158, 163, 292
  Human Rights Act 1998 64, 85, 152, 154, 228, 292
  and local authorities 64
  model of disability 41–4
  night-time assistance case 85–7
  Universal Declaration of Human Rights 37, 41, 44
Hunt, Jeremy 142

I

inclusion 161, 162, 296
  digital exclusion 264
incontinence 86, 88
independence and relationality 31–2
independent living 14, 67, 94
  L. Davey case 70–1
individuals in Western philosophy 35
inequalities 39, 40, 46, 49
  and digitisation 58, 271
  health inequalities 57, 243, 296, 300
  structural disadvantage 39
infectious diseases strategy 129
influenza pandemic planning *see* pandemic planning
information and advice 65, 132
  at day centres 275
inspections of care homes 5, 109
institutionalism 273

integrated working 65, 206, 262, 303
  Integrated Care Boards 11, 83, 103, 106, 123, 300
intellectual disability 296
international disease control 139, 146
  International Health Regulations 119, 120
internet access 269, 271
isolation 1, 5, 194, 246, 274
Italy 147

J

Jenrick, Robert 148
Johnson, Boris 3, 141, 232, 256
Journal of Public Health 134

K

Kerr, Lord 86

L

Labour Government 121, 288
  health/social care legislation 10
  personalization agenda 53
Law Commission 6–7, 12
leadership, absence of 144
learning difficulties 205, 271
learning disabilities 6, 88, 226, 240, 266–7
  abuse in care homes 18
  and day centres 273
  and isolation 246
Liberty 170, 183
life, right to 53
life expectancy 15, 57
  in Stoke-on-Trent 218
Lloyd, Lord 87
local authorities 20
  challenges to decisions 85–90, 101–2, 115, 229
  complaints 113–14
  and co-production 51
  duties and powers 63–5, 83–92, 282
  and easements 170, 173, 228, 254–5
  future intentions of 226–7
  and hospital discharges 166–7
  legal protection for 172
  limited resources 69–70, 71, 81, 87–8, 115
  maladministration 114, 259
  mental health aftercare 106
  and non-easement 174, 223, 235–42
  and notifiable diseases 120
  oversight for social care 63, 99–101, 108–9, 288–9
  public communication 164–5, 294–6
  safeguarding 95–8
  and third-sector/volunteers 251–2
  see also accountability; assessments of need; care market; professional codes/regulations; staffing/ workforce; transparency
Local Government Act 1974 113

INDEX

Local Government and Social Care Ombudsman 21, 63, 101, 113–14, 278
Unprecedented Pressure 259
Local Government Association (LGA) 97, 160
and funding 297–8
Localism Act 2011 63, 64
Local Outbreak Management Plan 169
Local Resilience Forums 123–5, 148, 176
and influenza planning 131
lockdowns 1, 3, 5, 59, 148, 231, 232, 280
long-term health conditions 15–16

M

Making Safeguarding Personal 97
market, the *see* care market
Marmot, Michael 243, 296, 300
Marxist arguments 46
mask wearing 232
May, Theresa 141
meals and food 7, 133, 181, 187, 252
means testing 12, 13, 92
media 14, 227, 229
  coverage of care abuse 18, 135
  coverage of easements 170–1, 238, 284
  coverage of hospital discharges 260
medical model of disability 38
Mencap 16, 165
mental capacity 36
  Mental Capacity Act 2005 34, 36, 68, 293
mental health 6, 59, 66, 80
  aftercare services 106–7
  Mental Health Act 1983 63, 106, 168
Middle East respiratory syndrome (MERS) 139–40
Middlesborough Council 170
minimum income guarantee 93
Ministry of Housing, Communities and Local Government (MHCLG) 124, 160
Minority ethnic backgrounds 28, 174, 176, 243, 249
mixed economy 11, 12
modelling predictions 147
modern slavery 257, 261
morality and care 28, 30
  war veterans 38
multi-agency practices 140
  in Walsall 209–10

N

National Adult Social Care (COVID-19) Group (NACG) 160
National Assistance Act 1948 10, 12
National Framework for Responding to an Influenza Pandemic 130–4
National Health Service (NHS) 10
  Capacity Tracker/Care Home 167
  and community care 11
  and Community Care Act 1990 63, 102

Continuing Healthcare (CHC) 63, 102–5, 166
Integrated Care Boards 11, 83, 103, 106, 123, 300
pressure on hospitals 132, 133, 259–60
recognition of pandemic risk 116
tensions with social care 115
see also hospital discharge
National Institute for Health and Care Research (NIHR) 79
National Insurance 256
National Risk Assessment/Register 126, 145
  flu seen as greatest risk 141–2
National Security Council (NSC) 126, 136, 141, 300
  biological security 144
neglect 66, 95–8
  self-neglect 96
Nightingale hospitals 177–8, 180, 197
night-time care 85
Nimbus, Exercise 146

O

Observer, The 16
older people 6, 14, 49, 132, 174, 274
  and day centres 272
  and online access 264
Ombudsman *see* Local Government and Social Care Ombudsman
Omicron variant 232, 253, 254
online/phone services 181, 183, 192, 203, 207, 211, 228
  online services 205, 213, 264–6
operational changes 173, 185
outcomes 74, 78, 82
oversight for social care 63, 99–101, 107–14, 288–9

P

pandemic *see* COVID-19 pandemic
pandemic exercises
  Alice 140
  Black Swan 181
  Cygnus 140–1, 144
  Nimbus 146
  Perinthus 210
  recommendations from Inquiry 288–9
  Winter Willow 130
pandemic planning 24, 116, 129, 130–9, 283, 285–6
  draft Pandemic Flu Bill 142, 148, 171
  expected phases 136–8
  Influenza Pandemic Strategy 126, 135–9, 141–2, 147–8
  lessons from 2, 20, 145
  recommendations from Inquiry 288–8
  see also pandemic exercises
Partners4Change 79–80
paternalism 37

patient choice 53, 245
paying for care 11, 176, 258
  cap on costs 13, 297
  charging suspended 202, 204
  deferred payment 93
  direct payments 7, 12, 70, 90, 93–5, 170–1, 259
  eligibility criteria 81–3, 152
  financial assessments 92, 151, 183
Perinthus, Exercise 210
personal assistants 7, 14, 247, 250
personal budgets 7, 70, 91, 93–5
personal hygiene 82, 96
personalization agenda 53, 273
personal protective equipment (PPE) 3, 4, 185, 188, 247
person-centred approach 156, 213
philosophies, different 29, 30, 35, 42, 46
phone services *see* online/phone services
police powers 168
Poor Laws 10, 37
population 17, 174, 176, 181, 186, 189
  of Dudley 210
  of Herefordshire 198
  of Shropshire 212
  in Stoke-on-Trent 218
  of Telford & Wrekin 203
  of Walsall 206
  of Warwickshire 193
  in Wolverhampton 215
  of Worcestershire 216
'postcode lottery' 82, 299
poverty *see* deprivation
prescriptions 92, 252
Primary Care Trusts 300
prioritisation of services 150, 157, 160, 188, 199, 220, 237
privatisation of care 9, 11, 12, 14
professional codes/regulations 7, 281
  Ethical Framework for Adult Social Care 161–3, 195, 283, 285
  Professional Capabilities Framework (PCF) 45
proportionality of response 139, 156, 161, 287
public, the
  awareness of social care 255–6
  public consultation 101, 164, 165, 215, 303
  public criticism 114, 229, 235, 239
  public interest 172, 236
  public trust 29, 121, 165
Public Administration Committee, on non-use of CCA 128–9
public health 118–29, 124, 287
Public Health (Control of Diseases) Act 1984 120, 148
Putting People First 53

Q

quality of care 17–18, 257
quality of life 5, 133

R

recreation 82
  holiday support 89
recruitment and retention 188, 255, 256, 281
Red Teams 288, 289
Rees-Mogg, Jacob 127
relationality 24, 26–8, 31–5, 278
  nested relationality 60, 281, 301, 303
religion and disability 38
research project 19–23
  interview selection and process 20–2
resources, limited 81, 87–8, 115, 155, 172, 282
respect 29, 37, 161, 162
respite care 7, 59, 82, 184, 228, 248, 275–7
restrictions, pandemic 1, 6, 53, 59, 87, 120, 232
resuscitation orders 5
rights *see* human rights
Rights in Peril report 276–7
risk assessment *see* National Risk Assessment/Register
Royal National Institute for the Blind 16

S

safeguarding 60, 82, 88, 95–8, 133, 170, 266, 282
same-sex marriage 9
Sandwell Metropolitan Borough Council 200–3
SARS 119, 173
scandals of care home abuse 18
Scientific Advisory Group for Emergencies (SAGE) 117, 136
Secretary of State for Health and Social Care 2, 71, 141, 148
  and appeals 100–2
  and easements 150, 160
  and Exercise Nimbus 146
  and oversight bodies 107–11
self-isolation 6, 136, 188, 193, 208, 257
Sen, Amartya 46
Severe Acute Respiratory Syndrome (SARS) 119, 173
shielding 1, 6, 59, 187
shopping deliveries 181, 252
Shropshire Council 174, 212–15
Social Care Innovation Network 49
social distancing 120, 201, 228
  impacts on services 204–5, 207, 218, 220, 291
social exclusion 40
social justice and care 30, 31, 40, 300
social model of disability 39–40
Social Services Act 1970 10, 62, 63, 108
social workers 2, 12, 155–6, 159
  and assessments 75, 78, 103, 292
  BASW 44–5, 67, 160, 163
  digitisation of services 3, 263–72

INDEX

and easements 13, 151
ethics/professional standards 7, 44–5, 161–2, 244
and home working 263–5
and hospital discharges 105, 184
re-organisation in Birmingham 176–7
and safeguarding 97–8
three conversations 79–80
values and training 67, 221, 293
see also Association of Directors of Adult Social Services (ADASS)
socio-economic factors 28, 57, 174, 181, 206, 218
solidarity 34, 301
Solihull Metropolitan Borough Council 186–9
staffing/workforce 4, 131, 211, 263
 Brexit and recruitment 256
 capacity 6, 158, 177, 197, 247, 252, 254, 261
 extended hours 219
 illness/absences 187, 189, 191, 193, 201
 impacts of pandemic 133–4, 280
 information flows 135
 recruitment and retention 188, 214, 250–1, 255, 256, 281
 see also carers/care workers
Staffordshire County Council 189–93
stakeholder reflections 221–7
state, crisis of the 16
State of Health Care and Adult Social Care in England 2022/23 261
statutory oversight body 288–9
stay at home orders 120, 232
Stoke-on-Trent City Council 174, 218–20
strengths-based approach 78–81, 214
 criticisms of 80
structural disadvantage 39
Sunday Times 148
Sunderland City Council 170
surge capacity 131
Swine Flu pandemic 134–5

T

tanker drivers' dispute 121
technical care devices 263, 268, 300
Telford & Wrekin Council 203–5
terminal illness 103
terminology 7–8, 290
Thatcher Government *see* Conservative Government
Think Local Act Personal (TLAP) 51, 160, 197, 285
 report on easement impacts 234–5
third-sector organizations 16, 23, 162, 170, 251
 filling gaps in care 276
 during pandemic 210, 225, 299
 and planning 278, 285

Three Conversations 79–80
transparency 97, 121, 163, 229, 233, 288, 295
trifurcated market 17
Tronto, J. 27, 28
Truss, Liz 256
trusted assessors 167, 292
tuberculosis 120

U

Ubuntu 29
UN Convention on the Rights of People with Disabilities 38, 41–4, 51, 67, 70, 95
Universal Declaration of Human Rights 37, 41, 44
University of Birmingham Ethics Committee 19
unpaid carers 14, 30, 185, 246–8, 258, 297
Unprecedented Pressure 259

V

vaccine development and supply 132
 mandatory vaccination of workers 256–7
 vaccination 136, 139, 232
values 45, 221
virus testing 6, 166
 test and trace service 4, 169
virus transmission 3, 14, 131, 136, 181, 217
visas 257
voluntary sector 9, 14, 106, 195, 250
 and hospital discharges 166
 VODG Commission 249
 volunteering 18–19, 162, 180, 191
vulnerability 26, 53–60, 172, 274, 282
 and COVID-19 Inquiry 145, 300–31
 and inequalities 57
 and volunteer scheme 191
 in West Midlands 174, 182, 187, 207, 211, 219

W

Waiting for Care 257
Walker, C. 127
Walsall Council 205–10
 multi-agency practices 209–10
Warwickshire County Council 193–7
welfare state 10
well-being principle 13, 35, 65–74, 154, 303
 broad holistic approach 79
 Health and Well-being Boards 108–9
Western philosophy 42
 and legal assumptions 35
West Midlands easements 2, 170, 175, 197, 220–1, 283–6
 Birmingham City Council 176–81
 case study 20–4
 City of Wolverhampton Council 215–16
 Coventry City Council 181–6
 Dudley Metropolitan Borough Council 210–12

Herefordshire Council 198–200
Sandwell Metropolitan Borough
   Council 200–3
Shropshire Council 212–15
Solihull Metropolitan Borough
   Council 186–9
Staffordshire County Council 189–93
stakeholder reflections 221–7
Stoke-on-Trent City Council 218–20
Telford & Wrekin Council 203–5
Tier system 231
Walsall Council 205–10
Warwickshire County Council 193–7
Worcestershire County Council 216–18

White, Alan 189
Whorlton Hall, County Durham 18
Winterbourne View, Bristol 18
Winter Willow Exercise 130
Wolverhampton Council 174
   communication 165–6
women 9, 27–8
Worcestershire County Council 174,
   216–18
workhouses 10, 37
working-age with disabilities 15–16, 50
World Health Organization 136, 142,
   146, 147
World War II 37, 38

www.ingramcontent.com/pod-product-compliance
Lightning Source LLC
Chambersburg PA
CBHW051524020426
42333CB00016B/1771